382.44
C762s

Phillips Library
Bethany College
Bethany, W. Va. 26032

DISCARD

A SLAVER'S LOG BOOK

or 20 Years' Residence in Africa

The Original Manuscript by
CAPTAIN THEOPHILUS CONNEAU

PRENTICE-HALL, INC., Englewood Cliffs, N.J.

A Slaver's Log Book, or 20 Years' Residence in Africa
By Captain Theophilus Conneau
Copyright © 1976 by Howard S. Mott, Inc.
All rights reserved. No part of this book may be
reproduced in any form or by any means, except
for the inclusion of brief quotations in a review,
without permission in writing from the publisher.
Printed in the United States of America
Prentice-Hall International, Inc., London
Prentice-Hall of Australia, Pty. Ltd., Sydney
Prentice-Hall of Canada, Ltd., Toronto
Prentice-Hall of India Private Ltd., New Delhi
Prentice-Hall of Japan, Inc., Tokyo

10 9 8 7 6 5 4 3 2 1

Library of Congress Cataloging in Publication Data
Conneau, Théophile.
    A slaver's log book.
    Transcribed from the author's newly discovered
manuscript.
    1.   Slave-trade—Africa—Personal narratives.
2.   Conneau, Théophile.   I.   Title.
HT1322.C59   382'.44'0924   [B]   76-17301
ISBN 0-13-788752-3

Introduction by Mabel M. Smythe

For more than a hundred years, historians have relied upon the Brantz Mayer-edited version of Captain Theophilus Conneau's account of his adventures in the African slave trade as a source of authentic information about that infamous traffic in human beings.

"Canot," the spelling of the author's name in the earlier versions, is a homonym meaning *dinghy* in French, a clever pseudonym to disguise the Captain's association with an illegal calling and so avoid embarrassment to his family. According to Malcolm Cowley's introduction to the 1928 edition, which leaves out or shortens some of Mayer's passages, "Canot" was "lounging about the wharves of Baltimore cadging . . . drinks" when he renewed his acquaintance with Dr. James Hall, philanthropist, founder and first governor of the colony of resettled slaves at Cape Palmas in Liberia. Dr. Hall, whom Conneau had met on the Guinea Coast a decade earlier, suggested that the Captain write his memoirs, introduced him to Brantz Mayer, a "prominent" journalist, and—Cowley speculates—probably provided funds for the cause.

Cowley was undoubtedly misinformed about Captain Conneau's condition. He could hardly have been a drunkard on the waterfront in 1853 and only a year later the possessor of a work based on the present manuscript ready for publication (after extensive further editing by Mayer), having successfully arranged for publication in England and France as well as in the United States. His presentation to Napoleon III by his brother, chief physician to the Emperor, and his subsequent conversation with the Empress Eugénie—who, like her husband, expressed interest in the book—suggest a totally different human being from the "physical wreck" put forward by Cowley.

If Phyllis and Howard S. Mott, customers of the respected old bookselling shop of W. H. Lowdermilk, had not been favored by the owner, Parke Jones, the manuscript of *A Slaver's Log Book, or 20 Years' Residence in Africa* might well have been lost when the building was razed to make way for construction of the Washington, D. C., subway. Fortunately, Mr. Jones permitted the Motts to poke around in the small back room where he kept his old books and manuscripts. It was there, according to Mrs. Mott, that they found the original Conneau manuscript in a dust-laden "pink cardboard box, tied with an orange woven tape," looking as if it had not been disturbed for years.

Some years before, Jones had purchased the papers of the Brantz Mayer estate. Mayer, in editing the 1854 edition of the "Canot" iii

382.44
C762s

memoirs, had "improved" on the original by omitting some incidents and details, as well as by rewriting in his own somewhat florid style Conneau's simpler and more direct account. (Mayer had also written to a number of Maryland Colonization Society officials and to ex-governors of Liberia, all of whom attested that Conneau's recollections were authentic as far as they knew.)

A great many popular accounts of slavery say little of the slave trade, partly because the legal prohibition against it after January 1, 1808, had driven its operations into secrecy and forced American traders to seek other flags for their ships. The British laws against the slave trade in 1807 and 1811, like their American counterpart, could hardly be enforced effectively without patrolling the seas, preferably with international cooperation. The British naval strength enabled the British to engage in search and seizure on the high seas; and in the absence of a clearcut agreement which might have been proclaimed in the Declaration of Vienna in 1814, bilateral treaties were concluded between Portugal, Spain, Brazil, and others on the one hand, and Britain on the other. An 1845 treaty between Britain and France established some cooperation; the United States, however, refused to allow British search and seizure until 1862.

With this legal background the reader can better understand Captain Conneau's possession and use of Danish, Portuguese, and Spanish flags. On several occasions he was threatened by or even forced to submit to search and seizure by French and British ships. His entire career in slave trading was illegal, according to American and British law, since he was born after January 1, 1808, and made his first voyage in 1819 in an American ship. By the 1820s, when he became involved in the slave trade, the British and Spanish governments had agreed that each would have the right to search and seize (in specified waters) ships engaged in the slave trade. The Spanish flag vessels used by Conneau were clearly vulnerable.

Why did the slave trade persist in the face of the laws and international treaties against it? Why would a man of Captain Conneau's abilities and apparent sensibilities engage in such a calling? Why would he be received, as he reports, with cordiality and kindness by officials with reason to suspect or even know the source of his income and its illegality?

In the welter of philosophical arguments for and against the slave trade, the one cogent and inescapable argument in favor of it is easily hidden: in spite of its risks, illegality, and blighted social status, slave trading was enormously profitable. Despite the popular assertion that free labor was cheaper, the price of slaves continued to go up and to compensate for the risks of the trade.

The economics of the slave trade implied the profitability of
slavery in at least some of its uses, notwithstanding the elaborate
assertions of planters and others that slave labor was financially
more burdensome than its free counterpart. Given the cultural
context of a slave society in which social status was related to the
size of slaveholdings and a child slave might be a suitable present for
a lady, decisions regarding the purchase and use of slaves were
frequently made on a social or psychological, rather than an
economic, basis. On the other hand, defenses of slavery were particularly forceful when abolition threatened the sometimes dazzling
profits in sugar and cotton.

Although Conneau's arithmetic leaves something to be desired,
he demonstrates satisfactorily that profits were enormous. On the
Fortuna, fitted out in 1827 and used for a voyage in which he had an
interest, his calculations of a four months' round trip can be sum-
marized as follows:

Income:		
Sale of cargo (217 slaves)		$77,469
Proceeds from vessel sold at auction		3,950
Total Income		81,419
Less expenses:		
Vessel, fittings, cargo, wages		39,700
Net profit:		$41,719

A profit in excess of one hundred percent in four months obviously sufficed to stifle a great many scruples. The profits were so
high that a missionary from England "abandoned his profession for
the more lucrative slave traffic" (p. 60), deserting his daughter and
her mother, a mulatto woman, in Sierra Leone. On the other hand,
the risks were great. Conneau describes an experience with another
slave ship, the *Areostatico*, with a "choice cargo" of eighty adult
slaves; the ship was never heard of again after she sailed.

Slave traders are easily imagined as evil, sadistic men, inured to
human suffering and unmoved by the appeal of the vulnerable and
helpless. The memoirs of an actual slave trader are a very different
matter. Confronted with an ordinary human being who believes
himself "civilized" and humane, who is horrified at being thought
willing to let his slaves starve to death, but who is nevertheless able
to deprive other human beings of their liberty, what is the reader to
think?

For one thing, it is clear that Conneau—humanly enough —strives to present himself in a favorable light. For another, he does not even seem aware of his tendency to sensationalize reports of tribal wars and ceremonies—tribal wars are considered cruel and barbarous—while reacting defensively or insensitively to equally objectionable actions by whites. For example, the murder of a black boy who stands in the way of an extra profit on a damaged ship arouses little more than a casual comment from him.

The overriding lesson of *A Slaver's Log Book* is that there is in a human being an enormous capacity for rationalization. Captain Conneau is no exception; and the motivation for rationalization was profit, so huge a profit that the avarice of traders could gloss over repellent conduct inconsistent with their protestations of Christianity: the flaunting of law, the dangers to their own lives and liberty, the viciousness with business associates, and the brutality to other human beings.

The rationalizations come easily—the assumption of white racial and cultural superiority, the titillating interpretations of tribal customs which indicate little or no curiosity regarding the values those customs expressed, the presumption that African behavior can appropriately be judged by the values of western civilization. Yet when the Captain judges the treatment of slaves, it is not by the standards that western civilization would apply to its own members, but by the conception of what slaves might expect or deserve—in the judgment of whites, of course. The notion of democracy does not interfere with his thinking; the application of such a concept to black "primitives" is out of the question. Nor is the sanctity of the family a problem: people who are not "civilized" are not expected to defend their wives and children from slavery—in fact they are punished cruelly for betraying any impulse in that direction.

Conneau is honest enough, however, to set forth the facts as he sees them. When he visits the Bager people in Africa and finds that they respect private property far better than the Europeans he knows, he indulges in a bit of irony and wonders, "Why . . . civilize this people and teach them Christian selfishness!" (p. 101). He obviously can hardly credit the fact that the possessions of a dead visitor to Africa have been kept for twelve years in readiness for the owner's friends to call for them (p. 102).

He is less forthright in yielding information regarding his personal feelings. Apparently a private person, he does not even allude to his marriage in the log proper, although the letters following the narrative mention a wife, Eliza.

Yet Conneau himself reports recoiling from the cruelty of slavery at his first experience with it in the East Indies, at the age of
seventeen: "The sight of such barbarity made me blindly sick with

passion," he recalls (p. 9). Yet such is the temptation of high profits that he goes into the slave trade, prospers, and quickly becomes rich—and defensive about "my abominable traffic," arguing that it is to a slaver's advantage to keep his human cargo clean and properly fed in order to maximize profits (pp. 266—268). At the same time, he concedes that a plentiful supply of food for slaves is not usual, and alludes to such "forcible cruelties" as stowing slaves in a space too shallow to allow them to sit up and so close together that the head of one must be in the lap of another—this on one of his own ships, which he sees as considerably superior to the general run of slave vessels.

He understands that it is cruel to beat (with a cat-o'-nine-tails) a slave who refuses food in an attempt at suicide, but adds this custom to the list of "unpleasant necessities," along with the "disgusting duty" of branding slaves when several shippers consign them on the same ship. As a presumed Roman Catholic in his early years, Conneau might be expected to react in some horror to the enormity of desperation that could drive a captive to prefer the mortal sin of suicide over life as a slave. That he instead calculates with little emotion the alternative courses of action to prevent slaves from starving themselves or leaping overboard suggests economic rather than religious concern on his part and calls into question his protestations that he is "humanitarian" and "civilized."

Like other ethnocentrics, Conneau sees his own standards as absolute and applies them selectively. He refers to the "perfect state of nakedness" in an African ritual as "obscene" (p. 281), ignoring the inconsistency in his position when he and other slavers insist that slaves be shipped naked for reasons of sanitation, despite the protests of the women, who want to cover themselves with at least the small customary garment (p. 82).

People have asked why Africans themselves engaged in the slave trade. Given the function of slavery in African societies, the origin of their participation is not too difficult to understand.

First and foremost, slavery was not confused with the notions of superiority and inferiority invoked as justification for black slavery in America. On the contrary, it was not at all uncommon for African owners to adopt slave children or to marry slave women, who then became full members of the family. Slaves of talent accumulated property and in some instances reached the status of kings; Jaja of Opobo[1] (in Nigeria) is a case in point. Lacking contact with American slavery, African traders could be expected to assume that

---

[1] E. J. Alagoa, *Jaja of Opobo: The slave who became a king* [sic] (London: Longman Group Limited, 1970).

the lives of slaves overseas would be much as they were in Africa; they had no way of knowing that whites in America associated dark skins with sub-human qualities and status, or that they would treat slaves as chattels generation after generation. When Nigeria's Madame Tinabu, herself a slave trader, discovered the difference between domestic and non-African slavery, she became an abolitionist, actively rejecting what she saw as the corruption of African slavery by the unjust and inhumane habits of its foreign practitioners and by the motivation to make war for profit on the sale of captives.[1]

Slavery in Africa was punishment; as Conneau recognizes, it was meted out to violators of serious tabus, to criminals, and especially to enemies captured in war. Muslims in particular used slavery in lieu of a death sentence. Bondage instead of death was the punishment for truly heinous offenses, as well as a solution to the problem of getting rid of one's captured enemies, who might attack again if set free.

Conneau's attitudes toward color are suggested by a remark early in the narrative (p. 2) that he "could not endure" the black cook, "never having seen a Negro before but at a distance." His view of African culture is generally seen through a European filter; he constantly contrasts indigenous values and folkways with those of the West. He does not hesitate to make such sweeping generalizations as ". . . in all savage nations, the woman . . . has to support . . . her husband" (p. 323) or "all native Africans have an antipathy to hard labor" (p. 311).

Conneau, like many of his contemporary whites, is less horrified by the inhumanity of whites than by equivalent conduct from blacks themselves. He is also more concerned for property than for black persons, as is usual in the slave trade; he is more horrified by a counterfeiter's plan to steal the jewels of a monastery than by the death impulses of slaves. Again, he wishes to leave the slave trade, but has "still too great an amount of property under my charge . . . which could not be given up till invested in slaves" (p. 293). The pull of such gain is irresistible!

There is danger as well as information in the Conneau narrative: in describing for the reader the risks, travails, and experiences of a life so fraught with peril and rich rewards, the Captain's account —told by a natural story-teller who is not without humor and well-placed guile, and who takes care to portray himself with sufficient popular *machismo* and intelligence to excite admiration, yet not

[1]Nigerian Broadcasting Corporation, *Eminent Nigerians of the Nineteenth Century* (London: Cambridge University Press, 1960).

to appear excessive—may invest slave trading with the lure of
romantic derring-do, color, and excitement. Yet, his sensitivity is
not so high as to alert him to the contradictions and inconsistencies
in his account; he blithely transmits what was, in the first half of the
nineteenth century, conventional wisdom about "primitive" peo-
ples, propagating unexamined stereotypes as truth and anthropolog-
ical misinterpretations as authentic history. (Note, for example, his
concept of cannibalism as a matter of everyday nourishment.) The
reader, meanwhile, may be drawn to accept the most bizarre tales of
primitive behavior as truth.

For example, Conneau relates an incident in which a wife and
sister watch as their husband and brother is put to death for trying to
escape. His implication is that they are unmoved by grief. In 1951,
an American soldier in Japan made a similar remark about a mother
who held her composure at the accidental death of her child; after a
longer residence in that country he learned of the pride Japanese
mourners take in reserving for private moments those displays of
grief which in other cultures may be regarded as appropriate in
public.

We have to examine the culture before we can interpret human
behavior, and Captain Conneau falls neatly into a category with
those television shows of crime and violence which, in portraying
the "good guys" as followers of the viewer's values and the "bad
guys" as transgressors of those cherished beliefs, ignore the fact that
both have good and bad impulses and equal capacity to suffer pain,
and thus leave us willing to accept and even applaud atrocious
treatment of the "bad" and unfair privilege for the "good."

This is the ultimate danger of the Conneau treatise: it presents
slavery as an understandable error, acceptable because the people
enslaved were "barbarous" anyhow. It may make us view the human
suffering of the slave trade as so variable that the abuses of "better"
slavers (like Captain Conneau, of course) are really not worse than a
good many other evils we see around us. As the Captain retorts to
British officers examining his barracoon and "factory" (p. 268), he
would be considerably more critical of the slave trade if the British
were not doing worse things in India. This insidious poison—looking for worse offenses for comparision, so that one's own sins appear
less significant—is all too human a technique for sidestepping responsibility, and Captain Conneau is thoroughly human.

It is understandable, but deplorable, that even in the last quarter
of the twentieth century, American audiences may yet accept the
Conneau that is presented to us as a popular swashbuckling hero
without challenging the premise that if our hero is personable, then

the slave trade is somehow more acceptable. If he were less appealing, we would presumably be entitled to challenge his claim to humanitarian instincts and more likely to point out that they are certainly weaker than his cupidity.

Let us hope that historical scholars will be more analytical and will make full use of the detailed account of shipboard life and arrangements, of relations between slave traders on ships and those on shore, of the kinds of risks they ran and the human suffering they encountered or promoted, of the brutality extended on occasion to the crew as well as the cargo, and of the at least occasional pangs of guilt and shame that attended the complicity of an avowedly human person in a system of illegal and inhumane trade which he could not hope to control and therefore had to accept unless he also rejected the tempting rewards. In making his "honest" case, our author has, unwittingly or not, been effectively self-serving. We see what happened through his eyes, colored by his prejudices and predilections. And our own avarice and inhumanity may respond with empathy to his.

So to read Captain Conneau's account requires a tough, sophisticated, and disciplined mind, wary of the ready excuse and easily-swallowed racist beliefs in the story. But it is the immediacy of the narrative, the detail, the management of daily life; the risks, problems and physical inconveniences; the shortcomings of alternatives to the slave trade for a person of Conneau's background and experience, and ultimately his capacity to make us feel that we are witnesses to a historical period of immense interest that catches and holds us and makes us, for a time, his contemporaries.

For the historian, particularly the student of slavery, there will be particular interest in his discussion of the 1836 Martinez de la Rosa treaty and its effects on the slave trade, as well as of the descriptions of routines in managing slaves on board trading ships and on plantations. Conneau's not altogether disinterested view of the treatment of slaves, while expanding on the slave's more pleasant impressions at the expense of the more distressing experiences and feelings, nevertheless provides the kind of daily detail which is not easily found in one place. When slaves arrive on the plantation, the use of a bit of pageantry to foster the erroneous impression that slavery is a happy state of affairs, the technique of offering or receiving bribes, the procedure in feeding slaves on board ship, the method of landing slaves in Cuba, the segregation of menstruating women, the accustomed menu in the barracoons—all flesh out the information about

the life of the slave between captivity and arrival in the New World.

Conneau's emphasis is on the general orderliness and on the logic of humane treatment, to be sure, but there shines the glow of truth in the picture of slaves lining up to pass by the rice pot at mealtime, scooping up a handful under the eye of a supervisor intolerant of hesitation or an attempt to get more than one handful. In the description of cramped space and inadequate ventilation on the slave ship one sees the growing frustration and desperation and horror which prompt men and women constantly treated as animals to become animals, scratching and pushing each other for a pitiful inch of space or a bit more distance from someone else's lower parts. The inhumanity of being perceived as cargo or chattel, to be stowed away in a ship like so many odd-shaped parcels with no room for personal choice or difference in habits or taste, hits the modern reader with a clarity unimagined (although perhaps not unimaginable) by Conneau in 1853.

Of the first-person accounts of slave trading which have survived, Conneau's is remarkable for its fullness of detail and sense of completeness in covering the entire process of capture, slave factory, Middle Passage, and sale. Richard Drake[1] and Thomas Branagan[2] document more of the cruelties suffered by slaves, as well as the freedom of the slave owner to abuse his/her chattels; they and others confirm some of the procedures (e.g., packing) described by Conneau. But their accounts are briefer and—particularly in Branagan's case—more entangled with polemic. Ultimately it is Conneau's account which offers the most abundant details about the slave trade, the source of tragedy for some fifteen million African captives—not to speak of additional millions of families disrupted or with members killed in the process—over a span of some four hundred years.

[1] Captain Richard Drake, *Revelations of a slave smuggler: being the autobiography of Capt. Richard Drake, an African trader for fifty years—from 1807 to 1857; during which period he was concerned in the transportation of half a million blacks from African coasts to America*, with a preface by his executor, Rev. Henry Byrd West, of the Protestant Home Mission. (New York: Robert M. DeWitt, Publisher, 1860.)

[2] Thomas Branagan, *The Penitential Tyrant; or, Slave Trader Reformed: a Pathetic Poem in Four Cantos*. (New York: Samuel Wood, 1807.)

The beginning of Chapter 79th in the original manuscript.
Conneau's hand is very neat, and his frequently odd spell-
ings make better sense when read with a French accent.
(For example, he uses "this" and "these" interchangeably,
probably since he pronounced both words as *theese*.)
Throughout the book, his own style has been retained
wherever possible.

Chapter 5

~ "Three Months in London" ~
~ A Slave in London ~

As I had never had, visited England I proposed. to See London above Stairs and below Stairs: my three years economics in Africa, placed me in a State to enjoy this wish in moderate extent.

My Black boy which I call'd Lunes, (Monday) I habited in a Suit of Marine Blue with a profusion of Anchor Buttons, his Vest was of well velvet Slightly edged with a gold Chord. this was intend with his cap of blue Cloth and a neck band to denote his valet occupation. With this subject of aristocracy after me, I visited the Directory in hands the principal places of the Celebrated capital. I shall not intrude on the

My Monday who was a well built boy, of 15 years with a pleasant Countenance, often attracted much notice, by his naive remarks when I visited any of the institutions, I remember one day I took him with me to Greenwich Hospital, and while on board the Steamer I called his attention to the Cupola of St Paul, and remarked to him, that the day before, we had both been in the Golden Ball. My explaination was carried on in an African English which caused the boy to collect in number around us. My argument could not convince the boy, when he answered " no, no, my father, you lye, true, I be black, but I no be dam fool! which way, two men men can live in tat small thing! his incredibility caused great merriment to the company and for the rest of the short trip he was the line of

The Author's Preface

This memoir having been written at the request of several friends who have known me during my residence in Africa—to them I dedicate it. And if, in the perusal, the reader should not find the interest which the title indicates, I beg him to lay the blame to those same friends who have overrated my life of vicissitudes.

By affixing my true name to these memoirs, I hope my friends will see the intention I have to restrict myself to the purest veracity, and as my motive for publishing them is solely for the object of profit, I shall not trouble the public with but two apologies.

First, as I am writing in a foreign language, I have to apologize for the odd and ungrammatical style in which I describe my narratives; and as I intend to portray Africa as it is, the reader must pardon those expressions which a delicate ear is seldom accustomed to. The public also must not expect an historical, botanical, or scientific description of Africa, but the simple facts; of the events of a mariner who has no pretension to the necessary faculty or education of a public writer, or wishes to arrogate to himself the prerogative to annoy his reader with technical phrases, Latin and French words, or the too-often repeated and tiresome practical quotations. My object is simply a description of a traffic now considered immoral and out of fashion.

Second, as these are no confessions or protestations of repentance, the reader should not look for an extra dash of philanthropic sentences today so much à la mode. I describe events such as the world's vicissitudes brought me in contact with, and publish them with the flattering expectations that it will bring harvest to my empty treasury.

*CHAPTER 1ˢᵗ

*My Parents · To Boston on the Galathea · Lord Byron

In order to account for the numerous adventures which I am about   *1808—1819
to describe, it is indispensable to inform the reader of the place of my
native birth, likewise several episodes of my early life, which with
my name I give with reluctance. But they are strictly necessary to
establish the positive fact of my distance and the truthfulness of my
narrative. Had I been born sixty years before my time and published
these memoirs then, no one would have read an account of
every day's occurrences. Philanthropy was not à la mode, and the
slave traffic was not piracy, but a privileged monopoly powerfully
practiced by the Christian potentates of Europe and the fathers of
our present generation.

My name is Theodore Canot, born in 1808 in Italy (City of
Florence, Tuscany), from French parents. My father came to Italy
with the Republican conquering Army under General Bonaparte
and married my mother in Nice (Piedmont), who followed him in
many campaigns, till the Emperor Napoleon abdicated and was sent
to the Island of Elba. On the Emperor's return, my father followed
him like a true Frenchman to Waterloo in his old capacity as Captain
Paymaster, where he died, leaving a wife and six children. My
mother, although not rich (as soldier's wives seldom are), managed
to keep me at school until near 12 years of age, where I was taught
Latin, geography, arithmetic, and history. Being now near 12 years
old, it was necessary to choose a profession, and in my studies
having perused many books on travels, I preferred the seafaring life.
No objection was made, as two of my uncles on my father's side had
been naval officers under King Murat of Naples.

In 1819 I made my first voyage at sea in the American ship
Galathea of Boston, belonging to Mr. William Gray, commonly
called Billy Gray.

I would not pretend to describe all the hardships I endured in my
first voyage, a stranger ignorant of the language, without assistance
or pity in my seasickness. I was made more than miserable. No one
sympathized with me but the Captain, to whom I was bound as
apprentice. But as I could not speak English, I could not complain of
all my grievances. Indeed, for the first three months I was made the

*Only later in the manuscript did Conneau begin dividing his text into chapters.
Chapter divisions and titles preceded by an asterisk have been added by the tran-
scriber. In the margin, dates preceded by an asterisk were not supplied by Conneau
himself, and are based on internal evidence.

butt of every joke, and as I lived in the cabin, every plate or glass that broke was laid to me by the cabin boy. Even the men and officers annoyed me at every occasion when the Captain was below, and with the exception of the Black Cook (whom by-the-bye I could not endure, never having seen a Negro before but at a distance), I was without a friend.

Besides three officers, the *Galathea* carried a Clerk whom the Captain obliged to teach me English, and by the time we arrived at Sumatra, I could plead my own cause. Not finding a cargo of pepper at this island, we proceeded to Bengal. On our arrival at Calcutta, the Captain—being his own agent—took apartments on shore, and the Clerk and myself followed him there.

It was the custom then for Masters of ships to hire a furnished house. Ours was a Spanish one, and with twenty servants to attend upon us, we lived like Nabobs, and sore incensed was I at the end of our three months when we returned on board, our ship being loaded.

At this place I found an Armenian who had been a long time in Leghorn as merchant. I accosted him in the China Bazaar. I took him at first (by his dress) for a Turk and addressed him in the *Lingua Franca*, a mixture of bad Italian and Spanish languages. But to my astonishment, he answered me in excellent Tuscan. Perhaps my Florentine accent had singled me out as an Etruscan to his quick perception. This man had left Italy long before the conquests of Napoleon, and although well acquainted with the history of the Emperor, was wholly astonished at the description I gave of the great General. My store of information induced him to offer me a situation in his house which I could not accept. However, this good Armenian loaded me with presents at parting.

On our passage home, I was placed in the steerage, being considered sufficiently strong to do duties before the mast, and was inscribed in the ship's articles as a light-hand at six dollars per month. In this capacity, I was under the immediate orders of our Chief Mate, being in his watch. This man had been reprimanded on several occasions by our Captain for his misconduct, and had become very unfriendly with him; and his spite was often discharged on me. I was ordered to every disagreeable job, and one day he even attempted my life.

It was four o'clock after meridian, the ship going about five knots. The Mate ordered me to loose the flying jib, which I immediately obeyed, but had not quite finished loosing the sail. This officer ordered the men to hoist away. One of the men on the ship remarked, "The boy is not off the loose jib." Intent on his vengeance, he replied, "Mind your business, you son of a b--ch," and cried out, "Hoist away!"

Off the boom I went, carried away by the clew of the sail, and after turning several somersaults in the air, I was thrown some fifty yards from the ship. In the hurlyburly of this mishap, some cried, "Man overboard!", others ran to the braces, some to the quarter-boat. The Cook, hearing his protégé in danger, leaped overboard after me, while the man who had advised the Mate of my danger and had received such an abusive answer, seeing me in the water and safe—as he expressed himself afterwards—clenched the Mate with the intent to throw him also over the boards. In this tumult the Captain came on deck and immediately layed the ship to. The boat was not sent, as I was alongside a few moments after I touched the water and never losing my presence of mind, the fall did not hurt me as I took care to fall on my head.

The poor darky had a big swim, however, in his anxiety to save me. He had jumped from the windward side and swam in a contrary direction to my fall. In the confusion, no one had taken notice of his generous act, till we heard his voice asking for a rope. The Chief Mate was rescued from the sailor's strong grasp by the Second, but not till both had received a sound drubbing by the men in general.

Order being restored, the men one and all protested against the First Mate and refused to obey him any more. The Captain consented by placing the Second in the place of the First.

This accident made me a favorite with the men. Our Cook was from that moment intimately permitted to share the Saturday nights with the white lords of the forecastle, and our Captain presented him with fifteen silver dollars and a certificate of his good actions. From this moment my situation became pleasant, I took a liking to the sailor's life and made rapid progress in navigation, which Captain Solomon Town very judiciously did not neglect to instruct me in.

A few days after, we made St. Helena but were not permitted to anchor. Napoleon was still alive and prisoner. No vessel was allowed to go within five miles of the island. A British frigate supplied us two puncheons of water. At the Island of Acension, we took a few more puncheons of water, some pumpkins, and a quantity of turtles. Here our sailors exchanged tobacco and cigars for English flax, clothes, and shells.

We arrived in Boston in July 1820 at night, and made fast to the wharf. Our Captain, who belonged to Salem, immediately left the ship. After making the ship fast, our crew also left. The new-made Chief Mate had a wife in Boston, and under that plea left me and the

Cabin Boy to take care of the ship and cargo, valued at at least 120,000 dollars. The boy being a Bostonian, he soon after followed the Mate. Therefore, by midnight I was the only one left. The Mate had ordered me to keep a good watch; I never left the deck. When morning dawned, I was anxious to see the City of Boston, so highly boasted of by the men during the passage home. Therefore, I drew the door of the cabin to and went up to the main royal yard to see the town. My expectations were not realized; I expected to see a second Calcutta. However, I liked very much the red brick houses and the very white frame buildings. All seemed so neat and clean compared to our European style that it made a favorable impression on a new-arrived stranger. To describe the beauties of Boston Harbor and its marvelous green fields would waste no few pages of paper.

My attention was soon called to my duties on the deck, as I saw an elderly man, not over-well dressed, promenading on the decks. I did not count on the rattlings[1] for my descent but slid down the back stays, just in time to meet this unceremonious stranger whom, in my then foreign notions, I considered by his freedom more of a suspicious character than a gentleman; and without ceremonies, ordered him off the ship. This individual corroborated my suspicions, as after surveying everything around in half a smiling way, asked me if I was alone. To this question I dared not answer, but ordered him off again, and calling for a dog which did not exist, tried by this ruse to frighten him away.

However, I did not succeed; on the contrary; and with the same smile, this stranger continued inspecting the ship fore and aft. I followed him all the while, close on his heels and twitching now and then the stranger's terrible long surtout[2] to enforce my order. During our short promenade he questioned me how the Captain was, about the Mate and the cause for which he was broken, the nature of our cargo, and the number of days we had been from Bengal; and many more questions to which I answered very shortly and, I may say, impertinently, still considering this intruding stranger a rogue.

By this time we had arrived close to the roundhouse which covered the tiller head. This place was adorned on the outside with a handsome set of water buckets artistically painted with a spread eagle and the name of the ship on each. As two of these buckets contained a dozen of small turtles which we had got at the Island of Ascension, these animals attracted his notice and he offered to purchase them. I informed him that only six belonged to me, and I would dispose of them if he paid me well. The contract was struck at

[1]ratlines
[2]overcoat

a dollar each, which he paid down in bank notes, but the bargain was not over, as he insisted on taking the bucket, which of course, I resisted and offered the money back. *1820*

The stranger, not acceding, still held the bucket, and with his ugly smile was enforcing his bargain by pushing me aside. Finding that his grip was stronger than mine and likely to succeed in his evil intentions, I dextrously shook it with all my might, which caused the water and turtles to fall on the deck, and wetted the old sinner's faded coat and feet. But to my astonishment, his cursed smiles not only continued but were transformed into an immoderate laugh which was joined by that of a second, still more suspicious person who had accosted the ship during our dispute.

This aroused my temper still more, and I began to feel mad with passion. I imagined myself in danger, and fastening my teeth on the hand which held the bucket, caused him to loose his hold; and in the scramble the banknotes were partly destroyed. Being now the conquerer, I took up my turtles and again insisted on his leaving the ship immediately, using those phrases peculiar to sailors and which foreigners learn faster than the more polite ones.

This abominable stranger, nothing daunted, made then for the cabin doors, which were ajar, and would have gone down to the cabin had I not quickly placed my back against them. Of course another battle issued, attended with a vacarme[1] of laughs from a crowd of laborers who had gathered on the wharf. This time I could not bite, but kept the apparent thief off with my feet, kicking him whenever he accosted too near. As this dire dilemma could not continue longer, and tears began to fall from my eyes, I threatened to shoot him if he did not leave the ship, and springing down the cabin steps, took up a musket which was kept loaded in a rack. The jocose stranger, prognosticating danger, left the vessel before my return on deck. I found him on the wharf surrounded by sailors and laborers who continued to laugh at my expense, but no one dared to venture on board.

I paraded for a quarter of an hour shouldering my musket and ramming the charge, bidding defiance in my bad English to them all to accost.[2] At last our Second Mate made his appearance, and to my great astonishment, I saw him take his hat off very respectfully to the hated stranger and escort him on board.

This shabby-looking old fellow was no other than the celebrated and highly respected Mr. William Gray, owner of the *Galathea* and her cargo, and a hundred more such vessels. On leaving the ship, the

[1]din, racket
[2]daring them to approach

old gentleman presented me with fifty dollars in exchange, as he said, for the six destroyed in the protection of his property; and on the day of discharging the crew, he not only paid me for the voyage round, but added fifty dollars more for my navigation schooling.

Four years after, I was presented to him at the Marlboro Hotel in Boston by my uncle, who had come to the United States on a commercial tour; and when informed that my first voyage at sea was made in the *Galathea*, he immediately recognized me and addressing my uncle in his jocular manner, told him that in all his life he never had received such cursing as I had given him, and particularly mentioned the fight and the several kicks he had got; further remarking that in nothing I had offended him more than in calling him, "puck-gut-son-of-b--ch," as he knew he was rather inclined to corpulency.

The reader may consider the black look my uncle gave me at the exposition of this behavior, and addressing me in French, demanded an explanation. I explained the matter in English by observing that if I had cursed Mr. Gray on that occasion, it was my first debut in the English language on the American shore, and that Mr. Gray valued it so much he presented me with twice fifty dollars.

This small anecdote brought to my uncle's mind a quarrel I had once with Lord Byron in Leghorn. As it caused some merriment to our company, I take the liberty to repeat it.

The House of Messrs. Webb & Co. of Leghorn, in which my uncle was a partner, were agents for the great English poet. One day, Lord Byron and my uncle were inspecting the landing of some boxes containing curiosities from Greece. I was called to see that they should be properly handled. Lord Byron had occasion for a pencil. My uncle, having none to offer, requested me to hand mine over, which by-the-bye was the first silver pencil I ever before possessed. Of course I handed it with bad grace. My Lord, in a moment of abstraction (I must suppose) very unceremoniously put it in his pocket and went off with my uncle. I saw him depart with some surprise.

Next morning, unknown to my uncle, at an early hour I presented myself at the Poet's house, and after great difficulty was admitted in his room. He was still in bed, and asked me what my business was. I informed him that the day before, I had lent him my silver pencil (strongly articulating the *silver*), which he had forgot to return. He considered some time, then assured me that he had returned it. I insisted to the contrary till I annoyed him, and in his English pride, commanded me to leave the room. I obeyed with reluctance. Till then, our dispute had been carried on in Italian, but at the door, I looked round and called him, *"Sacré cochon d'Anglais."*

The words were hardly out of my mouth when my Lord, in his shirttail, had me by the collar. A second explanation took place in regard to the pencil, and I referred him to my uncle. When I named the relationship, it caused him to give credit to my demand, and after searching all his pockets to no effect, he presented me with his own gold pencil and desired to know why I had cursed in French. I informed him that my father was a Frenchman.

"No wonder," said he, "you called me, *'Sacré cochon d'Anglais.'* The hatred runs in the blood. You do not like the English, eh?"

I answered, "No."

"And why?" said he.

"Because my father died fighting them," I answered.

"You have a right to hate them." And with a sigh he saw me to the door.

Next day[1] he left for Greece. A few days after, one of the store porters offered to sell to my uncle, at an exorbitant price, what he called "Lord Byron's pencil," which he said the Lord himself had presented him with. (It must be remembered that all classes in Italy looked on Lord Byron as a rich nobleman and a great man for the generous cause he espoused in favor of the Greeks; and any trifle of gift of the Poet was considered of great value.)

My uncle was on the point of bargaining with the man when he perceived his own initials: it was the identical pencil he had given me a few weeks before. An explanation took place. The porter received a trifle and myself, after relating the whole story, was deprived of my gold pencil in return for my silver one.

We must return to the old ship. All hands being paid off, I followed the Captain to Salem and became a member of his family.

[1]Byron sailed from Leghorn on 23 July, 1823, which dates Conneau's meeting with some precision.

CHAPTER 2nd

Education in Salem · Ruin in Antwerp and Paris · My First Shipwreck

1821—1825 This town of Salem was not a city in 1821. I experienced more kindness, I enjoyed more juvenile pleasures, and found more affection than I can describe. Every boy in the neighborhood became my friend. My foreign accent fairly captivated everyone I was presented to, and strange to say, no one ridiculed my poor English; on the contrary, my acquaintances even liked my way of pronunciation.

I remember one day I was called in an apothecary shop in Essex Street, I believe. Mr. Webb or Webber, having heard much of my Latin education, desired to ascertain the fact. I was asked whether I could translate Latin. I modestly answered, "A little." A Latin book was presented to me and I was requested to translate it. Fortunately for me, this book was no other than The Fables of Aesop, which but two years before I had translated while in my two Latin classes, and I even knew some of them by heart. Therefore, without a blush I read several of these fables as correctly as I would have done in Italian, and inasmuch as I made the translation in French as I could not then write English sufficiently, in ascertaining the correctness a neighboring confectioner was called in to translate the French into English, which he did badly enough, but satisfied the apothecary and his friends that this Italian boy was certainly a Magister. And though a good deal of fault was found with my Latin pronunciation, none was found in the translation. The Galatian and Spaniards pronounced the Latin quite differently from the English. From this moment I was pointed out as a scholar.

I can observe that in this town, I was taught navigation and sailed in different vessels out of this place for five years. Therefore I entirely owe to Salem and her shipowners my profession as a sailor and master mariner.

I will skip my other voyages in American vessels to India, but this one occurrence I must annoy the reader with, as it will illustrate the different changes time and circumstances operate in a man.

It was on my second voyage to the East Indies in the brig *Phoenix* of Boston, Salem owners, Captain Daniel Bray. The place was called Qualibatoo. I was on shore with the Captain, assisting him in weighing of black pepper, when a war proa (or canoe) arrived with prisoners from one of the Palau Islands and landed them to be sold out as slaves. I saw a young female dragged up the beach by her long

8

hair. The poor creature could not walk, having been cramped up in a narrow log canoe over twenty-four hours. The sight of such barbarity made me blindly sick with passion, and with my boathook I struck the Malay brute down to the ground. This act of rashness of mine obliged us to leave this port with all haste. I have mentioned this occurrence to show what my feelings were at the age of seventeen in regard to slavery.

A few more voyages to the East Indies finished my apprenticeship. I then sailed two voyages in the brig *Malay* as Mate, till a disappointment in my affections caused me to foresake the United States, and I left the brig in Antwerp.

At this place I followed the footsteps of dissipations that many others have done; Antwerp being a noted place for young sailors to spend their hard-earned salary. I did the same, and fell in love again with a Belgian beauty who made a complete fool of me for three months. I visited Paris. At the gambling table lost my all and left my empty trunk to pay the hotel bill.

Cruel necessity compelled me to embark on board an English vessel bound to Rio de Janeiro. The Captain was an Irishman, and his wife ditto, both of the same age, both stout and handsome persons; likewise both hard drinkers.

At my first introduction on board, the Captain presented me with the key of the spirit locker and ordered me under no circumstances whatever to give himself or his wife more than three glasses per day. This injunction I hardly comprehended at first, but on the second day out I was made aware of the necessity of such an order. The Captain's wife came to me about eleven o'clock while I was engaged in drawing the men's grog (gin) and requested I would fill her a tumbler. I did so, and on my return from the deck with the bottle, she again applied for another equal dose, which I reluctantly complied with. At dinner she drank porter and passed the gin as water to her simple husband.

The deception lasted till the porter was exhausted, and every day I continued to supply the Madame with a triple allowance of gin. The Captain never broke his order; three glasses a day were his regular quantity. With few exceptions we had a pleasant passage out, but here in port, both gave full scope to their drinking propensities; both quarreled, made friends, kissed, and quarreled again, often twice a day.

On the fourth day of our arrival at this port the Captain gave me orders to steer the vessel at the inner harbor. The sea breezes coming in, I was preparing to obey the order and had the vessel under sail, when the Captain made his appearance from shore and took command, steering the vessel himself. We were amongst the shipping, and although sailing with fair wind, it required a vigilant eye and a steady hand. Unfortunately the Captain was quite the contrary, being well intoxicated.

My duties called me forward, and observing a vessel ahead, I cried out, "Port your helm," which was not attended to. I then ran to the wheel, but my drinking Commander, with the stubbornness of a true Irishman, refused to give it up and persisted in his course till we came up plump upon the midship of a Swedish ship, smashing her quarterboats and monkey rails. This blunder caused all the vessels in the vicinity to toll their bells and hoot at us in token of contempt, while the Swedish officers called us "drinking lubberly soldiers"—an epithet no sailor can well digest.

This gross act of stupidity sobered our Captain, who immediately left the ship, observing to me, "Had you the command of the vessel and done what I did, I should say you was drunk." And with the assurance that none but his countrymen can assume, he let me clear the wreck, apologize as well as I could to the irritated Swede, and shoulder up the mortifying abuses from the Harbor Master.

For two days the Captain and his wife did not make their appearance on board. On the second evening they returned fresh from the theater. I perceived that both had been drinking and of course, quarreling as usual. Tea was ordered and set under the awning of the quarterdeck. Finding their difficulties increasing, I returned to my hammock under the main boom. They both sat down in a most unconjugal vis-à-vis, when a lie given by the Madame brought a loaf of bread in contact with her head, propelled by the loving Captain. And not content with this demonstration of resentment, he picked up the four corners of the table cloth with all the tea paraphernalia and threw it over the board.

This exhibition of matrimonial friendship put the Madame in a fury, and springing up like a Bengal tiger, she got hold of her lord's scanty locks while she pummeled his eyes with her right hand. The husband, having too much generosity to use his pugilist power, clinched his better half in one of those embraces worthy of a grizzly bear and neglecting a due regard to my modesty, with one hand clewed up her dress, while with the other inflicted several spanks that by their detonations, must have left high ridges on that delicate part.

In fifteen minutes, the tornado had blown over. I was called to give the key of the spirits—a resource that never failed in settling their difficulties—and all parties retired to a sweet repose.

Next morning before daylight, the Captain went ashore without giving me notice. At breakfast the Madame inquired of me if I had seen the last night of the fight. I politely replied in the negative, when she informed me that the quarrel arose in the theater: that when the old gentleman was in his cups, he was generally jealous. She further said it was not the first time she had given him a black eye and obliged him to hide himself for days, which in this instance he certainly did. She also informed me in an apologizing manner that she would not have been so rude, but for his throwing her silver spoons over the board, which had caused her to lose her temper; that she was sorry to have abused such a good man and would go ashore to nurse him, begging me if I had seen *anything* that I would not mention it to anyone; and concluded with the hope that if ever I married, I should meet with such a loving wife as herself.

To this last remark I was silent, reserving to myself the consideration of such an event. Present appearances certainly did not demonstrate the bliss of the marriage state so much boasted of.

Not long after, we made sail for Europe and anchored at Dover for orders, which when received, sent us to Antwerp. The night proved boisterous and squally, which caused us to anchor in the Downs next day and the day after. We proceeded for the entrance of the River Sckelde, but on account of high winds and the approach of night, could not effect it. We took no pilot at Ramsgate, confident of getting off Flushing. After seven the wind arose to great fury from the northwest. Before midnight it blew a gale. All exertions were made by us to run back, but to no purpose, as we could not carry sail. At two o'clock in the morning we ran aground on one of the numerous banks off Flushing, the sea sweeping over us and covering the deck with sand.

Next moment the spars began to fall, and the prospect became frightful, our sailors availing themselves of the confused state in the forecabin and from there, in the spirit room.

The vessel having bilged, I ran below to acertain the quantity of water she had in her hold. On my return I found the Captain dead across the rail, killed by a top gallant yard falling on his head, and his senseless wife near him.

Our situation was most dangerous. A longer stay by the vessel would have been rash madness. Therefore I ordered the longboat over the side and gave the command to the Second Mate, allowing the whole crew to embark, only reserving to myself the Steward and Cook. Unfortunately, I allowed them to take a beaker of gin; this boat was never heard of.

With the assistance of the Cook and Steward, I lowered the

quarterboat with the broken-hearted woman in it and succeeded in pushing off the vessel without accidents. The gale continuing to the northwest, I drifted nearly before the wind, with the expectation of making the lower lands of Belgium, the same direction I had given to the Second Mate.

Our boat being very small, I had placed the Captain's lady between my knees and covered her with all the coats I could get. I managed to steer the boat until daylight, while my two men were constantly employed in bailing her. Shortly after eight o'clock we made the land. Our boat was perceived by the villagers of Bragden, and signal made by them for us to run our boat on the beach, in token of which several of the men took their coats off and went knee deep into the sea, while others threw their hats in the air, demonstrating their willingness to rescue us from the surf. No hopes were left us but to push through this avalanche of breakers, and throwing my hat in the air as a signal to those on shore, I kept off for the shore, propelled by the swell of the sea and wind; and in we went with such rapidity that after the first breaker took us, we saw nothing more till the bold Belgians had us high and dry on the beach. But what was our surprise to find the Captain's wife dead. I could not account when she had departed. During the whole of the trajectory from the wreck to the beach (more than four hours at least), her head had rested in my lap, and no symptoms of pain or convulsion had taken place to denote the struggle of death.

Let me here first pay a tribute to the Captain and his lady, as both were excellent persons. With the exception of the immoderate use of liquor, their habits and morals were faultless. My next tribute of gratitude is due to the very poor villagers and the priest of that parish: the first fed us and clothed us, the last buried the lady and collected a contribution to defray our expenses to Ostend.

Here ends my first unfortunate voyage.

*CHAPTER 3rd

*The Bloomer Captain · We Run Aground ·
The Treacherous Fishermen

On my next trip, I shipped on board a Dutch galliot brig on a voyage to Havana. On taking charge of my office, I soon perceived that I was under the orders of two masters, male and female. The Pantaloon Captain navigated, while the Bloomer one had full control of us all. She was the total owner of this craft, and from Skipper to Cabin Boy, she controlled not only our actions but our stomachs also. Not content with arrogating to herself the scanty distribution of the provisions, she also assumed the prerogative of regulating our conscience, enforcing a strict fasting on Friday and abstaining from meat on Saturday. And never a week passed that her Catholic Almanac did not point out the vigil of some Saint to deprive us of our beef. This petticoated Captain was not only a strong member of temperance, but a Grahamite,[1] as white bread and sugar were abominations to her.

The reader will justly ask why I engaged on such a voyage and under such prospect. My answer is this: I had two motives. First, I was destitute. Having lost my all on the last voyage, I was forced to accept the first offer. Secondly, since my love disappointment in Salem, I had become restless. I had given up all ideas of returning to the United States, and made up my mind to engage in any adventurous expeditions that my profession offered. In 1824, Mexico and the Pacific Ocean were places known for young sailors to make rapid fortunes; therefore this Dutch galliot going to La Havana offered the nearest point of my imaginary El Dorado. These are the causes of my shipping under this marine female termagant.

We left Flushing in a convoy with several vessels, some very sharp American-built ships. Our old galliot, with the shape of Noah's Ark, beat them all out of the channel, and with fair winds no one could touch us. I anticipated a short passage to the Queen of the Antilles, but I was doomed to disappointment.

On the night of the seventh day out, while beating out of the Bay of Biscay in a beautiful moonlight night, myself on the watch, our vessel running about six knots, we ran afoul of a vessel running on the opposite tack. The concussion was terrible, knocking every man on the watch flat on the deck. I know not what damage we did to the

---

[1] Follower of Sylvester Graham (1794–1851)—American dietician who advocated temperance and vegetarianism. Graham flour is named for him.

other vessel, but it must have been great, as I heard someone cry out, "Oh Lord, we are sinking!" However, none of her masts had fallen when we last saw her. As we were completely dismasted, the wind soon drifted her out of sight. At daylight we could not see a vestige of her.

Fortunately I escaped the blame of this misfortunate affair, as a few minutes before the collision took place, I had called the Captain to take in sails.

This accident caused us to make for the nearest port. With jury masts and the assistance of a Spanish vessel, we arrived at Ferrol, near Finsterre, on the fifth day. This catastrophe had the good effect to open our female Captain's heart, as from this moment our crew had no more fasting days or short allowances and provisions were served out freely. For my own part, I had cause to rejoice at the collision, as during the repairs of the vessel, my importance was duly appreciated by our female commander. And in the absence of the Navigating Master, I became with her consent a third Captain *de facto*.

In this port we remained four months. Although Ferrol is the largest and the best arsenal of Spain, we could get no mast for a vessel of two hundred and fifty tons; part of our spars were sent for at Coruña.

Here I was arrested one morning and carried before the Alcalde.[1] An old woman and her two daughters had laid claim to me; the first as her natural son, the others as their younger brother.

A few days before, I had gone by the order of our gentleman Captain to purchase some sides of leather for the use of our riggings: as the tannery was on the other side of the harbor, I had taken with me the boat and four men. We made the purchase, and as I was killing time with my crew, I stopped at a house, calling for water as an excuse. It was handed to me by a young female who immediately ran back and returned with her mother and sister, who eyed me for a short time when, to my astonishment, they all fell on me, kissing and calling me "My dear Antonio, my dear soul, brother," and I know not what, forcibly dragging me into the house, where another great astonishment was in store for me. I found a still older lady who also claimed me for her grandson, and in her grandmotherly affection, slavered my moustache with her toothless mouth.

On the spot, and in the presence of my four shipmates, I was made acquainted by these female relations that six years before, I had left them on my first voyage on board of a Danish vessel; that my

[1]Mayor

daddy "the poor old man" had died two years after I left, and that I was the only male left of the family of Antonio Gomez de Carrasco, and that after such long absence, they hoped I would never more depart. Another kissing match took place. When it came to my Spanish sisters, I responded to their hearts' contents, as they were really cunning looking brunettes. For half an hour, this female quartet continued pouring such a volley of information, and with such volubility, that I was not permitted a word of astonishment or contradiction. At last finding a second of vacuum in their conversation, in a jocular manner and in very bad Spanish (as I could not then speak the language), I asked my affectionate and talkative mother what amount of property my papa Don Antonio Gomez y Carrasco had left me, and where it was. Taking it for granted that all this personification of Mother, Grandmother, and Sister was a joke, I wished to put an end, as time was fast approaching for my return on board.

My pertinent question brought tears in the old lady's eyes. I then saw that the drama had the appearance of veracity. Therefore I hastened to explain their error, but to no purpose. I protested with all my Spanish rhetoric against the relationship. They persisted and brought forward their neighbors, who corroborated the fact in favor of my Galician relations. Finding things had taken such a serious turn and the sun near the horizon, I again assumed the appearance of a credulous son, kissed the girls, and promised my female genitor a prompt return on the next morning.

As I did not keep my word, and two days had elapsed, these affectionate parents had made use of the law to claim their truant son. The Alcalde, after hearing my protestation, dismissed the claim, but my loving relations summoned me before the Admiral Governor of the province, and it was with difficulty that I proved false their maternal title, as my would-be good grandmother had also put in her claim. As I had no document to prove my nationality, I was called on to make display of my education, as my Spanish parent had acknowledged that their son had never received any. At parting I asked the old lady if she ever had a French sweetheart. By her answer I wished to account for the great resemblance I must have had with her son, as my father had been in Spain during the wars.

Our vessel having completed her repairs, we sailed for La Havana and continued without anything of importance, till in the neighborhood of the Bahama Banks. I had cause to chastise the cabin boy for some insolence, who in revenge whispered in the sailing Captain's ears some mysterious words whose magic aroused the green-eyed monster in his soul. In brief, a dispute arose between the Female Commander and our Male Skipper. Explanations took place, and a plump denial was given by her to all the boy's accusations, which in part satisfied him. However, it was but for a short time; jealousy could not rest. The treacherous boy was again questioned, but fearing my presence, refused to rectify what he had said before. His taciturnity, of course, excited still more the offended husband, and prompted by a revengeful curiosity, he tied the boy up and with the end of a rope applied now and then to his posterior, caused him to repeat his first declaration, adding at every blow something more piquant to himself and uncomfortable to his wife, who with myself stood by in astonishment.

The inquisitorial declaration over, I was called in the cabin by the husband Captain, and requested to own every word the boy had said in his agony. Of course my proud silence was the only satisfaction my guilty conscience could make. The Madame, who knew her man, assumed such strong innocence interlarded with a few tears that she fairly cooled the irritated husband's dander, and in his perplexity he ordered me off duty, and to my stateroom.

I know not what passed between them, but the next morning the boy was again well thrashed and turned forward. Our Bloomer Captain was herself again. So much for woman power!

In the course of the day I was invited to my duty, but with stubbornness refused. This refusal caused great uneasiness to the Captain, as he was a poor navigator, and now that we neared the Banks of Bahama, my services were mostly required. He insisted on my resuming office. But no prayer would prevail, as his wife had secretly advised me not to accept, as on deck I was in danger.

The next day we passed the Hole in the Wall and steered for Salt Key. No meridian observation could be had, and no one but myself could determine the latitude by the altitude of the moon, which in our position amongst unknown currents, was of the utmost necessity. I knew this difficulty troubled the Captain, but after the very significant and mysterious word of "danger" uttered by his wife, I dared not take charge. However, I could not imagine then that my refusal would cause the loss of the vessel and the life of every soul on board.

I still made my calculations and silently kept the course of the ship. Another day was passed without ascertaining the meridian latitude. At 10 o'clock that night I furtively took the altitude of the moon, and in the result I found that the vessel had drifted amongst the keys of the Island of Cuba, as my observations gave me five miles
to the northeast of the Cruz del Padre.

Confident of my work and certain of the danger, I proudly resumed my office. Without delay I gave orders to the Second Officer to call all hands, and tack ship. In the meantime, I commanded the Helmsman to luff and bring the vessel to the wind. The officer, proud of his new command, refused to obey till the Captain should be informed, and seeing no danger in sight, would not call him.

Time admitted no delay. I again ordered the Steersman to put his helm down, but, following the example of his Dutch countryman the Second Officer, he did not obey. In this difficulty I let go the lee main brasses and brought the main topsail aback. As the men of the watch came off, I ordered them also to clew up the mainsail. But no one would obey me; one and all had turned against me since the cabin boy affair. On being turned forward, the boy had reported some droll stories to Hollanders of the forecastle, which had ruffled their somewhat apathetic temper.

This fracas brought the Captain from his bed, and on being informed of my resumed duties without his order, and ignorant of the present danger, he ordered me back to arrest, and with the dignity of a most ignorant presumption, informed him crew he well knew how to navigate his own ship, without the mock necessity of lunar observations.

Order being reestablished, the vessel sailed on her former course for twenty minutes, when the lookout reported rocks and breakers right ahead. The helm was put down, but with too much rapidity. The vessel lost its way and took aback, shaving the rocks and falling stern foremost on a reef with seven feet of water.

Here the greatest confusion issued. The Captain returned on the deck with his wife. Everyone gave an order, no one obeyed them, and strange to say, the worst order issued was the only one obeyed: Our Lady Captain had assumed her prerogative and gave the order to let go the anchors. Down went best and second bower.[1] By this time the vessel had swung round and fell on both its anchors. No one thought of clewing up the sails; everyone looked around in perfect Dutch astonishment and stupidity.

This disaster took place about one in the morning. In the dilemma, the Captain's wife called on me to save her ship. Her tears and the dangerous position of the vessel caused me to resume my duties. Every sail was immediately clewed up and anchors weighed. Having lowered the boats, I went with one to find a channel to take the ship out, while the Captain did the same in another boat in the opposite direction.

[1]anchor

This operation lasted till daylight, when we ascertained that we had come over a reef at the top of high water, and that it would be useless to pretend to force her back, as she was then half a foot imbedded on a coral flat. At daylight a boat came alongside from a neighboring key, apparently deserted. On board, they called themselves fishermen, and certainly their appearance denoted such. They spoke Spanish only, the Boss of these five men spoke French. Their boat was an excellent one, well furnished with fishing implements. The whole of them wore their flannel shirts outside the pantaloons; this, I found afterwards, was to hide their long knives.

The head man of these fishermen informed us that if we would land our cargo on the key and lighten our vessel—in which operation they would assist us—we could get her off at the full of the moon; that the place to deposit our goods was a safe one, as they had only a hut there and would answer for all losses and pilot us out free of all dangers, for which, in renumeration of their services, we were to pay them one thousand dollars. Here I may observe that while the head man of these fishermen was conversing with us, some of his men were inspecting very minutely ever part of the vessel, while others busily inquired of our crew, the nature of our cargo, and the quality and quantity of our armaments. Myself acting as interpreter, it was agreed by the Captain, with his wife's consent, that if we could not get off by evening and return of tide, we should accept his offer.

The principal fisherman then made a new condition: once the vessel was afloat, the money should be paid him on the spot in hard cash, and not on a draft on Havana. To this the Captain too readily and imprudently agreed. This last part of the agreement was received with palpable satisfaction by the Boss, as I perceived him nod to one of his men who had approached us.

Shortly after, they left the vessel on their fishing excursion—as they said—promising to call back in the evening. We offered them a bottle of gin and a Dutch cheese which was indifferently accepted, but they disdainfully refused our black biscuit. As they were about pushing off, the Chief of them asked me if I was a Frenchman, our conversation having been in that language. I informed him the name of my native place; he then inquired of my name. I gave it also, which caused him much surprise, and he left the vessel, eyeing me as I then thought very suspiciously.

After breakfast we lowered the boats and again went on an exploring and sounding expedition, and returned sorely disappointed, both agreeing in one opinion to discharge the cargo.

Long before sundown, our apparently friendly fishermen came back and neglectfully tendered again their services, which were accepted. The place designated to deposit our goods was inspected by the Captain. As everything appeared correct and honest, it was agreed that the next morning the landing should begin.

At daylight next day, the appearance of two strange boats at anchor near the key gave me some uneasiness, and I mentioned my apprehensions to the Captain and Lady, but it was overlooked. We then began to discharge part of our heaviest cargo. The fishermen assisted us with their boat, but evidently with little progress. At sundown we compared accounts and found great differences in favor of the fishermen. I was ordered on shore to ascertain the error. On my landing I saw several new faces, and in particular a Frenchman who addressed me as his countryman and offered me some refreshments. His manners and language were those of a well-educated man, his person and physiognomy inclined more toward the aristocratic than the French plebian. Still, his features strongly denoted a long life of dissipation and a premature age. After conversing some time, he invited me to spend the night on shore, which I declined; and having rectified the error, I was about embarking when the Frenchman again insisted on my remaining on shore. As I positively assured him such could not be the case, he remarked that he had orders to do so by my countryman, the head man of the boat, and I would probably repent it if I did not remain.

On my return on board, I found that in my absence, the Captain had very injudiciously informed the *soi-disant*[1] fishermen of the rich nature of our cargo, and at one time I saw one of them pointing to a box which contained gold laces and epaulettes, wink at his companion, and rub his hands in token of complete satisfaction.

Before leaving the vessel, the Boss asked me in very pure Italian why I had not remained on shore and accepted his invitation. I answered in the same language and said my duties did not permit it. He then beset me with many questions as to my age, my parents, and my expectations; I remarked[2] that once or twice he exclaimed, "Poor boy! Why did you not remain on shore?" And when about stepping over the side, he wished me good night, so I offered my hand. After first having made a motion to take it, he forcibly rejected it.

These demonstrations, with what I had seen and heard on shore, caused me to suspect some future danger. At tea I again fully explained to the Captain my apprehensions, but unfortunately they were ridiculed.

By nightfall I had taken good care to place below every case containing valuables. I suspected some treachery, and had we had

[1]self-proclaimed
[2]noticed

arms, I should certainly have armed our crew, much to the annoyance of the Captain. Unfortunately, we had not even a single firelock.

At 8 o'clock I set two men in the watch with positive orders to call all hands at the least appearance of a boat. The Captain, wife, and crew having retired, I went to my stateroom, but as I found it occupied by a myriad of mosquitos, I took refuge in the forestay sail netting and covered myself with its sail, well tired of my day's work.

It must have been about one or two o'clock of the morning when I was awoke by a dreadful cry from the deck. On looking about, I saw the decks full of men, but as the moon had just set I could not make out their movements. Still, I could hear the cries and moans of the dying men. I aroused myself from what first appeared to me a dream, and once convinced of the reality, by the help of the gasket, dropped myself into the water and struck out for the shore. It was time. My fall had made some noise, and my flight was observed, as I distinctly heard a rough voice calling out in Spanish, "Stop, or I fire."

I dove, swam, dove, and went ahead, not knowing what would be my fate, but following the impulse of nature—self-preservation. After five minutes' hard swimming, I turned on my back to rest and take a fresh departure. I could not see the key, but saw the mast of the vessel, which was sufficient mark to guide me for the shore.

I continued by the assistance of this beacon to make for it, and as the sea was perfectly calm, in a short time I touched ground. I had divested myself of my shirt; shoes I had none on when I left the vessel. Therefore, when I landed I had on only a pair of trousers. I immediately made for the bushes—sort of dwarf mangrove trees and yacca[1] plants well stoked with briars. I had not been but a minute in this refuge when I was beset with an abundance of mosquitos that obliged me to make for the beach and hide myself in the water.

I was tormented in this manner the whole night. At daybreak I returned to the bushes and climbed the highest tree, only twelve feet. I saw my former home dismasted to the deck with several boats alongside, and about twenty men busily employed throwing cases and bales into them. Here then, my suspicions were correctly and too truly realized, but the meaning of the head man's conduct toward me was still a mystery. I could not solve why he had shown such sympathy or pity by singling me out from this murderous intent, as by the appearance of our ship and the cries on the deck of that night, I could not but believe that everyone had been butchered.

[1]a West Indian relative of the yew that bears pulpy fruits

*CHAPTER 4th

*My Capture by the Pirates · I Meet Don Rafaelin, Who Takes Me for His Nephew

I continued in my position, watching their movements, eating now *1826* and then some of the yacca berries, the most insipid and flattest-tasting of all fruits. About two o'clock I saw several boats towing the hulk of the unfortunate galliot to the southeast of the key, and shortly it disappeared. Till then I made all efforts to restrain myself from tears, but when all hopes were lost of ever seeing my friends and companions, nature resumed its dominion. If these narratives were confessions, the reader would see in them the description of a guilty conscience. Yes, I am not ashamed to say that I found no consolation till I prayed to my Maker, as the loss of so many lives could not be imputed but to my improper conduct.

I then collected a quantity of the berries and was looking out for what we sailors call a soft plank to lay down for the night, having previously devised a sure method to escape the annoyance of mosquitos—which was to bury myself in the sand and cover my head with my pants—when a noise in the neighboring bushes caused me to look about. Briefly I saw a ferocious dog, nose to the ground in search of some game. I could not mistake the nature of his hunt, but with the agility of a grasshopper, I sprang to my friendly perch just in time to save the seat of my pants. The disappointed animal then gave the alarm, which was cheerfully responded to by other canine hunting notes. Then came three of the same breed, followed by two men with guns in hand. They were not surprised at finding me, as I was the game they were in search of.

I was ordered down, and made to walk before them. They advised me not to attempt to run, as the bloodhounds would tear me to pieces if they commanded.

We crossed the island to the south and arrived at a rancho, the habitation of these men. I was ordered to sit down til the whole party would collect. As my captors also sat down to eat, I was allowed to partake of their meal. They then informed me that from an early hour in the morning they had been in search of me and wondered how I could have swum a mile or more. I ventured some questions, when I was informed that it would be good for my health to be quiet.

At sundown, the whole community of this unpopulated island collected, forming two parties, each headed by their respective Chief. One was the apparent leader of these two gangs and proprietor of the rancho; in this man I recognized the "Patroon" of the boat, the same that had inquired so minutely into my personal affairs. His associates addressed him, "Patroon Rafaelin"; they all surveyed me very suspiciously and then retired to the rancho, a hut made with ships' planks and old sails. Only one person was left to watch over me, who amused himself in whetting a knife on a stone.

The conversation was a long one. I could overhear every word, understood but few, but one in particular did not escape me. The meaning was so significant and interesting to me that it made my hairs stick out to the end, and as I understood it perfectly, I will give it here in Spanish: "Muertos no hablan." The English, verbatim, is "Dead men tell no tales." Let anyone imagine himself in my position: half naked, my skin covered with blisters from the bites of mosquitoes, with four bloodhounds at my feet, and a pirate, knife in hand, as my sentry, and the above conversation repeating the sickening, deadly words; to him I would ask, can hell have worse torments?

The piratical conclave lasted over three quarters of an hour, in which I was the sole topic, and coming to no agreement, the principal, Rafaelin, burst from the rancho with a blunderbuss in hand. He called me to him, and placing his strong grasp on my shoulder, whirled me round behind him. Then facing both bands, with a dreadful oath he swore destruction on the whole band if they persisted in the death of his nephew!

At the mention of the word "nephew," everyone drew near and agreed to respect his new-found relation, but desired I should take a solemn oath never to divulge either by word or writing to anyone the present or hereafter occurrences, during my whole life. I did what I was forcibly desired to and shook hands with everyone except my sentry, of whom I shall speak hereafter.

Friendship begets generosity. Each one vied in offering me some clothes, and in a few minutes I was rigged *cap-en-pied*.[1] We then all sat down to a cold supper such as fried fish, olives, sardines, ham, and cheese, with an abundance of red wine. The repast nearly over, the conversation fell on me. Everyone wondered (not without some cynical jokes at my protector Patroon Rafaelin) how such a mushroom relationship had sprung up, and ironically demanded of me some explanation.

My pretended uncle answered them thus—"Caballeros, you all seem to doubt my word. Therefore, you do not treat me as your superior. For many months we have broke bread together, shared the same dangers, and equally divided the same spoils. Have you ever found me in a lie? As your Chief, have I not always led the way?

[1]from head to foot

Have I not at times taken the most dangerous post? Was it not me that brought down the Commander of the American schooner *Grampus*? And for all this, what payment do I receive but black ingratitude? You dare doubt my word; yes, your sneering countenances denote it. Can this wine have intoxicated you?" (dashing the bottle before him to the ground). "Or has the blood of last night rendered you blind drunk to doubt my word? Have I not said it? And what Rafaelin says is the Gospel, and no one shall doubt it. I tell you, Caballeros, the moment any one of you doubts my word, him or I must die, and here I stand ready to give you all satisfaction, one by one or in a mass."

This speech was delivered with vehemence and a most daring emphasis. No one interrupted him to the last, when the Patroon of the other party, laying his hand on his arm, said to him in a coaxing mode, "Amigo Rafaelin, you take the joke in too serious a manner. No one here wishes to injure the boy or disbelieve you. Calm yourself, and let us drop the subject."

"No, Caballeros, I will prove to you that Rafaelin never lies." And calling one of his gang, he said to him, "Take him" (pointing to me) "out of hearing distance of this place, and I will condescend to narrate to you the tie of our parentage. I will tell you the name of his family and the place of his birth. Then you, Patroon Mesclet, who speaks Italian, shall interrogate him, and if his answers do not corroborate my narrative, then call me a coward."

I was sent out, and in ten minutes recalled, when the following questions were set to me: First, "What is your father's and mother's name?"

I answered.

Second: "How many uncles have you on your mother's side?"
I told them.

Third: "Was any one of your uncles a naval officer? And where is he at present?"

I answered that the only uncle naval officer I had I saw but once, and that was in 1815 on his way to Marseilles to embark on the Spanish Main, and that since that time, I had never heard a word of him.

My answers gave full satisfaction to the unbelieving crew. With a few more bumpers, we all retired to rest, each one under a mosquito net, leaving the four sagacious Cerebuses to watch over our slumbers. I laid me down thankful that so far, my life had been spared, but could not sleep; my agitated mind wandered from topic to topic. I could not account how this man Rafaelin could be so well informed with my family affairs as to pass himself off for my uncle. I knew I   23 had one in South America; I had seen him but once in all my life, and his appearance was much different from the one present. My mother's brother was a small-statured man, and strongly marked with the smallpox. The present, to the contrary, was a very handsome and smooth-faced man, and nearly six feet, with fine proportions to match. Still, his motives were good; his daring in protecting me had sufficiently shown it.

My slumbering rest was tormented with frightful dreams. The phantom of the butchered wife in her bloody clothes would rise before me, and with her arms round my neck implore my protection, then tearing herself away, would curse and accuse me as the author of her ruin, and till the morning dawned I was the slave of a conscience-struck nightmare. These dreams haunted me all the while I remained with these filibusteros.

At daylight, they all took coffee and left in their boats with axes and saws. On leaving the rancho, Rafaelin gave orders to the man who had performed sentry over me the night before to have breakfast ready by eleven o'clock, and for me to assist him.

I shall here give a description of this man, as he made some figure during my stay in this key. His name I never knew, but he was called Galliego, being a native of Galicia (Spain). Born of poor fishermen parents, he had received no education. Nature had stamped him with one of those physiognomies disagreeable at first sight. His speech and manners were of the very coarsest kind, his dress and general appearance were also of the most disgusting; to this man I was appointed as Cook's Mate.

A fire was made under some dwarf bushes and a large kettle put on to boil. Galliego then beckoned me to follow him to a thick cluster of trees some distance from the rancho, where under a cover of tarpauling we took our butter, onions, salt codfish, lard, rice, and all necessary for a breakfast. This spot was their pantry, and a large one it was. It contained not only an abundance of provisions and wines, but strewed pell mell I saw charts and spy-glasses, with a quantity of cabin furniture. We then returned to our camp kitchen, and I took my first lesson in Spanish cooking. Water we got from holes dug in the sand, which yielded enough for cooking and drinkable purposes, and when cooled in porous water monkeys, it lost much of its brackishness. Wood we had in abundance from the wrecks of vessels; tomatoes, mint, and peppers grew by our water diggings.

Breakfast was made ready in accordance to orders, and on their return we all sat down to eat. No one could find fault with our *déjeuner*, as it consisted of stewed codfish, boiled rice, and ham.

Wine was distributed liberally; coffee, brandy, and cigars completed our repast.

By two o'clock, some had retired to take a siesta, others took muskets to shoot gulls and sharks. Galliego and myself returned to our culinary duties and scullion-like, washed the dinner paraphernalia. Being the youngest in the cuisine department, I had the feeding of the dogs.

My duties over, I was preparing to follow the example of my piratical masters when Rafaelin made a motion for me to follow him, and handing me a musket, we made for the Interior. At a solitary spot we both sat down. Rafaelin then addressed me thus: "Well, young man, how old are you?"

I answered, "Nineteen."

"You must be surprised at all the events that have taken place these four days past. I have brought you here now to explain to you a mystery. I was obliged last night to pass myself off for your uncle to save your life, and would have fought them all to carry my point. When I first saw and interrogated you, I recognized in your face the countenance of your uncle Luis, and from that moment I swore the blood of my comrade's nephew should not stain my hands."

After a long pause, he resumed. "Young man, although you see me here at the head of a set of desperados, I am not in reality what I appear. I am the unfortunate slave of circumstances. I am a wretch, forced to become a bloodhound. I am—oh God!—a pirate and assassin," and with both hands he covered his convulsive face while his strong chest shook with remorse. This burst of repentant passion over, taking me by the hand, he again resumed.

"Nephew of my friend," said he, "your uncle was for a long time my brother in arms, in this American continent and in Europe. We fought side by side. We had but one purse, his enemies were my foes, and his friends my brothers. We had no secrets from one another, and our friendship dated from school. We both emigrated to Mexico, fought for their freedom, and received the reward of mercenary soldiers. Mexico once free, their pusillanimous legislators drove us from their soil. Five years after, your uncle died in my arms. A fatal duel robbed me of my companion and my dear friend Luis. You understand now why and how I personated your uncle so well, and you may comprehend why I have saved you alone out of the Dutch crew.

"I have much to say to you, but time will not admit of it. However, this I recommend you at present: you must school and guard your conduct according to circumstances during your short stay here. I intend that you shall not remain here long, and I will carry my point. You see I lack of no power over those ruffians. Still, I must use circumspection, not one of your actions must mar my projects. Therefore hear me well, and follow my instructions, and I will answer for your life, and short captivity."

He further resumed and said, "Young man, if I saved your life, it was to return you into the world and society, untainted with blood or dishonor. But to attain this object, we must both act our part. Present, I fear them not, but in my absence, if they should, by some misplaced word of yours, find out that you are not in reality my nephew, I would not answer for your life. Therefore hereafter you must call me Uncle Rafaelin, and I will call you Theodore. Next, I wish you to bear in mind, never ask questions. Make yourself useful about the rancho, and be civil to everyone. And this I particularly beg of you: be as cheerful as possible. Let not the recollection of your mother and sisters move you to tears—I saw them yesterday. Men of our stamp, whom present circumstances oblige you to associate with, do not understand them.

"I also require of you to form friendship with no one. Not one here, including myself, are your fit companions even for one single minute, and as your present occupation will bring you in contact with them, avoid all superfluous conversation: their society cannot be yours. Shun the smooth-tongued Frenchman, never attend our revels, and forsake wine.

"Our Cook Galliego, of him be on your guard. He is a great coward, but revengeful as a cat; he is our man of dirty work. If you should come in collision with him, strike first and well. No one will care for him, even his death would create no importance. Here, take this knife"—presenting a long cuchillo—"Keep it by day and night at your side, and make good use of it in safe defense. In a few days I shall say more. Keep good heart, and adieu."

We then parted and returned by different ways to the rancho.

Next day, finding a chest of carpenter's tools amongst some rubbish, I went to work and made a rudder for one of the boats. At their return at breakfast, they admired my mechanical handiness and Rafaelin, availing himself of the opportunity to separate me from Galliego and these servile occupations, proposed that I should repair the boat throughout. I accepted my new office, as I was better acquainted with the adze than the ladle.

*CHAPTER 5th

*Galliego a Thief · We Become Honest Fishermen
While Awaiting the Authorities from Havana

A few days passed. The men left at daylight to their work of destruction, as I found out afterwards, returning at midday. I employed myself at carpentry and sailmaking till one morning, the two large boats were manned, and my countryman informed me that they were going to the mainland of Cuba on business, and that I was to remain with the Cook in charge of the place, and be of good cheer, as he would not remain away but five days. To the Cook he recommended the care of the dogs, and to keep himself sober.

This day, Galliego would not cook. The poor dogs suffered most, as they would not eat dry biscuit. Next morning, this man of all dirty work, whose passion for fishing was a necessity, took a canoe and left me alone on the island. I passed part of the day in hunting for the dogs and cooking for myself. At night the Cook came back, prepared his own supper, fed the dogs, intoxicated himself, and retired without speaking a word.

At midnight I observed him leave the rancho with a bundle. He did not return till nearly daylight. The next night again, a bundle was taken out, and in the same furtive manner he left, returning at the same hour as the night before.

His taciturnity and his industrious night excursions made me suspicious, and on the fourth night I followed him at some distance, but took the precaution to take a loaded musket with me, with a fresh priming. Keeping at convenient distance, I saw him enter a very thick low bush and disappear. I returned, convinced that I could remember the spot the next day.

After coffee, as usual, Galliego left in his canoe with fishing apparatus. I watched till he anchored some two miles off the reef. Then calling for the dogs, I directed toward the bush, and in the object of my search, the dogs were of great assistance, as they would scent the footsteps of the Cook, after being placed on his track, better than I could see them.

After some trouble, I came up with a large patch of sand with many heaps of stones which had the appearance of graves. On a more minute inspection, I found one had the form of a cross, which I suppose must have been the grave of one of their comrades. I lingered here some time, wondering who these graves must have belonged to.

On entering this small deserted field of sand, I had observed a large quantity of land crabs take flight, but after a while they had returned and introduced themselves into all the graves but one. It struck my curiosity. I ventured closer and found that the sand nearby had been freshly smoothed down with a cloth. This evidence assured me in the belief that I was on the true track of Galliego's hiding place. Certain that I could not be detected, and with my musket by me, I began to remove the stones, taking care to mark their position in order to replace them.

I worked for ten minutes, when I discovered two boards which covered two pitch barrels on their head. One was filled with several bundles containing many pieces of silks, linens, and handkerchiefs; the other contained a chronometer, several pieces of lace, and a well gilt-bound Bible. One bundle in particular struck my observation. It was tied up in a madras handkerchief I had seen before. I loosened the knots and found several trinkets belonging to the Dutch Lady. I knew her silver comb, and a large silver pin mounted with diamonds; the Captain's wife wore it the last day I saw her. Sick at the sight, I replaced everything with precision, and smoothing the sand with my flannel shirt, returned to the rancho.

My agitated mind found no rest. The manual labor, which I used in former days as drunkards do narcotics or intoxicating drink to allay their troubled minds, in this instance failed me. My melancholy was not relieved till tears came to my support.

Kind reader, forgive these tears again, I was but nineteen. With these past events and such a prospect before me, could I restrain them? At the sight of a jewel which but few days before I had seen on the head of a dear friend and who now lay a murdered corpse, what eyes could remain tearless?

Just before sunset, our well-trained hounds gave the alarm of the approach of strangers. Not long after, four boats made their appearance. The first two of them belonged to the rancho, with Rafaelin and his crew. The other two boats contained two strangers to me, and their appearance was more that of a landsmen than sailors. Patroon Rafaelin denoted them by the appellation, "amphibious Jews." The boats were filled with provisions and a large quantity of fishing tackle; one of them contained a dead bullock from a plantation, which had been very unceremoniously shot. They had also brought fowls and pigs to stock the rancho.

These things landed, a supper was soon prepared which ended in a perfect orgy. As I attended the sober part of this repast, I found that the "amphibious Jews" were speculators—half thieves, half
bagholders—and had come from Cardenas to purchase the wrecked

goods. During the supper, many jokes were passed in regard to the last wreck, but none of the strangers ventured any questions; of course they knew the whole affair.

Next day I was sent out fishing with Galliego, and on our return, the strangers had left. Some days after, the Frenchman informed me that they had purchased the whole of the Dutch cargo.

After supper, Patroon Rafaelin requested me in French to take a long walk. I promptly obeyed, as I supposed they were to settle and divide the spoil with Mesclet and his party, who belonged to Galindo, a neighboring key some seven miles east of Cruz del Padre. While on the mainland, Patroon Rafaelin and his party had received information that the authorities in Havana were about sending an officer to inspect these keys, and in advance had procured for himself and his party a fishing license.

The loose ships' timber about the island was collected and burnt. The canvas roof of the hut was taken off, and leaves substituted. The furniture and armament was hid in a creek whose labyrinthine entrance defied all search. It took us two days' hard work to complete our transfiguration, and with the fishing apparatus and with several alterations in the huts, our rancho was transformed into the somewhat-looking semblance of a fishing establishment.

This work at an end, we began to fish in earnest. Every day two boats were sent a-fishing. Rafaelin headed one, the Cook—as the best fisherman—headed the other. I belonged to the Patroon's boat. On the return of the boats at midday, Galliego's was generally full, while ours was only a quarter loaded. We then cleaned, split, and salted the fish to dry them next day in the sun. This fish is called pargus, and when full grown, it weighs from 12 to 20 pounds. When dry, it sold at eight cents per pound.

We continued collecting fish for a week, and had piled up over a thousand when one morning at daylight, the hounds gave notice of the approach of a stranger. It gave no uneasiness to them, as everything was placed in the appearance of a well-conducted fishing establishment. We awaited the arrival of the strangers by preparing breakfast, as by appearance we supposed them to be Government boats. It so proved when their pennants hove in sight.

On landing, the Commanding Officer demanded of the Patroon his fishing license, which was produced, and every man responded to his name, myself included. This gold-lace magnate inspected the rancho, our pile of fish, and the great quantity of nets; and the apparent scantiness of our poor provisions quite satisfied his official credulence of our lawful occupation. He was then regaled with a fish breakfast.

I observed that Rafaelin at every occasion pleaded poverty and complained much of the hard times. This finesse was necessary, as a sort of tribute, or more vulgarly called hush-up money, was to be paid. Uncle Rafaelin's deception proved effective, as on embarking, this important inspecting officer signed the license with the gratification of only six ounces. I understood afterwards that this visit was not made by the authorities of Havana to inspect the keys and drive out the piratical stations established there, as it was publicly given out, but to impress sailors for the Navy. The six doubloons bonus was paid to the officer for the easy manner he endorsed our salt water and whitewashed license. As the boats disappeared, the men gave three cheers, as this inspection would not be renewed for six months.

Next day we brought back the furniture, armament, and cooking apparatus. We still continued to fish, and added to the establishment one more branch for our fishing speculation—which was fishing for right turtle, more commonly called the hawk's bill turtle, though more correctly called tortoise. This animal is caught in a floating net with a decoy shaped like a turtle fastened to it. The net is then anchored in 10 to 15 fathoms of water and allowed to float with the current. The turtle, on seeing the decoy, naturally takes it for one of its species, and in its sport entangles itself in the treacherous meshes. Once fastened by a flipper, the animal involves itself in the net and sinks exhausted, captive to man's ingenuity.

The season favored us, and we caught 26 right turtles and a quantity of loggerhead and green turtles. The shell of the tortoise brought over six hundred dollars when sold. We continued fishing for six weeks, when the Patroon received information that a French vessel, richly laden, had got ashore at Callo Verde, one of the keys some 40 miles east of us.

That evening, both boats were manned, and leaving to me the care of the establishment, departed armed to the teeth.

Once sole lord of the premises, I began forming plans for an escape. I matured my flight in a few moments and set to effect it too, as the darkness of the night favored me. I launched the canoe—the only embarcation left—and placed the sail, sculls, and grappling iron in it. I then returned to the rancho for some clothing. As it was dark, I lighted a candle. I then observed some chalk marks on the floor, and read the words: "Patience. On my return I will free you. (Destroy this.)" These words caused me to reflect and postpone my departure till next morning.

At noon the next day, a small pilot-boat made its appearance from

the west, sailing inside the reef with the assurance of a perfect pilot.
The dogs, as usual, had given notice before sunrise. I hastened to fasten them, as I could not manage them on such occasions when Galliego was away.

Two men landed and inquired for the Patroon Rafaelin. I told them I believed he had gone to the mainland, when they informed me that they had come from that quarter and had not met him. As I would not give them the direction the boats had taken, the principal of the two informed me that he had brought provisions for his countryman Rafaelin. I gave him the canoe to land them.

This man also informed me that Rafaelin had engaged him on his last trip to the mainland to bring the said provisions down and take me to Havana. But it was to be done with much caution, as his men would not consent on my leaving them until I had become as guilty as they. What I learned gave me full confidence in what Rafaelin had promised in the chalk inscription, and in gratitude I made my mind to await the ratification of his engagement.

I remained alone three days longer and amused myself in shooting possums for the dogs, and harpooning sharks. On the fourth day, the boats returned in company with the pilot-boat. I observed some quarrel had taken place, as they appeared discontented. The pilot-boat seemed now loaded. Next day they took her to the mysterious creek, where the fruits of their depredations were concealed.

The Frenchman, who had returned wounded in the head, remained behind, and with the volubility natural to his countrymen, informed me that on their arrival at Callo Verde, they had found the French vessel had been taken possession of by the fishermen of that place. (Of course he meant pirates.) As the dirty work was done, they had therefore arrived too late and lost their part of the plunder. A quarrel had taken place with the first possessors, himself had been wounded with a handspike, and Rafaelin, with his knife in hand, had secured their retreat to their boats. But on the pilot-boat's arrival, they again boarded the French vessel and carried her. In the second engagement, two men of the other party had been killed. They had then taken what goods of value they found remaining, but he really believed that the best part had been taken away. "Thank God!" he then added, "we have now the assistance of Bachicha" (a nickname for Francisco) "who is as brave as Rafaelin. And with his schooner, which is a real Baltimore clipper, we can carry on our business in grand scale. We can now cruise under the Colombian flag, and as Rafaelin says, 'rob Paul to pay Peter.' "

During my further conversation with this man, I found out that this small craft had brought down a large amount of ammunition, and a long 12-pounder to be placed in midship. He then recounted me his life, which I will reduce in few words.

His name was Alexandre B., born at Marseilles. His education had been classical and his family rich. His father had entrusted him with a cargo of wine and oils, which product he squandered at the gambling table; had got in debt, took to drink and vagabondage, was pressed by the police of Havana, made his escape, joined Rafaelin's party, and liked the present mode of living. One month after this conversation he died of his wound; we could not keep him from the bottle.

CHAPTER 6th

I Am Captured Yet Again Aboard the Cara-Bobo

1826

On the return of the party, they again prepared to depart for the mainland to sell—they said—the product of our fishing excursions. The fish and tortoise was packed in the boats, and soon next morning they took their departure. On parting, Rafaelin proposed to me that during his absence, I had better continue fishing with the Cook and assist him in setting the nets, that by so doing, I should be entitled to a share of the proceeds. Of course I consented. He also assured me that his promise would be soon ratified.

As the nets had been neglected, it took us two days to mend them. On the third, Galliego and I took the canoe, and according to orders, went fishing. By breakfast time we dropped anchor in 18 fathoms to take our repast. Shortly after, we saw a large schooner apparently steering full sail for us. My taciturn companion, after observing the vessel some time, pronounced her a Colombian privateer, saying we had better up anchor and go inside. I remarked that she was not making for us, and even if she did and wanted fish they would pay us, for it was cowardly to run and I would not go. I made many more remarks to induce Galliego to remain. I had heard so much spoken of Colombian privateers and the Patriot Service that I thought this a good opportunity to make my escape.

The Cook insisted on going in. I remonstrated *con furore*. High words issued, and Galliego, who was in the fore part of the boat, took his knife to enforce his argument by cutting the anchor rope. I gave him no time to effect it, but with one blow of an oar laid him senseless in the canoe. The schooner had neared us within a musket shot when this happened, and the Commander had seen the dispute. As he passed us at the rate of four knots an hour, a grappling[1] was dropped onto our canoe, which forced us in tow after the schooner.

Once into deeper water I was ordered up, while Galliego was hoisted up insensible to the deck. The Commander then questioned me about the dispute. I told the truth, reserving that which I thought unnecessary—my desire to ship. He also inquired if I could procure him a Pilot for Key West. In the meantime the Cook, who had come to and heard the conversation, answered "Yes," and pointing to me, assured the Commander that I was a Pilot.

Mistaking the word "Pilot" (which in Spanish means "Navigator"), the Commander, who was French and spoke Spanish very

[1]grappling hook

indifferently, took it literally for "Pilot," and believing me such, impressed me on board. I remonstrated, protested, swore, but all in vain.

Galliego, who saw the mistake, enjoyed the *jeu-de-mot* and mocked me for not believing him. On parting, he gave me to understand that his report to Rafaelin would not be much in my favor. They paid him for his fish and towed him back near the reef.

Once the vessel was under full sail, I was ordered to give the course for Key West. I informed the Captain Monsieur Laminé of the mistake, belabored him for comprehending the word "Pilot" for "Port Pilot," and referred him to anyone on board for the translation of "Pilot" which in Spanish was *practico;* and that Galliego had been prompted by revenge in availing himself of the Commander's imperfect Spanish to press me in his service. I acknowledged that I was a Navigator, but could not without danger undertake to pilot his vessel in a place I never had been.

Nothing would convince the French scamp, and with a kick where the coattails should be, he told me that "Sauce for the goose was good for the gander," and Pilot I must act. The First Lieutenant, an ignoramus and a brute like himself, repeated the blow, which sent me abaft the wheel. Here, then, I was in a worse predicament; I had fallen from the pan into the fire.

This privateer was called the *Cara-Bobo.* "Booby's Face" had a commission from the authorities of Cartagena to burn, sink, and destroy all Spanish property. She registered about 200 tons, and her crew consisted of 75 men of all nations and of all colors. The First Lieutenant, a Creole of Pensacola, spoke Spanish and French well, but little or no English. The commander was a native of the Island-of-France. Both were no Navigators, and this accounts for their impressing me; two of the Navigators had been sent away with prize ships, while the third was sick below with the fever.

Forced to take charge, I called for charts and instruments and shaped my course for the desired port. Key West was then a very small place and indifferently marked on the charts. It required all my seamanship to take a vessel drawing 12 feet of water over shoals that I knew nothing of.

We steered west-northwest the whole day. At sundown I ordered the vessel to for the night. Many objections were made by the Commander and First Officer, who insisted on carrying sails; however, I presented and carried my point. But to punish me for my obstinacy, I was ordered to keep watch the whole night.

To obey had been the order of the day for some time with me. I
promenaded the lee side of the deck till nearly eleven o'clock, when

exhausted with fatigue, I sat myself down on a long brass chaser and incautiously fell asleep.

I know not how long I remained in this position, but a tremendous shock knocked me off the cannon, and I found myself sprawling on the deck with my nose and both ears bleeding, and the First Lieutenant, cigar in hand, kicking my sides.

I soon saw the bad joke: the gun had been fired off by him with his cigar. My blood did not flow fast enough to cool me. I sprang to my feet, and with a rammer in hand, made for the aggressor. His hasty descent in the steerage saved his skull. The Commander, finding the joke too serious, reprimanded him in very severe terms.

At daylight we made sail and at 4 P.M. I succeeded in taking the *Cara-Bobo* in the narrow harbor of Key West. As the Commander was leaving for the shore, he ordered me on no account to land. Sentries were placed to prevent boats from approaching.

The Captain had not been gone but a few minutes when two men seized me while in the act of looking to the shore with the spyglass. They carried me below and put me in double irons. I would have been kept on bread and water, but for the kindness of the sailors who clandestinely supplied me with food from their kidd.[1]

On the third day, Monsieur Laminé returned with an American Pilot. I was set free and the vessel was got underway on another cruise. I was ordered to resume duties as Navigator, but I promptly refused till I had received satisfaction from his Lieutenant. But as he had told his story fresh, and as dogs do not eat dogs, I was not heard. The First Lieutenant, who felt the sting of mortification from the public reprimand the Commander had given him on my account, took the first opportunity to revenge himself, and to support his conduct had reported that he only secured me as I was making my escape for the shore.

The cruise had lasted a week, making only one sorry prize of a coasting craft, which was burnt. One morning, however, we caught a Tartar. A Spanish packet gave us fits and our long legs (as we sailors call it) saved us from a visit in the Moro Castle.

By this time I had become intimate with the American Pilot. I had before this intentionally assured the Pilot that I had been naturalized in the United States. This deception had a good effect, and through his influence with the Commander my condition was much ameliorated, but still I refused to do duties. The Third Mate, who had recovered from the fever, attended to the navigation. He was a native of Spain; to him I made known my intention to avail

[1]sailor's mess tub

myself of the first opportunity, in case we should meet with an American or French man-of-war, to claim their protection for my forced detention.

The Spanish Mate, who sympathized with me for the cruel treatment I had received, admonished the Captain to keep on his guard, as I would prove a dangerous customer when under the battery of a man-of-war.

That evening the course was shaped for the Cruz del Padre; I was called in the cabin and was informed by Monsieur Laminé that if I would sign a document which he presented, I should be landed at the same place I was taken from. I refused signing any document and demanded to be set on board of any vessel whatever; that all I wanted was to be free from him and his Lieutenant. We could not agree on this point, he alleging he dare not board any vessel but Spaniards'; but his true motive was to land me back in the same place, to keep me from lodging complaints to either Government and endanger the safety of his vessel.

The document presented me to sign was so construed as to exonerate the Captain and his officers from any compulsion or ill treatment on their part toward me. A receipt was also extended for two hundred dollars for my services, and the gold exposed on the table. After a long discussion, finding I could not carry out my point, I accepted the terms, signed the document, and pocketed the cash.

*CHAPTER 7th

*My Return to the Rancho, and Galliego's End

Next morning we closed in with the reef of the Cruz del Padre. A 1826 boat was manned, and I left the vessel. On my departure the Third Officer, to whom I had confided my misfortunes under an oath of secrecy, knew my destitute state and presented me a set of charts, spyglass, and a quadrant, with a large bag of clothes. He also concealed in a very fancy silk vest a silver watch and three ounces, which he begged me to wear on my arrival at Havana. Some portion of the white crew also presented me with some clothes; and a Black fellow, who had the charge of the boat and called himself an officer, in a most brotherly manner forced me to accept his mite—two sovereigns. He was a native of Marblehead and pretended having known me in Salem.

On approaching the rancho, I perceived everyone under arm and heard Rafaelin's strong voice ordering the boat off, or he would fire. I saw at a moment that Galliego had misrepresented me according to his promise, and that my countryman of piratical memory was laboring under a falsehood. I ordered the boat to backwater and threw myself knee deep into the water. On reaching the beach, I accosted my would-be uncle and offered my hand.

It was grasped with eagerness. Rafaelin had perceived even at a distance my innocence, and in his joy he clasped me to his arms and in a reproachful manner told his men that I could not be a traitor. The boat was called to the beach and many presents landed. I made one of the privateer's crew recount in presence of the whole party the manner I had been impressed by the instigation of Galliego. Rafaelin presented the boat's crew with a case of Chateau Margaux and a large quantity of fish.

I was called to give a detailed account of my trip in the Colombian privateer, the Patroon enjoining me to be precise and exact in my narrative; and requesting his party, Galliego included, to pay particular attention, remarking that his honor was at stake.

We then sat down on the sand, and I related my adventures in the patriot cruiser, avoiding with care implicating Galliego, as by Rafaelin's remarks I foresaw that this was to be nothing more but a court martial for their ill-natured, ill-born Cook. At the conclusion of my narrative I arose and deposited my presents, the two hundred dollars, and the two sovereigns by the Patroon.

A long silence issued, everyone looking up to my countryman for a speech. He then arose, and taking the two hundred dollars, went round the circle and divided that sum equally amongst the company; himself, Galliego, and me included. In his usual commanding tone, he then informed them that the two sovereigns, the clothes, and instruments were mine; that he had shared with them the profits of my labor as it was agreed that I should share the products of their lawful earning (meaning the fishing profits), but as to my presents, no one had any business with them. And again he added, "I am now doing an act of justice by making this division. Fair accounts make good friends, but this is not all: I demand a hearing. Caballeros, my nephew during his absence has been accused by one of us as a traitor, a thief, and a coward—three blasphemous vituperations which cannot be found in my prayer book and never existed in the blood of my family. Therefore, men, inasmuch as you have at all times found me just in my dealings with you, I now expect reciprocity to me and mine.

"Let that cowardly rascal" (pointing to Galliego) "repeat and prove his accusations. You all shall stand judges in the case, and if he cannot make good his charge, let him be dealt according to our code. This night this youth shall either be found guilty, or his reputation washed clean with blood. I further inform you that if you prove my nephew innocent, his reward shall be his freedom. His voluntary return warrants you his honesty, and tomorrow he shall depart."

Galliego was now ordered to repeat the accusation he had uttered in my absence. But no answer would he make. He was then required to say something in his defense, but he persisted in his doggish silence till someone proposed corporal punishment to induce him to speak. The threat brought circulation to his tongue, and he then informed the party he considered his defense useless, as they all feared Rafaelin, and could not expect justice at their hands. But if they would allow him to support his own cause, knife in hand against Rafaelin, he was ready to prove his innocence.

This challenge was accepted with disdain by my countryman, but opposed by the whole party. I then asked that inasmuch as the present difficulty had arose on my account, I was the only person that should take up the proposed challenge. But here Rafaelin interposed, and drawing his knife, made for the Cook, who took to his heels and disappeared.

The escape of Galliego caused some uneasiness, as should he be able to procure a boat, in his cowardly disposition it was feared he would turn King's Evidence against them. Therefore all the boats and canoe were secured with a chain, and a sharp watch kept during the night.

38 Order being restored, I inquired of the Patroon to give me an

explanation of the three accusations the Cook had made against me.
My countryman informed me that I had been accused by Galliego of having shipped in the privateer, that I had returned with her boat and robbed the rancho, and many more false and absurd stories. The only word of veracity in his charges was the blow I had given him with the oar.

I then told him of the hiding place amongst the graves, which I supposed must belong to Galliego, but said nothing of the madras handkerchief and its never to be forgotten contents.

In the morning a search was instituted in the graveyard, where all the lost objects of no importance were found. But unfortunately, Galliego had been before us, and many things taken away, and to my despair, the so much valued hanky.

On our return to the rancho we divided into two parties, each taking two dogs, and proceeded on the hunt for Galliego. Shortly after, we found him under a bush, a species of laurel noted for its aromatic smell[1], asleep with two empty gin flasks by his side. We aroused him with but little success; he was too much intoxicated to mind or care for anyone.

A kind of drumhead court martial was instituted, and with one opinion all agreed to chain him to the spicy tree on the spot, and there to remain to starve. The execution having been performed, he was left to his fate. One of the men, having found a case of gin nearby, returned with it to his doomed companion and left it near him to solace his exit out of this world.

Next morning he was found dead with four empty bottles out of the box. His body was never removed, but left to be devoured by the insects and crabs.

This afternoon, my proportionable part of the fishing operation was handed me by my countryman. It amounted to 324 dollars and was delivered with much feeling and in an emphatic manner. "Take it, young man," said he, "there is no blood on it."

A few days after, the schooner returned. As I was making preparation to depart, he called me aside from the rancho and in the presence of Bachicha the Master of the pilot-boat, addressed me thus:

"Countryman of mine," said he, "you are about to leave this cursed place. It must be so, as it is no place for you. At your age, and with your education, your spirit, and your profession, you cannot fail to go through the world with success to yourself and honor to your relations. All these minutes you have remained on this rock and amongst us have been hours of torture for me. Go then, you that can

[1] known as a bay rum tree in the West Indies

leave it with a clear conscience! Go, Theodore, never to see me more, and if I mistake you not your gratitude, never mention my name, and when you think of me, forget my abominable occupations. Look on me as you see me now, an isolated, poor, broken-hearted man, doomed to perdition and infamy.

"I have recommended you to a friend in Regla, a small town in the harbor of Havana. He will see you comfortably situated. He is a countryman of ours and will act with you as such." And handing me the ounces, he said, "Take this—it is my share in the fishing. I would not offer you but the coin of an honest labor. It will help you appear in Havana as your situation deserves it." He then shook hands with me, recommended me to his friend Bachicha, and left us.

At sunset, we set sail for Havana. During the passage Patroon Bachicha informed me that Rafaelin, after having been driven out from Mexico some years back, had established himself near Havana and did good business in the coasting trade, when a noted privateer, commanded and manned by Americans, had captured his vessel. The loss caused him to become insolvent. His property seized by his creditors and his person sorely abused in prison, in desperation he swore revenge on the authors of his misfortune; this caused his horrible mode of retaliation.

*CHAPTER 8th

*I Sail for Havana · Fitting Out the Areostatico

We reached Regla on the third day. I was presented by the Master of the vessel to an Italian grocer. As he could not read, he was made acquainted that I had been recommended to him by his friend Rafaelin, for whom he entertained great regard and in token of which, I was installed in his house and made as comfortable as a bachelor's cold home can make anyone.

Finding that my Italian landlord did not question me on any subject, I informed him that when I left Holland (Antwerp was not Belgian then), I had made my mind to go to the coast of Mexico or the Pacific, and would feel exceedingly obliged to him if he could place me in a way to find a vessel for either of those places; that if he could not find me a situation as an officer, I would work my passage as a sailor; that I could not think of abusing his generosity by a longer stay in his house free of expense; and that in consideration of the recommendation I had had to him, I could not apply but to him with propriety for such a favor.

The kind grocer, whose heart was excellent but whose language did not correspond with his good nature, replied he was ready to give me all his assistance and that I had no need to trouble myself about the intrusion or expenses of his house, that he had plenty of rooms in it, and that which fed five fed a half dozen. He finished his tirade of kind but rash offers with the assurance that I was welcome. About my proposal of going to Mexico or anywhere else, he could find me a passage every day in the year, but he could not recommend me any of those places suitable to make a hasty fortune. And as he had been there himself, he well knew the disposition of the Spanish Americans for their jealousy to strangers and that since I had asked his advice, he strongly recommended me to remain quiet for a while and make myself easy by studying Spanish. In a short time, no doubt something would turn up more advantageous than going to Mexico.

He then told me that Patroon Bachicha had informed him how honorably I had behaved with his friend at the Cruz del Padre, and that under all the present circumstances he was my friend and his purse was at my disposition.

I did as he wished me, and was introduced that day to an old Padre (a priest) who pretended to teach the Spanish language. Two lessons sufficed me of his incapacity but as he was very intimate with the kind grocer, and as his impudence in pretense to learning was such that he had become an influential person in the neighborhood, and in his capacity of priest he lorded it over the whole village with high hand, I resolved to continue as his pupil, in regard to my landlord.

As my Spanish teacher was a great lover of fish, I often went out in the canoe of one of his parishioners to fish, and when my excursion was attended with good luck I generally divided it with my friend the grocer and the old Padre. In extenuation of his great ignorance in grammar, I must here record with pleasure that while he lacked in schooling education, he certainly highly comprehended the Epicurean profession and could manage the *casserole en Maître d'Hôtel*. On such occasions I dined with him; therefore I speak from fact when I attest that my black-cloth gentleman perfectly understood the art of cookery. And let not the reader imagine I neglected his Spanish lessons; on the contrary, I courted them on account of his good pantry and well-supplied cellar.

During my idle hours I often sailed about the harbor, amusing myself at the sight of the men-of-war and the sharp-built slavers. On my return, I would inform my countryman of the sight which had most forcibly struck me. The slavers in particular attracted my curiosity. I described with the admiration of a sailor the models, the rig, and the neatness of the crafts I had seen.

I continued my sailing peregrinations for a month, when my friendly landlord invited me to accompany him next morning to see a vessel off in which he owned two shares. That said vessel was bound to Africa. I accepted with pleasure, and next morning we went on board.

She was a schooner of about 140 tons, and what is called Baltimore built. Her whole equipment was new, her crew consisted of 30 men beside the Captain, three Mates, Boatswain, Cook, Steward, and two cabin boys. She mounted a long twelve-pounder on pivot.

The vessel was towed out of the harbor by several boats, in sight of a large concourse of people congregated on the wharf. On our arrival on board we met all the owners of the vessel, some nine in number. The Captain, who had a share in her, gave us a superb *déjeuner* prepared from the shore. It consisted of all the varieties the market could afford. Champagne and Lafitte were the only succulent liquids used to moisten the luxurious repast. As she passed the Moro we left the vessel with three cheers, wishing them a successful voyage.

On our return home, I importuned the grocer with a thousand questions in regard to the slave trade, the mode of obtaining a cargo, the outfitting, the compensation to the Captain and officers, the dangers of the cruisers, and the requirement necessary for an officer to sail in such vessels. My numerous questions were patiently satisfied by a long explanation to all my demands. That night my dreams placed me on board a slaver hard chased by John Bull, so much had my ideas been quite captivated by what I had seen on board.

Next morning I informed my friend that I had given up my plan of going to the Costa Firma, and if I could get a situation on board a vessel bound to Africa, I should venture on such a voyage. He promised me to inquire for a berth and, if necessary, he would take one or two shares to secure me a situation as an officer.

A few days after, I was informed that probably I should realize my wish, as a very fast vessel from the Canary Islands was soon to be sold at auction, and a friend in company with himself would purchase her if sold cheap, and would send her to Africa. The said vessel was sold, and my friend became her owner for 3,000 dollars.

On my arrival on board I found she was a miserable Balahi,[1] about some sixty feet long and about 35 to 38 tons burden. Indeed, her rig and model well denoted her Canary Island construction. She was nothing more than a hermaphrodite brig rigged by fishermen, and a perfect wreck.

In astonishment I inquired of my friend if he really intended to send such a calabash to Africa! He informed me that he only bought her for her good sailing qualities, and that with the repairs he should put on, she should alter her appearance to such an extent that her former owner would not recognize her.

We then took her to the Casa Blanca—the merchant arsenal—for repairs, and in a few days, with the assistance of carpenters and painters, transmuted this ignoble craft into a respectable-looking pilot-boat. Her pompous name of *Globo* was changed into the more significant *Areostatico*, on account of her "flying" qualities, as it was supposed.

A culverine[2] was placed in her midship to protect her from the self-styled Colombian vessels, who made it an excellent business by cruising around the Island of Cuba and even the coast of Africa, capturing Spanish and Portuguese slavers, now under the Cartagenian flag, but then under the Brazilian colors. Many vessels sailed and captured Spanish property without license or letter of marque. It was believed that these vessels were fitted out from New Orleans, Baltimore, and St. Thomas, and when a prize of slaves fell into their hands they disposed of it in Florida and Pensacola.

[1] a member of the Untouchable Caste in India
[2] heavy cannon

The *Areostatico* having been made ready, a Captain was selected amongst the grocer's Catalonian acquaintances. I was presented to him as his Second Officer. The vessel was bound to Rio Pongo, and the Captain not knowing the English language my countryman had made use of this prerogative of mine to recommend me as very useful in the double capacity of officer and interpreter.

The shipping of our crew caused a good deal of demoralization. The Spanish squadron, being short of men, pressed every hand they could. Therefore sailors kept concealed, and when, with much difficulties and time we succeeded in shipping a crew, we found but too late that it consisted of jailbirds and the refuse of the press gang.

During the difficulties of selecting our crew, our vessel lay at anchor opposite the mole between a French and English merchantman. One afternoon I heard a great cry on board the English collier, and instantly saw a small boy issue from the cabin, his face full of blood. A man followed him, inflicting blow after blow with his clenched hand.

I called on the man to desist, but my interference raised the choler of the man to greater passion, and in his madness he picked up a large broomstick. Seeing the boy in greater danger, I then called on him to jump over the board and save himself, giving orders in the meantime to my only two men on board to man the boat. The boy, being hard chased by the infuriated man and having observed my boat at hand, did as I had desired, and with one plunge freed himself from the murderous attack. The Englishman, who was beastly drunk, gave vent to his rage in a most invective language, and I believe had he had a boat at his command, he would have attempted a rescue.

As the boat brought the boy on board I found him much bruised about the face and one rib broke. I took him to Casa Blanca and hid him under the care of an old Mulatto woman who cured credulous sailors' complaints by charms. The boy informed me the cause of his being beaten in such a manner by the Mate was that he had refused him the key of the spirit locker entrusted to him by the Captain.

That evening, the master of the English collier came to claim his boy, but as he was petulant and arrogant in his demand, I refused till he promised me better treatment to the boy in the future. But on the contrary, he impertinently insisted on an immediate restitution. I then began my turn to show displeasure and with no little humor ordered him off my vessel.

A complaint was lodged next morning by the British Consul to the Captain of the Port. I stated the case such as it was, with no great credit to the Mate and English Captain, but as he insisted on the boy being produced, and in my last interview with him he had begged me with tears not to deliver him up, I disculpated myself from complying with the request of the Captain of the Port by pleading ignorance to his whereabouts. Foreseeing this demand, I had ordered the Mulatto woman to remove him, therefore, I was really ignorant where he could be found.

As no further call was made the affair dropped, and after the sailing of the English vessel, with the consent of my Captain, I brought him on board our vessel as Cabin Boy. I have fully narrated this occurrence, as this boy was the only English subject I ever knew to have shipped on a slaver.

The Spanish squadron having sailed, in a few days sailors made their appearance. We shipped 15 men before the mast such as I have described. We then took in our provisions, with all the necessities for the comfort and maintenance of a slave cargo. With our powder and ammunition came four kegs of specie.[1] This was designed to purchase our cargo. Two days before we made sail, each of the men and officers received one month's pay.

On the day of sailing, we gave a grand *déjeuner* and left La Havana under a shower of blessings and good wishes from the generous grocer.

Here, then, commences the true beginning of this book. Having made one or two apologies in my title page, I will only add that I shall still continue my work in the same style of narrative, describing the slave trade not in a routine manner, but representing it such as it was and took place during my voyages and residence in Africa, promising that every episode of note will not be neglected on my part.

[1]coins

*My First Voyage to Africa, and First Taste of Mutiny

2 September, 1826

I return to my first voyage and the schooner *Areostatico*. It was on the second of September 1826 that we left the port of Havana with a customhouse clearance for the Cape de Verde Islands. Our vessel proved an excellent sailor, but not such as described. Our crew consisted of 21 hands all told, and as I said before, some of the worst kind of men. We had Spaniards, Portuguese, a Frenchman and two Slavonians. Our Captain was from Majorca—a poor sailor but good navigator, and of very timid disposition without the least confidence in himself; of everybody's opinion and giving up a point without argument or contradiction; finely a poor tool for Commander of a slaver. Our Chief Mate was Catalonian, a relation to the Captain, with no pretension but the perfect whiteness of his feminine hands, and like his relation the Captain, a good mathematician and freshwater sailor in manners, voice, and speech—an identical mademoiselle. Our Boatswain, who was in his watch, assured me that when he gave an order for a maneuver, it was always on the tune of La Norma or La Gaza Ladra. These were my chief superior officers.

We sailed for nine days without any incident. I had observed that our crew were a set of desperate fellows, while our Captain was too pusillanimous to subject them to any kind of discipline, and I foresaw that our voyage could not end well; I kept a watchful eye, but still wished myself on shore.

On the tenth day it began to blow from the northwest. We moderately took in sail; before 4 P.M. it turned into a gale, and the sea began to rise mountain-high. On being relieved of my watch by the First Officer, I had signified to the Captain that it was time to lay the vessel to. We were then scudding before the wind under close-reefed foresail, but the Captain, with his usual complacency to everybody's will, chose the advice of the man in the helm (a person much older than I was), and the vessel was allowed to continue at a frightful, immoderate rate; as she was then going a good ten knots an hour, and for a vessel of only 56 feet of keel, it was incredible. Once more I proffered the impropriety of carrying sails, but still, others' opinions were preferred.

As the deck was covered with water all the crew had collected abaft on the trunk, pell mell with the officers and naturally in hand-and-glove conversation with the Captain. Before sundown, I repeated the strong necessity of laying to, but here again, the men

46

who did not like the job assured the Captain that the wind would lull
as the moon would rise. Their opinion prevailed, and on flew our
strong little craft.

The moon soon made its appearance, but contrary to the prediction of the crew, the gale increased. Now then, the danger appeared
with all its horror. It blew a hurricane. Each sea submerged our
decks, but our noble *Areostatico* rose victorious from the heavy load.
It became necessary to avoid the seas which came rolling avalanche-
like on each quarters. Confusion became the order of the day. Every
begger gave his opinion but the Captain, who stood in the midst of
his danger-frightened crew without an opinion or a word of command.

As the danger increased, more absurd propositions were offered
by the crew, till at last one proposed to cut away the foresail and try
to bring the vessel to the wind. I was conning[1] the vessel when this
mad proposal was made, and fearing the Captain in his ignorance
would adopt it, I called on the Boatswain, who was a tolerable
practical sailor, to take my place. I then addressed the congregated
crew, officers and all, and told them that should they cut away the
sail the next sea would send us to eternity, and that our salvation lay
in driving our vessel with stronger force before the seas, that by
taking in or cutting the sail, we should lose command of the vessel
and the next wave would turn us keel up. Therefore I advised that
the balance reef should be let out as the only remedy to save us. I
enforced my argument of such necessity by telling the panic-struck
crew that I had seen such dangers before and succeeded by the same
method.

Cowards with danger before their eyes are soon brought to order
and obedience. I availed myself of their silent consent and ordered
the tallest of them to cut away the reef, requesting him to be mindful
of not cutting the sail.

My order was attended with success. The vessel, having acquired
more sail, scudded before the seas with greater velocity. This maneuver saved us from perdition. In time the wind abated, and we
repaired the damages of the gale.

Our sailors, once allowed to come aft and sit on the trunk, took
advantage of this liberty, and continued to do so in the future, much
to my dislike. I also saw that the whole crew had taken a peculiar
dislike to me. They could not abide the idea that the youngest
person, and a foreigner to boot, should have proved the best sailor.
As I would not mix with them, they called me arrogant. My orders,

[1]giving orders for the ship's course

if complied with at all, were gone through with nonchalance and in a neglectful manner.

I saw a great alteration in their behavior from the last gale. It proved so, as in time they formed a complot to throw me over the board, but I knew it not till the danger was passed.

We continued on our discontented voyage till we made the coast of Africa, and after 41 days' passage, we anchored before the River Pongo, or Rio Pongo. As no one on board knew the entrance of the river, the Captain and four well-armed men went ashore in search of a Pilot.

A 2 o'clock P.M. the boat returned with the Pilot. The Captain had sent him off with orders to take the vessel up the river; himself had proceeded up to the factories. The wind and tide being favorable, we entered the river about 4 o'clock, and at sunset we anchored midway upriver.

Our native Pilot spoke the English language tolerably well; I spoke with him on many subjects. He told me he had been to the United States and liked the country; he then inquired if anyone near understood English. I told him that no one on board spoke the language but the boy and myself. Seeing he wished to say something, I encouraged him by informing him that the boy was my brother.

He then whispered very secretly that some of the boat's crew, while on shore, had attempted at the Captain's life by snapping a carbine which had missed fire. This had been told to him by a native boy who had followed them up the beach, and that the Captain was not even aware of the attempt. He also informed me that on his way out to the vessel, the tallest man of the boat's crew had asked him such questions as to induce him to believe the whole crew had the intention to take the vessel. This information of the Black Pilot corroborated the many hints the Cook had given me during the passage. It was then one hour after sundown. The attempt on the Captain disturbed my mind, and I could not but imagine that danger was at hand. I had taken the precaution to see everything secured, but still I was not easy. A thought struck me to inspect the carbines returned from shore, which I had put away in the arms chest, and which stood by the trunk. On applying the key to the padlock, I found that it had been forced open, and several pistols and cutlasses taken away.

Astonishment-struck, I stood for a few moments in deep thought but could not reflect; the present danger had bound me dumb with surprise. With one effort I shook off the apparent nightmare and was myself again. The crisis had passed, and I almost rejoiced that the

intended revolt would take place that night; I hankered for the moment. 13 October, 1826

I looked about the decks. Everything was still. I saw but two men lying about the decks, apparently asleep. This was an unusual silence. The guitar and song had been abandoned to cavil[1] the revolt. Machiavelli-like, I had made my mind to strike the first blow.

As I was Second Officer I could not command, but still, with the determination that I was right I called the Chief Mate, Boatswain, and Cook as silently as possible into the cabin, leaving the English boy to watch at the cabin door. Once congregated there, I informed them of what I had heard from the pilot, and the missing of arms from the chest. I also told them the determination I had taken, if they would assist me, which was to secure the crew and give them battle.

Here the Mate, who as I said before had more of the female quality than nature intended, refused to take any rash step till the return of the Captain. The Boatswain and Cook I knew to be men of spirit, and their silence sufficiently convinced me of their consent.

Finding that my arguments could not arouse my pusillanimous superior, I told him to remain below, that I would take the blame on myself, and that I was decided in taking the first step, which would be to shoot the ringleader (the one who had attempted at the Captain's life). This I thought would silence the revolt, and taking two horsepistols from under the Captain's pillow I called the Boatswain and Cook to follow me, and mounted the deck.

The Mate, who had followed us, called on me to desist and clinched me in his anxiety, begging me not to commit murder. In the scuffle to shake him clear of me one of my pistols went off. One minute after, the well-known voice of the boy called out from the starboard side of the deck to look out for myself, and on looking forward I saw the towering stature of the ringleader within two paces of me, brandishing a cutlass at my head. I aimed and fired. We both fell—he of the cutlass with two ounce balls through his abdomen, myself with my eye and face cut by the concussion of the pistol.

Neither blow deprived us our senses. I was up in a moment and so was my antagonist, who although knocked down with two balls through his body, rose to his feet, and placing his hands to his bowels, ran forward saying he was killed. But in his descent to the forecastle he was met by the Boatswain, who stabbed him in the shoulderblade with a bayonet. The blow was such that the instrument could not be extricated.

[1]trump up

49

As I said, I was up in one moment, and placing my hand to my face, felt a mass of blood down my cheek. I hastily tied my neck-handkerchief over one eye and opened the arms chest, when I heard the report of a pistol and immediately after, the cries of the English boy, who had still watched near me.

The shot that struck him was designed for me. The fire had come from forward but it had hit his leg. I took him up, laid him on the trunk, and returned to the arms chest. What followed is not my report, but that of the Cook. I saw no danger, felt no fear; I must have been spellbound. I mechanically discharged carbine after carbine, throwing away the useless arms as they were fired. All moving objects fell by my unfortunate aim, and unhappily, it was not till the firearms had all been discharged that I was awoke from this mad stupor by the Cook, who found me still searching the fatal chest.

As the smoke evaporated the fore part of the vessel appeared uninhabited. On inspection, two dead men and one in agonies proved how mortal the firing had been. Still, it was not all; the ringleader and another man were dying in the forecastle.

It appeared that the crew had been aroused at the accident of my pistol going off, and the chief of the complot, sword in hand, came aft to ascertain the cause. My next fire began their meditated attack. The Cook, who they believed one of their party, was not fired on, and strange to say, out of six pistols found discharged forward of the galley, only one had taken effect on the poor boy's leg. The Boatswain found himself forward when the firing began, and seeing no chance of escaping from the murderous reports of the carbines, took refuge over the bows.

On coming to my true self again, my first care was to the boy, who with a cheerful inquiry asked about my wound; my next was to the dying men, to whom we could do but little. The ringleader lived long enough to acknowledge his crime, and in agony called on my name and begged my pardon.

Order was hardly restored when a boat hailed us in English. It was Captain Sharp of Philadelphia. The report of firearms had attracted his notice; his brig was lying at only the next turn up the river. His assistance was very welcome. On stepping on board with his men, I looked on them as my countrymen—not that I had anything more to fear, but still I needed someone to sympathize with me after such a horrible affray. I wanted an eyewitness to approve of the high-hand manner in which I had quashed the revolt.

Fortunately Captain Sharp came in time to see the last moments of the dying leader, and although the Captain could not understand Spanish, still he could comprehend the agonizing words of "Pardon,

pardon, Don Theodore!" Captain Sharp and his men kindly helped us to wash the deck and lay the bodies in a *requiescat in pace* manner.

A word about our Mate, who the moment the first shot was fired, ran below and never appeared on deck till the arrival of the American Captain. No description can represent the poor fellow's fright. His gasping appearance strongly denoted his terror. On his return to the deck, he embraced the American Captain and with tears protested himself innocent of all murderous occurrence, and at the sight of the five dead bodies, fainted in his arms.

The American boat was sent to Bangalang, the residence of Mongo John, to apprise the Captain of the occurrences of the night, while Captain Sharp kindly volunteered to keep me company till morning.

At daylight I caused the dead bodies to be thrown overboard, and the decks cleared of the gore. Shortly after, we heard a voice from the shore. It was the Black Pilot, whom I had forgotten. In the melee he had jumped overboard. At morn our Captain made his appearance accompanied by Mongo John, several Mulattos, some sixty natives, and an American, Mr. Faber.

Since the commencement of the fight I had assumed command of the vessel; and as the Captain and his company arrived I received them at the side and gave him full account of the proceedings, leaving the Mate to exculpate himself for his cowardly conduct. A kind of declaration was extended and signed by me, the Cook, the Boatswain and two of the men, who protested they had not taken part in the fray.

The wound of the Cabin Boy was inspected, and it was found that the ball had passed between the two bones without injuring them. My wound was also inspected, and although not severe, still it was thought dangerous to the eye. The flintlock had inflicted three gashes on the left side of the face.

As all the company desired to know the cause of the revolt, I recounted to them the whole affair; and when I described the attempt on the Captain's life, he rose in his fright and demanded to see the man. I pointed to the water.

In the course of the investigation it was found out that one of the men, a Slavonian, had fired the pistol which wounded the boy. He was put in irons, to be sent on shore. Our Mate, who had nothing to say, was pitied for his haggard look, and to avoid any further mortification the Captain took him on shore with him.

The vessel was got underway and brought to an anchor before Bangalang, a pleasant spot fronting the head of the river.

On leaving the vessel, Mr. Ormond—or Mongo John—offered

me his friendship and promised to send a Country Doctor to cure my eye and my protégé's leg, making me promise in the meantime to visit him as soon as my business would permit. The four kegs of specie were taken ashore by the Captain, and I was left in charge of the vessel with orders to strip, repair, and provision her for the return trip home.

That afternoon the Black Doctor came on board, and after examining my eye, recommended woman's milk fresh from the breast, which was immediately sent me by Mongo John in the shape of a stout Negress and her black babe, with orders to remain and bathe my eye with her milk every half hour. I know not if nature or this remedy cured me, but in a few days the broken flesh had consolidated and the inflammation from the eye disappeared.

*CHAPTER 10th

*I Visit Bangalang and the Seraglio of Mongo John

It took me ten days to water and wood the *Areostatico*. The necessary provisions to feed the live cargo we had brought in the vessel. It was only required for me to distribute them in their proper places. Slave deck we had none, the vessel being too small. It would have taken too much room; therefore, mats were spread instead on the firewood which filled the unevenness of the water casks.

24 October, 1826

At the end of my tedious job I went ashore to report to the Captain that the vessel was ready. But it was not so with him, who could not collect a cargo of boys but with great difficulty. And although sixty dollars were given per head, which was ten dollars over the price of full grown prime men, still we were delayed twenty days longer than we had contracted.

According to invitation, I visited Mr. John Ormond, called by the natives Mongo John. He treated me with much kindness, showing me his town, barracoons, stores, and injudiciously introducing me in his seraglio. I also dined with him and assisted the old gentleman in the consummation of a couple of bottles of wine.

Mr. Ormond had been a sailor; I was one. We spoke of the different countries we had both visited, and another bottle was called to refresh our memories. Wine begets friends. By sundown, our electric memory had visited nearly the whole globe, and our intimacy was at the highest point.

The fluid had operated on the Mongo's legs, which kept him glued to his chair. In me it had a contrary effect; it went into my head, giving me a disposition to rove. The cursed seraglio, which I could not forget, was the first place I made for. It was nearly dark then, no one observed me till I had got in nearly the center, when a handsome Mulatto woman, the second in the affection of the Mongo, called the attention of thirty-one more colored ladies of this establishment, saying, "Ho, here is the white man. Let us have some fun," and invited me to her apartments—a small veranda with a hammock—in which I took a seat. In a few minutes the place was filled with the inhabitants of this not very moral harem. Every female wanted to see the white man who had fought so well on board the Spanish vessel. My eye's wet-nurse, who was a slave to one of the damsels of this establishment, had made me out a hero, and everyone wanted to see me and her cure.

The usual dance was proposed. A large bonfire was made in the yard, and a circle formed by women and children. A female drummer soon made her appearance, and a tam-tam struck their national dance, accompanied with song. Each one by turns stepped out and danced according to their nation. I cannot well describe this dance, as the fumes of the wine had taken possession of my head. However, I fancied my turn had come. I boldly stepped out, and desirous of showing the Black barbarians a specimen of my dancing power, I began with an *avant-deux, chassez balance*, finishing with a grand flourish of a double pigeon-wing.

They all applauded me very much, which had the effect to embolden my assurance, and taking one of the *danseuses* round the unveiled waist, insisted on a waltz. The effect was magnificent. We were encore'd, till my colored beauty was giddy. I returned her to her mat, parting with a kiss. But the waltz had created a furor. Each lady desired to have a dance with the enjoyable white man. I was in great demand. With one I danced a *sauteuse*, with another a reel, and another a fandango (polka and schottische were not known at that time), and, of course, at parting every one received a buss.

The cause of this unusual merriment was reported at the headquarters, and shortly Mongo John made his appearance with the Captain. I was the most capriciously engaged in showing his youngest wife, a charming quadroon, my favorite dance, the Cachuca, when lo! turning round, I saw the Mongo and my Captain ocular spectators of my frisks. I sobered at once and apologized for my intrusion.

Mr. Ormond readily forgave me for the violation of his seraglio, but as I only had had a dance, no more was said. We returned to the hospitable board, and again under the lee of a decanter, the Mongo began one of his long sad yarns, much to the annoyance of the Captain, who could not understand a word.

As we parted for the night, Mongo John advised me to steer a straight course for my quarters, as he said his cruisers kept a strict lookout in the premises. I took the hint and understood the meaning.

Next morning my Captain informed me that as Mr. Ormond had taken such a great liking to me, and even had insinuated to him his great desire for me to remain with him as his Clerk, he thought it his duty to give me his advice on this subject. He then stated that as I had taken upon myself the first hostility on board the *Areostatico,* and that the unfortunate result had caused the death of five of its crew, he was bound on his return to Havana to make a statement to the Commander of the Port of the whole affair, and that although I had truly saved the vessel, and cargo, I would have still to undergo a rigid examination and, of course, remain imprisoned during the time, and that probably the remaining crew and the friends of the defuncts would prove troublesome to me. Therefore he thought 25 October, himself justified in advising me to accept the present offer as one, not *1826* only very profitable, but advantageous under every consideration. He added that he could not answer for what decision the court would give if the case was carried to the Admiralty, and that for his part he was very sorry to part with me, but it was his duty to impart to me his fears.

I saw at once the drift of his long discourse. His object was to reinstate his relation the Chief Mate, and with a mortified pride I thanked him for his advice and with no very flattering words upbraided him for his ingratitude and cowardice.

I need not say that that same day I left the vessel.

The parting with the English boy was affecting. I had contracted a strong attachment for him, and the youth would not part with me; in his affection he would have followed me on shore.

Mr. Ormond gladly accepted my services. That same evening we regulated my salary and next morning I entered in my new capacity as Secretary to Mongo John, King of Rio Pongo. In our agreement, Mr. Ormond was to pay me one slave per month or its value at the rate of forty dollars per head, his table, and a private establishment with the accessories not necessary to mention.

A short time after, one of the traveling traders returned from the neighboring rivers with 18 boys and girls purchased for account of the *Areostatico*, which completed her cargo. Therefore, the next day she left with a full cargo of 108 boys and girls. The oldest was not 15 years of age.

This vessel arrived in Havana in 28 days with 105, losing but three. I was glad to hear of her safe arrival for several reasons. I could not conjecture how so many human beings could draw breath in a vessel's hold where her between-decks had only 22 inches height, and as I had stowed them myself, I knew them to be well cramped. As they were not fastened it was found necessary to secure them under deck while the vessel descended the river, to prevent their escaping by jumping over the board. As the height did not admit of allowing them to sit, we made them lie down spoon fashion, one in the other's lap; on the starboard with the left side down, and on the port vice versa.

I left the *Areostatico* a few miles out of the bar with no cruiser in sight. I wished them every success and a safe arrival. On my return to Bangalang the Mongo showed me my establishment. It was a mud house with two rooms and veranda. As I expected something better, I shall describe the interior in order that the reader may not be disappointed by the pompous name of "private establishment." 55

The floor was carpeted with a strong coat of mud and manure. The odor reminded me of my father's stable. The ceiling of the rooms was a leaky thatch roof. My bed consisted of a two-musket chest with a mat over it. A German paper-mounted looking glass adorned a deal[1] table in company with a greasy tin palm-oil pan for a lamp. A bamboo stool with one piece of crockery completed the rich furnishing of this comfortable abode of mine, and my trunk, mattress, and blankets showed to advantage in this establishment.

I must now introduce Mr. John Ormond, or Mongo John, to the reader, as he will become the hero of a few pages.

Mr. Ormond was a Mulatto native of Rio Pongo, the son of a white man and the daughter of a native Chief. His father, John Ormond, a rich slave trader from Liverpool, sent him, when young, to England to be educated. He remained there some years, but made little progress in education.

In consequence of the death of his father, the agent to whom he was entrusted refused him any further supplies, which obliged him to shift for himself. Poverty induced him to ship in a merchant vessel, but the press gang soon claimed him (and he an African!) as a British subject and forced him to serve, now in the capacity of servant, then in that of sailor, during five years in the West India and Mediterranean Station.

On his return to England, he procured a passage back to his country Rio Pongo and at once claimed his father's property. Fortunately his mother was still alive and publicly recognized him as her first born.

A grand palabra[2] was called and his father's property, which only consisted of a great number of slaves then in the hands of his brothers, sisters, and uncles, were returned. At the time of his arrival the inhabitants of the river were in a state of civil war, occasioned, as nearly all African quarrels are, by family disputes.

Some of the influential Mulattos had taken part for a Chief, while others for another. The war had continued for years, devastating and depopulating the neighborhood and driving the Interior trade to other rivers, Rio Noonez and Fourcaria.

On the arrival of Mr. Ormond one of the contending Chiefs had died, leaving his ally the Mulatto, a Mr. Lawrence, in very poor circumstances. The other Chief, being a second uncle on his mother's side of Mr. Ormond, for a trifling bonus soon came to terms with his nephew.

Availing himself of the times and the quarrels, with the assistance

[1]plank
[2]palaver, parley

56

of his mother's friends, brothers, and numerous slaves, he soon
declared himself Chief, or Mongo, of the river.

The Mulattos Lawrence and Curtis abandoned the contest, having expended all their means.

Bangalang had been a noted English factory where many fortunes had been made. Mr. Ormond chose the place of his residence and formed a town which retained the ancient name of Bangalang. Peace being reestablished, Mr. Ormond informed his friends in Sierra Leone of the happy termination of the war. In a brief time trade poured in from the Interior, and in abundance. Vessels from Sierra Leone and Goree also began to find their way to the river, and in a short time his stores were filled with English, French, and American manufactories; hides, wax, gold, ivory, and palm oil were the produce returned for those goods, and slaves were exchanged with Spaniards and Portuguese for their doubloons and Spanish dollars.

In a few years Mr. Ormond became not only rich but a popular Mongo with the great tribes of the Interior, the Foulhas and Mandingos. Knowing his generosity, the neighboring chiefs also flattered him with the title of King, and knowing his Solomon-like poligamic propensities, forced on him wife after wife, which he could not well refuse. The indifferent-looking ones he kept only for a short time, while the handsomest he cooped in his seraglio.

He invariably accepted these numerous female presents, as this is one of the greatest tokens of friendship with which a native can compliment his superior—by presenting him his sister or a daughter, which cannot be refused without offense. (By-the-bye, my patron the Mongo had the constitution of a Samson.) This accounts for the thirty-and-odd women his harem contained.

On taking possession of his stores, I did not find them as well filled as I had cause to suppose. His books, kept by previous Clerk, accounted for goods which did not exist and were not booked as disposed of. Therefore my first step was to take an inventory.

Captain Sharp, who was an old trader in this river, and knew the manner Mr. Ormond had neglected his business for a few years past, suggested to me the idea of making a correct list of all the goods in store. He also recommended me to keep a watchful eye on the stores, never allowing anyone else to enter them.

When I presented to the Mongo the statement of the deficiency, he received it with indifference and begged me not to annoy him with my accounts. I saw at once that his affairs were on the decline.

As I returned to the store, mortified at the neglect of my employer, the chief woman of the seraglio, an old black hag, desired me to give her admittance to a cloth chest, and *sans compliment* let her help herself with several fathoms of blue cotton cloth. As she could not speak English nor I the Sosoo language, the point could not be well argued as to the propriety of such liberty. Therefore I took the cloth and presented her with a pencil and told her in as pure Nigger English as I could, to go to Mr. Ormond and bring the order.

This refusal caused high indignation to the mother abbess of the harem. During the absence of other clerks she invariably had the possession of the store keys, and of course assisted herself to the best, and without economy. She left the store in a passion with a volubility of black words horribly difficult to repeat.

At dinner I informed the Mongo of the conduct of his chief woman toward me, but in his neglectful manner he gave me no redress. In disgust with my employer I retired for the night, sorrily repenting my having left the *Areostatico.*

I had just stretched myself on my hard pallet when the boy servant informed me by signs that someone at the door demanded admittance, but desired that the lamp should be blown out. I consented, and shortly a female covered *cap-en-pied* made her appearance. I led her to my sofa bed and begged her to uncover. After some hesitation she did so, and although we had no light, the door gave sufficient for me to recognize one of the wives of my employer, the same female who had danced the Cachuca with me. After apologizing for her untimely appearance, she informed me that she had heard the dispute I had that day with the head woman Unga Fatima, and had come to put me on my guard against her, as she had sworn to be revenged. Therefore, out of pure friendship and compassion she had ventured out, much against the rules of Mongo John's establishment, to make me aware of my danger and tenderly hoped I would take heed.

I inquired the nature of the danger in order to guard against it. Her answer was not to eat anything from strangers or out of the Mongo's table, that Unga Fatima was of the Mandingo, and therefore well acquainted with all the ju-jus peculiar to her nation. She then begged that happen what may I would never mention her name, that if it was known she had visited me at that hour, her enemies would construe her present step to quite a different motive. And with a modest blush (which I could not see), she assured me she had only followed the dictates of her heart and very dangerously placed herself in a very critical position, but as I was a stranger, she had blindly exposed herself to public blame.

I thanked her kindly, promising her all she desired, and without
falling on my knees, swore eternal gratitude—I believe love—and a

thousand more words of such stuff. Suffice to say that from this moment we became friends.

2 November, 1826

As she was on the point of departing, I begged her to recommend silence to my servant. She bade me be easy on that point; the boy, being a slave, would not dare say anything injurious of a free person, and she left me promising to return whenever danger was at hand.

*CHAPTER 11th

*Esther's History of the Mongo's Seraglio

Friendship begets confidence. From this female I learned all the secrets of the seraglio. As she was a near native of Sierra Leone, she spoke the English language tolerably well for a native.

In our second interview, which took place next night (although no danger at hand) she gave me the history of herself. She was born in the islands of Los from a Mulatto mother and a white parent. Her father, a missionary from England, had abandoned his profession for the more lucrative slave traffic and, after collecting a large quantity of slaves, left for America, and since that time was never heard of. In respect for his first profession her father had given her the Biblical name of Esther, which she well deserved.

Her color was neither of the repugnant albino whiteness, nor of the displeasing Sambo color. Hers was that peculiar clean blushing quadroon so highly praised by the wealthy Creoles of New Orleans. Her shape was that of the Venus of Medici and her face seraphic; as to her hands and feet, the first must have belonged to a Duchess, the other to a gazelle. Her modesty made her the favorite of all her lord's wives.

Let not the reader shrug his shoulders at the word "modesty," as I beg him to consider she was only seventeen years old, with such an example as the morals of a seraglio her *faux pas* should be considered with forgiveness and the unknown word of modesty not taken literally, as that virtue is not much practiced in Africa.

As I have often made use of the name of "seraglio" let me explain what it was. The reader may have anticipated a Turkish harem with its high walls, double-locked strong gates, guarded by a troupe of Black eunuchs, et cetera. Nothing of the kind existed here. This was only an enclosure formed by a cluster of mud houses uniformly placed in a quadrangle form, leaving a large square in the center and one entrance, which was indifferently guarded at night only.

Fatima, who was the oldest, was the sole guardian of this enclosure. Every department of the establishment was under her control. Besides being the police of the place, she distributed the provisions and singled out the number of servants each lady should have. Her power was very great, as she distributed her lord's favors at pleasure, and of course those of the females that most humbled themselves to her or made her more presents, were preferred for the Mongo's affections. But strange to say, these privileges were never sought by the colored damsels.

Mongo John during his younger days and in the pride of his glutted prosperity, ruled the establishment himself, with the severity and power of a Grand Turk. But as time came on, his strong Samson's constitution declined. Nature became exhausted. Even the stimulating narcotics failed to supply him what debaucheries had robbed him of, and his women ridiculed him for his impotence and despised his touch. In his despair he had recourse to intoxicating drinks, neglecting the chastity of his wives and his pecuniary affairs. In this present state of affairs I came on the tapis. Both harem and store were in disorder and my patron, indolently heedless of the future, abandoned affections and all worldly cares for the bottle.

In my conversation with Esther, I found out that of all the inhabitants of this well-managed female establishment, each one had one or more lovers, Esther excepted. She swore she had none and wanted none (of course I believed her), but could not help bringing my thumb to my nose. In her African ignorance, she did not understand why my nose itched at the moment; she believed in my European credulity. One and all having lovers, no jealousy existed, and now and then, invitations to attend the Mongo's repose were forcibly and reluctantly complied with.

Fatima, in her great prerogative, made the lovers pay a tribute for her condescension and silence. As it often happened, children were born when the mother had not participated in the Mongo's caresses for a period longer than nine months, and likewise it came to pass that from these ladies babes came into the world whose color did not warrant the paternity of Mr. Ormond. In all such cases, Madame Fatima, who amongst the many charges held also the important one of midwife, immediately improvised some resemblances to the credulous Mongo, who in this impotent lost pride wished to believe himself still a man. On the occasion, in his cuckold joy he welcomed the newborn with a good spree, rewarding the mother for her fecundity with a slave and eighteen months' discharge from the matrimonial duties incumbent to her husband. These vacations were as much sought by them as holidays are by schoolboys; it gave them an opportunity of visiting their friends and full freedom to their actions.

I have said there were no jealousies in this Babylonian and polygamic department. I was wrong—I meant literal matrimonial jealousy, as even in an educated Christian society it would be difficult to find two females friends without some lurking jealousy of one another. Often disputes arose in this place when the Mongo distributed presents to them, such as cotton cloth for wear, looking glasses, beads, tobacco and pipes. Then if the least preference was apparent, adieu to order! Fatima's power became null; even the Mongo's authority stood below zero. The self-supposed injured party became furious, and if not promptly redressed, her rage became unimaginable.

I was the involuntary witness of one of these feminine impetuous jealous fits. The aggravated lady entered the store where the Mongo was, and throwing a Dutch looking glass to the floor demanded a larger one, hers being only one inch smaller than the rest. Her request was not taken notice of by Mr. Ormond, who when half sober had pride enough not to allow his women to molest him, and in answer to some further impertinences, ordered her out of the store. The claimant became mad with fury, and throwing all her covering off, demanded of her lord the Mongo if she was deficient of any charms to be slighted more than the rest, and parading herself before poor blushing mortal me, demanded my opinion also. This model artist demonstration brought the old gentleman to terms. Her demand was immediately attended to.

I had till then envied my employer's dominion over such a quantity of females, but after such a demoniacal demonstration I thought myself happy in my single state of loneliness, and silently vowed never to become a slave to female caprice.

At another time, years after, I saw another instance of African female temper. Her lord having preferred another of his wives' babes, she threw hers into the fire.

When a quarrel arose amongst these women, on account of their lovers, a meeting was appointed out of hearing of the Mongo, and both parties, throwing off their waistcloths, settled the matter in a gladiator-like costume, but without much damage. Lovers would at times take up the cause, and if the antagonist accepted the challenge, the duel would take place publicly. The belligerent parties each came out armed with a three-tail cat made of rawhide, stripped themselves, and threw three cowries in the air to determine the head or tail. The favored by lot then began to inflict so many number of blows with the cat, which his antagonist, according to agreement, received with the fortitude of a martinet and without a groan the stated number of lashes. The one that has received the flagellation with more fortitude is proclaimed the victor by the seconds.

This sort of duel leaves their backs much lacerated, with large ridges and scars. Youths often make boast of their courage by exhibiting these marks to strangers. It often happens, however, that after one or two blows the sufferer runs, to the great merriment of the seconds.

With this, I finish my tedious narrative of an African seraglio.

*CHAPTER 12th

*Ama-De-Bella Visits Our Factory

I had now been three weeks in the store and understood the value of all the goods, likewise the measures and quality of the country produce. My employer very seldom molested himself by visiting the stores, but as I did not understand the language, a trade man who understood English and several native dialects was appointed as my interpreter.

30 November, 1826

My time was employed nearly the whole day in retailing goods in exchange for rice, ivory, and palm oil, with other provisions for the establishment. Mr. Ormond attended himself to the purchase of slaves and gold, as I was not yet initiated in this important branch of traffic.

The dry season having set in, large caravans were expected from the Interior. One of our messangers had returned from the Fullah with the news that Ama-De-Bella, the son of a Fullah Chief, was about to visit the river with a large caravan.

Preparations were made for him and the strangers. Barkers were sent on the paths (there are no regular roads in Africa) with presents of colas[1] and tobacco to welcome them. Barkers are men that on account of their fluent tongue and volubility of language are employed by factories or chief traders to seek and meet strangers in the Interior and induce them to bring their produce to their patron. They are not called traveling clerks or agents as in civilized country, but perform the same duties, magnifying the prosperous state of their patron's affairs with as little regard to veracity as their Christian brothers. To give more charms to their persuasion, these talking agents—I mean barkers—are supplied by their employer with a small quantity of tobacco and colas, one to make snuff, the other to chew, with one or two bars of soap for the Chiefs of the caravan to wash their garments, as is strictly necessary after sixty or seventy days' traveling.

Some days after, the report of firearms were heard from the hills, giving us notice that our barkers had the desired caravan in tow. Our cannons gave a loud response to the signals of our traveling Clerks, and by the time the smoke had cleared, Ama-De-Bella and his party entered the town, marshaled by our ministers sent by the Mongo and who in loud voice sang the praise of the young Chieftain.

Next came the principal traders and their slaves, heavy laden

[1]kola nuts

with produce, followed by some forty captive slaves secured by rattan bands. Then came some fifty bullocks, a large quantity of sheep and goats. The women followed next, and a large tame ostrich closed the procession.

Mr. Ormond received this Chief and his committee of head traders on the piazza of our receiving house, commonly called the factory, a building 150 feet in front, built of mud, and fireproof; this building also contained the stores. As each one was presented they shook hands and snapped fingers with the Mongo several times. The introduction took a whole hour, as every trader and petty peddler wanted to shake hands with the rich man, for luck.

On the arrival of a caravan to a factory, as soon as the compliments are over it is customary for the strangers to deposit in the stores the merchandise that thay have brought. This is done, in the first place to secure it; next, to ascertain the whole amount, as by its value the calculations of welcome is determined. Although not acquainted with St. Paul, the Africans follow his maxim: seeing and feeling is believing, as it often happens that Interior merchants declare on their arrival much more gold and ivory than they really have, in order to receive a greater welcome.

The produce once secured, a couple of bullocks with a quantity of rice was given them, and the heads of the caravan were billeted about amongst our townspeople, while the *canaille*[1] made temporary huts for themselves with bushes on the outskirts. Ama-De-Bella was a strict Mahometan and had two wives with him; three separated houses were given him, with several new mats.

The caravan consisted of seven hundred strong, principally men. The manifest of their produce brought was as follows:

3500 bullock hides	valued at $1,750
19 large prime teeth of ivory	valued at 1,560
Gold	valued at 2,500
600 pounds small ivory	valued at 320
15 tons of rice	valued at 600
40 slaves	valued at 1,600
36 bullocks	valued at 360
Sheep, goats, butter, shallots	valued at 100
900 pounds beeswax	valued at 95
The whole value	$8,885

We gave notice to the Chief that we should open trade the next morning. These large caravans are very expensive, as during their

[1]riffraff

wait, their goods remain unpaid. They have to be fed, therefore the sooner the exchange is made the more profitable for the factory.

That evening Mr. Ormond, Ama-De-Bella, and some of his headmen stipulated on the prices to be paid for the produce, leaving a certain percentage as a duty for them. Likewise the customary presents were agreed upon for each head man. These preliminaries are necessary before trading, as it would be impossible to traffic with the petty traders and mob without the assistance of the headmen.

Next morning at daylight a crier went round the town announcing that the exchange would first begin with the hides and rice at the salt house, as these articles are generally exchanged for salt. Once this exchange was gone through, the crier again announced that the cattle and other animals would be purchased. This operation ended, and a day was put aside for the gold, ivory, and slaves to be exchanged.

On the day appointed, Mr. Ormond, Ama-De-Bella, and myself locked ourselves in the store and traded through a window, our barkers passing the goods to the interested party, often using their whips to keep order. Ama-De-Bella pretended to inspect the measurements of cloth, powder, and tobacco, but in reality attended more to his own interest in collecting his percentage.

The rice we purchased at the rate of a cent per pound, a hide for 18 or 20 cents, a bullock for twenty or thirty pounds of tobacco, a sheep or large goat two pounds of tobacco or a fathom of common cloth worth 25 cents. Ivory we purchased at the rate of one dollar per pound for prime and half for scrivilla,[1] making about 150 percent profit on our goods. The gold we paid at the rate of 16 dollars to the ounce, making only 70 percent, as this valuable metal commands the very best of goats.

Slaves we purchased at the rate of one hundred bars each. The bar is calculated at a half dollar value, but one pound and a half of tobacco is a bar. One fathom of common cloth is a bar, a pound of powder is a bar, a common soldier's musket is 12 bars. Therefore when slaves were purchased for tobacco (150 pounds), the real value paid was eighteen dollars; when made in powder, 100 pounds each, 20 dollars; and as we paid three dollars for English muskets, we seldom purchased slaves for that article alone.

On women slaves, we made a deduction of 20 percent when above 25 years old, but if young and well built with favorable appearances of fecundity, they commanded a price equal to a prime man. Boys measuring above 4 feet 4 inches were valued the same as full grown men. Children are seldom bought by factories, but are

[1]small elephant tusks, suitable only for billiard balls and scrimshaw work

disposed of with advantage about the native towns. A pregnant woman, or one with a baby at the breast, brings a trifling more.

The ostrich was an Indian gift to the Mongo; it was sent by the Ali-Mamy, the father of Ama-De-Bella, begging Mr. Ormond to return him some muskets as he needed them. The animal cost Mr. Ormond nearly sixty dollars—a chest of twenty muskets.

Every person on finishing his trade received a bugnee or a dash—a small present according to the value he sold. In a week the majority of this caravan had departed, and but few head men remained with Ama-De-Bella.

This Chief was a second son of the Ali-Mamy, or King of Foutha Yalloo. Having attained the age of 24 rainy seasons, his father had allowed him the prerogative attained only at that age, to head a caravan to the seaboard. This privilege is only granted as a great favor by the Ali-Mamy to his favorite sons and immediate relations, on condition that half of the products of this lucrative office shall be paid to him. The privileged son or relation departs from Foutha Yalloo at the first beginning of the dry season with full power of life and death, and squats himself and his party in one of the most frequented paths to the seaside, often sending small squads of his party to the different paths and blockading all passages to the beach. This blockade is sometimes kept up for a month or more, according to the quantity of traders they may have detained, as the object of this blockade is instituted not only to collect a large caravan and give the Chief himself the more importance, but to sequester a certain tribute due to the Ali-Mamy by small tribes which never could be collected otherwise. The privileged officer avails himself of this blockade to stop malefactors who may have avoided the justice of the law. Absconding debtors are eagerly seized on this occasion and their goods sequestered, and if not sufficient to pay the claim, his person becomes the property of the offended Justice if a Caffree.[1] But if he is a true believer, he is set free with a bastinado.[2]

Traders resort to all manner of subterfuge to evade these roads' interceptions, as it not only subjects them to a disgusting obedience, but it is often the case that the intention of their purpose is totally frustrated. When seized by one of these blockading Chiefs, they are made to go to a town or factory they perhaps never intended to visit, and when such a seizure lasts any time, it causes them to expend all their provisions, diminishing their profits and capital.

During Ama-De-Bella's stay in Bangalang, I visited him every evening, and through the assistance of an interpreter we amused

[1]Kaffir; a non-Muslim
[2]whack with a stick

ourselves for many hours in conversation. I would recount my voyages and my seafaring life, but could never successfully make him understand the rotundity of the world or its diurnal revolution. As I could refer neither to the Bible nor the Koran to prove my statement, I failed in my effort; still, I came off victorious, as he allowed me to be the better instructed, having traveled so far. But it was not so in religious matters. My African friend, who I really believe had swallowed the Koran and knew it by heart, would not be convinced on any subject. His prophet was the true prophet and his god the Great God; and as nothing is gained by disputing with a fanatic, I allowed my Mahometan Chief to retire with his self-satisfied ignorant opinion.

My condescension in religious matters was well repaid, as Ama-De-Bella in his confidence believed me quite convinced of the superiority of his religion, my silence at his long quotations of the Koran giving him cause for as much. He repaid my visits with interest; he even visited me in the store during my hours of business, and with the fervency of an enthusiast would spout his devotions in my ears. Out of mere caprice I made him believe that I would be willing to become a Mahometan, but only on one consideration— that I should be dispensed with undergoing the ceremony of Baptism of Blood.

My Mahometan devotée took the joke at a word, and from that day we became intimate friends. He then assumed the authority of a teacher, and when on the next day I could not repeat the whole of the Arabic Lord's Prayer which I had wrote off, he would chide me and in a very pathetic manner admonish me to have more regard for my salvation—much to the amusement of our interpreter, who was neither Mohometan nor Christian and enjoyed the joke.

Time arrived for Ama-De-Bella's return to Foutha and I now saw too late the effects of the bad joke I had practiced on my pious Mahometan friend. In his faith he had truly and sincerely believed my promises of apostasy, and now at the moment of parting he required me to bind our friendship by an oath of the Holy Book to continue in my new-found faith. I avoided the solemn affirmation till I had acquired better knowledge of the Koran and his religion, and by this excuse I gave him no offense.

I must retrogress a few lines before I allow the Chieftan to depart, and give the reader a short sketch of part of our conversations. The day appointed for the purchase of slaves, Mr. Ormond took the business on himself, as I was not yet initiated in the quality of this living commodity. It came to pass that out of the forty slaves the Mongo rejected eight of them. After some slight altercation Ama-

De-Bella agreed to discard seven, but one he insisted should be shipped, as he could neither kill him or send him back. Mr. Ormond refused him still, on account of the fellow's old age, and on no account would he accept him. Each one insisted, and nothing was done that day, as the Chief would not consent to go on with the trade till this difficulty was arranged.

In the evening I inquired of Ama-De-Bella the nature of the crime the slave in question had committed, as he could neither be killed nor taken back. He informed me that the man had killed his own son. The Koran described no punishment for such crimes, and the judges had condemned him to be sold and transported as a slave to a Christian country, this being considered greater punishment than death to a Mahometan; and till the Mongo agreed to his request, he should not go on with the trade.

As I had seen two women brought down with ropes around their neck, while others came loose and to be sold for the same purpose, I naturally inquired why were they secured in such a manner. He replied that two women would have been burnt for witchcraft but that his father, who needed powder, had spared their lives to replenish his magazine. One of the slaves which had been brought fastened in company with the two women was a Mahometan who had abjured his religion and had set fire to a dwelling, to the great danger of the whole town. He would have been killed, but his having renounced his creed, and the great want of powder amongst his nation, had caused the court to spare him and order his sale.

The rest of the slaves were all Caffree and unbelievers, either culprits or prisoners of war. On account of the scarcity of powder Ama-De-Bella had not succeeded in bringing more slaves in his caravan this season, but with the supply he now could carry on his return home, he hoped in the next rainy season he would be able to carry on a large war against different small tribes, whose sale would enable him to replenish his stock of cattle destroyed by the distemper two years before.

I then made inquiry in what manner they disposed of Mahometan culprits not condemned to death, since they could not sell them. His answer was that in his native country Foutha Yalloo, they had two codes of law, one taken directly from the Koran and adapted solely to born Mahometans, the other, made on the occasion by the head men of his father's counselors, was applied to unbelievers and slaves. He also added that a Mahometan is never sold in slavery; capital crimes were punished with death and small offenses by confiscation of property or corporal chastisement. Debtors were stripped of their cattle and slaves, and the affair ended thus.

Female Mahometans have also a separate code. As many of them can read the Koran they are regarded nearly on the same footing as their lords. For any small peccadillo in a married woman, the husband uses the rod of correction. No courts or pettifoggers[1] have jurisdiction over matrimonial affairs, and divorce is not known. But if a Mahometan woman committed incest with a slave or an unbeliever, death was her portion.

Infanticide is also punished with death, but is seldom resorted to, as fecundity and maternity are better appreciated in Africa than amongst our more civilized nations. The more children the woman brings into the world, the greater the influence she has in her husband's household. The Foutha Mahometans can have only four wives, which they cannot either reject or sell, but they can have as many concubines from other tribes. These are treated more as servants than mistresses. However, the children are free from their birth and brought up in the same creed as their brothers of lawful mothers.

Slaves and Caffrees are considered by the Mahometans as unbelievers, therefore as mere ignorants. Their punishment is applied with less vigor but with more contempt, and a crime which would be visited by death on a Mahometan is only considered a case of slavery on an unbeliever. This last sentence is invariably resorted to, as it never fails to be compatible with the interest of the courts, and the smallest crime is considered capital—an abuse which is no less palpable in our civilized and Christian community in cases when the parties are poor and friendless.

I then begged to know in what manner they could have collected so many slaves in a Mahometan country where a true believer was a free subject. His response was that the Koran permitted the sale of their bondservants, and from that source many were yearly exchanged for European goods, which in return supplied them with the means of carrying on the wars commanded by the Secret Book—to conquer and subjugate all tribes to the true faith. In order to carry out more fully the commands of a true Mahometan to destroy all unbelievers, they had recourse to the cupidity of the white man, whose milder religion authorized its votaries to enslave the African.

My curiosity prompted me into further inquiry, and I desired him to tell me if these wars of devastation commanded by the Holy Book, were not more frequently instigated by interest in the great profits his Mahometan countrymen reaped from the results. I gently insinuated my belief that he himself would not undertake to storm

[1]shyster lawyers

one of the well-fortified Caffree towns if not prompted by a success-ful booty of slaves. After a minute's consideration he replied with some humor that Mahometans were no better than Christians; the one stole, the other held the bag; and if the while man—the elect of God, whom he had taught how to make powder and guns—would not tempt the Black man with them, the commands of the Great Allah would be followed with milder means. Somewhat convinced on the subject, I retired from the field of controversy with a flea in my ear.

The daily disputes did not diminish our friendship. Ama-De-Bella loved argument, and I wished to be instructed; this caused us to seek one another's society, and till it became necessary to part, we saw each other as often as my business would allow me. On the last meeting we exchanged names, a friendly usage in the country. I presented him with a double-barreled gun in return for a volume of the Koran illuminated with the sandals of the Prophet. (Images are prohibited by the Koran.) I accompanied him some miles on his way, and parted with a promise that the next dry season I would visit his father in Foutha Yalloo.

*CHAPTER 13th

*I Take the African Fever and Am Nursed by Mr. Edward Joseph

As I wished to be instructed in the rudiments of my profession, I watched my employer with avidity in all his operations when the purchase of the slaves took place. As each slave was brought in, the Mongo examined them from head to foot, and as they were perfectly naked no part was spared. Male and female, young and old, all underwent a long manipulation. This was done to ascertain the soundness of their limbs. Every joint was made to crack; hips, armpits, and groins were also examined. The mouth was duly inspected, and when a tooth fell short it was noted down as a deduction. The eyesight was minutely observed, the voice and speech was called into request. Nothing was forgotten; even the fingers and toes had to undergo similar inspection.

Full grown women were as minutely inspected, and questions asked which are not necessary to know, but for a purchaser of slaves. Several passed this rigid muster without a noted defect, while on many others large deductions were made; one for having lost two front teeth, another for an insignificant squint in his eye, and a third for having imitated the French conscript who in order to unfit himself for service cut off his first finger.

A large powerful man was brought in. This poor fellow was strongly pinioned with two double rattan bands to his waist, with both hands fastened to it. The conducter held him by a rope fastened around his neck. To my great astonishment I saw him put aside as discarded by the Mongo. I naturally inquired the cause, and was told that the apparent strong man had been medicated. In such cases they bloat them and give them powder and lemon juice to make them perspire. Mr. Ormond told me that these medicines were nothing more than jockey-tricks practiced by a sharper to sell off a sick slave, and to enforce his argument desired me to feel the man's pulse. I did so, and found him in a high state of fever. The securing of his person was only a hoax.

I was told that in the Interior, whenever a slave becomes useless to his master on account of sickness, they deliver him to a slave peddler or broker to be disposed of. Such men are familiar with drugs and eagerly undertake the job of puffing the sickly creature with a mineral drug peculiar for its power to bloat the flesh. And while he is in a state of operation an additional dose of stimulants

—either lemon juice and powder, or rum and red pepper—is given, which gives a luster to the skin. In this state of bodily fermentation he is sold to the first greenhorn in the trade. But the experienced slaver will soon detect the cheat; the yellowish eye, the swollen tongue, and the feverish skin soon denote the trick of the quack human jockey. Five days after, I found the poor fellow a paralyzed skeleton, abandoned by his Master.

Two more lessons from the Mongo, and I was considered sufficiently instructed in the slave traffic. I was left the sole manager of the stores while Mr. Ormond gave himself up to his drinking propensity. But although he neglected his commercial business, still he attended to his country palabras, which in his ambition to be called a King he delighted to settle, and let it be said to his credit that his decisions never were deficient of sound judgment, but impartially and correctly given.

As I began to understand something of the language, having been in the country three months, I could dispense with the interpreter, who the Mongo often employed as his trusty messenger. At parting on a long journey, this man advised me to make up with the head woman Fatima, as she suspected of my intimacy with Esther, and by all means to make her a present to purchase her silence, as in her animosity to me she would undoubtedly denounce her to the Mongo, who entertained for her a mad but powerless passion.

I did as I was advised, and held the candle to the devil in the shape of a string of coral beads. This golden key opened the gates to her black heart, and in the future she silently tolerated our nocturnal interviews.

I had been in office some weeks and thought myself proof against the fever so much dreaded by the whites. I neglected all the admonitions from the natives—to keep within doors at night, not to go swimming in the heat of the day—when a violent pain in the loins with a swimming of the head announced to me the powerful grip of the African Fever.[1] The second day I became delirious. Mr. Ormond paid me a visit, but in my incautious delirium, I knew him not. I called on Esther for water, giving her the appellation of *inkele* (dear). This caused some surprise to the old gentleman, who interrogated the abbess Fatima on the subject. The coral beads had made a strong impression on the old hag's delicate feelings, and with an extempore adroitness peculiar even to colored ladies, she fabricated such a rigamarole story which not only quieted the well-contented Mongo, but brought out Esther's character with fresher luster.

72   [1]Dengue fever

The easy-believing old gentleman, finding Fatima so well disposed toward his previous Secretary-Clerk, gave her back the charge of the store, which was the height of her ambition; in gratitude for my sickness she gave full permission to Esther to attend my sickbed. I became unmanageable. Several other females volunteered their services, but as no one could speak English but Esther, they could not be of much service.

The old native Doctor was called in, and I was cupped after his African *materia medica* fashion. This was done with a hot knife blade; he inflicted several small gashes on my back, on my neck, and on my stomach, applying plantain leaves after. As one nail drives the other, this operation allayed the fever for a couple of hours, but it returned with greater fury. It became necessary to inform the Mongo of my very dangerous position. Mr. Ormond sent for an Englishman lately settled on his own account in the neighborhood of Bangalang, and who had been his former Clerk.

Mr. Edward Joseph soon made his appearance, and finding me abandoned by my employer, very generously took me, insensible as I was, to his place, Gambia. I had been introduced to Mr. Joseph the morning after the fray on board of the *Areostatico*, when as resident in the river he had offered his services, and he now put them into practice.

Another Mandingo Doctor was called in, and all incantations were resorted to without effect. (My English friend, strangely, believed in such fooleries.) I remained in this state of torpid stupidness till next morning, when Esther made her appearance conducting a very old white-headed woman, the greatest enchantress and fortune teller of the Kiwan Country. This female Aesculapius had been induced to perform my cure for the reward of a slave paid by Esther in advance.

No time was lost. The floor of a mud house was made hot with a large fire, and when considered sufficiently heated, a large quantity of lemon leaves were strewed on the floor in guise of a couch. A cloth was then spread over it. When I was placed to steam under cover of blankets, my medical attendant then extracted from some most bitter herbs (also by the steaming process) half a tumbler of doubly disgusting and abominable tasting green juice which I was made to swallow. The operation of barbequeing on wet leaves and poison drinking was repeated during five consecutive days and, strange to say, it baked the fever out of me. But the recovery was not so hastily gone through: I remained a *chétif*,[1] emaciated, poor ambulating liv-

[1] feeble

ing skeleton whose stomach could never be satiated and whose limbs underwent for a long period a diurnal concussion of two hours' duration, caused by the fever and ague, an invariable sequel of an African Fever.

Days after days passed on, and my convalescence made no progress. My voracious appetite had made me a glutton, and the continued fever and ague had created such an indolence that I only rose from my bed to walk to the dinner table, and I was again considered in a dangerous position. The advice of a French Doctor, Monsieur Dumaige, restored me to health by making use of a cold bath at the crisis of fever. It proved good to me and I have used no other person's orders since, and consider it better than the use of quinine.

On my recovery Mr. Ormond requested I should resume my charge. I refused, as Esther had informed me that Unga Fatima, foreseeing my restoration, had looked out for a rainy day and of course had made herself free with the goods in the store. As I demanded a settlement from the Mongo for my services, we parted with coolness on his refusal.

I returned to my friend Joseph, who had established himself in a very pleasant spot of this River Pongo, called Gambia, and with a small capital carried on a tolerably good business.

My English friend had also been a Clerk in Bangalang with Mr. Ormond, and like myself, had accidentally found a female friend in the Mongo's Mulatto-Black harem. But not knowing the pilfering passion of Fatima, he served in the stores for a year when the losses became too palpable, and, harboring the same fears, gave up his situation. This young man was born in London and had come out to Africa with General Turner, Governor of Sierra Leone. On the return of the Governor to England or at his death—I forgot which—he remained in the Colony and for a time occupied the place of Harbor Master.

His first visit to Rio Pongo was made as supercargo of a small coasting craft. He succeeded in disposing of his goods, but not so in collecting the payment, as his principal creditors were the females of the seraglio. The deficiency on the balance sheet of his account caused him to abscond from his creditors. In brief, he never returned to Sierra Leone; finding himself deprived of goods and in want, he accepted service with Mr. Ormond.

As I said, he continued one whole year in that employ, but finding himself sufficiently instructed in the mode of traffic and the language of the country, he proposed to his creditors in Sierra Leone a full payment of his debts, provided they would still advance him capital enough to begin trading on his own account. An Israelite merchant accepted the proposal, and in short time Edward Joseph 27 *February*, numbered as one of the factors of that river. *1827*

On my first arrival at his place, I found him well stocked with English goods. Having nothing to do, I employed my time in the acquisition of the native language and made a rapid progress in the Sosoo dialect, which derives its origin from the Mandingo language. This dialect is very easily acquired as nearly all the verbs end with a vowel, and when well spoken it sounds very soft to the ear. I also found that many words were taken from the language of the Portuguese, the first discoverers of this continent.

*I Obtain a Cargo for the Fortuna, Consigned to Me · The Eventual Profit of Her Voyage

15 March, 1827

On the 15th of March 1827 a Spanish vessel arrived, and to the astonishment of all the magnates of the river, the Captain addressed himself to me.

The vessel belonged principally to my old friend the grocer, and as the *Areostatico* had arrived in 28 days from the Pongos in safety, the owners had sent out a larger vessel and consigned her to me. My old friend the Boatswain was in command; her name was the *Fortuna*.

With a letter of instruction, the owners had sent me out my wages for the voyage round and a present of thirty ounces in consideration for my conduct in defense of their property. The Captain of the *Fortuna* informed me that the English boy had been paid off and, at my request, the grocer had procured him a berth in a Liverpool vessel.

My letter of instruction authorized me to load the *Fortuna* with an assorted cargo of slaves, for which they had shipped 200 thousand Havana cigars and 500 ounces or doubloons in Mexican coin. They did not limit the price I should give for a slave, but it was thought sufficient to purchase two hundred. My commission was limited at 10 per cent and an assurance of the command of a vessel whenever I should get tired of Africa.

Let me deviate for one moment. As the reader may naturally wish to inquire of what utility cigars would have been to Africans, in due time I will answer this question.

As agent of the *Fortuna*, I called all the traders on board. I made known to them the instruction of the owners to me and offered to divide the cargo amongst them, on condition that at a given day they should all make payment according to the proposal I would make. After much discussion the division was made, but only with the gold. No one would take any portion of the cigars. Mr. Ormond took a quarter, Mr. Faber another quarter, two native Chiefs took the rest. It was agreed that in 30 days from that date the vessel should sail; therefore the payment should be made on board the day before, and that no pregnant woman should be considered as fair tender. No boys or girls under 4 feet 4 inches should be accepted as prime. Also I reserved to myself the privilege of rejecting any slaves which I might consider in fault.

As this was my first assay in the management of a slave cargo, I only studied the interests of the owners and, knowing the importance of dispatch, I divided the cargo amongst the different factors to hasten the shipment. I had not even regard for the price; dispatch was my object. I allowed the traders the exorbitant price of 50 dollars to the slave.

My friend Joseph, who had till then only traded in produce, could not now stand the temptation any longer. He came on board with the rest and took a proportional part of the doubloons. The 500 ounces, valued at 17 dollars each, brought only 170 slaves; the cigars were invoiced at $12 per mill, but no one took them. I had recourse to my friend Joseph, who proposed to send them to his friend the Jew in Sierra Leone and exchange them for Manchester goods. Accordingly, that evening I hired a canoe and sent my cigars to the Colony. On the 10th day the Israelite merchant arrived in the river with a cutter full loaded with superior English manufactures. The charms of 500 doubloons in the hands of natives had already allured him from his home. For my cigars he paid me at the rate of sixteen dollars, which profit enabled me to pay the expenses of the vessel while in the river, and purchase the rest of the cargo.

These cigars were shipped at the request of the Captain of the *Areostatico*, who finding the grocer was about sending me a vessel before his own could be refitted, had maliciously induced them to believe that cigars would fetch a great price in the river, in order to put me into difficulties. However, a few days after the sailing of the *Fortuna*, having boasted too loud of his duplicity, he was discharged and another Master appointed to the *Areostatico*.

I have said that the report of a slaver with doubloons as cargo had spread all over the English settlement. Jew merchants, as well as their Christian brothers, flocked to the river in droves. In a few days English goods fell fifty percent, such was the demand for slavers' gold.

This concurrence[1] made me well known amongst the merchants of Sierra Leone, and the arrival of the *Fortuna* sealed to my consignment stamped me as a great Spanish slaver. I had not as yet been five months in Africa.

On the given day, the *Fortuna* left the river with 220 slaves. Three months after, I received information that she had landed in the Bay of Matanzas 217 slaves, which were sold at 21 ounces each by the lump. (Let me here remark it was a choice cargo.) This high price realized her owners in less than four months forty-one thousand dollars.

[1] transaction

27 March, 1827   As the reader may with difficulty credit such enormous profit, I will give here a full statement of the fitting out of this vessel in 1827:

First cost of the *Fortuna*	$ 3,700.00
Fitting sails, carpenters' and coopers' bill	2.500.00
Provision for crew, $765.00,	
ditto for slaves, $350.00	1,115.00
Advance to 18 men 'fore the mast @ $50	900.00
Ditto Captain	100.00
Ditto Mate	80.00
Ditto Second Mate	70.00
Ditto Boatswain	70.00
Ditto Cook & Steward, $60 each	120.00
Cargo: 200 mill cigars, 500 doubloons	10,900.00
Clearance, and hush moneys	200.00
	$19,755.00
Commission on the amount, 5%	987.00
Fortuna's full cost on her voyage out	$20,742.00

Expenses on her return:

Captain's head money, $8 a head	1,746.00
Mate's head money, $4 a head	873.00
2nd Mate & Boatswain, $2 a head	873.00
Captain's wages 66 days at $100 a month	219.78
1st Mate's wages 66 days at $80 a month	175.56
2nd Mate & Boatswain wages 66 days at $70 a month	307.12
Cook & Steward wages 66 days at $60 a month	264.00
18 Sailors wages 66 days at $50 a month	1,972.00
	27,172.46
Government officers, $8 per head	1,736.00
My commission on the 217 slaves,	
expenses deducted	5,565.00
Consignees' commission 5% on the value	
of the slaves, $77,469.00	3,873.00
217 slaves dresses, $2 each	434.00
Expenses—full amount	$38,780.46

Returns

Value of the vessel at auction	3,950.00
Cargo: 217 slaves at 357 dollars	77,469.00
	$81,419.00
Extra expenses, such as doctor, fresh provisions, landing, boat hire, etc.	1,000.00
	$80,419.00

Costs as above	38,700.00	*27 March,*
Net profit	$41,719.00	*1827*

The above statement is a correct valuation of the outfits, expenses, and returns of this vessel, fitted out in Havana in 1827. At that time the Government only received—I may say, clandestinely exacted—eight dollars' bonus each head. But of late years, the responsibility being greater on the Governors of Cuba, the importers of slaves have been made to pay as much as three ounces per head, besides a few dashes to smaller Government satellites.

*The £30,000 Treaty and Its Effect on the Slave Trade

March,
1827

The *Fortuna* was fitted out for only 220 slaves, and that quantity was then considered quite a full cargo for a vessel of ninety tons burthen. But since the Treaty of Martinez de la Rosa in 1836 with the British Government, all vessels under Spanish flag have been made liable to be seized on the Coast of Africa, if only thought apparent or suspicious of being engaged in the slave trade. The danger becoming greater by this treaty, it obliged slavers since that time to have recourse to greater economy in the stowage of slaves or in the fittings out. A vessel of the size of the *Fortuna* could now stow 400 slaves, and the fitting out would amount but to one half of what it cost then. Slaves have also become much cheaper in Africa, and as the vessel that lands them in Cuba cannot but with great difficulty return to the ports of clearance, they are generally destroyed. Therefore this accounts for the economy in the fitting out.

This mortal treaty the Spanish slavers called "The 30,000 Pound Treaty" as it was reported that the Spanish Minister Martinez de la Rosa had received such a premium from the Court of Saint James. I will here state the effect such a treaty had on the reduction of slave trade.

Primo: as this arbitrary law was put in force by the English cruisers (I suppose with the consent of Mr. Martinez de la Rosa) a good four months before it was promulgated in the Spanish possessions, it gave an opportunity to the British cruisers to seize in that time over eighty Spanish vessels, one third of them never intended for the slave trade.

Second: as this treaty condemned slave vessels to be broken up after seizure and not sold by the Captains as formerly, fast-sailing vessels came more into demand. Faster clippers were built which gave them a better chance to escape.

Third: Spanish slave merchants had recourse to other nations for the protection of their property: Portuguese and Brazilian vessels carried on the Spanish slave trade for a long while, and French, English and Americans took the Spanish cargoes out to Africa for the purchase of the slaves.

Fourth: As this law entailed greater expenses to Spanish slavers, every method of economy was resorted to, but principally the crowding of slaves on board in lesser space was the most prominent feature of its effect.

80   Fifth: As slavers could not be fitted out from the Island of Cuba,

other nations sent their vessels, ready equipped, to Africa, and there under the jibbooms[1] transferred their vessels to African traders, the Captain and part of the crew taking passage home with their registers in any other lawful trader.

Sixth: As this law of destruction deprived the cruisers of their share of prize money, the Government in consideration granted them so much a ton for every vessel captured, and from that time hence, the English foot rule was diminished to 10 inches and sometimes less. This method in the gauging of prizes, therefore, certainly gave greater shares to the captors. Not a few slavers were sunk as unseaworthy by the cruisers when their measurement would not amount to much if sent to the Maritime Commission Court for adjudication, and the Carpenter's salt water report was the only measurement sent to this Admiralty.

Last, this philanthropic law (if it was such) did not diminish the slave trade one iota, but on the contrary, it drove slavers to use harsher treatment with their slaves, as it became impossible to take the same care of them while on board. When lesser numbers were shipped, the ration of water was diminished and food the same. Slaves were not only allowed less room and free air, but irons were put on when not needed before, sentries were doubled, and gratings constantly kept barred. These restrictions caused frequent disease, and mortality was augmented six and ten percent.

My object is not to criticize others or disculpate myself, but to describe such episodes as I was witness to. If in my former chapter I have mentioned in too correct terms the contrary effects of a law which I believe was dictated by pure philanthropic motives, I have done so to prove the abuses it created and the forcible cruelties it produced. By abuses and forcible cruelties I mean those inevitable necessities which attend all forced trade, and which owners and masters are involuntarily reduced to use those means unpleasant to their feelings. I will hereafter describe such of these necessities as came under my notice.

As I am on the chapter of cruelties, let me describe the shipment of cargo of slaves on the Coast and the middle passage.

In the first place, the factor takes great care in selecting the slaves for shipment. Those whose appearance denotes the least contagious sickness are never shipped. Women in a far state of pregnancy are also reserved; children at the breast are rarely put on board. A few days before the embarkation takes place the head of every male and female are shaven. They are then marked; this is done with a hot pipe sufficiently heated to blister the skin. Some use their initials

[1]bowsprits

made of silver wire. The object of this disagreeable operation is done only when several persons ship slaves in one vessel, otherwise when only one proprietor is sole owner it is dispensed with.

This disgusting duty is one of those forcible cruelties which cannot be avoided. When several proprietors ship in one vessel it is indispensable to mark them, in order that on the arrival the consignees may know them. Also, when death takes place in the passage, by the mark it is ascertained whose loss it is, as every Negro thrown over the board during the voyage is registered in the log book.

But in extenuation for this somewhat brutal act, let me assure the reader that it is ever done as lightly as possible, and just enough for the mark to remain only six months; when and if well done, it leaves the skin as smooth as ever. This scorching sign is generally made on the fleshy part of the arm to adults, to children on the posterior.

The appointed day for shipping having arrived, they are plentifully fed and shipped in canoes to be transported on board. Once alongside, their clothes are taken off and they are shipped on board in perfect nakedness; this is done without distinction of sex. This precaution is necessary to keep them free from vermin. This also is an unpleasant necessity, and forcibly attended to, as the females part with reluctance with the only trifling rag that covers their Black modesty. As they are kept in total nudity the whole voyage, cleanliness is preserved with little trouble.

In this state they are immediately secured below, the women in the cabin and the men in the main hold. The children and boys are kept on the deck and distributed about the boat, but they are kept below till the vessel is clear of the land. At mealtime they are distributed ten to a mess.

Thirty years ago when the Spanish slave trade was lawful, Captains of slavers were somewhat more religious than they are at present. They made their slaves say grace before meals and thanks after, but in our days they have no time. Masters of such a vessel, with the fear of John Bull only before them, content themselves with a short sentence such as "Viva la Habana" and a clapping of hands.

This hurrah over, a bucket full of salt water is given to each mess and *bon-gré, mal-gré*,[1] they are made to wash their hands. Then a kid is placed before them full of either rice, fariña, yams or beans, according to what country they belong, as Negroes from the south do not eat the same food as those from the north. At a signal given they all dip their hands and in rotation take out a handful, a sailor watching their movements and the punctuality of the regular turn.

It is the sailor's duty to report when any one of the slaves refuses

[1]willy nilly

to eat, and if by the reconnoitering of the officer it is found that stubbornness is the cause of a voluntary abstinence (Negroes often starve themselves to death), the cat is applied till a cure is effected. (Here then is another instance of those unpleasant necessities resorted to, but it is only given as medicinal antidote.) If the loss of appetite is caused by indisposition, he is singled out for further inspection and a glass head or button is tied round his neck as a sick list ticket.

The feeding over, another bucket of water is given for a second washing, and everyone is then allowed to retire in single file manner to their favorite plank about decks or below. This duty of feeding takes place twice a day, at 10 in the morning and at 4 in the afternoon. Water is also given three times a day, a half pint each time. Pipes and tobacco are also distributed with some economy, as they cannot all be allowed a pipe. Half a dozen boys light a pipe each, and they go round the decks giving so many whiffs each person. Thrice a week their mouth is washed with vinegar, and nearly every morning a dram of spirits is given them, both used as preservative against scurvy. Every afternoon, wind and weather permitting, they are allowed to sing. Women, men, and boys join in chorus in African melodies accompanied by the tam-tam on a tub.

Men and women are ever kept separate, but permission is granted to converse together during the daytime. Corporal chastisement is only inflicted by order of the officers, and then the culprit is made to understand why he is chastised. Once a week the barber goes the round with his attendants and scrapes without the assistance of soap their wiry chins, free of expense. The fingernails are also cropped every shaving day; in this operation all the penknives and scissors are called in requisition. This operation is well attended to, as in their nightly disputes when contesting for an inch more of room they generally vent their passion in scratching one another, the narrowness of their quarters seldom permitting a pugilist settlement.

The sick are separated as soon as discovered. The whole of the forecastle is appropriated exclusively for the sick slave. (Sailors on board of slavers have up quarters. Sick or well, the deck is their only habitation.) The Chief Officer generally officiates as Doctor. He inspects each Negro every morning before breakfast and with his medical staff performs all cures, and in serious cases reports to the Captain.

The Boatswain's duty is to keep the ship clean, and this is attended with the greatest scrupulosity. Every morning at daylight all the filth of the night is removed and the tubs scrubbed with chloride of lime. The upper deck is washed and swabbed, the slave deck scraped and holystoned. By nine o'clock the Captain inspects every part of the ship, and no vessel, except a man-of-war, can compare with a slaver in cleanliness and order.

In a well-conducted vessel, Captain, officers, and crew are constantly employed in preserving and safely conducting the vessel and cargo. Much has been said in regard to the stowing of Negroes on board of slavers, and the words "packing and piling" invariably used to denote the mode they are carried during the voyage. Permit me to describe this operation also, one of those forcible cruelties necessarily resorted to and inevitable on board a slaver.

Two of the officers have the charge of stowing them. At sundown the Second Mate and Boatswain descend, cat in hand, and stow the Negroes for the night. Those on the starboard side face forward and in one another's lap, vulgarly called spoon fashion. On the port side they are stowed with face aft; this position is considered preferable for the free pulsation of the heart. The tallest are selected for the greatest breadth of the vessel, while the short size and youngsters are stowed in the fore part of the ship. Great precaution is also taken to place those such as may have sores or boils on the side most convenient for their distemper. Tubs are also distributed on the sleeping deck and so placed that both sides can have access. (The sick are never placed below.)

This lower deck once full, the rest are stowed on the deck, which is prepared with loose boards to keep the water from under them; they are then covered in fair weather with spare sails and with tarpaulins in rainy nights. In this manner they are made to remain all night, if possible. This discipline of stowing them is of the greatest importance on board slavers; otherwise every Negro would accommodate himself with all the comfortability of a cabin passenger.

As it is necessary to keep order and silence during the night, out of every ten slaves one is chosen as Constable. To him is delegated his watch, and in order to enforce his commands he is supplied with a cat. As a remuneration for his services, which are well done when the cat is called into requisition, he is supplied with an old shirt and sometimes with a pair of terry trousers.

Billets of wood are sometimes distributed to them, but as slaves shipped are often of different nations this luxury is not granted till well assured of the good disposition of the Negroes, as in many occasions slaves have been tempted to mutiny only by the opportunity at hand of arming themselves with those native pillows—indeed a very destructive missive in case of revolt.

As it may appear barbarous that slaves should be made to lie
down naked on a hard board, let me inform the reader that native

Africans know not the use of mattresses, and it is only the free and rich that indulge now and then in a loll on a mat or a rawhide. Even the Chiefs of Mandingo, the most industrious and civilized nation of Africa—their beds, divans, and sofas are but mud couches with an untanned skin as cushion and a billet of wood for bolster. Therefore slaves cannot find great inconvenience in laying down on hard boards. I consider their position on the above subject much better than that of a soldier who half of his sleeping life is made to lay on boards as hard as a ship's deck, and with the additional inconvenience of his clothes and shoes.

The ventilation also is an object minutely attended to. Every slaver's hatches and bulkheads are grated, and additional small hatches are cut about the decks for the greater circulation of air; wind sails and every communication with the hold are constantly kept up, unless in a chase, when every comfort is sacrificed for the safety of the vessel. When in light winds or calms and the wind sails are useless, the gratings are taken off and a portion of the slaves are allowed to lay on the deck, under guard of the whole crew which are ever armed on such occasion.

For the security and safekeeping of the slaves on board or on shore in the African barracoons, chains, leg irons, handcuffs, and strong houses are used. I would remark that this also is one of the forcible necessities resorted to for the preservation of order, and as recourse against the dangerous consequences of this traffic. Irons and handcuffs are used on board with as much frugality as possible. Slaves are generally brought on board chained ten in a gang. This is the mode they are secured in the barracoons on shore, but as these chains are very inconvenient on board, they are taken off immediately, and leg irons put on which secures them two by two, the right of the one fastened to the left of the other. They consist of a bolt a foot long with two shackles, and are only put on to full grown men. Women and boys are let loose on their arrival on board. The refractory ones are doubly secured with handcuffs (an iron shackle which secures both hands) and taken off as soon as possible. It is often the case that these fastenings are taken off long before the arrival, when the behavior of the slaves warrants it, and many Brazilian slavers never use irons. Slaves from Anjuda, Benin, and Angola are of milder disposition and not as given to revolt as those from the east of the Cape of Good Hope or north of the Gold Coast.

I have used the word "frugality" in regard to the irons used in this traffic not as a mere phrase, but with all the meaning it conveys, as I mean to signify that they are only put on but when powerfully compelled to. As a proof, I will add that the longer a slave is kept in

March, 1827

irons, the more he deteriorates, and as the sole object of a slaver is to land his cargo in perfect healthy order—not only because his pecuniary interest is at stake, but because his character would be impaired—it becomes him to be sparing when using the means of security.

My object (as I said before) is not to disculpate the inhuman traffic, but to correct the exaggerated reports made on the heavy and ponderous chains said to be used on board of these vessels which not only subject slaves to a continual reclining position, but at will they are made—according to these false accounts—to be drawn up, by a jerk of this supposed chain, feet uppermost, to the ceiling of the upper deck. I know not where these unfounded accounts originated from, unless they were used before my time on board of vessels whose nationality permitted these barbarities, and who now condemn the same trade as felony.

*CHAPTER 16th

*The Landing and Sale of a Slave Cargo

As I have fully described the mode of shipping, feeding, sleeping, *March,* and securing of the slaves on ship board, I shall next narrate the *1827* manner they are landed in the Island of Cuba. But before I do so, let me crave the indulgence of the reader if I again correct many remarks made by public newspapers and pamphlets on the filthy condition that slaves are forced to be subjected to during the middle passage. I have said before that slaves are shipped and kept naked for the sole object of cleanliness; I have also described the policy of the slaver in regard to washing and scraping of the slave deck. Let me further inform the reader that whenever the weather permits, they are also made to bathe, and it's invariably done once a week. The women during their periods are kept in the cabin, where no person violates their secrecy, as during the night the keys of the cabin grating are kept by the Captain, who as Chief never gives bad example.

This duty being one of the most important on board of a slaver, it is never neglected. A Master on such a vessel is made accountable by the owners for every death, and when it can be proved that through his negligence or disregard the health and the comfort of the slaves have been impaired, or if he has used unnecessary cruelties toward them, such a Captain is not only immediately unshipped, but his commission or head money stopped and his reputation blasted.

If Masters of emigrant ships could be made answerable for the life of every passenger, the hospitals of New York would number less deaths of ship fever caused by filthiness, putrid provisions, and want of pure airs; a palpable neglect in many such transports where the absence of every policy is indolently neglected. It is with satisfaction that I can assure the reader that in not one instance have I seen or heard of ship fever on board of a slaver.

The landing of slaves is generally made now on some given point of the coast where the absence of habitation is apparent, but some hidden hut denotes the spot of the persons appointed to await the arrival. As soon as the anchor is let go, one or more boats are sent off and the landing is effected while some of the crew dismantle the vessel in order to avoid notice from inland or in the offing. Once the cargo is landed, it is hastened in the Interior as soon as possible, escorted by the Captain and part of the crew all well armed, and made to walk at a rapid rate. In this manner they are conducted to the nearest plantation whose consent is purchased before, and there *87* deposited, which secures them from the grasping power of the petty magistrate of the district (called *capitan de partidos*) who in imitation of his superior the Governor would exact a remuneration for his consent.

In the meantime, a dispatch is sent to the owners in Havana, Matanzas, or Santiago de Cuba, who arrive post haste at the plantation with coarse dresses for the new-arrived Africans and the necessary gold to pay off the crew.

Messengers are sent off to the different slave brokers, who inform the needy purchaser that a quantity of Bossal slaves are to be disposed, mentioning the nation but not the owner, Captain, or the vessel that landed them. As gold is expected, nothing is said of the terms.

The vessel, if small, is either dismantled or so disfigured as to warrant a safe return in a port of clearance with a cargo of sugar or molasses and under the coasting flag. But if the vessel is a brig or rigged ship, she is either burnt or sunk. Sometimes she is sent to St. Thomas, Curaçao, or Spanish San Domingo as a distressed vessel, to appear again perhaps transmuted under another rig, paint, and name.

On the arrival of the slaves in a plantation, they are well fed with fresh provisions and abundance of fruit, which greatly astonishes the African who in his joy forgets his country, friends, and relations. But his wonder rests not there. The new clothes, the red cap, and the blanket (a civilized superfluity not yet accustomed to) dumbs him with surprise, and in his amazement he puts his clothes on the wrong side out, or the hind part before. The arrival of a carriage or cart creates no little confusion on this benighted Ethiopian, who has no idea that animals can be made to work, and in his African ignorance admires the white man's ingenuity.

But the grand demonstration of the surprise of surprises is at hand: a Black postillion in his red jacket and silver spurs alights from a prancing horse and in the language of their mothers bids them welcome and in the name of Allah blesses their safe arrival. A furor takes place. Every African wishes to embrace and snap fingers with the equestrian civilized African brother, who by his Master's order preaches them a well-learnt sermon on the happiness of being a white man's slave, cracking his whip on the well-polished boot to enforce his untruthful arguments.

Should this be a cargo owned by a company, every one takes his share away with him to his house or plantation, but if owned by speculators who need them not, they are sold on the plantation to the planter who, gold in hand, chooses what best suits him. The operation of disposing of them is gone through with as great a haste as possible, before the Great Britain Argus[1] makes his report to the Governor General, who not in respect of treaties but in fear of the Proud Albion Consul, promises to put the laws into force and with the dignity of a grandee of Spain orders the comandante of dragoons or lanceros to proceed at a gallop to the plantation designated by the representative of England, who awaits in person to see the order given.

While the sale takes place, one of the owners or his agent pays a morning visit to the Palacio, knocks at the Captain General's Private Secretary who is ever on attendance on such an occasion, and in comfortable vis-à-vis relates the happy landing of the contraband (such is the cognomen[2] given to the traffic), depositing in the meantime on the table the necessary rouleaux which contain the 51 dollars head money. As the man in the office draws the gold into the drawer with a patronizing manner, he offers a cigarillo to the cringing offerer who, hat in hands, awaits the order to depart. But not so, the gold is only for private purse of the Governor; the private factotum must have a share of the pie. But it must be done indirectly, and availing himself of the passing cloud of smoke he in an insinuating manner demands the price of a small slave which he has an immediate demand for. The hint is taken by the owner. In contraband transaction, it is not only necessary to hold a candle to the Devil but to his imps also. Next morning a small slave is sent, or its equivalent in Spanish ounces, as it is well known that government officials prefer the gold to mortal flesh.

Having described the landing of slaves in Cuba, I will return to my younger days of African memory.

[1]mythological giant with a hundred eyes
[2]nickname

*I Lose a Native Wife to My English Partner

March,
1827
The prompt dispatch I gave the schooner *Fortuna* started new ideas amongst the trading community of the River Pongo. Everyone agreed that my method of dividing the slaver's cargo amongst the different factories was not only the best mode for a quick dispatch, but it also favored every trader, as it gave them a chance in the purchase of the cargoes; while it remained in one hand, it was monopolized by only one person. A palaver was called at Gambia, the place of Mr. Edward Joseph, where it was agreed that for the good of the river, all slavers' cargoes should be divided to a certain number of traders. The division should be proportionable to the slaves on hand and subject to the consignees to determine the prices and other terms.

To this meeting Mr. Ormond did not attend, feeling offended at our presumption, and it was with difficulty that his people kept him from sending an armed party to destroy our factory. The knowledge of this act of hostility was soon spread in every town of the river. Every chief trader sent messengers to Bangalang informing Mr. Ormond that any steps from him taken toward the injury of the Furtidee (white boys, Joseph, and me, Theodore) would be resented by them. Our landlord, a descendant of the Foulah Nation, told him in the presence of his own people, that himself as well as others were well tired of a Mulatto Mongo, which gave him great offense. And from this day forward his power dwindled away by degrees into an insignificant mockery, a light respect only granted for his age and for the memory of what he had been.

The return of the *Areostatico*, which arrived during these difficulties, and the division of her cargo, which was also cash, settled all question. My *modus operandi* was made a law, and the Mongo sealed it by accepting part of the cargo.

As I am about to describe three years in this river, let me dispatch the *Areostatico*, which went off in twenty-two days with eighty full-grown men and women. This was a choice cargo. I was authorized to give sixty or seventy dollars per head and instructed to pick them well made and of the Mandingo race; that nation having come into fashion in Havana, every lady had the mania for a stout Mandingo or a Sosoo servant. I did as I was ordered, but unfortunately the *Areostatico* was never heard of after she left the river.

This last consignment fully confirmed me in the notice of the natives. Every day the neighboring Chiefs sent me friendly messages with small presents, which I accepted. But one in particular, more friendly and more generous than the others, insisted on becoming my father-in-law.

As the offer was made personally, with the boon present, it was with difficulty I declined the honor, alleging many excuses for the refusal, as a direct denial is an unpardonable offense amongst those natives and, I may say, all over Africa. To reject a wife is considered a great insult, and to avoid quarrels, high-born natives accept them for a week, pay all expenses, and pass her over to a relation, often in the same state of purity as she was presented.

My officious would-be father-in-law would not be conquered into a true sense of refusal; no excuse on my part would he accept. If I declined on account of her youth, he would shock her modesty to prove the contrary. If I rejected under pretense of my still-existing convalescence, he would urge that a wife was the sole restorative for declining health. Finally this good Chief in his fatherly affection for me would not accept my excuses; in this dilemma I was on the point of sacrificing myself when my good friend Joseph relieved me from this unheard-of trouble by offering himself as my substitute.

This generous offer was accepted by the father with no difficulty. His interest in the transmission of the valuable present did not diminish—a rich white son-in-law he must have, no matter if he was of the Saxon race or of Roman descent. All his African affection consisted in gaining a rich relation, and my partner and myself were considered such.

I have said in some former pages that my English friend Joseph had imbibed many of the natives' superstitions. I might also have said he acquired a taste for native habits, and I will add without any intention to stigmatize his character that there can be no account given for a man's taste. I say with propriety that in his Epicurean taste for the flesh, he regarded amalgamation with the eye of a true philanthropic philosopher.

My partner was in every sense of the word a true admirer of African beauties. He not only loved the country, but admired their customs and their language (which by-the-bye he spoke well). Native dishes he preferred to roast beef and plum pudding; he delighted in the African melodies and would fall in ecstacies at the philharmonic sound of the discordant tam-tam. Even African barbarity had its charms, but what captivated him most to an African life was the Asiatic custom of polygamy and the *dolce far niente*[1] of the natives.

As I have taxed Joseph with indolence, let me retrieve my word;

[1]live and let live

in the future marriage preparation, he certainly neglected his siestas, and till everything was completed for the matrimony, no one in the factory had a moment of rest.

As the parents of the bride were magnates in the upper part of the river, the family had insisted that the ceremonies should be performed with all the formalities appertaining to the bride's high rank. To this my partner readily agreed, although I remonstrated against it. Esther, who acted as my mentor in every country difficulty, had suggested that it would be much against my friend's interest to ally himself with a family whose only motive was cupidity, and strongly urged that if Joseph would take the girl he should not consent to have a *Colungee* (the ceremony or feast).

If the reader wishes to hear the tedious description of a marriage in high life in Africa, let him read the following lines, as I will delineate my partner's nuptials with all its preliminaries. But I would beg the female reader to nerve her ears to some unvarnished words, as in my description of an African matrimony I shall have to use such as require an apology. Upon the whole I would have them tax their curiosity and skip this chapter, as I would not offend their delicate sensibility by a description of African manners as they are.

My Cockney friend wished to do the thing in tip-top style, and as the manners of the country required a formal demand from the groom to the bride, the most respectable matron was chosen from my friend's Black acquaintances to be the Cupid of this love message. This messenger proved to be the head wife of our landlord, an uncommonly fat woman. Such is the reverence natives have for flesh that this female's corpulency made her the most respected lady of our Ethiopian parish. I ever found during my travels in Africa that the fatter a woman, the more she is prized; and in many places the most ponderous female was the *bonne-bouche* of the seraglio. The Moorish matrons of the Deserts of Zara glut their daughters with cuscus[1] to make them plump and valuable.

Let me return to my corpulent Black Cupid, who in her important charge had selected several female attachées to give more importance to her mission. On her departure she was furnished with the following presents to make her *dantica*[2] proposal. (Here in the Pongos as well as most other parts of Africa, no demand is made without a present, and this is one of the greatest barriers white travelers in Africa have to encounter.)

These presents consisted as follows:

First present: two demijohns of trade rum for the community of the bride's native town.

[1] a North African hot cereal of cracked and steamed wheat
[2] demand

Second: a piece of blue baft (cotton cloth), a musket, a keg of powder, and a demijohn of pure rum for the father.

Third: for the mother, a young female virgin slave, dressed in a white tontongee (this is a strip of cloth three inches wide and four feet long which is used to cover their nakedness. It hangs part before and drags behind, suspended by a few strings of showy beads round the waist. This is the only covering maids are allowed to wear, and in some places, none at all.) With this slave was added a pure white piece of cloth, a white basin, a white sheep, and a basket of white rice; all presented in token of the purity of her daughter.

Fourth: to the bride, a Dutch looking glass, several bunches of beads, a coral necklace, a piece of turkey-red handkerchief, a white country cloth, and a white decanter of white palm oil to grease her black body after bathing (a part of the toilette invariably attended to by African belles).

With these presents, this female messenger was dispatched on that important mission.

During the while, my now indefatigable but indolent partner set to erect a house for his bride, and it took just as many days as was employed to make the world. With the assistance of a little mud, a few bamboos, and a half dozen bundles of straw, the building was erected; and as my friend said there should be darkness, there was abundance of it. No windows encumbered the wall; white grooms as well as Black brides desire not light to witness their *tête-à-tête*, even in Africa.

This building done, it was furnished with all the luxury of African taste; a four-poster was put together, and being of bamboo, it had all the elasticity necessary. Two or three pieces of crockery indispensable to a well-furnished nuptial apartment were disposed about the room with perfect taste by the happy Joseph, and as Negroes love looking glasses, the largest that could be selected from our store was nailed against the door (the only illuminated part of the room).

Nothing was wanting. On the seventh day I rested, well fatigued at the expenses of these matrimonial preparations (as a partner, I had to suffer part of the bitter without a portion of the sweets) while my partner retired to meditate on his future happiness.

Next day our corpulent Ambassadress returned, proud of her success. Her mission had been prosperous, and this happy information caused no small joy to the white groom. The delivery of the bride and the Colungee Day, so much wished by all parties, was to take place on the tenth day of the moon; such was the oracle time appointed by the fetish. From this day onward all was bustle and confusion till the expected event took place.

On the appointed day in the afternoon, a discharge of musketry from the waterside announced the arrival of the bride, and the sound of the horn (not a French horn) with the tam-tam of the country drum corroborated the fact. As the damsel was expected from the river, my English friend and his Italian partner proceeded to the waterside, our fat *chargée d'affaires* and her attachées with our servants heading the procession.

Five large canoes loaded with people formed the committee that accompanied the happy African maid. Boat after boat disgorged its passengers, but to our astonishment, everyone had the appearance of displeasure. As the last boat, decorated with flags, and which contained the bride, was approaching the head man of the committee commanded her off and not to approach.

This order, so unexpected, struck terror in our Black factotum and dismay in my white friend. Both inquired in one breath the cause of this contra-order. After much palavering which I could understand but little, I found out that they considered themselves slighted and not treated with the courtesy due to the rank of the girl. This complaint was based on two points: first, we had not saluted them with our guns; and second, we had not prepared the landing for the bride, neglecting to spread mats for her virgin feet to walk upon—a formality seldom neglected and tenaciously insisted on by the grandees and upper ten thousand of the river. The result of the palaver was that the maid could not land without the fulfillment of this etiquette.

Here we were, in a perfect state of perplexity, as we could not collect mats enough to carpet the road from the water to the factory some 500 yards' distance, and the stubborn commandant of the matrimonial committee not relaxing an iota of his demand. My crestfallen partner disculpated himself by urging his ignorance of the country customs, but to no avail. But when our bulky manager threw herself on her knees and cried "Peccavi!"[1] it had some effect. At length it was proposed that as Joseph had employed a person to conduct his matrimonial affairs, himself ignoring the manners of the natives, and as that person was considered well vested in all such matters, the same should suffer all the penalty of the insult. Therefore the matron directress was condemned to pay the value of a slave for the benefit of merrymaking at the Colungee, and to carry the bride on her back from the waterside up to the groom's apartment (the law prohibiting any man to touch the bride while on her way to the nuptial couch).

The salute was fired, which soon settled one part of the difficulty,

94   [1] I have sinned!

but the performance of the other was not gone through with the same facility. This was no small job for our landlord's wife, who with difficulty could hardly carry her own bulky substance. According to the penalty, the Ambassadress was saddled with the bride veiled from head to foot, and with the load was made to mount the Calvary Hill up to the bathhouse. The operation caused a good deal of merriment to all parties, while it cost many grunts and much perspiration to the weary matchmaker.

The taking off of the veil from the damsel cost my friend a slave, the regular price all princely grooms pay for this ceremony. As I have not described this African beauty as yet, I will now, as her veil is off, attempt to portray her. She was a maid of the Sosoo Nation, but a descendant of the Mandingo race; her age about fiteen, and well developed in her forms, which were as round as chiseled by Canova's[1] powers. Her features were angelical, her stature such as could be expected at her age, her feet and arms in accordance with her beautiful form, which might be called a *chef d'oeuvre* in black marble.

Her dress was that of all maids of the country: beads at the ankles, at the waist and neck, with a quantity of bracelets from the wrist up to the elbow. These ornaments contrasted well with the white narrow tontongee, which was to be exchanged hereafter for one whole fathom of cottonade.

As the veil came off, a shout arose from the crowd accumulated before the house, and the mother handed the girl to our female manager, who with her feminine chargées retired to the bathhouse to perfume her. Each lady (I mean those initiated in the matrimonial secrets) had an inspection of the profumigation, and as the lady inspectors came out from the bathhouse they all shook hands with the mother in compliment for the purity of her daughter. The groom also received the same civilities from the ladies in compliment of his good luck.

From the bath the bride was taken wrapped in a very white sheet on the matrons' arms to the nuptial couch and there deposited. The door was then shut and two of the chargées placed as sentries. The matron, then assuming all the importance of a newly nominated plenipotentiary, called the happy Anglo-Saxon groom and handed him the strip of cloth, or tontongee, that covered the nakedness of his future Ethiopian wife, saying in a loud, commanding, and consequential voice, "White man, this authorizes you to take posses-

[1] a renowned nineteenth-century sculptor, who portrayed Pauline Borghese, Napoleon's sister, among others

sion of your wife. Make haste, and return with the proof of her virginity."

On the groom's arrival at the door the sentries, in order to carry out to the letter all the desired formalities, demanded the sign which my friend still carried in his hand. The tontongee being delivered, the Sesame opened, and he was lost sight of.

A long pole was planted before the door and the virgin tontongee was hoisted as a signal of privacy, and there allowed to float in similarity to an admiral's night pennant. As soon as the door was shut the house was surrounded by all the female community, and with the sound of song and instrument they danced a kind of Carmaniole, causing a continued clamor which drowned all other voices. On my first voyage to Calcutta I had seen nearly such a bacchanalian dance round the flaming pile of a Brahman husband, and was told that the great tumult was created to drown the cries of the burning widow. But at this wedding I could not see the utility of so much uproar, till I was told.

The men made merry the while round a bonfire, discharging musket after musket and emptying tumbler after tumbler from a well-filled demijohn of New England rum.

The rest of the night was passed in eating, drinking, singing, dancing, and firing. At daylight the matron factotum announced to the community that the groom was satisfied, and in token of the same, the white sheet once pure and unsoiled, was unfolded on the same pole with the tontongee and transplanted in the middle of the yard in full view and for the satisfaction of all parties.

At sundown the pole was taken down. The tontongee pennant was returned to the contented husband while the virginity flag was rent into small pieces with the exception of a quarter, the most noted for its stains, which was next day sent to the father publicly paraded on the horns of a bullock. The small pieces were distributed amongst the circumcised and married women who then congregated into an out-away house and locking the door, performed that mysterious dance which no man can witness.

In due time next morning, the bride was taken to the bath by the matrons and annointed from head to foot with a peculiar vegetable butter which although it smelled good to them and to my would-be-African English friend, had a contrary effect to me. She then made her appearance led by the hand by the Matron in Chief. Her waist and loins were now covered with three yards of French print.

Her arrival was saluted by a discharge of musketry, and all her friends and relations salaamed and thanked her for having proved what every bride should be.

A temporary bower having been rigged by the pole, she was

seated under the proud banner of her purity and her breakfast was served out there. It consisted of a bowl of broth boiled from a virgin pullet boiled whole and with the intestines. This dish is the only food a bride is allowed to partake; my mentor Esther informed me in a whisper that such a dish—in such cases—encouraged progeny.

The matrimonial fête, with all its African pageantry, lasted three days, and as everyone returned to his former occupation, I returned to my ledger and in amazement summed up 550 dollars in the wedding bill—not much for a Princess, but quite enough for a Black maid. On showing this enormous account to my phlegmatic partner, he coolly remarked that when we are in Rome we should do as the Romans. Now, then, Esther's advice became more lucid. I understood the dangers of an African matrimony; I saw but too late that my friend Joseph had paid too much for his whistle.

As I shall not describe any more marriages in my future pages, let me inform the reader that in high life as well as low life, such ceremonies are nearly similar, with the exception of the expense. The same formalities, the same rum drinking, the same firing, but in less quantity—but should the bride not prove a virgin, she is then returned with disgrace, and the friends that brought her receive a good beating from those of the groom. The presents are invariably demanded back, and if not promptly returned, a war of pillage is the consequence, whence it often degenerates into one of carnage. The position of the poor girl on her return home is not an enjoyable one; the disgrace she brings to her relations is visited by the severest punishment. Parents often avail themselves of this excuse to sell such of their children as commit a similar *faux pas*.

My friend's honeymoon did not last long. One of his Sierra creditors who had not been notified at the arrival of the Spanish doubloons informed the Government of that Colony that an Englishman named Edward Joseph had set up a factory in company with a Spaniard for the purpose of purchasing slaves.

An expedition was immediately fitted out by the Governor to destroy our little factory. Happily the friendly Jew gave us timely notice, and an opportunity offering, my friend left the river in a slaver for Havana, carrying with him sixty slaves and leaving his disconsolate wife to return to her parents.

As the hostile visit from Sierra Leone was expected hourly, I went to work and made out a set of new books all in my name, and dated them three months back. And when Lieutenant Findley of His Britannic Majesty's army arrived with his armed force I had just finished my last entry.

According to the information of the expected day, three boats made their appearance bearing the well-known cross and colors of St. George at their masthead, making up the creek for my factory.

On their arrival the Commander inquired for my partner Joseph, showing me an order from the Governor of Sierra Leone and its dependency to burn and destroy all property belonging to him and to capture his person. To this document I presented Lieutenant Findley another, which was the bill of sale of our establishment for all the property and chattels of the Gambia factory; and for his further satisfaction showed him the fresh-made books which could not be contested.

Our native landlord, who was numbered as one of the Chiefs of the river, was questioned by this officer in regard to the true proprietor of the factory, and as he reported just what I had taught him but few minutes before, no proofs could be preferred against me warranting the destruction of the property.

After dinner this officer retired without molesting our establishment. Indeed, his conduct during his visit at my place was most strictly gentlemanly.

A visit from three armed boats with the mighty royal flag created no small surprise in the river. My enemies (a prosperous new beginner never lacks of such commodity), and the Mongo principally, could not hide their joy when this bellicose naval force directed its course towards Gambia, and not knowing my preparations or the hasty exit of my friend, looked out toward my establishment for the smoke which should give them the expected and gratifying signal of the destruction of the place.

*I Visit the Bager Nation · My Opinion of That People

During the rainy season which begins in June and lasts till late in October, the produce sadly diminishes. The Foulhas and Mandingos are impossibilitated from traveling to the seaboard with produce from the Interior on account of the great torrents the continual rains produce. Therefore the factories have recourse to other rivers where vessels cannot enter, and there in canoes collect such produce as the Interior traders have left during the dry season. (Small traders frequent those rivers to escape the blockades of the Foulah Chiefs.) Canoes are also sent to the mouth of the river to purchase salt and palm oil from a peculiar nation called Bagers, whose only employment is to boil salt water into salt and make palm oil. It is not very profitable trade, but it furnishes them the opportunity of disposing of their refuse goods.

October, 1827

I have said these Bagers are a peculiar nation, inasmuch as I found them so, and as I have never read an account of these worthy Africans, which in honesty could be compared with the most civilized nation of the world, I will with permission of the reader burden his patience with a concise account of the manners and the unheard-of honesty of this people.

This Bager Nation have a language of their own, nothing resembling the soft, gentle, Italian-like dialect of the Sosoo. They live and intermarry in their own solitary tribes, they inhabit the muddy shores of the rivers, and as their occupation is boiling salt in the dry season and making palm oil in the rainy, their abodes are necessarily built in the flat and swampy entrance of the river borders.

Their appearance and the favorable reports of them I had so often heard from the Sosoos tempted my curiosity. I resolved to pay a visit to one of my traders who I had sent there with a small invoice of goods to purchase palm oil. Having prepared a canoe with a waterproof awning and the necessary provisions for a week, I started for the mouth of the river.

After a very tedious pull we arrived at a narrow creek, and with difficulty pushed our canoe through the mangrove branches which intercepted it and finally landed on a mud bank which we had to waddle through knee deep before we reached the more solid shore.

The town lay some hundred yards from the landing in a desolate savannah. On my arrival the oldest man of the town, who invariably acts as the Chief, welcomed me to his hut with a truly hospitable cordiality. Having made my *dantica*, or declaration of the purpose of my visit, I demanded to be shown the house of my trader.

The old patriarch took me to a distant dilapidated hut whose roof was supported by only four posts without walls. Here I recognized a large trade chest, a rum cask, and my trader's grass hammock. In wonder I demanded why my property was thus exposed.

I was informed by my conductor that this was my trader's habitation, that my property being under the shade of the sun and rain it was perfectly safe, and that my man had gone to a neighboring town to purchase some oil and would be back that afternoon. Laboring under astonishment and doubt I opened the chest, which to my still greater surprise I found unlocked. And lo, I saw it nearly full with the same goods I had filled it. I shook the cask, and its weight opposed my desire. I turned the cock, and behold, the rum spouted on my feet.

Nearby stood another temporary shed where I saw a pile of hides and several casks of palm oil. My venerable friend told me that this hut and its contents were my property. Struck with amazement, I again questioned the head man and wished to know why my trader was not supplied with a better house, and my goods a safer place free from theft.

The old gentleman (I shall name him thus, as he could not be but one) answered with a gentle smile and said that they, the Bagers, were neither Sosoos nor white men; that a stranger's property was as safe as their own; that their labor supplied them with food and all the necessities of life; that they had no need to steal from their guests or to sell one another. At this last assertion, which he made with some stress, I broke the conversation as I saw he was becoming personal. My white dignity could not brook the offense and I took refuge in silence, glad none of my friends were there to witness my blush.

On a second consideration, I shook the noble man's hand and presented him with a piece of cloth. I thought then, had Diogenes traveled in Africa in search of his man, he would have extinguished his lantern here.

As we returned to the old Chief's house he presented me with a large ram goat peculiar for its head ornaments, a distinguished present amongst those artless natives, and which he called my supper. He then sent a crier about the town, informing the women community that a white stranger had arrived and would be their guest during that night.

In a short time the hut was visited by all the matrons, or the female heads of families, one bringing a small quantity of rice, another two or three roots of cassava, this one a few spoons of palm oil, the other a handful of peppers or a little more rice. The oldest lady made herself important by presenting me with a fine capon fowl. In half an hour after the crier had gone his round, my reclining mat was filled with presents for myself and my eight gromets (a name given to men employed in boats or canoes, equivalent to seamen in the Sosoo language and taken from the Portuguese *grumetes*, "young mariners"). This contribution was not forced, but voluntary, as I found that even when a poor Black stranger demanded hospitality everyone in the town shared in the charity. Why then, civilize this people and teach them Christian selfishness!

As I had arrived about two in the afternoon, I found the town nearly deserted, with the exception of the old gentleman, one or two more old men, and a dozen of old women. On inquiry I found that the townspeople had gone on an excursion of palm-nut gathering.

Two hours before sundown my man returned, and shortly after the people made their appearance, singing and loaded with the palm nuts. On hearing of my arrival, men, women, and children surrounded my hut till it became necessary for me to come out and shake hands with them all. The women in particular gratified themselves with a *sumboo* (a smell at my face—the native kiss) and folding their black arms in a firm and long embrace round my neck, which is ever attended with some detriment to the white man's clean shirt. By stratagem I avoided the oldest of this affectionate crew by throwing myself amongst the youngest community who fairly took possession of my hands and led me to the rum barrel, there to treat them to a dram. This juvenile desire once satisfied, I sat down with the old patriarch to a mess of properly and well-boiled rice, prepared by my landlady of the capon.

On uncovering the small bowl that contained the stew, its powerful effluvium spoke right out the name of Billy; it contained choice parts of the goat presented me before. I refused to partake of the French dish, apologizing my dislike to water and mountain oysters.

My true philanthropic landlord gave orders to another of his wives to bring her supper in. Her stew was what is called a palavra sauce; its looks and smell were inviting. I inquired the nature of the ingredients and was told by my trade man it was wild hog. This condiment was highly flavored with red and malaguetta pepper, and with the seasoning of eight hours' fasting; it was devoured by me with the gastronomic appetite of an alderman.

Two days afterwards, my trade man informed me that the wild hog was nothing more but the spareribs of an alligator. Had not the digestion hours passed, this information would have had the effect of an emetic, as I never loved wild game.

As the sun went down, a myriad of mosquitos made their appearance; in a few minutes it was impossible to breathe without snuffing a handful of them. I inquired what precaution they took against such pests, and was told that the natives had recourse to palm oil by anointing themselves from head to foot, but for me they had prepared an alcove made of green weeds which mosquitos abominate. In my trouble I demanded to be shown to my place of rest; I was led to another hut in the center of which I found my fresh weed quarters. It was a low bower in which I crawled on my knees; the entrance was immediately blocked up, and I passed the night much better than I had anticipated.

In the morning I took an inventory of the goods, which correctly balanced with the produce in store of my man. As I still doubted this never-to-be-forgotten public and national honesty, my trade man led me to a neighboring lemon tree and there showed me a pair of English brass steelyards[1] hanging on its branches. He told me that they formerly belonged to a Mulatto trader from Sierra Leone who had died in the town on a trading trip, and that the steelyards as well as a chest half full of goods which was deposited in the palavra house had been kept above 12 years in expectation that some of his friends from the Colony would call for them.

I thought then that few of these Bager natives would not come amiss as missionaries at the Five Points of New York or at the mummeries of London, where the words of *tuum* and *meum*[2] are synonymous. After this perfect proof of probity, I did not see the necessity of a better security of my property than the ignorant morality and good faith of these naked and benighted Africans.

However, as a cloud of doubts still remained in me, I inquired of my man if these natives, to maintain the safety of property or to resist the great temptation of the inciting barrel of rum, did not make use of some sort of fetish or ju-ju in guise of the tabooing of the Sandwich Islanders. To my great wonder I was told that it was not but a natural virtue. I was also informed that these natives had no ju-jus, fetishes, or gris-gris. They had no idea of God or evil spirits, neither prayed to the one or feared the other, and their dead are buried without pomp or tears, but put underground as an incumbent refuse, doomed to eternal oblivion.

An attempt to describe further the manners of these natives would be a presumption on my side, as I only remained two days in this place; the mosquitos drove me off. But I will end this chapter by an attempt at picturing their appearance. The Bager man is of a dark black color and middling in size, but broad in the shoulders. They

[1]hanging scales for weighing suspended items
[2]thine and mine

are neither brave nor war-like, and as they live separate from the contact of other tribes they are never at variance.

A Foulah law protects them from foreign violence (being salt-makers, this is their prerogative). Salt is regarded in the Interior as one of the greatest necessities of life, and its makers are under the safeguard of this law.

The men also have an indolent cast caused by the great quantity of palm wine and the little labor they perform, and most of them at the age of thirty suffer from the hernia, also caused by the effects of palm wine. Their dress is a single handkerchief or a strip of country cloth 4 or 5 inches wide, very neglectfully put on.

The females, even when young, have none of the sylph-like appearance of the Mandingos or even the well-shaped form of the Sosoos; every limb about them has the appearance of bloatedness. Hard work and palm oil, interiorly and exteriorly applied, relaxes their limbs and flesh. Their dress is that of Adam and Eve before the fatal apple, with the exception of a small strip of hide which is of still greater detriment to their pudicity.[1]

As the bump of curiosity is strongly developed in me, I could not refrain from asking my old landlord the cause why the men were better covered than the women. Young girls and boys go perfectly naked till the age of marriage. Males and females all shave their heads, but combs are still in great demand. Youths of both sexes wear rings in the nose and lower lip, with small sticks, reed tubes, or porcupine quills stuck through the cartilage of the ears. I have said that they do not sell one another, but they often buy children of both sexes and adopt them, and I am not aware that they dispose of them afterwards.

As they live in a small community, the labor and profits are divided, and when one family starves, the other certainly does not luxuriate, but one and all fare alike. I may compare this tribe to the Mormons in polygamy and the way they live retired from other tribes; and to the Fourierists[2] in their excellent method of living in community and brotherly partnership.

[1]modesty
[2]followers of Charles Fourier, a mid-nineteenth-century advocate of utopian cooperative communities

*How the Free Black Becomes a Slave

October, 1827

During this rainy season, I bought many slaves from the neighboring districts. It must not be understood that slaves are only supplied from the wars. Many are exchanged for commodities which the whites have introduced, and a native will sometimes dispose of a slave for a barrel of rum to celebrate a marriage or a funeral. A female will sell her domestic to ornament herself with a new string of coral or any other gewgaw.

The bad crop of rice is also the cause of many exchanges, where a favorite slave is made to pay for the needy provisions. In my narrative I shall mention where the parents sell their own offspring, but still I would not lead the reader to believe that it is often the case; when natives part with their children they are thus induced by strong forcible necessities. Very few of the native Africans will dispose of their own flesh and blood. And in extenuation of such barbarity, let me inform the reader that an African mother never has recourse to forced abortion or abandons her newborn to the mercy of a stranger or the public.

No, Christian civilization has not introduced the necessity, and well-patronized acts of a Madame Restell[1] or the highly valued professors of infanticide. No encouraging foundling asylum is there to open its trap doors for the unnatural mother to hide her shame with heartless eyes. The descendants of Cain regard procreation as more a command of God than as a sin, and the ignorant African society has not condemned woman's best quality as an unnatural gift.

To give a full account of the whole process and manner in which the Negro becomes a slave, it would require the work of many pages. Suffice to say that three quarters of slaves shipped are the product of native wars, which are partly brought about by the great inducement and temptation of the white man. I inculpate all nations, as all the principal nations have had a share in fomenting the slave traffic and introducing wants, desires, and luxuries, with a view to encourage the then humane trade. These wants, desires, and luxuries have become an indispensable necessity to the natives and the traffic a natural barter.

England today sends to Africa her cheap Birmingham muskets and Manchester goods, which are exchanged at Sierra Leone, Accra, and the Gold Coast, for Spanish or Brazilian bills on Lon-

[1]Madame Restell (Caroline Lehman), a brothel keeper, was the subject of two sensational trials in New York 1841 and 1847 for abortion.

don. France sends her cheap brandies, her taffeta reds, her Rouen cottons, and her *quelque-chose*, the United States their leaf tobacco, their one-F powder, their domestic spun goods, their New England rum and Yankee notions, with the same effect or the same purpose. Therefore I say it is *our* civilized commodities which bring the cause of the wars and the continual, now called inhuman, traffic.

In the first category of slaves I shall name the prisoner of war. Other wars also take place, caused by family quarrels which also tend to slavery; I shall place these captives in the second category. Having described one of the principal causes of the wars in Africa, I will show how a Negro often becomes a captive without being a prisoner of war.

In Africa, where coin is not known, the slave is made a substitute for this commodity, and in each district a positive value is given him which is passed for currency and legal tender. Therefore if a man wants to purchase a wife, he pays the amount in slaves; another wishes to purchase a quantity of cattle, he tenders in payment slaves. Fields of cassava, rice, or yams are paid in slaves. The African court also taxes all forfeitures and pecuniary penalties in slaves, and in all country palavra and crime the culprit is made a slave of. The creditor or bankrupt shares the same fate. The murderer, the manslaughterer, or the highway robber is condemned to the same punishment, with the addition that his family and near relations follow him in his captivity. The Spanish barracoons become the malefactor's gallows, his State's Prison, or his Botany Bay.[1]

I shall place the above in the third class. In the fourth quality I will include those inculpated with witchcraft, the Crim Con[2] cases (not few in Africa), orphans of culprits, vagabonds who dare not to return to their tribes, and unruly sons.

By the fifth quality I will designate the gamblers, which requires a small chapter by itself. In my future pages I will describe this class of African industrials by a short anecdote.

As there are in Africa no madhouses, no hospitals, or houses of refuge, the brother often times sells his mad sister to avoid broils[3] in his family. The father barters his sickly child to purchase another wife to reproduce a better offspring. The mother also is reluctantly driven to dispose of her imbecile, or deaf and dumb child, to avoid shame and ridicule from her neighbors. (It is the custom amongst the Africans to look with scorn on the parents of a crippled or deranged child, and one of the most mortifying curses a person can vituperate

[1]British convict settlement in Australia 1757–1840
[2]Criminal Conviction
[3]imbroglios

another with is to upbraid him or her with the infirmities of his offspring.) Africans, in their un-Christian ignorance, never swear, curse, or abuse their Maker's name; their uncivilized passion is let forth in the abuse of the defects of the contesting party, not daring to attempt in their vituperation the presumption of the white man. The above invalids I will select as the sixth category of slaves.

The Ethiopian Lord of Creation also, while in search of a house of refuge, also finds in the white man's barracoons a safe and profitable deposit for his unfaithful better half. The disconsolate husband of a barren wife (ignorant of the civilized and accommodating law of divorce) also has recourse to the cupidity of his more civilized brother, and both find in the stores of the slaver supplies in abundance to furnish themselves; the first with a more loyal wife, the second a more fruitful one. I will place these unfortunate females in the seventh and second to last number, ending the catalogue with the born slaves, which are used by the natives as pawns or deposited. But many end their life in a plantation, their speculating Masters failing to redeem them.

As I have so far explained the manner in which the slave mart is supplied, it is further necessary to inform the reader that being an African currency, the slave's value is estimated at a higher rate than any other walking commodity. The proprietor avails himself of his slave to transform him into a draft on sight, with the advantage that it carries itself.

To facilitate these banking slave operations; there exist also in Africa a set of native brokers, but which I shall call slave dealers —such as exist in all countries where slavery is permitted and whose business is to run the country in search of this or that kind or quality of slaves for different patrons; the strong man to replenish the phalanx of a War Chieftain, the neat boy for a servant, or the adopted child for some old unfruitful Queen, or the handsome maid for the harem of an African Lord, or those that are not Africans. These slave dealers are very useful in the country; they collect and pay debts, and in emergency they take the place of the Bailiff and kidnap in the shape of sequestration.

As I have designated them with the honorable name of brokers, let me prove them so by stating their occupation in this regard. Suppose a native Chief wants such a quantity of cloth, guns, tobacco, or powder, and he does not understand the manner of trading with the beach factory. He employs one of these brokers to effect his barter and pays him his commission just the same as a planter would exchange a horse for a quadroon girl, the child perhaps of his Christian friend, and would naturally pay his broker for the delicate

but not difficult transaction.

*CHAPTER 20th

*The Arrival Into Gambia of Mama-De-Young

As the rains began to disappear, now and then a small caravan would make its appearance. As a newcomer, I had a small share of their trade, but I consoled myself that I should do better in the dry season.

About this time a Spanish vessel arrived and brought me the information of Joseph's safe arrival in Matanzas. My partner had sent me out a Clerk, knowing my great desire to visit the Interior. As this vessel was only loaded with rum I refused her consignment, and she went to Benin. As I had employed myself during the rainy season in building a boat, I now launched her and sent her to Sierra Leone with palm oil to be exchanged for English goods. (Crafts without full deck could enter the Colony's harbor without register.)

With November came the dry season, so much desired by all the traders. On the first of this moon I received a message from the head man of a caravan informing me that on the full moon he would arrive at my place with all the produce he could press till then; that he was the bearer of a message to me from his nephew Ama-De-Bella, and that he kept back only to blockade the path, so as to swell his party and make his arrival more interesting to me.

I immediately sent my interpreter with presents and availed myself of his stay to build him a neat hut, as no true Mahometan Fullah will abide in the same house with an unbeliever, and furnished it according to their customs, with a green hide and a few new mats.

Mama-de-Young, true to his word, made his appearance on the very day that the moon had attained its full diameter, and the moment he espied the river from the high hills, he turned to the east and with arms extended toward Mecca returned thanks for his safe arrival at the seaside. After many genuflections in which the head ever touches the ground, he rose and made toward my factory, himself and his people singing the loud praises of Mahomet.

His entry in Gambia was saluted by my people, who with muskets in hand awaited his arrival. As I had no minstrels or music to welcome him, as Mr. Ormond would have done, I ordered a few more fusillades instead.

My landlord. Ala-Ninfa, proud of his origin as a descendant of Mahometans, preceded him, chaperoning the distinguished stranger to the house of the white man. As this was the first caravan and the first royal Chief that visited my place, I gave this reception all the importance possible. My long piazza was lined with mats fore and aft (as we sailors would say), and opposite my stool I had there spread at a convenient speaking distance a sheepskin of pure white color as a reserved seat for my noble stranger.

I received the princely guest on the steps of my house and accepted his credentials standing; this was Ama-De-Bella's snuffbox (a silver-mounted gazelle's horn), a token he had agreed to send me this dry season. As I took the horn I carried it to my forehead and passed it to Ala-Ninfa, who acted in this important occasion as my Secretary. The salaam over, I led him to his private seat and we both squatted, him on the sheepskin, the humble writer on a ship's stool.

According to custom, Mama-De-Young began his *dantica* (declaration), first invoking the Allah-Hoky-Bara (or the Great God) and giving his message all the pomp and importance possible. He said he was not only the bearer of his nephew Ama-De-Bella's message, but the Royal Envoy of the Ali-Mamy, King of Foutha Yalloo, who at the desire of his son had sent him with an escort for me to visit Timbo[1] as I promised Ama-De-Bella. And himself, Mama-De-Young, had orders to remain in Gambia till my return; this was done to protect my place during my absence from the Mongo of Bangalang, whom they had heard had become my enemy.

I allowed him to finish his long message, when I presented him my credential to Ama-De-Bella's friendship. I brought forward the Koran of his nephew, which I had previously wrapped in a white towel. At the sight of the Holy Book, Mama-De-Young gave a long aspiration of astonishment, and striking his breast with one hand, took the book with the other and falling on his knees, bent his head to the earth and in this humble posture remained several minutes there in fervent devotion (this was no mockery).

As he rose, his forehead full of dust and his eyes streaming with joyful tears, he opened the book and showed me and his people some of his own writings which translated, meant this: "Mama-De-Young gives the Word of God to his son Ama-De-Bella." At the reading of this verse all his followers chanted a response in honor of the Great Allah and Mahomet too. I then, in presence of my people and his whole caravan, swore on the said Koran that with the help of God, I would accept the invitation of the Foutha King.

Having disposed of the caravan to their alloted quarters, I presented my guest with a small portable kettle much valued amongst the Mahometans, as it is used for frequent ablutions; they never attend prayers or the most simple calls of nature without washing. I also sent him a portable inkstand and paper in compliment of his profound learning; quills I did not send, as they use reeds in prefer-

[1]not Timbuctoo, but a town some hundred miles southeast of Gambia, just north of Sierra Leone

ence. I also authorized my landlord to supply all his wants and that of his immediate committee.

The next morning I paid him a visit, coffee kettle in hand. I intended to surprise him (his nephew had never drunk coffee before I presented it to him). But the odor of the boiling steam had preceded me, and before I entered the hut, Mama-De-Young's olfactory organ had detected the aroma and he had mentioned the name of the beverage to Ala-Ninfa. On my presenting him a bowl of it, he remarked that he had drunk coffee thirty years before in Timbuctoo, which he said "the Moses People" (meaning the Jews) drank with milk and honey.

Long before the arrival of Mama-De-Young, fame had pronounced him a learned book man and a great traveler. The name of Timbuctoo from such a person filled me with curiosity, and I begged him to give me a description of the Capital of Capitals, as the learned Africans call it.

My Royal Messenger kindly granted my request, but as he was then giving a lesson to the Mahometan children of his caravan, he postponed it till after breakfast, when he promised to call at my house and there with an interpreter satisfy my curiosity. On entering Mama-De-Young's quarters, I found a dozen of children, Foulahs and Mandingos, surrounding a fire, himself at the corner of the room with several old manuscripts, his kettle and inkstand by him; and Ala-Ninfa, the backsliding Mahometan, pretending to give an interested ear to a description of the precepts of the True Prophet. The apostate! When no Mahometan was present he would partake, and with abundance, of the forbidden swine flesh, and water he only used in making his ablutions. But why should I abuse him? Joseph and I had partly civilized him.

In silence and with slate in hand, the boys took down notes from Mama-De-Young's reading. By the slate I mean a piece of very thin hard board which has the two sides well smoothed with sandy leaves. On this board Mahometan children write their lessons with a small reed cut in the shape of a quill. Their ink is made by dissolving a little powder which does not penetrate the pores or grain of the wood. The lesson once learnt, the wooden slate is washed and dried by the fire.

Mahometan teachers prefer giving lessons one hour before daylight and one hour after sunset, and invariably by a large fire which serves them as a light. Their method of teaching is very poor, as it takes a youth several years before he can read, and I believe but few can transmit their sentiments in writing. Although after years of schooling they can tolerably well read the Koran and other religious writings, still I have ever found them very deficient in reading letters. In such cases when a letter is to be read (which by-the-bye is an event, as even these great book men seldom write to one another), I have seen them mum and yaw over the missive and often fail in giving the true meaning. However, such was not the case with this distinguished messenger; his erudition was superior to any other African I ever met.

*CHAPTER 21st

*The Messenger Mama-De-Young Gives Me a Description of Timbuctoo[1]

Mama-De-Young, true to his promise, called the same morning at my house with an interpreter and sat down to perform a task which all Foulha and Mandingo travelers do with pleasure and exaggeration. Having evoked the Lord's name, as customary, he took from his servant a small bag of fine clean sand and spread it on the floor, making it very smooth with his hand, and when one quarter of an inch in thickness, on this sand he chose the westmost spot and dotted a point with his finger for Timbo, the starting point on his voyage, east nearly 45° North, to Timbuctoo.

As he went on describing his long journey to the grand capital, he continued spotting the principal territories he had traversed and their principal towns; he also chalked by a thick or a light line the rivers or streams he had crossed. The great savannahs he would describe with a slight pressure of the palm of his hand, the mountains he would form with an additional handful of sand, the woods he marked by spreading a quantity of snuff on his sandy map in extent to what he considered their length and breadth.

His description of his travels to the great city was very long, but amusing: at such a town, he would describe the kind or bad treatment he had to endure; at such a river he recounted his troubles in forming rafts or building bridges in order to cross it, or the time lost in awaiting the currents to abate. Then he would mention the fine fish and soft-turtle with which this or that river abounded. In some great rivers he had seen the hippopotamus and the enormous alligator in tremendous combat. In the extensive savannahs he had met with the father of snakes glutted to a helpless position, the horns of a large deer protruding through his throat; or the viper red-tape snake whose sting is a sure and immediate passport to the next world. The first of these reptiles he described as thirty feet long and of the size of a man's body (it must have been the anaconda), while the second was only 14 inches long and the size of a pipe stem.

In the mountains he had seen the zebra, the wild jackass, droves of wolves, and the rapacious hyena, the vulture, and the daring eagle who often attacks the sleeping traveler perched in a tree (in the woods, himself and his party sought refuge on high trees to escape from a drove of elephants). Of the lion and the leopard he had shot a

[1]From here on, all chapter divisions and unmarked titles are Conneau's own.

2 November, 1827

111

dozen or more, these being the only animals worthy of a Chief's trouble; of other animals he spoke with contempt and were only shot by his attendants or slaves. African Mahometans do not eat wild game; the deer only if brought down and still alive when taken, is eaten by them if his throat can be made to bleed. The elephant as well as other animals are called unclean, and all vultures or carnivorous animals are food for unbelievers.

With such narrations he occupied the whole morning, and the hour for prayer and ablution having arrived, he begged permission to retire, leaving a person to protect his drawing. On his return a few minutes after, I treated him with a *déjeuner* of biscuits and sugar, being the only food that his religion allowed him to partake. As he resumed his narrative, I requested him to shorten it and delineate at once the City of Cities.

My request was granted with little humor. Story tellers one and all, Black and White, all love their own way of telling their tales. Therefore, placing his snuffbox (the sharp end of a buffalo horn) opposite of Timbo, on the other extreme end of his chart he landed himself at Timbuctoo. It was my time now to invoke the Great Allah! and this sacred exclamation reconciled me to my narrator, who with his former grace and kindness again took up the thread of his recital.

Mama-De-Young, as I said, was a great traveler, having visited all the European Colonies on the North Coast, and his description of this great city varied much from those of others of his fellow travelers, as he invariably acknowledged the superiority of the Europeans. He had not the presumption of his Mandingo brothers to prefer the buildings of Timbuctoo to those of Senegal and Sierra Leone. In his modesty he calculated that the capital of the Interior had more extent and more population than Sierra Leone, which in 1825 could not exceed over 15 thousand.

The Ali-Mamy's palace he represented as a large enclosure of mud walls, built without order or taste, and the inside a labyrinth of an infinite quantity of buildings for his great family of wives, children, and relations. The houses of Timbuctoo he would not dare to compare to the well-built and magnificent structures of the French and English Colonies. The magnitude, elegance, and comfort of European architecture he spoke of with admiration. Of the streets of Timbuctoo he also spoke with contempt when compared with those of the colonies. The only preference he gave to Timbuctoo was its markets, which exhibited every five days large and variegated assortments of merchandise, provisions, slaves, and

produce. The Moors and Jews from the North Coast of Timbuctoo he represented as the wealthiest merchants there; he also spoke of a set of traveling merchants wearing a kind of turban and called them "Joseph's people" (I presume he meant Armenians).

Of the Government of Timbuctoo and the police of that city, he represented it with the same disgust as an Hungarian would speak of the Government of Austria or a Milanese would of the inquisitorial police of Lombardy. According to his account, strangers are very much taxed there.

Many of the Interior tribes visit Timbuctoo to procure salt, which is abundantly found a few miles from the city and is dug up as a mineral, this being the greatest production of the country.

When I questioned why he preferred the markets of Timbuctoo to the well-filled stores of the European establishments, his answer was that where a trader could not exchange his slaves for goods, or vice versa, he considered it a poor trading place. This answer solved in my mind one of the difficult questions of the political problem of African civilization, and which I shall make mention of in the last pages of this work.

CHAPTER 22nd

I Start for the Interior

Having repeated the long and tedious description of Timbuctoo by a Black man, I will discharge the narrator by giving him the charge of the landlord of the premises, as a protection against the machinations of Mongo John during my absence.

My preparations being made for the voyage, I visited Mongo John with the object of ascertaining his feelings on the subject and as I expected, found much opposition on his part. He left no argument unspoken to dissuade me from my project. I saw that my trip annoyed him, and his jealous heart could not brook my seeking friends amongst the Chiefs of the Interior. At parting I informed him that Mama-De-Young was in charge of my place by order of the Foulha Ali-Mamy. The information caused him great surprise and his anger was such that he left me without a word.

The next day, after taking leave of my Foulha landlord and having written instructions to my Clerk, I bid adieu to my people and neighbors, requesting to them the care of my factory and bullocks. Our caravan consisted of 30 persons belonging to Ama-De-Bella, headed by one of his distant relations, 10 of my people to carry my loads and provisions; Ala-Ninfa, my native landlord, with my two interpreters, were also of the party; with my servant boy and hostler, we formed a procession of 46 persons.

As we started, my Mahometan friend put into my hand a verse of the Koran which I was to exhibit to all good Mahometans as a passport (the interpretation of it was, "Hospitality to the wearied stranger is the road to Heaven"), and taking a handful of dust from the road, he threw it over our heads and proclaimed our voyage prosperous. We left him in prayers, prostrated to the earth. As we passed the neighboring Sosoo towns, my caravan was saluted with a discharge of muskets. Children and women followed their *Cupy* (white man) a little way out of the towns.

The nature of the 550 miles of country I traveled was so variated that my memory cannot now correctly describe it. From the beginning of my journey we struck a foot path and seemingly continued the same narrow road till the end of our journey, seldom meeting any other roads but such as leading to small towns, brooks, or cultivated fields.

When in thick forest, we traveled for hours without having a glimpse of the sun, which indeed was a great desideratum, inasmuch as our men of burthen suffered less from the heat, but our greatest journeys were performed in the open country, the valleys, and

marshy savannahs. The sun, which was the greatest inconvenience
to me, to them the natives was but a secondary slight annoyance.
Our great troubles were when the road followed in parallel some dry
brook whose torrents had left bare the live rock with its flinty picks,
or a bed of large pebbles where the human foot or hoofs of horses
rolled off as soon as pressed.

The endless prairies with their sword grass were often to our
caravans a source of continual punishment, although the path was
the best and smoothest of all others, as it was straight and perfectly
clear of rocks and roots. This grass grows from six to nine feet high,
and its wiry edges, when dry, cut the flesh like a saw. On such
occasions our men made rough baskets of willows which they wore
as a mask, thus protecting their faces.

As I traveled in the dry season, I had not to contend with fording
rivers or swimming across brooks and lagoons, which we encountered in abundance, but only knee deep. My personal troubles were
weariness, fatigue, and heat. In that season of the year in every hut,
village, or town we found abundance of provisions, and my caravan
being Ali-Mamy's own, we commanded a despotic obedience.

The woods furnished our caravan with several refreshments
unknown to the more ignorant civilized nations: berries, roots,
barks, buds of peculiar quality were picked and used; the first was
eaten raw, the second was broiled or boiled, the rest were used in
drinks, sometimes palatable and refreshing, and often peculiarly
abominable.

The open country and valleys supplied us with many vegetable
and animal luxuries which a white man would pass unnoticed. The
marshes and savannahs never failed in regaling my conductors with
toads, snails, iguanas, or a jumping young alligator.

I believe I have said that all the roads in Africa are nothing more
than goat paths, just sufficient for the stepping of a single man. Our
caravan marched in single file. The loaded slaves formed the van-
guard; two men escorted them, cutlass in hand and each armed with
a well-loaded gun. The duties of these men was to scour the path,
give notice of any danger, and cut the protruding or fallen branches
obstructing the road, walking at a hearing distance from the caravan.
I found this an excellent precaution, as the men under heavy load
would suffer much from the inconvenience of such obstructions had
they not previously been removed. The two guides also gave timely
notice when a nest of hornets, bees or ants obstructed the passage.
Either of those insects are very annoying to travelers, in particular to
the cattle, as a sting from them infuriates the animal and it is often
lost.

The center of the caravan was occupied by the women and

children; the rear was commanded by the proprietors and the Chiefs, who with whips in hand stimulated the wearied or lazy straggler to his station.

The first day we made little progress, as we passed five small towns and at each I was obliged to accept their *bugnee* (a small present). Therefore we lost much time. The second day, our people having got, as we sailors would say, their sea legs, we walked merrily on, our party at times singing, joking, and praising the Lord. Even the slaves were allowed a familiarity that was never relaxed in the town, and the Master would often take part of the load to relieve his slave. When we rested, the men of burthen were never called to attend on any service; the women distributed the provisions, cooked, and brought the water.

The second night we rested at an abandoned town and comfortably passed the night. I calculated that we had performed 18 miles, and no one appeared tired. At daybreak we again took to the road, our Chief having informed the men carrying loads to exert their limbs, as that night he intended to sleep at Kya, the first Mandingo town on the road, urging the necessity that it being the pineapple season, they might expect a visit during the night of the wild elephants which are attracted by the aroma of this delicious fruit and perform many miles in search of it.

We rested only twice this day, at different brooks. At sundown we saw several piles of alvine[1] discharges from the elephants, and as it prognosticated danger, our caravan one and all took to a trot, and in one hour we arrived at Kya, a well-barricaded town owned by Abrahima-Aly, a Mandingo Chief of some note.

[1]intestinal

CHAPTER 23rd

Arrival at Kya, a Mandingo Town · A Mandingo Stew · Abrahima and Ala-Ninfa Drunk with Cordial

It was some time before we could be admitted through the gates; Abrahima-Aly, being at prayers, could not be disturbed. Annoyed at the delay, I fired my double-barreled gun, which I knew would awake the devout Aly from his devotions. And it proved so, as the next moment the war drum was heard and a voice from the porthole demanded the *qui vive*. Our Chief responded imperatively, "The Ali-Mamy's caravan, loaded with goods." Ala-Ninfa also informed the questioner that it was himself, with Mongo Theodore the Furtoo of Gambia (the white man of Gambia), and requested that his friend Abrahima should be immediately informed of the important arrival.

Shortly after, the trap door was drawn and one by one we entered the town, Abrahima-Aly attending at the gate. His welcome was sincere to Ala-Ninfa and myself, but to our Foulha Chief, cool and formal; Mandingos digest with mortified pride the power of the Foulhas. As my landlord had been a playmate of Abrahima, their friendship still existed in its primitive sincerity, and to honor the guest of his friend was the height of his ambition. His whole pack of wives were called on to prepare my quarters, while some of his servants were sent in search of a fat sheep and other provision for my supper. In the meantime, a hammock was given me, while both friends retired to recount events of past days.

As Abrahima had set a sentry to prevent the approach of the multitude, I remained quiet till supper was made ready, when the two cronies and myself retired to his private sleeping apartment and partook of an excellent supper. Ala-Ninfa, who knew my taste and, as he called it, "white man foolish delicacy," had stood *maître d'hôtel* and ordered my dishes boiled and broiled. But as both were partaking of a rich stew which a French cook would call *sauce blanche*, I desired a taste, which engendered a wish for more. The delicious mess was made of mutton minced up with roasted ground nuts (or peanuts) and rolled up into a shape of forced-meat balls, which when stewed up with milk butter and a little malaguetta pepper, is a rich dish if eaten with rice *en pilau*. Monsieur Fortoni of Paris might not be ashamed to present a dish of it to his aristocratic gastronomes of the Boulevard des Italiens.

The boiled, broiled, and savory stew satiated our appetite, but water alone could not quench our thirst. Knowing the propensity of my landlord for strong drinks, I called my boy with the canteen and offered the two Mahometans the flask, which out of courtesy for their religious feeling I called cordial, a term used by them to disguise the prohibited liquor, and the sanctimonious excuse of our strict temperance men when using the alcohol as a medicine. My case bottle being full of 4th proof brandy, and the libation often repeated, soon arouse the mischievous feelings in my two landlords. In Ala-Ninfa, liquor excited his religious feelings and in Abrahima-Aly his generosity; one took to praying while the other offered me and his friend his slaves and children; his unbounded generosity extended to his harem, forgetting the honor of his bed and the prohibition of his religion. As it was midnight, I clandestinely left them with the dregs of the bottle and, escorted by my servant, returned to my hammock.

Our Foulha Chief awoke us long before daylight, his cries calling the caravan to prayers before starting. In dismay Ala-Ninfa made his appearance, begging me to postpone the departure till the next day, as Abrahima was impossibilitated from appearing, and himself hiccoughing at every word, proclaimed himself vanquished by the cordial and implored my interference with the Foulha conductor for the accomplishment of his wish. As the caravan was my own escort, I sent for the Chief, and tying a handkerchief round my head, covered myself with my cloak and shammed a strong fever. On his appearance, I made it known that I could not start; therefore I begged him to countermand the order of departure.

My apparent state of suffering had the desired effect, and the good-natured Foulha, true to all their superstition and Mahometan bigotry, insisted on my taking a dose from the Koran diluted in water, a sure specific for my complaint. I readily consented, as I knew a little ink and water would not hurt me, and by seemingly accepting his medicine, I could better hide my shammed sickness. Accordingly the appropriate verse was chosen from the Holy Book and word for word copied on the wooden slate. This done, it was washed off with a glass of water, and I swallowed the black dose. Knowing that I required rest, my Mahometan doctor and conductor left me in the power of his religious charm and requested my boy not to allow anyone to disturb his patient.

Toward midday the two landlords made their appearance, somewhat chopfallen at the last orgy. Both confessed their guilt with confusion and promised never to partake of the intoxicating cordial. On inquiry, I found that in order to allay suspicion, Abrahima had sent a large goat with three baskets of rice to the Foulha Chief.

As it was past meridian and too late to make a start, I soon got better of the pretended fever and made a visit to a neighboring spring which the natives called the Devil's Fountain. As Abrahima in his drinking generosity had offered me his horse, I took advantage to remind him of it, and he good-humoredly gave it over.

CHAPTER 24th

A Visit to the Devil's Fountain · My Conversation With Him · Seizure of 15 Slaves

Mounted on the steed and followed by a guide and several of my own people, I ascended a small mountain and in a thick forest, in a cave of rocks, I saw a spring of water whose brackish taste denoted its sulphuric origin. Its temperature might have been 90°, and such was its bad odor that it was with difficulty I swallowed a spoonful. As I was inspecting the rocks in expectation to ascertain the quality of the mineral, the guide told me that the Devil who owned the fountain could speak all languages, and requested me to say something in my own dialect which he would answer word for word, provided the imp had not gone out.

I immediately called out, "Kya." No answer was given, but on a moment's reflection, I comprehended that this place, by its cavities and configuration and hanging rocks, could well form the echo, and changing my position, I told my people that the Devil was there, that I could call him by his own name, and requested them not to move. I walked several paces and called on "Caffra fure" (Black Devil). The echo resounded the words four times, which so frightened the conductor and my people that they left me alone to converse with the Devil.

I again changed my position, and the echo had lost its influence; as I neared the former spot, the sound gradually augmented. As I emerged from the cave, my people ran to me and shook me heartily by the hand; the guide had told them that the Devil would transform me into a rock for cursing him.

On my return to the town I inquired of Abrahima if he really thought it was the Devil who repeated the words. By his answers I found he was as ignorant as the rest, only he believed it was an evil spirit who was placed there to watch that fountain whose waters he supposed poisonous, as it had the property when drunk to physic the body. Many animals in the dry season and in great drought were found dead a short distance from the cave.

I allowed him to enjoy his ignorance, as my maxim was then to follow all the natives' customs, believe what they believed, and not to make myself obnoxious by too much erudition.

I had been long enough in the country to find out that many white men often created themselves enemies by despising or ridiculing their errors, and as I was not on a mission of civilization, I left things as I found them, never disputing or controversing their political or religious topics. I affected to believe in the Koran when amongst Mahometans, and when amongst the Caffrees, I respected their ju-ju, fetishes, snakes, iguanas, alligators, and wooden images.

Early the next morning our landlord had ordered another mess which the whole caravan partook of. It was made of rice previously boiled and dried in the sun, then pounded into flour which when boiled with milk or water to the consistency of thick gruel, makes a nutritious light food well adapted to travelers on long journeys. The *canaille* of our caravan was served out a large kettleful, simply boiled in water and a little salt. To the heads of the party was added some pure milk, and to myself, the new-created Mongo, was served a bowl expressly boiled with milk and honey. From this day forward I considered the Mandingo nation the Epicureans of Africa.

As we passed the gates I espied the horse caparisoned for a journey, and as Abrahima was to accompany us to the first brook, I supposed the animal was designed for his return. The etiquette of the Mandingo is to escort an honored or esteemed friend to the first brook, drink of the same water, toast a prompt return, invoke the Great Allah to grant a prosperous voyage, shake hands, snap fingers several times, and bid adieu. The one that remains never loses sight of his friend till he disappears. It is also the custom of these benighted Africans when they promise you anything, to keep their word, and when the gift is presented, the owner purposely absents himself and leaves you in no *embaras* to return him thanks.

As I crossed the brook some distance up the path, I found the horse in attendance for my service. The keeper informed Ala-Ninfa that no refusal on my part would be accepted by Abrahima. Before I mounted the horse, I wrote an order on my factory for two muskets, two kegs powder, two pieces of blue cloth, and 100 lbs. tobacco, requesting my Clerk to hide in the center of the tobacco a flask of 4th proof cordial. This I gave to the hostler for his master.

This day proving cloudy, we performed a long journey. I suppose we ran the distance of 20 miles. As there were no towns in the vicinity, we halted in a valley at the entrance of a wood, and near a rivulet. Our rice was soon boiled, and with a little dried beef, soon satisfied our hunger. A large tin pot of tea was my only beverage this evening, the brandy having given out. After prayers, we all lay down to rest, and here again I was surprised by Abrahima's generosity: my boy had been made to accept for my use a grass hammock, which next to a horse was a most convenient present. I crawled in my suspended couch and never awoke till midnight, when the Chief aroused me and told me to prepare for a defense or flight.

I was up in a moment, and so was the whole caravan. The greatest silence prevailed. The two guides had been sent out on reconnoitering party, as our night watch had previously heard the voices of several men and had awakened the Chief, who had dispatched the guides. This was all the information I could then collect.

A portion of our party had armed themselves with bow and arrow, while my men had newly primed their firelocks. My double-barreled piece was soon out of its case, and my pistols in their belt. On the return of the guides, they informed us that they believed it was a party of runaway slaves hiding from the search of their owner.

It was agreed to capture them, and our sagacious Ala-Ninfa (a determined warrior) proposed to await daybreak for the seizure, but on a second consideration, all concurred on an immediate assault, as by the light of their fire we could determine their hiding place.

Our party divided into two bands, my landlord heading one party and the Foulha Chief the other. They then, with great caution, crawling on their hands and knees, surrounded the suspicious party; and at a word from my Mandingo friend, they rose and pounced on the uncautious lurking party. Two escaped and fifteen were captured.

CHAPTER 25th

We Divide Our Capture and Proceed on Our Journey · Summary Proceedings Against a Village

The 15 captives having been brought to our camp, they were secured with cords till daylight, when we proceeded on an inquiry from whence they came, and were bound. The oldest of the party informed us that they were the property of the Chief of Tamisso, a town on our way to Timbo, and were bound to the beach. Their owner had died, and his brother their present owner had threatened to sell them in the Interior, which caused them to run away. They sincerely begged us not to take them back to Tamisso, as their proprietor would surely kill them.

Our Foulha Chief and Ala-Ninfa consulted what should be done in such a case, and with the consent of the whole caravan, they were divided in proportion to the men in both parties. And as we could not carry them with us, I suggested the idea to send them to my factory, giving them an order for the payment. The division and securing them for the trip to the beach took us the whole day.

As all were men, we made two gangs, securing them with rattan hoops round their waists, and their hands fastened to them with ropes. Then a long pliable braided cord (of which every native traveler carries a small coil for such purposes, as a Mexican muleteer carries his lasso to secure horses) was tied to the neck, seven in a gang, as I said.

As we could not dispose of many of our people, Ala-Ninfa proposed to take my two interpreters and four of my people with muskets, and he himself would escort them to Kya and deliver them to Abrahima-Ali to forward them to my factory; when with all haste he would return and overtake us, while we would go on performing small journeys till the River Sanghu, and there await his arrival. We then parted, each one on an opposite course.

For three days, we made about ten miles per day. On the fourth we arrived at a small village newly formed by a *parvenu*—a Mandingo trader who with the pride of his fellow countrymen gave the Foulha caravan a poor reception, allowing only one house for myself and the Foulha Chief. (I have not given his name, as he was called Abrahima, and I wished not to confound the two Chiefs.) This was considered a great insult, to allow a Mahometan and a Christian to sleep under the same roof.

I saw a storm brewing in the countenance of my chief conductor,

123

and hastened with my boy as an interpreter to inform the Mandingo trader that as I was a friend of Ala-Ninfa his countryman, I begged him to assign me any hut and allow the head man of the caravan to occupy the house alone. The proud *parvenu* took no notice of my request and told me he knew no Ala-Ninfa and did not care for a Foulha Chief or a poor white man. This answer brought an impertinent *repartee* from my servant, which caused the master of the town to inflict on the boy a blow with the flat of his cutlass. The boy in his rage called out to the Foulhas in general for a rescue, crying at the top of his voice, "They are killing my master."

In an instant the whole caravan was in arms, and the Chief with my double-barrel in hand made his appearance. Fortunately, out of precaution, I never allowed the caps to remain on the tubes, as my Foulha friend snapped both locks at the impertinent Mandingo.

I immediately prevented our people from doing any further damage, but could not prevent the securing of the upstart proprietor by our head man. He was immediately seized and fastened to a housepost. In the meantime, our men scoured the town, but it had been evacuated. At the first rising of the Foulhas, the townspeople—some 12 men and 30 women and children—had departed.

At my solicitation our people were recalled and the prisoner released, on condition that he should give up his new house to me and supply the whole caravan with provisions till the arrival of Ala-Ninfa, who would then determine any further proceedings. My boy was sent out to recall the townspeople and assure them that the palabra was settled. The town being placed in a state of seige, our people naturally took the best quarters and at every opportunity annoyed the proprietors for more provisions.

On the second day of this affair, Ala-Ninfa made his appearance with my people, and the proud Mandingo trader received judgment from his countryman which found him guilty on three articles: first, want of hospitality to strangers; second, cursing or abusing a Foulha Chief and a white Mongo; third, and the greatest crime, for not having respected the name of his superior and countryman, Ala-Ninfa.

As there was no appearance of slaves, and the private property had been hid by the townspeople, and the few cattle had been killed by our caravan, the culprit was condemned to receive 50 lashes and his town fence broken down, never to be rebuilt. The lashes were a chastisement for the abuse to the three, and the demolition of his barricade for the refusal of hospitality to head men. This is a long-established prerogative which Chiefs use toward small towns when they fancy themselves slighted.

It took three days' journey to arrive at the River Sanghu. The river being dry, my horse could not pass it on account of rocks which he could not overstep. Every man was set to, cutlass in hand, to cut long poles, while the women made ropes with the bark of trees, and by evening we had thrown a bridge half across the river. On the third day we had accomplished it, twenty-five yards long, and which structure would merit the approval of the polytechnical school.

As the whole fabric shook, we had much trouble in forcing the terrified horse over it. Once on the other bank of the Sanghu, the animal gave sign of greater terror and insisted on returning over the bridge. I could not comprehend the strage action of this quadruped, but our sagacious people soon informed me that some wild animal was near, and the horse had scented it. We fired three or four discharges of muskets, and proceeded on.

This night we encamped in a large flat space of ground, full of dwarf trees whose fruit resemble much the peach, but like other African fruit, has too much kernel and little meat. As this was considered a dangerous place on account of the wild animals, a continual fire was kept up during the night and the horse placed in the center of the caravan. Three men also kept sentry, walking the whole night around our sleeping party.

Some time before daybreak, one of my interpreters, a youth of 20 years old, being on the watch, stole from the camp and pursued a leopard loaded with a large deer. The report of his gun awoke our party, when our bold youth made his appearance with the strangled deer on his shoulders. He had seen the leopard leap on the deer while browsing at some of the fallen peaches, and the temptation being too great, he abandoned his post to dispute with the brute the dainty morsel. As we had not eaten meat for five days, we devoured the animal half raw.

CHAPTER 26th

Arrival at Tamisso · The Chief Mahamadoo Describes to Me the French Traveler Collier

Four days more of toil brought us to Tamisso. For three days the inferior people of the caravan had lived on roots and wild berries and a flowery bean called locust, very nutritious, while the head man would clandestinely eat flour made of boiled rice dissolved in water and drunk cold.

Before we entered Tamisso we stopped at a brook in its vicinity, and the whole caravan was made to wash their garments, while our women combed and greased their skin and ornamented themselves, head, arms, and ankles with showy beads and clean waistcloths. Our two interpreters, with a messenger from our Chief, were sent to the city to inform Mahamadoo of our arrival. Ala-Ninfa, who knew the pride of the Mandingos, thought proper to send such a message to prepare for my reception, well knowing that Mahamadoo would feel mortified if he had been surprised within the precincts of his court *en bourgeois*, squatted on a mat with a female scratching his vermined head.

About 3 o'clock P.M., our interpreters returned with Mahamadoo's son and a dozen women bearing large platters of boiled rice with small calabashes filled with shrimp sauce and pure vegetable butter. A fine horse was also sent for me to ride in town.

Having partaken of our hasty bowl of soup, we started for the town, our interpreters discharging their muskets now and then in sign of joy.

Halfway between the town and the brook, a band of musicians met us with a minstrel and harp. I was surrounded by the musicians while the minstrel chanted in flattering words the riches of a white Mongo. A buffoon or clown also met us in the vicinity of the town, and with the imprudence and familiarity of all fools insisted on leading my horse and capering about me, and with a dirty handkerchief would make attempts to wipe my face, after having done the same to the horse and himself.

At the entrance of the gates we found a large multitude of men, women, and children anxious to see the *Furtoo*, or white man. As I could not pass the low trap door gates, I dismounted and proceeded on foot to Mahamadoo's place. My progress was but slow, with the narrow street and the crowd; I could not make headway till several old men with whips dispersed the mob.

The palace of Mahamadoo was like all other Negro buildings—a large mud wall with a small gate, a large court, and a quantity of mud houses with verandas, the furniture, mats and couches made of rough bamboo, with a profusion of wooden platters, common washbasins (to eat rice in), and a few brass kettles. On a couch with a leopard skin spread on it I found Mahamadoo reclining on his pillow, awaiting my arrival with the pomposity of a European potentate.

He was a man of sixty with a long goatee. He had no hair and wore a light turban. His corpulent and stout-built body was covered with a pair of trousers, Turkish but very short, and a large Mandingo shirt embroidered with red and yellow. Worsted covered the rest of his body.

We shook hands, snapped fingers, and he welcomed me three times according to custom. Ala-Ninfa and the Foulha Chief made their *dantica* (declaration) in which they informed Mahamadoo that I was the guest of the Foulha Ali-Mamy and therefore was entitled a free egress and regress to all parts and cities, free of expense; and that he, the Chief, was the conductor of this important mission.

This information did not please the Mandingo Chief, as he had calculated on a heavy duty for my passage through his territory. Ala-Ninfa's sharp eye detected the displeasure, and he hastened to declare that this white man, knowing that he had to pass through Tamisso, had not come empty-handed, and that my visit to his territory and the Foulha King was for the object of trade; that I had also come to him for the express purpose of purchasing slaves, having several vessels on the coast with large assorted cargoes of cloth, muskets, and powder.

This long declaration in favor of the slave traffic dispersed the squall, and rising from his bamboo lounge, he again took me by the hand and presented me to his people, calling me his son—a title given by an elderly person to a young friend.

The best house within his enclosure was given me and fitted with his best furniture. As soon as the Foulha Chief had retired, Ala-Ninfa returned with the head woman of Mahamadoo acting as a confidential Clerk, and we handed her the presents for her lord—six pieces of cloth and 20 lbs. tobacco. My supper consisted of broiled chickens and the famed savory peanut stew with an abundance of milk. A bed was prepared with a green hide and several soft mats made of rushes.

A bath was also prepared in a small yard, but I could not enjoy it. I was pestered by the curiosity of the female community, who wanted to see the disgusting skin of the white man. As I attempted to go through the operation with as much modesty as possible, I took my shirt off first, leaving my pants. Till then these women had seen only my sunburnt face and hands, but the sight of the whiteness of my shoulders and breast took them by surprise, and several ran away in horror. One old lady, the boldest of the bold, advanced and with one of her fingers pressed the whitest part of my breast and then, looking at her finger, wiped it against the wall. As they appeared so much disgusted, I had flattered myself to be soon left to enjoy a full ablution, but Black curiosity goes ahead of all other curiosities when in the power of women, and piqued at their tenacity, I disappointed them by taking only half a bath.

The next morning Mahamadoo invited me to breakfast, and as we had a mess of rice boiled soft with milk, he handed me a silver spoon well worn. A *P* on the handle struck my curiosity, and I asked where it came from. After some reluctance, he informed me that it came from a white man who had died many years ago, further up in the Interior (it might have belonged to Mongo Park).

I also inquired how many white men had passed Tamisso. He only recollected four, but did not know the names. The last he said was a poor fellow who followed a caravan and could read the Koran and believed he belonged to Senegal. This surely must have been Collier, the French traveler who a few years before had traveled from Rio Noonez to Morocco by the way of Timbuctoo.

The town of Tamisso is a fortified place with a double fence of pointed posts. The space between the two fences, being some seven feet apart, is planted with a thick forest of smaller sticks pointed and hardened by the fire, which render them as durable and as hard as iron. This is done in case the enemy should climb the first fence; they would meet an army of wooden bayonets, difficult to surmount as they are pointed not only upwards, but diagonally and horizontally. The gates at the entrance are three in number through the thickness of the wooden wall, and the passage is made in a zig-zag manner, with loopholes to command every angle.

Three days we remained at this place to recruit. Mahamadoo at parting made a promise to prepare against my return a quantity of slaves; he also furnished our whole caravan with provisions for four days.

CHAPTER 27th

Arrival at Jallica in the Territory of Solimana · The War Drum · The Danseuse and Harmonica Player

As we neared the Foulha country our men traveled better, and some days we performed 20 miles. Between Tamisso and Jallica we met many parties with slaves and cattle, and as we passed them each said, "Salaam alecum," we responding, "Alecum salaam." *January, 1828

For three days we coasted the foot of a large ridge of mountains to the north of us, and as the country was very fertile and full of rivers, rivulets, and brooks, we were well supplied with provisions. With one leaf of tobacco we could purchase a fowl; for a dozen of eggs or washbasin of milk I gave a charge of powder each, and for a large sheep I paid a quart of salt or six-hundredths of a dollar.

On the fifth day we made Jallica and rested half a day to prepare for our reception. The Chief was called Suffiana and a relation of my landlord Ala-Ninfa. As my Mandingo friend had been absent from Solimana country for many years, his entry in Jallica was to be attended with all the ceremony accrued for the occasion.

The distance from Jallica to our resting place (a small stream) was about three miles, and in about one hour from the time that we had dispatched our messengers, the war drum from the town gave us notice that our message had been received. The second was so grateful to my landlord's ears that it affected him into tears. I presume it had the same effect as the church bells have on some people when long absent from a dear home. As the discordant noise died away, Ala-Ninfa, trembling with emotion, informed me that that instrument was to give notice to all the war men that an old Commander was about to arrive and called them to prepare their war accoutrements to receive him, insisting it could be heard five miles' distance. The war drum was never sounded in time of peace, but on such occasions; for five years Ala-Ninfa had had the command of that instrument, and it had never beat a retreat.

Our messengers soon returned with Suffiana's lance, or dart bearer, informing Ala-Ninfa that the gates of Jallica were open to him and his party.

No *fanda* (refreshments) were sent to welcome us, no music or fools did we meet on the road to the town. Our caravan marched in silence nearly the whole distance to the gate.

Some fifty yards from the gate a troop of war men met us, and taking Ala-Ninfa on their shoulders, carried him high through the gates, singing their war songs and attended with all sorts of instruments. As yet, no one had taken notice of us. We had got near the gate when someone espied me on horseback and cried, "Furtoo! Furtoo!" (white man!) The gates were immediately closed, and those that were outside remained so.

As my Foulha conductor came up and found the entrance closed, he flew into a passion. But fortunately Ala-Ninfa, hearing the name of "white man" mentioned, recollected he had left me outside and ran back to us, apologizing to me and the Foulha Chief.

Our caravan was conducted into a large square of this well populated city, and under the Palabra House (a large shed without walls) stood Suffiana with his court of old men, awaiting our arrival. The outside was crowded with men at arms; each carried either a musket, a spear, or bow and arrow, but all wore by their side a cutlass or a long knife hung up high to the neck.

Ala-Ninfa preceded us with several minstrels deafening the air with their unharmonious songs. As he entered the shed, Suffiana rose, drew his sword, and placing his left arm round the body of my landlord, gave him a long accolade, brandishing his blade with the other.

Each one of the Royal Council did the same. Then the war drum was rolled out in the center of the square and two men with slingshots covered with gutta-percha[1] struck with all their might a mighty reveille. This favorite war instrument of Ala-Ninfa and town family piece was the trunk of a tree four feet in diameter and hollowed or bored out to the consistency of two inches thick; its length was ten feet and only one end was covered with a bullock hide. Its sound, when nearby, was deafening, and I believe it could be heard six miles in a calm day.

As Ala-Ninfa took a seat, all the men at arms one by one saluted him by pointing down their war instruments at his feet. The operation lasted two hours, and as it was an honor due to a General it could not be dispensed with. But as soon as he could disengage himself he came, and assisting me to dismount, he presented me to the Court and His Royal Highness with the appellation of his son, addressing a long panegyric on my qualities, riches, et cetera that brought down a shower of admirations from the credulous courtiers.

Here I found better houses and greater order in the town. As a guest of Ala-Ninfa, no one annoyed me with visits or female curiosity, and although I was attended by young and handsome females, they took no improper liberties. I was allowed as much privacy as

[1]a hard, rubber-like tree resin

possible. But it was otherwise when I went out. Two men were sent with rattans, constantly hitting right and left to keep women and children from impeding my passage.

On the second day I paid a private visit to Suffiana with the customary presents, although I was not bound to pay any duties, being, as the reader is well informed, the Ali-Mamy's guest. Still, I wished to make friends and never deviated from the old customs, ever taking the necessary precaution to hide such gifts from my Foulha Chief, who would never have consented to allow me while under his protection to pay a leaf of tobacco as a duty.

As the Chief Suffiana knew this, he accepted my gifts with many thanks, and that day I partook of his dinner which was served in one of his wives' house. After dinner several female singers were introduced and amused us with a concert. I cannot say much in favor of their voices or melodies, but still, some of their instruments were certainly ingenious enough; the harp, or better called by its ancient Greek name the lyre, was an instrument about two feet long, made of three sticks tied together in a triangle of 35 degrees. Half a gourd covered with a skin with several small holes in it was secured to the sharp angle. The strings or chords were made of the fibers of cane; they came perpendicular to the obtuse angle. This lyre in the masterly hand of a Christy Ethiopian Minstrel would give nearly the same sound as an American banjo.

Another instrument I must describe, and I am silent on music for this chapter. But as it struck me for its peculiarity and sound, I believe the reader will patiently peruse its description. This was something like an harmonica: a board the size of a tea waiter with a light open frame at the extreme ends. On this frame were tied two strings made of cane, and on it reposed several pieces of bamboo well cleaned from the pith. These pieces were gradually made, one larger than the other, declining in size and placed in rotation; under them were placed seven gourds also gradually declining in size. This instrument was carried with a strap around the neck and played with two wooden hammers covered with gutta-percha.

Its harmony was peculiar. The female musician who played it had fastened to her elbows, wrists, ankles, and knees a lot of small bells which she managed to sound as she struck the harmonica and danced in the meantime. The effect was rather vulgar as she took many attitudes which required indispensables;[1] still, it amused the King and his females. The concert over, the Chief presented her

[1]underwear

with a slave. This musician was considered in the country a Jenny Lind in regard to her voice and a Mozart as a composer and instrument player, and a Fanny Esther or Taglioni as pirouette dancer. As she also made her obedience to me, I gave her my Bowie knife as a value for ten pounds tobacco which I promised to pay her.

CHAPTER 28th

Arrival at Timbo · My Reception by Ali-Mamy, Chief of the Foulha Nation and Brother of Ama-De-Bella · Ama-De-Bella Delighted at My Improvement in the Mahometan Faith

Our day of departure was postponed by my Foulha conductor, as the moon was to appear this day, and the journey could not be commenced. The next day we started, but my friend Ala-Ninfa would not accompany me, being taken sick by a sudden indisposition which I found out afterwards he had shammed to perfection. The cause was that he had duped so many Foulha traders and owed so many slaves that he did not dare to accompany me in the Foulha territory. My interpreters and the Foulha Chief were not sorry at his remaining behind, as they did not like the preference I gave him in every question.

*8—14 January, 1828

As I have described the different incidents of my other days' journeys, I pass over the six remaining days, as nothing of consequence took place worthy of notice during the time.

My conductor had dispatched a messenger from Jallica to Timbo, and as we descended into the Valley of Foutha Yalloo the road was intercepted by a horde of slaves headed by Ama-De-Bella, who had come to meet us with horses to make our entrance in town. As we met, Ama-De-Bella turned to the east and so did both parties (the writer not excepted), and in a long drawling voice, sung the usual grace for our safe arrival. I wished not to show my religious ignorance, therefore I kept time with the rest.

On rising from our prostrate position, I shook hands with my Foulha brother (the appellation Ama-De-Bella gave me in his prayer of grace) and I mounted a fresh horse. My interpreters and servant also were furnished with horses, while our caravan was discharged of their load by the slaves attendant on my royal brother.

We were still one day's journey from the capital of Foutha Yalloo, and as our carriers were relieved from their load, we made it in seven hours. Two mounted criers preceded us and drove travelers from the path. At a small village from Timbo we rested the whole night and early before daybreak entered the City of Timbo while its inhabitants were still asleep.

I was conducted to a house newly made for me and enclosed by a high wall. Here I found every accommodation resembling my own house at Rio Pongo: table, sofa, a very ingeniously made rocking chair of rattan, plates, knives and forks, tumblers, pitchers and basins; all had been purchased by my conductor at other factories and forwarded, unknown to me. This act of refined kindness was intended to surprise me and it did so, as no one of the above-mentioned articles are used by Mahometans.

Ama-De-Bella enjoyed my surprise, and as I returned him thanks for this distinguished mark of friendship, he begged me to be silent and told me that I had done the same with him at our first acquaintance.

As Ama-De-Bella while at my factory had much admired an old morning gown and spoke with admiration at the whiteness of our European linen, I had brought with me for the occasion a highly colored and fancy-figured morning gown, well faced with yellow lining (the preferred color of these people). My pants were large, without pleats at the waist, well bleached and ironed; my shirt suited the pants in purity. I also wore a Greekish cap with a blue tassel. My interpreters wore their new Mandingo dresses; one carried my double-barreled gun, the other my long pistols. My servant also wore the Mandingo costume and carried a highly gilted regulation sword, some of the intended presents for the Ali-Mamy. And at 10 o'clock I was escorted to Ama-De-Bella's father.

On our way we were followed by a grand concourse of people, but not interrupted as at other places. The crowd looked on and made room. As the Ali-Mamy suffered from dropsy in the feet, I was conducted to his private dwelling, and no pomp was displayed. I found the old gentleman in the veranda reclining on a sheepskin, and two young females fanning his feet.

Ali-Mamy, although a despot of his people, still ruled his dominions and issued his dictates with the consent of his Council, which is formed of his near relations and oldest son.

On my visit to Timbo I found him a man nearly sixty years old, retaining all his powers although much afflicted with the dropsy in his feet. His mind was still juvenile, as his questions to me were quite simple, but affable and friendly, ever dwelling on the nature of my amusements and wondering on my taste for information and curiosity. And he delighted to hear me recount my voyages at sea, not conceiving that a wooden bark could contain provisions for such a long voyage. The sea also was a mystery which only God and a white man could solve.

Ali-Mamy, as I said, was a man of sixty and strange to say in Negroes, quite bald to the temples, wearing a long white thin goatee a foot down on his breast. His physiognomy was certainly pleasing and never harsh or proud; his height was two or three inches above six feet, with a slight inclination to corpulency. As a true Mahometan, he never drank, but after sunset he indulged in a kind of mead made of roots which when well fermented acts on the brain somewhat like lager beer.

His habits were those of his co-religionists: devout to excess, full of salaams, genuflexions, and ablutions; quoting the Koran on every trifling occasion. His younger days had been spent more as a book man than a warrior; it being the custom amongst the royal family that the first-born is brought up as, we may say, for the Church, while the other children are never exempt from the field of battle. I suppose this is done as an excuse not to expose his life.

I have forgotten to describe the contours of his face, which were exceedingly regular, with an oval face, small mouth full of ivory, and pouting lips. The nose was somewhat flat, but not adorned with those frightfully large cavities so peculiar to the Negro race. His forehead was high and perpendicular, and his color was a spotless brown.

As his son presented me with the title of his "White Brother," he extended his hands, drew me close to him, and made me sit down near him, and looking me long and well in the face, he asked me my name. I answered, "Ama-De-Bella."[1] As I spoke the Mahometan name, he drew me still nearer to him, and holding both hands high upwards to Heaven, he repeated several times the great Mahometan expression of "God is great and Mahomet the true prophet."

Several questions were put to me in regard to my parents, my journey, and he scrupulously questioned whether I had been well treated on the road; what stay I should make in his country, and if I liked my habitation. He concluded with the desire that I would remain the whole rainy season.

I was about taking leave of him (as he was laboring under great pains) when he recalled one of my interpreters and distinctly told him to take anything in his dominion he thought I would fancy —slaves, horses, cattle; everything was at my disposal—and pointing to his son, said, "Tell your master he is our guest, and Ama-De-Bella will redress any complaint."

On our return to my lodgings, we called on Ama-De-Bella's mother, a lady of about forty who according to custom kept her head and shoulders covered and exposed her face as little as possible. She welcomed me with much kindness and called me "Ama-De-Bella-Theodory." As this was our breakfast place, we squatted on clean

[1]probably to emphasize that he and Ama-de-Bella had exchanged names

mats to breakfast. It consisted of milk and rice, clabber,[1] and honey. Each one had separate bowls and spoon; the mother did not eat but mixed our food and encouraged our appetite by her hospitable and kind words. After the meal, several calabashes of water to wash our hands were handed round by girls whose forms could well serve as models to the Roman school.

I was then conducted to the palavra ground, a grove of large cotton and tamarind trees, where Sulimany-Ali, the older brother of Ama-De-Bella, and the head men were awaiting my arrival. All were squatted on sheepskins.

As my Foulha brother presented me, Sulimany-Ali rose, saluted me, and carried me to a rock covered with a white cloth, the seat of honor for distinguished strangers. I was saluted by all the rest, who gradually rose and shook hands with me, bidding me welcome three times. Ama-De-Bella stood by me till everyone had returned to their seat, when taking a long cane from one of the oldest men and stepping forward, he saluted the assembly, invoked the Lord's name three times, and introduced me to them. In his introduction he said that with the consent of his father and his older brother, he had invited his white friend and brother to Foulha and hoped that I would be made welcome, giving the following reasons: First, I was nearly as good a Mahometan as many Mandingos, himself having converted me (as he supposed) I was entitled to that courtesy. Second, I was a rich trader from the Pongos; thirdly, I had come for the purpose of making arrangements for slaves and for which I would give a great price.

In African palavras, as well as in some of our religious congregations, it is the custom to give a groan or sigh at any remarkable or affecting description, and the African uses the same gutteral groan in token of assent, as he is not allowed to interrupt the speaker. In Ama-De-Bella's introduction, the necessary groans were given at the information of my arrival, at my supposed and doubted apostasy, and at my riches. But when they heard my purpose to purchase slaves, they all sang out, "Allah Okibarsa!" (The Lord be praised!)

My interpreters then opened several bundles containing white and blue cotton cloth, 10 yards of scarlet, six kegs of powder, 300 lbs. tobacco, 2 strings of amber beads, and six muskets. The gilded sword I placed aside from the other goods with a rug, and a small package of tincture of cantharides,[2] which I denoted as private for the King.

[1]bonnyclabber: thick curds of sour milk
[2]Spanish Fly, used as a diuretic as well as an aphrodisiac. Considering the Ali-Mamy's dropsy, the gift was hardly frivolous.

Sulimany-Ali, taking then the cane from his brother, informed the head men that his brother had brought a rich stranger amongst them, and pointing to the presents, said there was the proof. He requested that their hospitality should be according to my generosity. He also mentioned that these were no tribute, but a voluntary gift; as an invited guest, I could not pay duties. The goods, he added, his father would distribute next morning, and that during my stay in Foulha they should furnish for me and my people a bullock a day and two baskets of rice. As every Chief should partake of my generosity, each one should contribute to my comforts.

The goods were then examined by each one and the pieces counted. The sword, being a private present with the rug, was very gently handled, but when the vials of cantharides were unpacked and the contents known, each one declared that the valuable poison should not be private. A dispute arose on this subject which I cut short by offering to add to the public presents a dozen vials of the malignant noxious.

As I returned to my lodgings, I found several presents from the King, of fruits both dry and fresh, and two milking cows. Ama-De-Bella soon made his appearance with his younger brother, who he introduced as a learned divine, and we had a long conference on religious matters. But as I had made but sorry improvements in the Mahometan religion, I gave assent to all the arguments which my devout Black brother chose to entertain me with, and in this manner I escaped the detection of my ignorance. I suppose many others have done so before me.

A Stroll Through the Vicinity of Timbo ·
The Palavra Sauce

As I wished to see the country, Ama-De-Bella proposed we should mount our horses and visit the neighboring villages, all commanded by his relation.

Early next morning we left Timbo with a party of ten horsemen. As we came to the first brook, well shaded with high trees, our quadruped caravan stopped and the leader called out in a loud voice, "Take care! Strangers are coming." A few moments after, we crossed the brook and I observed several women awaiting our crossing. All appeared to have been either bathing or washing. Men in Foutha are strictly forbidden to cross brooks without giving notice to the females who might be washing themselves.

On our arrival at the village of Findo, we found it deserted. Fame had preceded me, and as it was a slave town, the inhabitants at my approach had escaped, fearing our mounted caravan with the dreaded white man at the head. The day of my arrival had been promulgated in all the vicinity, and as in the presentation the principal compliment paid me was my having come to purchase slaves, those ignorant dependents had imagined that my mission then was to seize them, and such was the panic that it affected even the free.

At Findo we only rested to breakfast, which the Chief of this village had prepared for us. At the next village, Furo, we met the same reception; as we came more suddenly on this place, we found in many sheds pots boiling with their provisions in them. As the head man was absent, not a soul did we find. Ama-De-Bella laughed much at their fear, but I could not but feel much mortified and insisted on our return.

These small slave villages were surrounded by plantations and patches of gardens, but as it was the middle of the dry season, everything was withered or cut down. But the immense rice paddy fields denoted the abundance of this staff of life. In their gardens the cassava root and sweet potato were predominant; the red pepper, onion (shallots), garlic, and a bitter tomato formed the rest of their vegetables. The squash and pumpkins also grew in the fences of their gardens. As I observed in each of these enclosures a pole with a piece of paper and writing hanging to it, I demanded the meaning and was told it was a scapulary to keep thieves off.

As I had spoken to Ama-De-Bella about the good messes I had in the Mandingo town on my way to Timbo, I was treated this night on my return from our long ride with a sumptuous supper he had ordered. Here I ate the palavra sauce in all its perfections. This mess is a stew of meat, fowl, or fish with the buds of a peculiar plant very finely cut up in it. The meat is allowed to boil to rags, and when dished up, it is served with a spoon and eaten with rice which by its peculiar way of cooking would bring to the blush all the South Carolina Negro cooks, if the black was not in the way. Let me inform the amateurs of this grain that African rice has more taste and solidity than the Carolina rice, although it is not so white.

CHAPTER 30th

My Opinion of the Foulha Nation and Their Character

Wishing to visit the city without molestation or *avant courier*, I begged Ama-De-Bella to send his criers out and inform the public that the stranger wished to walk the streets without a mob following me. Three criers with a triangle each announced at each corner the wish of the Furtoo and admonished the children and women of the punishment of the transgression—a bastinado.

This afternoon I took a stroll through the city, attended by my servant and two Foulhas. The order had been complied to the letter; each person that I met shunned me or made room for my party. Several times I called children and young girls, but in vain—they flew from me. Toward evening I went to the gate leading to the brook and sat there near the path. The physiognomy of the Foulha Nation had struck me very favorably and I wished to see the youthful portion in their occupations.

As each family at sundown sends their children for water, I chose this spot as the most proper for my observations. Here women and girls, not aware that the stranger was near, sallied out in their *deshabillé* or working dress, a cloth from the waist downwards, but the shoulder naked. No nation in the world can boast of better or equal forms. In general, all appeared to me to be made by the same mold. Their erect round forms with a small waist was a peculiar beauty in every female; their bosoms denoted no relaxity. Even mothers walked without inconvenience of burden. I saw here none of those outshaped breasts which the Sosoo working women exhibit. Their features also were fine without the flat and expanded nostrils of the common Negroes; I remarked their lips were rosy and not ever thick or hanging. The hands and feet were also very feminine. The men resembled their women too much to appear with advantage. I found them too delicate and small-limbed for the masculine frame.

I presume this evening I saw the best part of the female population and its youths, and on reflection I cannot say I saw a deformed or lame person. Blind I saw perhaps two or three; and pitted with the variola[1] but very few. I leave the philosophers to moralize on the subject.

Next I undertook to calculate the length and breadth of this city, but failed. The streets are so irregular, short, and full of cul-de-sacs that I either lost my way, continually returned on my steps, or

---

[1]smallpox (but Conneau has crossed out "syphilis," which used to be known as the "great pox")

found myself blockaded by some wall or fence. I also made the circuit of this place and rode round it in one hour. I could not be informed of the census of its population, but I believe it contained about ten thousand inhabitants.

The Foulha are a population of shepherds. Their large towns are a distance apart, and their dominions extend a large tract of flat land. Their wealth is calculated in horned cattle, and although they deal largely in slaves, still they seldom sell their home-born servants. The moral character of this population I believe to be superior to any other African tribe. The women are reserved and, I think, virtuous; they are also in both sexes industrious, as I never saw a man or woman idle or lazily basking in the sun. Here the females are constantly employed in spinning or cleaning cotton, when not employed in their household occupations. Many elderly females I met soon in the morning and late at evening, reading the Koran.

The men are generally employed in working leather, weaving cotton cloth, manufacturing iron implements out of the rough bar, cutting plantations, or reading and writing, for which they have great taste. What nature has refused in physical strength, their natural character has made up for, as they are naturally bold and brave and their unity constitutes their national strength.

CHAPTER 31st

My Return Home

Having satisfied my curiosity and being anxious to return to my factory, I visited the Ali-Mamy with the purpose of informing him of the same, but as I presumed strong objections would be advanced to postpone my journey, I prepared an excuse to carry on my point; which was that when I started, I had calculated on being gone two moons only from my place, and being then on the third, I was desirous of returning immediately, as I expected a vessel full of goods for a slave cargo, and which I could not delay. This was the only soft point on which I could conquer all objection.

Accordingly on the ninth day of my arrival I called on the King and with the assistance of my interpreter, whom I had schooled for the purpose, told him of my projected return on the third day. As I had forethought, many objections were made, but my excuse was so forcibly expanded on that on the fifth day I was allowed to depart.

Several parties were immediately sent out to blockade the paths, and that night the African press-gang made several recruits from the slaves about the town, and early next morning Sulimany-Ali sallied forth before daybreak with his troop of horsemen and returned by sundown with 45 captives taken from Findo and Furo.

As I took my usual walk every morning I found the children ran with great fright at my appearance. Since the seizure of the night before, all under the yoke of captivity on seeing me, thought their time had come, and I am certain the poor part of the population looked on me as their Satan. Once or twice I detected women pick up a handful of earth and throw it toward me, exclaiming a short sentence. This was done to drive the evil spirit from them.

My good Mahometan brother Ama-De-Bella lost no chance during my stay here at Timbo to Musulmanize me, and although his efforts were not successful all-together, still I managed to satisfy his anxiety in regards to my Christian soul.

On the fourth day, Ali-Mamy called a palavra and attended himself; here my presents were distributed according to each one's rank and called upon to make suitable returns. All his relations presented me a bullock or a barren cow, the rest a sheep or a goat. The King himself presented me five slaves, Sulimany-Ali a beautiful white horse; Ama-De-Bella two elegant female slaves. His mother sent a country bed covering, very ingeniously woven with red and yellow threads unraveled from Manchester goods.

At parting, a grand Mahometan *Te Deum* was chanted. I bid adieu to Timbo and its inhabitants, and preceded by a large caravan *1828 headed by Ama-De-Bella, left Foutah for Rio Pongo.

As my road was the same as I had taken in going, the reader will be content to know that the events of my return were similar to my going. At Jallica I found my landlord Ala-Ninfa ready with a large quantity of slaves and some large elephants' teeth, with some gold and wax. Here Ama-De-Bella left me, having been recalled by his father on account of some family dissension. At Tamisso our good friend Mahamadoo had also prepared his portion of slaves and ivories, which swelled our caravan to a thousand strong.

At Kya we rested four days, and our jolly Abrahima treated me with a glass of 4th proof cordial, a liquor I had not drunk for a month, my canteen having given out at Jallica on our way out, as I said before. On the fourth day from Kya we passed the village neighboring to my factory. Here Ala-Ninfa divided the caravan in four parts, taking the best and choicest for myself. This division was necessary as I had in our caravan many slaves which were unmerchandisable.

I had taken precaution not to send messengers to my factory, as I wanted to surprise my people by such a hasty return, but it was a fruitless attempt. The cannon of my hands soon announced to me that my arrival was known, and that afternoon, two hours before sundown, I saw the Spanish flag waving over my house (the joyful sign that everything was correct).

CHAPTER 32nd

Mama-De-Young's Sister's Captivity

*1828 Immediately on my arrival I purchased the produce of the caravan and sent Mama-De-Young back with suitable presents for himself and a kind token to my brother Ama-De-Bella. A slaver had also arrived during my absence and my Clerk had not completed her cargo. I made arrangements with her Captain for the remaining part of his goods.

Mama-De-Young, the royal messenger and temporary landlord, had only departed but three days when a messenger from my friend Ama-De-Bella made his appearance almost dead with fatigue; he had performed the route from Timbo to my factory in 21 days.

The bearer of this message informed that his master Ama-De-Bella had sent him to tell me that his own sister (by the same mother) was about being conducted as a slave to my factory, by order of his father and brother Sulimany-Ali, with the express condition that she should be shipped. Ama-De-Bella requested me not to refuse his request, but by our brotherly friendship not to ship her and await his arrival.

This information caused me much surprise, as I knew Mahometans never sold their caste unless the punishment was greater than death. However, I promised the bearer that I would prove a true friend to his master, even if I incurred the displeasure of his father and older brother.

This messenger had only preceded the unfortunate girl but a few days, as on the sixth day of his arrival Sulimany-Ali's courier arrived with the information that Ama-De-Bella's sister was in the next village, escorted by a relation and with express order to be shipped by me; and that till the chargee of this disagreeable business knew my intention, he would not start from his resting place.

I hastened to send back a favorable answer, but as the girl had sworn never to see salt water and refused to walk any more, threatening to knock her brains out against the rocks if they insisted on carrying her to the waterside, her refusal to proceed any further placed her conductor in a dilemma, as he dared not use but ordinary compulsion, and being of royal family, he dared not degrade her with the whip.

I availed myself of this opportune detention to send one of my landlord's wives to the spirited Mahometan girl, begging her not to make any difficulties but to come down and allow her jailer to

144 perform her tyrannical father's and brutal brother's orders; that my

brother Ama-De-Bella had sent me notice of her captivity and that I had sent him back word, to save her, that her oath did not bind her as the river was not salt water. This was a lie, but in such case I had no scruple, as I was telling it for her safety. I also sent her the token of friendship her brother had given me on our first acquaintance—the manuscript Koran, a book well known by all her family—and added that her brother was on the way to redeem her, but she must be guided by me and fully have confidence of my friendship.

My mission was conducted with satisfaction, as early next morning the young Princess was conducted by her Sir Hudson Lowe[1] to my factory with a rope around her neck. The preliminaries of the purchase were long and tedious, as I was obliged to promise many things which I intended not to keep. However, the principal point was agreed upon, *viz*, that I would ship her by the vessel then laying in port.

In order to disgrace her the more, her half-brother had commanded that she should be sold for salt (considered a contemptible sale, as cattle are exchanged for salt in the Interior). As the last tub of salt was measured I cut the rope from her neck and covered her naked shoulders with cloth, calling then apace the same female messenger who had the night previous transmitted my request to her, told her to take her to her house and treat her as the sister of my friend.

As her conductor was refusing to take his payment and insisted on taking the girl, I assured him that my promise should be kept and that in two days she would be put on board before his own eyes; but that while she was under my roof, I could not but treat her as a royal person.

As the reader will naturally ask what crime this young woman had committed to deserve worse punishment than death, the future chapter will tell.

[1]the English General who, as Governor of St. Helena, made Napoleon's final imprisonment needlessly unpleasant

145

Ama-De-Bella's Sister's Crime · Her Deliverance · Mahomet Performs a Miracle Through My Intermission

This young Princess whose age might have been 18 years had been promised by her half-brother Sulimany-Ali to a distant relation of her family's. This man, besides being very old, had acquired a cruel fame in the treatment of his wives and also bore the name of a bad Mahometan and was vulgarly accused of eating unclean flesh. Now this young girl, whose name was Belia, strongly refused to be united to this sliding Mahometan, but in the absence of her own brother Ama-De-Bella, she was forced from her mother's arms to be given into those of her disgusting lord.

On the arrival at her new home, she stoutly refused to share the matrimonial mat, and as the Mahometan law prohibits force in such cases, she retained her purity. Her lord having exhausted all fair promises and arguments, cast her from him and sent her to Sulimany-Ali with an insulting message. Her resistance was considered an act of disobedience by her father and half-brother, and as she still persisted in her refusal, she was condemned by the laws of the land, her barbarous parents, and the Koran to be transported and become a Christian slave. Such was her capital crime.

The slaver being ready for sea, I requested her Captain to aid me in the sham shipment of the Princess. I had also informed Belia of the farce I was going to act, and as everything now depended on her obedience to my injunctions, I begged her to fully confide in my management.

The appointed day arrived for the shipment of the slaves, and the vessel was sent out this time outside of the bar to take her cargo. The slaves were mustered on the beach and passed over to her Captain, who took on all, and they were sent off in canoes.

The last slave delivered was the Princess, who had been conducted to the beach by her jailor-conductor and my women. The Captain of course accepted her without the formality of inspection, and she was put into his boat, manned by five of my groometes (a name given to native boatmen) who immediately paddled off to the vessel. Her conductor and myself remained on the beach to see the boat alongside.

As the boat neared the breakers to the south of the bar, a heavy roller took the boat sideways, and she was capsized. At the sight of this disaster the jailor cried "Allah!" and buried his face in the sand.

So did his follower, while Ala-Ninfa's wife (who I had kept in *1828 ignorance of the expected event) tore her hair and beat her breast in despair, cursing the barbarity of the parents of poor Belia.

In the meantime, a light canoe which had been sent previously on the spot, picked up the girl and with the velocity only capable of such swift skiffs, made for the nearest spot on the opposite beach; this maneuver was executed so well that no one observed the deception.

The girl in safety, I shook the prostrated Mahometan crocodile and pointing to the spot, I upbraided him with their Musselman cruelty. And as it was a good opportunity to moralize, I preached him a long sermon on the subject, insisting that it was the Great Prophet who by a miracle had swamped the boat and destroyed Belia's life sooner than one of his daughters should become a slave. The repentant conductor acknowledged the fact and immediately took his way up to Foulha with the sad news.

As Belia was taken ashore in a fainting state, I caused her to believe she had been in the water several hours. This deception was also necessary, as it would hide in part the trick I imposed on her keeper. A few days after, I caused a Bager fisherman to take the Princess up to a friend of my landlord. Pretending he had picked her up on the beach and saved her life, he claimed her as his slave: she then became the apparent slave of another person, who was not bound by any promise, as her owner could dispose of her at his pleasure.

I have no need to say that shortly after, her own affectionate brother sent me ten slaves to redeem her, and *bon-gré, mal-gré*, she returned to her mother.

CHAPTER 34th

Arrival of a French Slaver · His Deception to Kidnap Mongo John and Myself · His Success

1828   Having disposed of the Belia affair with honor and some pride, I intended to take a long siesta, but the salute of twenty-one cannon awoke me from my lethargy. In wonder at the noisy intruder I sent a boy on the lookout tree to ascertain the nature of the extra-polite stranger who wasted his powder with such profusion.

It was reported that a schooner opposite Bangalang had anchored and sported a long pendant and a white flag at her pick. As I knew no man-of-war would salute a native Chief (the French are more economical and not so philanthropic), I concluded it must be some French Slaver and awaited his message.

That evening Mongo John sent me a note informing me of the arrival of a French vessel to his consignment with a rich cargo and requested me to call soon in the morning to breakfast on board, through the invitation of the French Commander.

I accepted the invitation, and next morning I met Mr. Ormond on board the slaver *La Pérouse*,[1] whose Captain welcomed me with the politeness of a true *dit-donc*.[2] As the Frenchman could not speak English, I interpreted for the Mongo, and as breakfast was not ready, we spoke about his cargo. The Captain exhibited some splendid samples of callicos, French guns, and superior cask brandy, adding that to complete his cargo he had 500 doubloons. The name of a doubloon had always a peculiar effect on Mongo John, and at his request I calculated the amount which summed up with his other goods made the value of his cargo about 17 thousand dollars, for which we offered 350 slaves. The offer was accepted and our boats sent off in search of the canoes for the discharge of the goods. We then sat down to a sumptuous *déjeuner* which was dispatched with an appetite that a good bargain generally engenders.

As the breakfast table was set on the quarterdeck under the awning, the coffee also was served there. The *plus café* made its appearance, and that was swallowed with a toast to la Belle France. Several toasts were given and attended with different cordials, and at the last glass the Captain called for his writing desk. This was the signal for four men armed with cutlasses in hand to seize the Mongo

---

[1] named after Jean-François de Galaup, Comte de la Pérouse, famous French explorer (1741—1788)

    [2] "agreed, then": an accommodating man

and myself. The carpenter was then called and a couple of darbies[1]
were riveted onto our feet.

As the operation was going on, the ever-polite French Captain informed Mr. Ormond that he had used this deception to decoy him on board in order to secure his person; that two years ago, his brother had left in Mr. Ormond's hands some 200 slaves which he could never get, although he had called twice for them, and opening his desk, he exhibited to Mr. Ormond a due bill for 200 slaves payable on demand. And as he refused to pay, he availed himself of this *ruse de guerre* to oblige him to honor his note.

As the note was properly endorsed, the Mongo had nothing to say. Besides, the excitement of the toast began to affect his understanding, and turning to me, he laughed at the joke.

I then asked the Captain what I had to do in the concern to be also subject to his ill usage. With a reverence worthy of a Marquis he informed me that as I was Mr. Ormond's Clerk when the note was signed, I had a share in the pie, and now that I had a factory to myself, I could assist my patron to pay a debt which I knew was correct.

I confuted his argument by representing that the writer of the document was an Englishman who was absent, and that I had nothing to do with Mr. Ormond or his affair, and insisted on him setting me free immediately. His answer was that on no condition would he liberate one or the other without the full payment of his due. He then called his men to man the cannons and prepare for action, as he had espied the canoes pushing off from Bangalang.

At the appearance of the first canoe, a shot was sent across its bow, which caused it to backwater-haul, the rest in dismay took ship for the shore again. Soon after, the war drum sounded at Bangalang, and the natives mustered in great number, but what could they do against a vessel with six six-pounders?

Before sundown my boat made its appearance with a white flag. My Clerk was in her. The Frenchman allowed him to come alongside, as he was attended with only two men. Having taken counsel with the Mongo, we agreed to let the Frenchman have his way, and told my Clerk to return next morning with a change of linen and by all means tell the natives not to attempt any rescue.

That evening we had an excellent dinner with a profusion of Lafitte and Chateau Margaux. A good mattress each was given us

[1]long boards with two handles each, used for smoothing plaster (in other words, Conneau and Mongo John were not shackled, but hobbled with the nearest thing handy)

and we passed the night in perfect calmness, but not little inconvenienced with our iron stockings.

Next morning *café noir* was served us with toast. Water and clean towels were also passed round, and cigars to Mr. Ormond. Our polite and hospitable gaoler then desired to know if we had passed the night comfortably and what determination we had come to, as it was very much distressing to him to keep us in durance vile. I would not condescend an answer; my Italian blood was too full of revenge to take notice of his French *parlez-vous*. The Mongo said that while on board he could not make arrangements, but if he would allow him or me to go free on shore, he could make payment in two or three days.

The Frenchman took one hour to consider, when he proposed that Mr. Ormond should send four of his children and two of the Black gentlemen that had visited him that morning from Bangalang, and he would allow him to go on shore. The Mongo, with my assent, accepted the proposition, and the flag was hoisted under the fire of a blank gun. A canoe came alongside with my Clerk, and speedily the six hostages were placed in the cabin, and a sentry at the door.

As Mr. Ormond left, I gave him a written order to my Clerk to press all useless and indifferent servants in the factory and deliver all with the slaves in the barracoon to the Mongo. This order I showed to the Frenchman and told him the hour of retribution would come; to this he answered with the usual frivolity of his countrymen, "Fortune de la guerre, mon ami."

A few hours after the discharge of the Mongo, my Clerk came off with 50 slaves from my factory and demanded my exchange, which was not granted. Next day forty more slaves were sent off by the Mongo, but the cunning French Captain would release none of his hostages. The collecting of the other 110 slaves was a difficult job. Slaves were scarce, and many household servants had made themselves scarce, not wishing to take the place of their betters.

Three days had I been in captivity, during which time my constant prayer was that God would grant the arrival of some well-armed Spanish slaver, and as the prayer of the wicked never avails and the humble is never exhausted, so mine was heard. The third afternoon a boat passed us bearing the Spanish flag. As she passed us, I gave three cheers and saluted her with the pride of a liberated Algerian convict. But as the boat was manned by Blacks, the Frenchman took it for some deception of the Mongo to frighten him into an immediate release of his prisoners.

During my captivity the Commander had at all times been very

polite, and everything that his pantry or canteen could produce was
ever at my service. Till then I had refused all extra refreshments and
partook in stubborn silence of my regular meals, but at the sight of
the Spanish boat, I called for champagne. The astonished steward
brought it, but with a trembling hand. The infection had spread to
the mates and the forecastle. The Captain alone stood firm, but
indecisive. I called on him and begged him to assist me by partaking
a glass of his champagne, which he *sans cérémonie* accepted. As I
drank the foaming liquid I wished that the next glass we should
drink would be under the Spanish flag, and hoped it would be
tomorrow. The toast was drunk, but with bad grace. My joy was too
sincere not to denote the aspiring revenge that flashed from my
burning cheeks. As he left me, I saw him retire to commune with his
officers.

CHAPTER 35th

Arrival of a Friendly Spanish Slaver, the Ninfa · My Deliverance

*1828 Next day as the sea breeze was lightly making in, the tall masts of a schooner made their appearance over the mangrove trees, and the tide soon drifted her past one of the sinuous bends of the river. Her masts were decorated with the Spanish flags, and as she neared within a musket shot, an anchor was let go and immediately two springs[1] were run out to the bushes to give her a broadside position.

The astonished Frenchman, who had till then wished to doubt the danger, now was convinced that "la fortune de la guerre" had changed patrons. As he espied the vessel, hoping to find her disarmed, the muzzle of a large brass piece in her midship and her decks full of white and Black men brought his glass to a vertical position, and calling to his Mate, he desired him to have my iron struck off. This officer was about to obey, his hammer in hand, his crestfallen Commander's orders when a voice from the Spanish vessel was heard, commanding the Frenchman to send his boat on board and threatening to fire if not hastily obeyed.

The French boat was lowered, but no one would man her. Even the Chief Officer refused the honor. Many of the crew, most of them Creoles and Mulattos from St. Thomas, had deserted the deck. The Commander in his trouble addressed me thus: "You are the favored by fortune; do as you please with me, and take your slaves or anything else you choose."

As the Spaniard was repeating his order, I told the Frenchman that I alone would go on board of the schooner, and lowering myself in the boat, pushed off, sculling myself to the Spanish vessel.

My arrival was hailed with a shout of joy, and as the Commander embraced me as a brother, the old Ala-Ninfa jumped in the Frenchman's boat, calling his men to follow. Fortunately my Clerk had observed him and gave me timely notice to stop his proceedings, or I know not what would have become of the French officers, deserted as they were by their pusillanimous and mongrel. crew.

The Spanish vessel was the *Ninfa*, consigned to me from Matanzas. Her Commander was not known to me, but I knew his officers and many of the crew. I informed my deliverers of what had taken place on board the Frenchman, expanded on his gentlemanly con-

[1]lines from the quarterdeck specifically designed to hold a vessel athwart the current

duct in regard to personal treatment, and begged the Spanish Captain to allow my own way of satisfaction, which with reluctance he did, much to the mortification of his crew who wanted a signal[1] revenge.

The Frenchman's boat was manned in company with the *Ninfa*'s boat, and I returned on board the *Pérouse*. I then ordered his own carpenter to spike his six small guns, which being done I then caused all the slaves to be landed. This also being attended, I begged the Monsieur to give me the list of his cargo, the 500 doubloons, and the document for the 200 slaves.

The document was handed, but no doubloons or list of cargo existed. The samples alone were the only goods that formed his cargo. I begged the French Captain to spare me the necessity of searching his vessel, and as he had in a manner acted gentlemanly with me, I wished to return the compliment.

As no persuasion could induce him to show me the invoice of his cargo, I sent one of my men for his writing desk and there found that he had shipped 600 doubloons in St. Thomas. I unscrupulously demanded them when the Frenchman made an oath that he had landed them at the neighboring River Noonez with his supercargo. I was in the act of retiring with my men when his treacherous Steward winked at me. I returned and begged to see his log book, which on examination did not make an entry of this money being landed. I questioned his Mate, but he pleaded ignorance. I then called on the Steward and ordered him to bring me the Captain's trunk, which I opened and found 250 Mexican ounces. As the gold was counted out, I asked of the Spanish Captain what was his charge for the loss of his tide and the extra work of his men. The answer was "250 ounces," which I allowed him to take.

As I left the *Pérouse* I informed her Commander, who with tears begged the restitution of his gold, to consider himself lucky, as had I allowed my Spanish friends their settlement of this affair, he would not then complain, as they would not have given him the opportunity.

[1]singular, memorable

*CHAPTER 36th

*The Ninfa *Engages with a Danish Brig*[1]

*1828   The *Ninfa* was discharged of her cargo, and as her Commander labored under a spell of fever contracted at Cape Verde, I gave him orders to go to sea on a recruiting cruise and return in two months, when his cargo would be ready. As preparations were going on on board for the cruise, the Captain fell worse and died.

As I had seen what I estimated then to be much of Africa, I wished to return and make arrangements with my friends for the establishment of a large mercantile concern. Therefore, the death of the Captain of the *Ninfa* gave me an opportunity of returning to Cuba as Master, and as the officers were inexperienced in the management of a live cargo, I took charge without creating any unpleasantness.

As a Danish brig had also arrived for a cargo of slaves, it became me to bestir myself to collect my cargo, and I visited my vessel but seldom. One afternoon, as I was dining with Mongo John in company with the Danish Captain, a native of Margarita[2], the report of a cannon announced some new arrival. Immediately after, the lookout announced that the Spanish schooner was firing on the Danish vessel. We all ran to the piazza when another shot from my vessel announced to us that my crew were the aggressors. I called for a canoe when we heard the report again, of smaller calibre. The Danish was defending herself with her small artillery.

As I pushed off in my canoe, the Danish Captain did the same in his small boat then in attendance. On my arrival on board I found the crew busily weighing the anchor and the small arms spread on the roof. My Mate was on the bowsprit urging them on, while my Second Officer lay on a mattress with his head bound in a bloody hanky. Another man lay nearby, wounded in the shoulder by a musket shot.

My appearance on board soon reestablished order, and calling the First Officer and men to an account for the assault on the Danish brig, I found that both vessels' boats having gone watering at the same brook, the crews had quarreled for the precedence of the stream. And as the Danish were seven in number against three of my men (our boat being small, while the Danish was a launch), my men had been beaten off. My Second Mate, who had charge of the yawl, received a blow from the blade of an oar which inflicted a very severe wound in his head and laid him senseless.

[1]Conneau failed to title this and certain later chapters
[2]an island off the coast of Venezuela

On the return of the boats, the Danish arriving first on board their vessel, very imprudently they ran their flag and pendant up. My boat arrived soon after, and the Second Mate, still senseless, was hoisted on board apparently dead. The affray was pictured to the Chief Officers in its worst colors, and when the flag and pendant of the Dane was observed by my crew, it was immediately taken as an act of defiance, and a cry was given by them for a fight which was responded to by the excited Danes. Unfortunately the Dane had not calculated the distance or the measure of his calibre; his grape[1] did not reach the *Ninfa*, while our 18-pound shot told a sad tale in his bulwarks and mast.

I know not what tale the Danish Mate told his Commander, but shortly after, a round shot came whistling over our head. Another and another followed in the same track, but being too elevated, did no damage. This second act of aggression gave me no time to reflect, and at 24 years, under such circumstances reflection was out of the question. I ordered the chain to be shipped and set the jib and mainsail.

It was done in a minute, and the next moment, placing my vessel in raking position with the Dane, I sent him a dose of grape and cannister which materially spoiled the looks of his poop. My second fire was a round shot to his mast, with no effect. The third I intended to send between wind and water and not miss my mark, but the Dane had struck his impertinent pendant; his flag had flown away by the effect of my grape.

We both remained in status quo till the Mongo arrived with his boat. As I was the nearest on his way, he called on me first, and ascertaining the state of things, he went to the Dane. His visit was a long one there, as night came on before he left. Fearing some treachery from both parties, I again weighed anchor and placed my vessel in a creek, broad side on, ordering my Mate to keep continually on the alert against surprise. I then took my leave and went to my factory to place my establishment in a state of defense.

Next morning the Dane had gone, and on visiting Mr. Ormond I understood he had gone to Sierra Leone to seek protection from a man-of-war or the British Government. As I knew such could not be the case—no vessel prepared for a slave cargo would dare enter that colony—it gave me no concern. I also learned that the infuriated Danish Master caused his three side guns to be discharged at us without any forethought, but repenting immediately as his carpenter was killed and three of his men badly wounded.

[1]grapeshot

Mongo John Connives at My Depriving the Danish Slaver of His Cargo

*1828 A few days later, the Danish brig returned, but without any protection from the British Colony. As he anchored some way higher up the river, my crew and his never more came in contact.

As we often met at the Mongo's, we cooly saluted each other, but never spoke. But still I perceived a kind of newly sprung-up friendship between Mr. Ormond and this Captain, which did not exist before. As I knew the treacherous disposition of the Mongo toward me, I set about observing their proceedings. To effect my purpose better, I purchased the friendship of the Mongo's private servant (who spoke English well) to sniff out the secret of this new-existing friendship.

Next day the unfaithful servant told me that the Dane had secretly made several presents to his master in provisions and all his remaining cargo, for which Mr. Ormond had promised him the payment of his cargo before mine.

Now the Mongo owed me 200 slaves on the *Ninfa*'s cargo, which debt was contracted before the arrival of the Dane; therefore my payment was due first. This the Dane knew well, but my peppering his stern and the death of his carpenter still stuck in his crop, and not being able to revenge himself, he had chosen the cupidity and the aversion of the Mongo to me to deprive me of the 100 slaves in the hands of Mr. Ormond.

I allowed some time to pass without taking the least apparent notice of their amity, but still keeping an account of all the slaves in the Mongo's barracoon, and the day that I found that he had just accumulated 300 slaves, I called on him and privately informed him of his treacherous intent.

As he could not exculpate himself (my information ·was too exact), he confessed the intent, alleging some poor apology in favor of the Dane, who had received such damage at my hand. To argue a point with the Mongo where propriety or impropriety of his conduct was the subject, I knew was labor in vain. I would sooner undertake to wash him white than discuss such a subject and convince him. His business affairs were too much on the decline, and his pride as Mongo still retained all his arrogance. Why should he stoop to honor his contracts? The affair of the Frenchman, Monsieur

156 M., strongly showed his inclination to pay his debts.

I resolved to outbid the Dane and offered Mr. Ormond his note of hand for the 200 slaves he owed Captain M., the same that I had taken from him; also the note for the 100 he owed me from the *Ninfa*, with 150 slaves that I would send him that night if he would consent to load the Dane on the next night.

The Mongo understood my meaning and the trick, therefore readily consented, looking forward to a good bargain to himself. It was also agreed that he would inform the Dane that by the next night he might prepare his vessel to take in cargo, and to recommend him to drop his vessel down the bar to be in readiness to make sail once the slaves were on board.

Without loss of time, I went on board of my vessel and gave orders to prepare to take cargo the next night, and secretly told the Mate to prepare the small armaments in fitting condition for a skirmish, likewise to double-load our pivot gun with chain shot. I then returned to my factory and there made preparation for an absence of four months, giving my landlord the care of my place, and the young Clerk the charge of the goods.

That afternoon, the Dane, in order to deceive us the better, sent on board a native canoe to borrow a small anchor to kedge[1] his vessel lower down the river, giving my crew to understand that he was only changing his berth to be nearer the sea breeze; and soon after his vessel passed mine with sails unbent.

On the next night, my large boat was manned with ten men, each armed with pistol and cutlass. At nearly the appointed hour the canoes made their appearance loaded with slaves. The first I boarded myself and commanded the men to pull for my schooner. The second was captured by my Mate, who did the same. The third, fourth, and fifth fared the same. In an hour my vessel had under her hatches 375 slaves. I then presented the patroon of each canoe with a document acknowledging the receipt of the number of slaves taken out and wrote an order in favor of the Danish Captain for the full amount of slaves borrowed from him, with an advice to be more on his guard in the future. I requested the principal patroon to deliver the same to the Dane.

As it was near daylight, I made sail with the land breeze and favorable tide. I soon passed the vessel of the Dane, who still expected the arrival of the canoes, but as he did not hail me, I followed my course out of the river and by midday I was plowing the salt brine, not a little proud of my having paid the Dane with his same currency.

[1]to drop an anchor and haul in the line, drawing the ship after it

CHAPTER 38th

The Ninfa's Engagement with the Boats of H.B.M. · The Conflict

*1828 We sailed on till the land wind gave way, expecting as usual the sea breeze, but we had light and variable airs. At sundown we could still see the mouth of the river, and at every moment expected the appearance of the infuriated Dane full in search of us.

Next day we made hardly any progress—the same light winds from the south-southwest, the highlands still in sight—and continued the same all night. At daylight on the third day our mast had cried out, "Sail ho." Our fire was extinguished and the sweeps rigged out and each double-manned. Our spyglass was pointed to the unwelcome stranger, which at first sight appeared a large frigate, but as the sun peeped above the horizon, I distinguished the two masts steering toward us. As I knew of no cruisers in these latitudes, it gave me no concern, but still fearing the Dane which I expected would become a troublesome customer if once alongside of us, I continued sweeping and encouraging my men to a greater exertion. But my Mate, who had mounted to the fore top masthead, called out to me, "It is the Dane. I see his flag." At this information my men swore they would sooner fight than pull at their sweeps, and giving three cheers, requested me to await the Danish brig.

As we had made but little progress with our oars and it was perfect calm, I called my Mate down, and collecting my men abaft, I inquired of them if they really wished to fight. I questioned each one separately, from the Mate to the boy. Having received an affirmative answer, I ordered breakfast, which of course was a cold one, but to make up its sufficiency I added three cases of claret. The breakfast over, the doors of the forecastle were nailed down and the gratings secured as for the night. Every Negro attendant was also sent below. The magazine and arms chest were prepared and covered with blankets; as I wanted to deceive the Dane, I put up the Portuguese flag.

Having appointed everyone to his station, I mounted the rigging with my spyglass, and taking a deliberate aim at the enemy I fancied I saw a row of ports which the Dane had not, and sweeping the horizon a little astern of the vessel, I saw three boats pulling for us and each bearing a flag.

I immediately returned to the deck and ordered the sweeps out again, the breeze helping about one knot. Once underway, I called the Chief Officer a second time and informed him that we had an enemy more formidable than the Dane; John Bull himself would be our antagonist, and that only our legs could save us. But if we could repel the boats, we might succeed in escaping the battery of our foe, who I calculated to be a vessel of 12 guns. I also asked his opinion as to the willingness of our people to fight the man-of-war's boats, which he did not doubt.

I then visited every man at his oar and informed them of the approaching danger, collecting their votes, fight, or no fight. All but two voted in favor of a defense. As I caused everyone to give his vote unknown to the others, I was very positive of their good services in the expected and dangerous trial.

As the wind was again abating and the oars being of very little service, I ordered them in. Then, as several water casks were in the way, I threw them over the board, and our boat was hoisted on the stern davits as a bulwark against boarding on that part of the vessel.

A few days previous to our sailing, a Spanish schooner had grounded on the bar of Rio Pongos, which so far disabled her that she sank the day after. Her officers and crew had taken a passage with us. Her armament, which consisted of two short twelve-pound carronades with a good supply of small arms, had been transhipped on board the *Ninfa* the night before sailing; therefore we now mustered on board 37 in all, and three cannons.

The British boats having neared us at a respectable distance, they lay on their oars for some time (I presume in consultation). As the distance was within range of my midship gun, I ordered the first fire, which was received with three cheers as the shot passed over their heads. The boats then parted company, the larger pulling directly for the center of our vessel, while another pulled to cross our bows, the third to board us by the stern.

As our carronades could not be used as yet, our pivot was the only arm attended to, and in order to point it at pleasure, I kept constantly two sweeps ahead and two astern to give my vessel a suitable position. But the largest boat, being the better target, to her I directed the most fire, which was returned, but without effect. Their boat carried a carronade whose caliber did not as yet reach us. Our sixth fire, being a double-headed shot, took effect for the first time, cutting short several oars from the starboard side of the largest boat, which disabled her from further advancement. We then directed our fire to the other boats, when the Commanding Officer called them to repair damages, and after joining, they all returned on board.

Till now I had not observed that we were flying the Portuguese flag, which I had hoisted to deceive the Dane. As the boats apparently retreated, I immediately struck my flag, and refreshing my people with light drinks, I called them to man the sweeps. The idlers I employed in making more *cartouches*.[1]

On the arrival of the English boats on board their vessel, they were allowed to remain alongside. This prognosticated an intention of a second attack. As it was still perfect calm, and the working of the sweeps fatigued my men too much, I took them in and ordered my men to dinner.

About 12 o'clock the enemy's boats again started from their vessel and made for us. The distance from each vessel might have been about five miles. As the ungrateful breeze refused us her services, we again prepared for a second attack, which I knew would be more terrible than the first. John Bull had his stomach full and had smelt powder. I had often heard say that give an Englishman his belly full, and he will fight his way to the Devil, and by their hasty strokes I saw we should have to contend with furious bulldogs. Such I consider English sailors, begging their pardon for comparing them to animals, when their national honor is concerned.

On they came again in three divisions with intent to board. Our long tom was kept continually discharging shot after shot, but with little effect and returned by the bold British with incessant har-ha's. Having neared us within grape shot, the murderous music was exchanged from both parties. Our carronades now spoke their might, and in two instances repelled the daring Anglo-Saxon from a nearer approach.

At 3 P.M. the Senior Officer made a signal for a second retreat and briefly returned on board, but by their hasty strokes, I could well see the intention of a prompt return. As my men saw them pull back, they gave a long "Viva!" which I immediately suppressed and requested them not to exult on a retreat which would be followed by a still greater, more furious advance. I then caused an inspection of our ammunition and to my great astonishment found that if we had repelled the boats, we had done it by the sacrifice of nearly all our artillery ammunition. Of powder I had still seven kegs, but of cannister and shot remained only a dozen rounds all told. Small arms ammunition we had in abundance, but I considered it a poor defense against the British carronade whose fire, if once allowed to come within musket shot, would prove murderous to us. Every locker was searched, and several bolts from the slaves' shackles were hastily formed with the assistance of a few rope yarns into a package

160   [1]cartridges filled with powder, to speed the loading of the ship's guns

just the size of our long midship gun, and all the loose musket balls were also put into small canvas bags to fit our carronades. In one half hour we were again ready for another attack, which I considered would be the last. My men began to refuse wine, and several of them made propositions to others to refuse fighting any longer.

As yet but two men had been wounded by muskets' shots which made but slight wounds, the balls being nearly spent. But discontent was plain in several of the passengers, and although my men kept them from an open revolt, still it was too visible for me not to take notice.

Perceiving the boats still alongside the English cruiser, I called my whole crew aft, and after describing the danger of giving up the ship while there was a hope, I offered them each two ounces cash down and a slave for each man on our safe arrival in port. As my offer was only accepted by few, I doubled the bounty and proposed that the discontented were at liberty to take the boat and seek refuge on board of our enemy, that myself and the crew would see the last of the *Ninfa*.

The last proposition touched the timorous in the right cord, and their Petty Officers taking up the defense, spoke for them, saying that they would fight to the last, and the hospitality that I had given them was sufficient reward for all they could do in the defense of my vessel.

The wine was again greedily drunk, and every man received three doubloons which reconciled their fainted hearts.

The marine phalanges again made a start from the enemy and in perfect order pulled directly in a body for our vessel. I perceived their determination to board me on one side and bravely stand our fire, which if not precise would give them the greatest of advantages. I allowed them to approach, awaiting their fire, but their Commander had also guessed my intention and reserved his fire till I should be involved in my own smoke, when his two other boats would board me under the fire of his carronade and ten marines. I allowed them to give a few more strokes at the oars. My pivot long gun then lodged in the midst of the flotilla a confusion of iron balls which for a few minutes paralyzed their proceeding.

The starboard carronade gave them a salute which told remarkably well. The boats were not idle; the carronade of the launch swept our bows, killing and wounding five men. The marines also poured in a constant discharge of musketry which was only silenced by our second carronade. A third retreat took place which gave us (for a time) some hope of escape. But to our astonishment, we saw at a distance of five miles another squadron of boats pulling direct for us.

The report of our cannons had been heard by the consort of the brig C., who although not in sight sent a boat toward the direction of the cannonade, and while the former engagement lasted, had had time to report and return with assistance. The dead calm which had lasted since the action began had assisted them. On they came with the rage of mad bulls, head on in two columns.

My men at times during the engagement had shown token of discontent. Now that the danger was greater and that five of our men lay stretched and bleeding on the transom, they became furious at the contest, and the greater part taking their shirts off and calling for rum, swore to die or conquer.

Every man returned to his post and again the long gun sent her round missive amongst the British boats. One of them was disabled, but the rest pulled and cheered at every one of our discharges. As they neared us, they separated and again prepared to board us on two divisions.

The awful moment had come, and although death stared us in the face, my crew still returned hurrah for hurrah and poured in several discharges. As the two columns had surrounded us, the signal was made by the Senior Officer to fire. In a moment several of our men fell. I myself received a musket shot in the left knee, but was not disabled. In the confusion, the Captain of the long gun had put in the cannister before the cartridge; consequently the priming burnt, but it would not go off. A round shot from one of the launches had dismounted our starboard carronade and the British, perceiving our disabled state, boarded us over the crippled starboard side. Our muskets for a moment kept them at bay, but before we could reload, they were alongside.

Cutlasses in hand, our fore part of the deck was cleared in one moment, the Commanding Officer urging his men to cut down everything before them. Down fell man after man, while others who had broken the gratings ran below amongst the Negroes.

I received my wound while on the roof and still retained that port, but at the blood and the disaster of our carronade, I perceived our total misfortune and called on my men to throw down their arms. I myself struck the flag.

The second boat that immediately boarded was the Senior Officer's, who seeing the men cut and slash at everything, called on them to desist and give quarters, and it was time. In their fury, the first boat, which had been twice maltreated during the engagement, had boarded with the revengeful intention not to give quarters; and had it not been for their Superior Officer, the writer would have been one of the victims.

CHAPTER 39th

My Escape from the English

*1828

Boat after boat boarded us till our decks were full of British sailors. The two Commanding Officers demanded my papers. I gave them to the senior, the same who had humanely ceased the massacre, and called myself his prisoner. This act of submission of mine annoyed the other Commanding Officer, who at three different times had been repulsed by our fire, and although junior to the other, insisted on being the captor in chief. Some very severe remarks were passed between the two officers, in which I was much abused by the junior. But the senior stopped the conference short by ordering his junior in his own boat and to assist in towing the schooner to the consort just in sight, the corvette *N.S.*

My boat, although much perforated by musket shots, was lowered down, and myself and my servant, a Black boy, were sent on board the corvette with my papers, and under escort of a midshipman. On my arrival on board, the Commander received us at the gangway, and as I could not come up by the side ladder, I was very gently hoisted up and immediately sent to the cockpit and my wound dressed. It was only a flesh wound; consequently I could walk but not bend my knee. I was called in the Commander's cabin and several questions were put to me which I correctly answered.

I was then made aware that in the report of his First Lieutenant, thirteen of my people had been killed and nearly all the rest wounded. I was also requested to say to whom I surrendered, which of course I said, "To the last reinforcement," as without the assistance of the consort's boats, I thought myself sufficiently in force to resist the first division of boats.

My papers were then looked over, and as they were Spanish, did not correspond to the Portuguese flag we had fought under. As I was not prepared to make a moderate good excuse for such violation on national privilege, I boldly told the truth so far as concerned the dispute with the Dane (which I called a Frenchman), carefully forgetting the last part of the quarrel—depriving him of his Negroes; exculpating myself with the hope that as I had first repulsed the *C.*'s boats with the Portuguese flag, I had flattered myself that I would escape with the expected sea breeze and avoid detection.

I was then asked if I was aware that my defense under the Portuguese flag could not be otherwise construed but into an act of piracy. The change of color in my countenance was sufficient answer. As this investigation had been in presence of the Doctor who by his looks strongly sympathized with my situation, the Commander remarked to him that it was a pity to condemn a man who so manly had fought in the defense of his property.

I was then requested to remain in the cabin till further order. As I felt hungry, I begged for food which was immediately and delicately supplied, and my servant was sent down to me.

Presently I saw the Doctor and the Commander's servant busily filling a basket with biscuit and cold meats. Several bottles were also put in, and a small line tied to the handle. Several other articles were also placed in it. The doctor then called for lights, and unrolling a chart, inquired of me if I knew the position of the vessel. I pointed out the spot, and by request I measured the distance from the nearest land, which was 37 miles to Cape Vergas. The kind Doctor put several questions to me, which I so precisely answered that I knew I had a friend.

He then informed me that he, in my place, would make his escape, having all the elements in my reach to effect it with safety. First, there was my boat towing astern, and the cabin window handy to get in. Second, there stood a basket of provisions almost ready to go in by itself. Third, my boy would follow me and assist me in my escape; and finally he remarked that darkness favored my enterprise and that there was nothing to fear, as the vessel was laying to and no sentries were on the quarterdeck. As he rose to leave me, he shook me by the hand and hoped never to see me. Passing by my servant, he placed something in his pocket which afterwards proved to be five sovereigns.

The Steward made his appearance and placed on the transom four blankets and bade me good night.

Availing myself of the Doctor's advice, I looked out of the window and although it was very dark, saw my boat towing astern. Presently someone pulled it up from the deck close under the counter. I lowered my boy into it, then the basket and blankets, and with the assistance of the boathook, slid myself into her. A small jerk at the painter on my part brought the coil slowly into the water. A few moments afterwards I had drifted some distance from my generous enemy.

CHAPTER 40th

My Crew and Officers Are Sent to Lisbon in Irons

The unlucky *Ninfa* was sent to Sierra Leone and there condemned as   *1828* a Slaver, but the officers and crew were sent by order of the Admirality to Lisbon in irons, where another tribunal condemned them to five years in the galleys. But they were shortly liberated by the clemency of Don Pedro of Braganza on his arrival in Lisbon. I am only sorry to add that my brave Chief Mate died in prison of his wound; of my men only one is now alive.

My Return to Rio Pongo · The Monkey Soup

1828 The moment I thought myself at a safe distance from the corvette, I put the oars out and pulled away to the east. At daylight I was apparently alone on the ocean. My basket underwent a thorough search. In it was found a part of ham, two bologna sausage, a large piece of salt beef, two bottles of brandy and four of water, biscuit in profusion. An elegant pocket compass, a corkscrew, and a hunting knife were well packed in a large table cloth, which our judicious and kind benefactor had no doubt placed there to make a sail of.

The humble master and his slave broke bread out of the same basket and drank from the same bottle. Only the day before this boy, now my companion, was the humblest of the humble, and today he was my equal, as without him I should have perished. My knee had become inflamed, and I lay helpless in feverish torment. Fortunately at midday the breeze arose from the southwest, and with the help of the table cloth and an oar, he rigged a square sail which wafted us at the rate of 3 miles an hour. With two blankets and another oar I rigged an awning. Half reclining, I steered till midnight, when darkness prevented me from seeing my compass. I layed to. The next day the breeze again favored us, and by sundown I came up with a friendly Mandingo canoe. I exchanged my quarters and never awoke till we landed at the Islands de Los.

Here my wound forced me to remain ten days. In the meantime I had sent to the Pongos for my boat, which in due time arrived equipped for my return. As I had lost my clothing, and my Clerk having neglected to send me a suit of clothes, I was forced to dress in the Mandingo costume. In this attire I returned to my factory.

As I entered the river, I perceived a French brigantine anchored near the bar. I called alongside and begged the Captain to give me a drink of claret. The stupid Frenchman, mistaking me for a native, inquired of me where I drank wine last, and pointing to the water alongside, told me to drink that. I thanked him kindly and was on the point of pushing off when, recollecting himself, he inquired where I had learnt French. I would have left him in the enjoyment of his ignorance when one of his men, who had been in the river before and knew me, whispered into his Commander's ears my name.

The astonished Frenchman leaped in my boat and taking both of my hands, begged thousands of pardons, and would not part with 166 me till I had dined with him. I readily consented, as he promised me a good plate of soup, and my men also wanted some rest. I mounted his decks, my dress causing some curiosity amongst his crew.

The goodhearted Frenchman insisted on dressing me out of his scanty wardrobe, but as he resisted all remuneration, I only accepted a clean shirt and the loan of his dull razors. While the bouillon was getting ready, I was informed that the Danish brig had left the river after a severe quarrel with Mr. Ormond, who only gave him 100 Negroes for his cargo, and that a Spanish brig was up the river waiting my arrival. My boy, whom I had sent from the Islands de Los, had reported my speedy return, my engagement with the English man-of-war boats, my capture, and my escape. The Frenchman also informed me that the Spanish Captain, hearing of my prompt return, had suspended all operations with the Mongo and now expected me with anxiety.

Le diner prêt, we sat down to a smoking tureen of soup. As it was *bouillon gras,* a dish with toasted bread stood in the middle of the table.

The officious Captain, having loaded my plate with two slices of toasted bread, poured on them two ladles full of the steaming broth, and as all well-cooked French dishes seldom require condiments from the caster,[1] I was requested to begin *sans façon.* Indeed, my appetite was sharp and the vapor of the liquid inviting. I did not wait a second invitation. Spoonful after spoonful was swallowed and the contents tasted very palatable. During the intervals (as the soup was very hot), I praised the Cook and French cookery.

Having begun first, my plate was the first empty, and I must say my diet of former days had made me somewhat greedy. I had dispatched my first plate in haste, calculating upon another ladleful before other calls. I again filled my plate with the toast and very politely requested a little more soup, still feeling in my palate the agreeable sensation of the last spoonful.

As the Master was on the point of helping me, he inquired if I would like a little of the thick. My answer was affirmative. Down goes the ladle and with a peculiar slue,[2] it was brought up in horizontal position, and rising above the rim of the tureen. The bowl of the instrument contained a very small human skull, face upwards, grinning at the guests with a cursed grimace.

The plate I dropped, but remained fascinated at the damned object. I looked at the mummy head and still could not make out if it

[1] a spicerack for pepper, sugar, etc. The closest modern equivalent is the rack of tabasco and horseradish served by restaurants to accompany cocktail sauce.
[2] the twist or rotation of a mast or spar

was a monkey or young Negro's head. I know not how long I would have remained in this state of stupor had I not been relieved by an oppression of the heart, much resembling seasickness. I left the table in some hurry and without the assistance of an emetic, dislodged the abominable broth into the river.

In disgust at this second insult, I left the anthrophagian Frenchman without accepting his apologies and returned to my factory.

CHAPTER 42ⁿᵈ

Mongo John's Suicide · The Cause of His Jealousies

Next morning I visited the Spanish brig *Feliz* from Matanzas, lying *1828 to an anchor before Bangalang. As my boat rounded a point and came in sight of the brig, the colors were set and a gun was fired. On stepping on board, I was cheered by the whole crew. The report of my long engagement with the boats had been magnified to a Trafalgar battle.

This vessel was also consigned to me, but as I had left the river, the Commander had partly made engagement with the Mongo; hearing of my return, he withdrew his bargain and now placed his cargo according to instruction into my hands.

Although a brig, the vessel was only 140 tons. Her cargo amounted to 350 slaves which I disposed amongst the different traders. Mongo John, who thought himself slighted, refused a share. This refusal caused much disgust in the town of Bangalang. His people, who did not understand the cause of his refusal and suffered by not participating in the trade, accused him of indolence and neglect, and many free families left his town for Gambia, my place.

His own brothers who materially suffered, abused him with no measured words for his misplaced arrogance. His women—headed by his head woman Fatima who at every new cargo of goods abundantly supplied herself of a portion—who lost their usual present, rose in a mass into an open mutiny and declared they would all leave him if he did not accept part of the cargo.

In all the seraglio's grievances, Fatima was the orator and the defender of its inhabitants. On this occasion she did not spare the Mongo, and finding herself well supported by 30 more female tongues, openly accused him of indolence, drunkenness, and impotency, and at every accusation her feminine crew responded "Amen." The revolt was such that many of these she-demons boasted in his face of their infidelities, while others brought their bastards to him and ridiculed him on their resemblance to himself.

The Mongo, finding himself set to by these rabid females, called on his people to subdue the revolt, but lo! His men were the lovers of these women; no one obeyed, and in his madness, Mr. Ormond found relief in the bottle.

On the afternoon of this insurrection, by request, I visited the Mongo, whom I found nearly drunk but cautious of the morning insult. His eye denoted something revengefully dangerous, and his quick movement bespoke a desperate, troubled mind. As he took my hand, his grasp was terrible and cold. He held it long, then requested me to take a glass with him. His offer I refused under a plea of indisposition, but I requested to be informed in what I could serve him. With many incorrect phrases he told me that he had changed his mind and would take a portion of the *Feliz'* cargo. His language and conduct strongly demonstrated a distracted mind. I thought prudent to give acquiesence to his demand and proposed to settle this affair the next day. I left him apparently more calm.

Before leaving Bangalang, I called on some of his people and was informed of the morning with his women and the appeal in vain to his men to quiet them. As I was on the point of embarking in my boat, the Mongo's servant—the same who had assisted me with the Danish affair—informed me that I had done well not to drink with his Master, as previous to my arrival the Mongo had medicated the bottle. He also requested me to be on my guard, as Mr. Ormond had often threatened my death, and that morning when his women attacked him in a body and one in particular mentioned my name with some pride, the Mongo had fallen in a fury and struck the woman, accusing me for all his troubles.

At midnight I was awoken from my sleep by the watchman, who informed me someone wanted to see me. I hastily rose and found Esther, the Mongo's favorite, in tears, with three more of her companions who had escaladed[1] the seraglio and taken flight from Bangalang.

The Mongo had entered it with two loaded pistols in search of her and Fatima. Fortunately they both made their escape, and fearing further search from the Mongo, they had left Bangalang and begged a night's hospitality, when in the morning they would determine on further proceedings.

An hour after, a messenger arrived with the sad news that Mr. Ormond had shot himself in the heart, the head man of the town requesting me to come over immediately.

Early in the morning I went to Bangalang, and there lay the Mongo, still in the same place where he shot himself. It appeared that in the state of inebriety which he was in at sundown, he forgot the medicated bottle which he had prepared for me and must have drunk pretty freely out of it, as it was found nearly empty. Finding out the mistake, and the poison operating, he resolved to shoot his two women Fatima and Esther, the first for heading the unmerciful abuse in the morning, the second for the cankering jealousy which he ever had for this female who unfortunately could not appreciate the lascivious caresses of a worn-out and impotent lord. A few

170   [1]used a ladder to escape from

moments before he committed the deed, he was heard to say that as he was to die, he wanted company.

The body was found in one of the vegetable patches, stretched out amongst the cassava plants, a pistol in the left hand still loaded. The other lay at some distance, discharged. The body was perforated right under the left breast, and the paper wadding lay in the orifice of the wound. The ball had lodged between the flesh and the cutis[1] on the shoulder.

It is customary in this part of Africa that at the burying of a Chief, a grand feast is given which is called "Colungee," when all neighboring Chiefs and relations send presents and provisions for the feast. This is a day when the poor and vagrants, pell mell with the better sort, get a stomach full of meat and rum.

Messengers had been sent to his brothers and other relations, and the burial was postponed till the third day. It was requested by the brother of the defunct Mongo that I would undertake the ceremonial burial service. I gave orders for the necessary preparations, and on the third day I returned to Bangalang, where a large concourse of people had collected. The body in the meantime had been given in the charge of his wives, who during the whole time kept up a continual cry of mock sorrow.

A grave was dug under a large cotton tree, and at 12 meridian a salute was fired by the guns of the town, to which the brig *Feliz* and my factory responded. The Chiefs having assembled, the body was exposed, and each had a view. The coffin was accompanied in procession to the grave by the wives, who appeared covered with torn rags, their heads shaven, and their shoulders and breasts lacerated with wounds inflicted with burning irons. At the grave they abandoned the awful yells which till then had been constantly kept up.

As no English prayerbook could be had, I read the funeral service from an old Latin book which only contained the common everyday prayers. Therefore the body was consigned to the dust with an Ave Maria and a Pater, which I calculated quite sufficient, considering the company present.

On the return of the procession to the house, several bullocks were killed, rice distributed, and demijohn after demijohn of rum served out. A sham battle was got up and two parties formed. Both retreated to an opposite direction, and in a short time, scouts appeared, crawling like reptiles on the ground. Having ascertained the position of the supposed enemy, the parties sallied out in small platoons bent to the ground, guns in hand, while other parties did

[1]skin

*1828   the same with bow and arrow and short lances. When apparently near enough, those with guns discharged them, while the others returned a volley of blunt arrows. Several prisoners were captured, and the war ended for a dance which lasted till morning, when the rum gave out and everyone returned to their home.

CHAPTER 43rd

The Fortune Teller

As I had reserved half of the cargo of the *Feliz* and slaves came but *1828 slowly, I undertook a trading excursion to the Matacan River, some miles' distance.

Having equipped my two large canoes with sails, provisions, and good armament, I left my factory with the amount of 50 slaves in goods.

At the Island of Matacan I only remained but a short time and the third day arrived at a town on the border of the Matacan, a narrow and short river not navigable to large vessels. On landing I called the Chiefs and exposed my goods, which quantity and quality had the effect which I expected.

Shortly after, that same day several young persons were brought to me for sale, which in the morning they never expected. They were born slaves; others who share the same fate had long forgotten their peccadillos, which my goods had now caused to be brought again to daylight. The jealous husband who had drunk of my rum also remembered the infidelities of his wife and exchanged her for more of the intoxicating liquid. Before night the town was in confusion. Everyone wanted to find any excuse to kidnap his neighbor under some pretense to have a share of my goods.

As the town was small and the fifty slaves could not be collected in this place, I had recourse to the villages in the vicinity. My barkers or agents did their work to perfection. With intent, they carelessly exposed their goods to the temptation of youths, and then hid themselves in ambush to watch the uncautious pilferer, when he was seized in the act and immediately hurried to the waterside as a slave. In this manner I had disposed of my goods by the fifth day of my arrival, and my canoes sent back loaded with 50 Negroes which certainly did not bless my arrival in their country.

While I remained at this place I heard much of a famous wizard who performed several wonderful tricks and astonishing cures. They spoke of him as the *ne plus ultra* of the fortune tellers, and his habits were described as astonishing. For miles around, the infirm would come and seek cures for his wound; the credulous warrior would also deposit at the shrine of this astonishing wizard rich and valuable presents for a fetish against muskets' shot. Others would do the same for a preservative against the bite of snakes or the influence of evil spirits, and the mother would consult this semi-devil on the prospects of her expected *accouchement*.

One of my interpreters, who had visited him in the morning, gave on his return such flattering reports of the wonderful and correct statement of his own fortune that it set all my people in great excitement, and everyone wished his fortune told. I was obliged to advance them goods to satisfy their curiosity.

On their return that evening, they all felt satisfied that a fortune was in store for them, but my Patroon in particular felt the most happy, as he could now defy alligator and shark, and exhibited a small deer's horn filled with dust, which was to protect him against all watery monsters, and for which he paid the value of a small slave.

As I was detained one day longer than I expected on account of provisions which could not be got ready before, I determined to see the far-famed African Doctor Rowback, and taking four yards of cloth and a few pounds tobacco, I sent for my landlord and called on the teller of fortunes.

Let not the reader here suppose that I was credulous enough to believe any part of this native's reports. My object to visit the Black enchanter was only to satisfy my curiosity, and to observe what means this Doctor used to convince his countrymen out of their goods.

This Negro necromancer had perched his abode in a cave on an elevated rock near the riverside, and the road to it was a dangerous zig-zag path amongst rocks and bushes. As we neared the place, my conductor gave several whoops, which I supposed was to give notice to the wizard that strangers were at hand. As we entered the cave, the man of importance caused us to make a good long *antichambre* before he made his appearance, when a long growl resembling the angry cry of a crocodile announced his arrival.

As he emerged from the inner part of the cave, a tall figure presented itself with a young leopard in his arms. His countenance could not be seen, as he was covered from head to foot with black monkey skins such as used in cheap muffs. A small blind boy followed him.

We all took seats on rawhides, and my conductor informed the black mask that I had come to have my fortune told, for which I had brought the necessary presents, which we exhibited. The young leopard, who had been taught to carry, dragged each piece to his master, which he duly measured and balanced in his hand to ascertain the correct weight. Taking then a bamboo, he placed it at the ear of his blind boy and whispered what the boy repeated aloud.

His first question was "what I wanted to know first," as one of the boasts of this learned Doctor was that he could speak all languages. I
spoke to him in Spanish. As his answer was not analogous with what

I asked, and I reprimanded him in the native language, he imperi- *1828
ously waved his hand and told me to wait, that he understood me
perfectly, but that his magic power would not allow him to make
answers but in rotation to the order of things.

I saw the trick and requested him to speak my language (the
Spanish) and let his boy repeat the answers in that tongue. I spoke in
the native dialect in order to let my conductor know what I demanded. This was a puzzler to the magician, and after a little
consideration he informed me that it not being full moon, he was not
permitted to speak foreign languages.

I requested him then to tell me my fortune by telling me the past,
of which, like all his brother magicians, he told a pack of nonsense.
But the future was somewhat romantic: I was to be a great Prince,
immensely rich, and have 100 wives. The most important fact was
that before six months my factory would be burnt, and that I would
lose my vessel.

As I had heard also much of his sleight-of-hand tricks, I demanded a performance of the same. A rope was produced and
several knots tied with it, when with a jerk they became untied. This
trick, which astonished the natives, was no new thing to me who
understood the manner of slippery knots.

A long knife was sunk deep in his throat and a glass of water
poured in, which was well done. Several other fooleries were performed, but the most remarkable was the handling of hot iron,
which he did remarkably well. However, in this operation he
anointed himself with a vegetable paste, apparently glutinous,
which frizzed when the red-hot iron came in contact with it. I have
since seen such operations done by the other natives, and invariably
when burning coals or red-hot irons were used, this vegetable paste
was besmeared on the hands or feet.

Years after, I visited another such necromancer at Gran Cavally,
east of Cape Palmas, but through the noncompliance of some formality, I was prevented from conversing with him.

The Burning of My Factory

25 May,
1828

On my return to my factory, I hastened to arrange my affairs in order to take passage with the *Feliz*. The loss of the *Ninfa* required my presence in Cuba, as I wished to report to the owner her loss myself.

I had just collected the necessary quantity of rice for the homeward passage of the *Feliz*, and everything was going on toward a prompt departure when the following catastrophe blasted for a month my future plans.

It was on the night of 25th May 1828 at 3 A.M. when the voice of my servant calling on me at my door to rise and save myself awoke me from a very pleasant dream. I sprung from my cot, and on opening my door, the brilliance of a red light told me that the premises were on fire. I stepped forward in the yard and there I saw the roof of my house on fire.

No time was to be lost. One hundred fifty kegs of power was a danger to be avoided, under a thatch roof 120 feet long. I could not for a moment think of escaping the blast by a prompt removal; the quantity was too great.

I hastily returned to my room and seizing my gun, fired the two barrels, which I knew would arouse my people, and running to the barracoon where 220 slaves were confined, I called the watchmen to open the trap doors. In the meantime my men had collected, and with the assistance of a few strangers who the report of my gun had alarmed out of their bed, I succeeded in marching off my Negroes in a wood till the danger should be over.

In my haste to depart, I forgot my servant, who not knowing the danger of the powder, remained behind and with laudable exertions made several trips back and forward to save my personal property. Having completed his first object, he returned to the house and insisted on saving the dog, a large bloodhound which resisted by several bites the friendly hand who exposed his life to save him; and fortunately the last bite was so severe that the boy retreated to watch the property he had saved.

A few minutes after, with a tremendous blast the powder exploded, shaking the earth for several seconds, even as an earthquake in Chile.

On my return to my factory, not even the coals of the fire remained; to the distance of a rod round the place was swept clean.

In a few minutes my boy returned, frightened to death, his nose and ears bleeding profusely. His hiding place had been over a musket shot away, in a deep former well; the concussion had been so great that the earth had fallen on him and nearly buried him.

The prediction of the Matacan fortune teller had been sadly realized. The detonation of the powder was sufficient messenger to the neighbors to inform them of my misfortune. In two hours my houseless factory was visited by all my friends, who according to the custom of the country, proffered their services to rebuild my lodgings.

Of all my rich goods which my store contained, I was left without even a mess or rice to feed my people and slaves, and thanks to my boy, a few clothes only were saved. I felt my loss much more, as in this fire was destroyed ten tons of rice, the provision for the brig. Having no goods, I was at loss how to replace it. In the emergency I exchanged Negroes for rice and in a few days successfully dispatched her with a complete cargo.

As the fire was discovered at the top of one of the gable ends, I conjectured with my old landlord Ala-Ninfa that some mischievous hand had set it on fire. This suspicion was corroborated by the fact that the conflagration was foretold.

Every method of investigation was resorted to, but our labor was fruitless till a stranger appeared at the next village and exhibited for sale my double-barreled gun. The Chief of the village knew the gun and requested to know where he had got it. The exhibitor pretended to have purchased it at some distant town from a stranger, but his answers were so confused that he was arrested and sent to me. On further inquiries, the true thief of my gun was divulged and proved to be a messenger from the wizard, whom I caused to be arrested and executed.

In his confession, I found that the brother of Mongo John was the principal mover in this affair. The last words of his brother had been reported to him, and believing me a too-fortunate antagonist in his future advancement, had resorted to adopt the vile incendiary to ruin my prosperous circumstances.

Disgusted at so much enmity, in a few weeks I left the river with intent at some future time to give the new Mongo of Bangalang the benefit of a free passage to Cuba. My proposed intent I never put into effect, as a few months afterwards my animosity had abated.

CHAPTER 45th

I Abandon the River and Seize a Portuguese Slaver

*1828—1829 Having made my arrangements to leave the river, I left every one of my servants under the care of Ala-Ninfa for the benefit of my partner Joseph and went in my boat to Sierra Leone. Here I purchased a schooner condemned by the Mixed Commission Court for the benefit of the captors.

At Sierra Leone in 1829, prize vessels were publicly sold and fitted out with very little trouble for the coast of Africa. Availing myself of the nonchalance of the Government officers, I fitted my schooner in perfect order to take in a cargo of slaves immediately on my leaving port. My crew consisted of prisoners from prizes and men of all nations; however I took good care that my officers should be Spaniards.

On the second day out, one of my crew, a smart young sailor, while at the helm informed my Mate that he had belonged to a vessel then in Rio Noonez, and that the Mate was supposed to have poisoned the Captain to appropriate to himself the vessel and cargo. He himself had left her on account of bad usages; the said vessel had been shammingly fitted out at St. Thomas on a coasting trade, but in reality for the Coast of Africa, and she had no papers. Her coasting register had been sent back to St. Thomas by a sailing boat, and she was then nearly loaded with slaves.

I believe that the slave trade was never carried on with the punctuality that all smuggling traffics should be, and gentlemen commanding slavers have in general forgotten that title when accidents or misfortune deprived them of their cargo. In order to receive a good reception from their owners on their return home, they have in many instances availed themselves of their superior force or ingenious cunning and unscrupulously deprived others of cargoes which they themselves had lost.

In 1828 and '29, many severe engagements took place between these kinds of smugglers, and Spanish slavers would attack the Portuguese when opportunity and prospects offered. Many vessels were fitted out for this purpose from Cuba, and safely returned home with a live cargo purchased with cannonballs.

As I was not different from others of the same cloth and I then loved a little excitement, my vessel also sadly wanting a cargo, I considered in my Don Quixotish opinion that my mission was to redress this Captain's death and chasten the villainous Mate. In order to effect my purpose I returned to Rio Pongo, and while I fitted out my vessel with a long nine-pounder cannon, I sent a native spy by land to Rio Noonez to ascertain the facts in regards to the Mate's conduct toward his Captain and report to me the true nature of the armament of this unregistered vessel.

The tenth day my messenger brought me intelligence that the sailor's declaration was correct, and that the said vessel lay up that river with 185 slaves; moreover, that in a few days she would sail with her complete cargo of 225.

The time was propitious, and every circumstance favored my enterprise. Even the number of her slaves was just the quantity that would conveniently fill my vessel. Such an opportunity could not be neglected. I hastened my departure, and on the fourth day, entered the Noonez.

As I had only a Portuguese pass to the Cape de Verde Islands, I hoisted that national flag whenever I passed some vessels.

I know not if my messenger had been imprudent and his indications had given suspicions to the crafty Mate, but at my arrival at Furcaria, the vessel was not at her former anchorage. Here, then, was a sad disappointment. I could not proceed any further with my vessel, as she drew too much water, and I was not acquainted with the river. I let go the anchor and seized on the first canoe that was passing. For a trifling reward I was informed that the schooner, the object of my search, was at Kakundy, the King's place, and hidden in a bend of the river; that my vessel could not be gotten there but by a pilot, and only a French Mulatto nearby could undertake the job.

This French Mulatto was a great rogue. He owed me five slaves which he refused to pay, and no offer of mine could induce him to give me his services. I made a resolution to seize his person by force and bring him on board. The tide being favorable, I landed about 12 o'clock that night with six of my crew. I surrounded his house and knocked at his door. My Mate called him by name, and on making his appearance, he was seized, gagged, and brought on board.

On finding out that he was under my power, his fright was great. He supposed I had seized him for his debt. However, I soon undeceived him and requested him with a sufficient reward to pilot my schooner up to Kakundy. But again the obstacle of my vessel drawing too much water was argued with full and convincing objections, and I resolved to board her without delay and bring my projected prize down alongside of my vessel.

My two boats were immediately manned with small arms and dark lanterns. The oars also were muffled, and with the pilot under the lee of my pistol, in twenty minutes we were alongside the schooner. With a frightful English hurrah we boarded her on both sides, and discharging our pistols in the air, drove every soul below. Two sentries were placed at each cabin and forecastle door, and the cable shipped. My largest boat took her in tow, myself and the Pilot at the helm.

Once over the danger and the rocks far on our stern, I recalled my boat and with the assistance of all my men, the schooner's crew was secured in irons. Great was their astonishment when they found themselves in the hands of a brother slaver. They had imagined themselves prisoner to some man-of-war. I was glad the self-made Captain was on shore, revelling with the King.

By morning I had transhipped 197 slaves into my hold, and the prize vessel was anchored in the middle of the river. Five of her men and the Second Mate, who appeared disgusted with their former Mate, now Captain, refused to remain with him and shipped with me.

At 10 o'clock as I was making sail, three canoes came blustering down the river full of men, the King at their lead. But one single round from my gun scattered their bellicose approach, and I proceeded out of the river. Captain Scarborough of Baltimore gave me three cheers as I passed him; being acquainted with the murderous conduct of the Mate toward his Captain, he was overjoyed at the punishment I had inflicted on him.

CHAPTER 46th

I Meet a French Cruiser · Narrow Escape · Mutiny on Board · Their Punishment

Being July, the rainy season had set in, and the winds continually blowing southwest with strong currents from the same quarters, I made but little progress toward getting off the Coast. On the tenth day I was still in the longitude of the Cape de Verdes, when at daybreak, under a shower of rain, the first lookout at the masthead called out, "Sail-ho, under the lee." From the deck the intruding stranger was invisible, but the Mate, who had mounted the crosstrees with a spyglass, corroborating the fact, I silently tacked ship, when the Boatswain's call from the unwelcome consort was distinctly heard on our decks, immediately followed by a musket shot which passed through our mainsail. This settled the question: the unwelcome and intruding stranger was a man-of-war, and had espied us nearly as soon as we did him. *July, 1829

Every sail was trimmed to the best advantage and the position of our slaves changed, sometimes a little more forward or more astern accordingly as I judged her best rate of sailing. The head stays were slacked and the wedges of the masts taken off. Every encumbrance from the deck was also thrown over the board. The enemy, who had imitated our maneuver and was in full chase of us on the same tack, gave us now and then a shot from his bow chasers which only perforated our sails but did not disable us from carrying a full press of sails. The wind had somewhat increased, and I perceived the enemy was gaining on us, when another shot took part of the rail and wounded our foremast three feet from the deck by taking a large splinter from it, which rendered it dangerous to carry on a crowd of sail on the same board. I again tacked ship in an instant, when to my astonishment I found the vessel sailed one knot faster on this port tack. A few more shots from our antagonist passed us without crippling any of our spars, and by 10 o'clock I was free from the troublesome cruiser.

The danger past, we repaired our damages and proceeded on our voyage without interruption. The death of my Mate, who fell overboard in the night while inspecting some work on the forecastle, is the only remark of note made in this journal. No assistance could be given him, as it was dark and a heavy sea running; my Second Mate took his place.

We were then near the Antilles, and instead of joy and cheerful countenances, I remarked a sullen deportment in part of my crew, even at times a disposition to question my orders. My Second Mate, the same who had shipped in the Noonez, I found several times in close conversation with his men on the watch, and his behavior of late strongly denoted discontent and disobedient feelings.

This conduct appeared to me strange, as the sight of land generally creates merriment both in the crew and the slaves, who at the sight of the first island are all liberated from their shackles and allowed (in daytime) free intercourse with the females. The tank of water is also left open at their disposal, and from this moment forward these men who were subjected to close confinement as dangerous enemies are now permitted to mingle with the crew their former masters. The cat-of-nine-tails has been cast into the sea, and its owner shares his biscuit with the Ethiopian passenger who now, free from his irons, stares with an avid look at the long-sought land, his future home.

The strong discipline which we forcibly compelled them to obey is relaxed, the sight of land dispels all danger of a revolt, and although order and obedience are still attended to, still the captive enjoys a new life till the day of landing.

Our sailor, with the generosity proverbial to his caste, distributes with the independence of a millionaire to his Black friends his last shirt, reserving to himself only a clean suit to land with.

The women, who most need a covering, are also soon rigged out from the Captain's, Mate's and Petty Officers' wardrobe, and sheets, table cloths, and spare sails are soon torn in strips to adorn their loins. Even boots, shoes, caps, and oil garments are sought with avidity by the now contented Black emigrants, who dress in this masquerade and with new expectations before them, forget in part their long privations.

The deportment of my Mate was such that I taxed him openly before the crew and told him to consider himself no longer an officer under me. His effects I sent forward and his doghouse—a temporary bunk on the quarterdeck—was immediately thrown overboard.

Having no other officer, I appointed two of the youngest sailors as my aides; the Cook and Steward who messed aft I knew to be faithful servants, and with four men at my back I felt perfectly safe, and from this moment I allowed no one of the crew to come abaft the main mast.

The same afternoon the Island of Puerto Rico came in sight. One of my aides, availing himself of the familiarity usual with Spaniards, offered me a cigarillo while I was employed over my chart. As I
never made use of tobacco in any shape, I good-humoredly rejected

the offer, when the man dropped it before my work. I then saw it was not a cigarillo but a small billet twisted in the same form. The contents informed me that a mutiny headed by the Mate would take place when in sight of St. Domingo, and I was then to be landed on that island. Six of my crew were implicated with the Mate, and my Boatswain who lay sick in the slaves' hospital (the forecastle) was to share my fate.

I immediately opened the arms chest, and ascertaining that all was correct there, I picked ten strong men from the slaves, whom I armed with a cutlass each and informed them in the Sosoo language that my Mate and crew wanted to run the vessel on shore and drown them all, therefore I wanted their assistance to secure them. My Petty Officers I also armed with pistols, and marching forward with my Black guard, I secured the Mate and six of his companions. A court martial where I was (like Captain Mackenzie)[1] the sole judge, was instantly instituted and the parties arraigned.

During the investigations, several flagellations took place, and the willful murder of my unfortunate Mate was exhorted when other means had failed. An excuse was made that the gammon lashing had parted. Being an important job to secure, the Mate naturally went over the bow to ascertain the best method to have it done, when he was knocked overboard with a handspike by the Second Mate.

The object of this revolt was to secure the vessel and cargo amongst the mutineers, regardless of the consequences.

At the summing up of the evidences I found that my life was to be spared if possible, on account of the good treatment that two of the implicated had received at my hands during their fever. The Mate would also have been spared, but being of a colossal stature, it was thought too dangerous to secure him, and he was disposed of by the advice and hand of the Second Mate.

The defense was but a poor specimen of the Second Mate's abilities in conducting into a safe harbor a slave vessel without documents or owners, and disposing of its cargo. The disculpation of his accomplices was based on accusing the Second Officer as the originator of the revolt.

After a severe reprimand, four of them were discharged. To the other two I inflicted a severe flogging and continued them in irons till our arrival in port. The Mate's punishment I left to the crew, who cast votes as to the punishment to be inflicted on him. After a long debate, they could not agree. Several were for inflicting the

[1] Alexander Slidell Mackenzie (1803—1848) hanged three would-be mutineers in 1842 and was exonerated in his ensuing trial.

same death with which he had treacherously murdered his superior, while others were for making a raft and setting him adrift.

As I considered both these punishments too cruel, I proposed to chastise him in the same manner as he wished to serve me; and next morning I landed him with two shackles on his feet on Turtle Island on the north side of St. Domingo, with provisions for three days.

CHAPTER 47th

A White Squall · The Landing of My Cargo

*1829

The same afternoon while I was still occupied with the recent events and the destitute state of my Mate, a white cloud which apparently rested on the distant horizon presently disappeared, and a fog instantaneously rose around us which was no other than the forerunning spray of a white squall. And before I could give the least order, the vessel was nearly knocked down on her beam ends. The shock was so violent and unperceived that it sent everyone to the leeward. Our slaves, who lay unrestrained about the deck, slid with a frightful cry into the lee scuppers, then a foot underwater. As I was near the Helmsman when the squall struck us, I did not lose my footing, and by the assistance of the tiller ropes kept myself to windward.

The only order I gave was to the Helmsman to keep her away. But the rudder, being nearly out of water by the diagonal position of the vessel, had no power in her actions, and there we remained, expecting to capsize or lose our masts, till our square sail broke and shortly relieved us of its pressure. Fortunately none of our riggings or spars gave away, and the squall passing over, we gently righted to our former position.

In this unforeseen accident I lost two slave children who were neglectfully allowed to sit on the lee rail. I have recounted this incident as few sailors can boast of greater neglect and still come off with less damages.

The following day brought us to the south of the Island of Cuba, and before sunset my cargo was landed on a small beach nine miles east of Santiago de Cuba. Some sixty yards from the beach lay a house whose owner gave us all the hospitality customary on such occasion. His barn was immediately appropriated to the use of our slaves, and all the family was employed in preparing a mess for them.

As this was my first voyage to the south of Cuba, I knew no merchant in Santiago to whom I could consign my cargo and my unregistered vessel, which now lay on the Coast discharged of her contraband cargo but unprotected by any flag. The cargo safely landed and secured from the grasp of the greedy cruisers, I prepared to depart for the city in search of an honest merchant to intrust with my live cargo.

Accompanied by a guide, I mounted a spirited horse and in a few minutes I was on the road toward the city. My guide, who pestered me with thousands of questions, in return informed me that only a month ago a vessel belonging to Matanzas had landed a cargo of slaves, which were consigned to a Mr. M., a Catalonian. I immediately formed my resolution to trust my all to this man. His only title to my esteem was his nationality.

The Catalonians, a numerous body of industrious merchants, traders, and mechanics, have been much abused by the natives and disaffected Creoles of Cuba. The Spanish papers edited in New York and New Orleans daily traduce them in the blackest color. I know not what political cause the editors of those papers may have against these Spanish settlers to villify them before the whole world as pernicious to their advancement. I can only say that had the Creoles half of the energies, the capabilities, the industry, the will and courage of Catalonians, they would not remain an hour longer under the yoke of Spain. Even the 30 thousand bayonets of Her Faithful Majesty's troops would only be a feeble obstacle to the enterprising, honest, enduring, and martial Catalonians.

With due apology for deviating from my narrative, I return to the subject. I introduced myself to Mr. M. and informed him of all the circumstances connected with my vessel, and her destitute state.

That day the Governor was informed of my arrival and the total number of the Africans (this is the name given for Bossal[1] slaves) was also duly reported. The Commander of the Port was also applied to, and in a blank page of his port register was inscribed the name of my schooner, as having sailed from that port six months previous. A registrar and a blank muster roll was then furnished to secure an unquestionable safe entry in port.

At daybreak next morning I returned in company with my agent to the place of landing with a suit of clothes, cap, and blanket for each slave. The schooner, now a Spanish property under the name of *Santiago*, was sent into the harbor under charge of a pilot who was to act as her Captain—a formality necessary for the satisfaction of the boarding officer, and as the man had been well schooled by my agent, no suspicion was entertained by the inferior officers of the port. A few days after, a sham public sale was effected and the vessel was perfectly secured.

At this time, the slaves once landed and the head money paid, no civil, military, or foreign force could interfere with them. Minc I allowed to remain 48 hours to recruit and acquire a stately walk. Part of my men who had been left on shore to guard them, acted ladies' maid to the females, and *valet de chambre* to the male part of the slaves to perfection, and the ill-shaped Lemburg-made garments were put

[1]Spanish slang for a horse's bridle; thus, a slave still new to captivity

on with all the ship-shape Bristol fashion style of a sailor's rough hand. The razor had closely officiated for the last time on all their black skulls. The old also, with the assistance of razor and soot from our scuppers (in the place of John Jones Hair Dye) were transmutated from grandfathers into decent prime fellows.

Under the escort of my men and two native guides, this cargo of slaves was marched into the City of Santiago at daylight and comfortably housed in a store to be sold at retail. My crew were paid off without exceptions or diminution made to the mutineers. In the punishment of their leader, I forgot their crime, and as I considered my business management in perfect hands, I took a stroll in the country for a month.

My crew, who had received a double pay as a renumeration for their daring action in seizing our cargo in Rio Noonez, now went about town half intoxicated, boasting of their good success, and one of them, a French sailor who had been swindled at cards out of his whole voyage, in his despair applied to the French Consul for relief. The incongruous vaunts of my crew had reached the ears of the Consul, and now that one of the said crew applied to him for protection, he availed himself of his destitution to use him as a witness against myself. I had been reported to him as a native to France, and the punishment of my Second Mate, who was also denounced a Frenchman, was magnified into an unjustified cruel act.

The French representative immediately laid the whole matter before the Governor, who gave orders to the Captain of the Port to arrest me and my vessel. As no such person by my name could be found, and my vessel, as I said before, had entered the harbor with Spanish papers and Spanish crew, the accused schooner had never entered port. Therefore the complaint of the Consul was reported to the Governor as a malicious fabrication; that night the press gang seized my braggadocio crew, and as no witness could corroborate the Consul's complaint, the whole affair was never more mentioned.

CHAPTER 48th

Loss of My Slave Vessel on the Bahama Banks

1829—1830   Three months after, I left Santiago in my schooner for Kingston, Jamaica, where I purchased a suitable cargo of English merchandises for the Coast, and returned to Cuba to fit out for a cargo of slaves, and in a week sailed again for Africa.

On the third day, after toiling against a severe gale for 24 hours, my main mast gave way just when most needed, and having the land under my lee I was obliged to run my vessel on shore. The night was dark, and the shore appeared a mass of sharp rocks dashed by continual high breakers. The land I knew to be one of the Enagua Keys, where no anchorage could safely be effected. Therefore in despair I coasted the breakers for a few minutes in search of a friendly nook to deposit my crippled vessel when a white spot denoted the appearance of a short beach. This was an invitation to save our lives, and I lost no time in squaring away for it, dead before the wind. At the first shock, our only mast went over the side, but the vessel was halfway up the beach, where she remained stranded forever.

At daylight I observed that we had been cast on the Small Enagua,[1] consequently uninhabited. Every valuable was landed, and with our sails, spars, and sweeps we rigged awnings and there deposited such of our provisions and cargo that had not been totally damaged by the bilging of the vessel.

By sundown we had succeeded in securing the most valuable part of the stores and cargo, and after a hearty meal we prepared to lie down to a well-deserved night's repose. And as the wind had totally abated, every one of us had anticipated a safe retreat from the night dews, when the buzzing of a well-known insect gave us notice that this solitary rock was inhabited by the dreaded mosquitos, and on they emerged from the crevices and the dwarf bushes with the voracity of hungry wolves. The expectations of a good night's repose proved a failure. Not a moment's repose were we allowed by these musical insects. No covering would keep them away, and till the sun rose, everyone was kept on his feet stamping and brushing them away.

After breakfast two reconnoitering parties were sent in opposite directions to scour the island, while the rest rigged a mast on the

[1]evidently Little Inagua, to the north of the Windward Passage between Cuba and Haiti

highest part with a flag as a signal of distress. On the return of the men, nothing had been discovered but an abundance of pools of rainwaters lodged in the concaveness of the rocks. A large dog was discovered with a collar on his neck, but he could not be made to approach, and I would not allow him to be shot.

For the second night we made preparations against the annoying mosquitos. Our tents were continually filled with tobacco smoke, but little rest were we granted, and our repose was deferred again till daybreak.

One of my boys of very light complexion was so much mortified by these voracious insects that he lost his senses and never recovered them till long after his return to Cuba.

Several vessels passed us at great distance, and no one took notice of our signal of distress. But on the eighth day, a couple of small crafts indolently made their appearance and their services could not be procured but at very exhorbitant price. Finally it was agreed that they would take my cargo and crew to Nassau, New Providence, and the average should be decided by the court.

I readily agreed to this proposal, having the greatest confidence of an English court, but the result proved otherwise.

Our cargo was landed at New Providence and put into the hands of a commission agent to be sold at auction. Three or four persons, proprietors of the wreckers, with one of themselves for judge, formed a court, and a document was given the wreckers and myself to sign which bound us to abide by the decision of the court.

I made my statement to which hardly any notice was taken. The wreckers did the same, when several notes were taken and many hums and exclamations made. This wise court then proclaimed that out of the proceeds of my cargo I should pay the wreckers 70 per cent for only shipping my cargo from Enagua to Nassau as a salvage. I could not understand why such salvage was allowed them, as I saved all the cargo with all my crew, but my document was there to stop all argument: the judges had decided in their favor.

Thus many unfortunate mariners find in New Providence a temporary asylum at the cost of four fifths of their property, an abuse practiced only on foreigners.

I Ship as Sailing Master in an Armed Brig
the St. Paul · The Smallpox

1829—1830 I returned to Cuba with very small capital, and as I could not get the command of a vessel, I accepted the situation of Sailing Master in a brig which I was to join in St. Thomas. Her Commander was a Frenchman, an experienced sailor but short-sighted.

On my arrival on board in the Harbor of St. Thomas, I found the *St. Paul*, a Brazilian-built brig over 300 tons burden with ten port-holes. In her hold were 16 twenty-four-pound carronades. Her magazine was well stocked with powder and hand grenades, and her keelson was lined fore and aft with round shot and grape.

Her Commander, who had been represented to me as a martinet and a Tartar, received me kindly and was much delighted at finding I spoke the French and English languages fluently. As a Danish man-of-war was expected in port, we made all the haste possible to leave the harbor before her arrival. Our stores were tumbled in anyhow, and our water tanks filled in one night, and before daylight, 55 ragged men of all colors, castes, and nations were sent on board as a crew.

By seven o'clock, with a coasting flag flying, we were two miles at sea when from a small schooner we took in six kegs of specie and several chests of clothing. The second day out two sets of uniform clothing was distributed to our men with the request that they should be worn on Sundays and when called at quarters.

The officers also were provided with a blue coat, anchor buttons, a single epaulet, and a gold lace cap with a side arm. Both in the officers and men, the style was of the French regulation.

The distribution made, the Captain called the whole crew on the poop and informed them of the object of our voyage, which although a slave voyage was not an ordinary one. It was partially explained to them, and they were dismissed with the promise that if our voyage proved successful, they would all receive a gratification of $100 each besides their salary.

After supper this same evening I was called in private conference with the Captain, when he informed me that he intended to take his cargo in a Portuguese port in Mozambique. To effect his purpose he had fitted out his vessel with a good armament sufficient to repel a man-of-war of equal size (an illusion I never believed in), and on all occasion except a French man-of-war, he would hoist a French flag

and pendant. He had distributed uniforms for the express purpose,
when necessity called, to appear as a French war vessel, and as the
crew was to receive a premium on our safe return, the officers also
should be entitled to double salary. And he handed me a certificate
for the same for the two other officers; I was presented with a
memorandum book where instructions for the whole week were
noted and a remark which instructed me, as next in command, to be
punctual, just, and severe with my inferiors.

In a few days I had mounted the 16-pound carronades, and with
the assistance of a little seamanship and paint, the vessel had undergone the appearance of a small sloop of war and according to
instruction, our men were called to quarters thrice a week to exercise
the guns.

Our small arms also had been put in order and placed in a handy
and appropriate place, ready for use twice a week at the exercise of
cutlass review or sham fight.

The wind favoring us, we made the Cape de Verde Islands the
27th day out. We took some water at St. Antonio, shipped ten men,
and loading our decks with livestock, we shipped our course for the
Equinoxial Line. The voyage proving prosperous, we rounded Cape
Good Hope in 66 days, and till this day we had passed several vessels
without speaking to them. But at midday a sail was described on our
starboard bow, going on contrary tack, and apparently with the
desire to speak with us.

We kept our course when we observed the stranger taking sails
and the French table cloth at the peak. Shortly after we perceived
she sported a long white pendant, which we well understood the
meaning of. Our drum called all hands to quarters, and the signal
chest was brought on deck. Presently the French transport (such
was the stranger) demanded our private signal, which out of our
hundred flags was immediately answered, while at our peak we
hoisted the Portuguese royal flag.

As we neared one another, our guns were double-shotted and
matches lighted. When within hailing distance, our Captain, who
considered himself superior officer to a Lieutenant in command of a
transport, hailed him first and demanded where he was from.
Several demands and questions passed, ours in Portuguese, the
others in French, when the Frenchman begged permission to send
his boat on board with letters to be forwarded to the Isle of France.
The request was granted, but the French Commander was informed
that we had several cases of smallpox which we had probably got at
Angola, and could not invite his officer on board.

The words were hardly spoken when the Frenchman squared

away, braced sharp up, and made off with all haste, not even giving
the customary salute.

In ten days we anchored in Mozambique amongst several
Spanish, Portuguese, and Brazilian slavers. The sails were clewed
up and a salute of 20 guns was fired under the French colors. In a
short time it was answered, and our Captain, in full uniform of
Commander, paid a visit to the Governor. I was left on board with
orders to mimic the man-of-war by firing a gun at sundown and
striking the yards at the same moment, and all such *mode de guerre*. I
had also orders to get underway the instant the fort would signal a
vessel, and meet him at a small beach off the port.

Next morning the cash was sent on shore in the Governor's boat,
and the fourth day we left for the government factory where we took
in eight hundred Negroes. Therefore, the eighth day after our
arrival we had completed our cargo and were underway on our
return home.

Our Captain, who understood the cupidity of the authorities of
this place, had hit on the idea of personating the man-of-war with a
double intent. First, in a port where many slavers were anxiously
and impatiently waiting for their cargo of slaves long due, the arrival
of a French man-of-war vessel gave them no suspicion and did not
interfere in their business. (It must be understood that at the time we
anchored at this port, there lay some 14 vessels of large size, all
awaiting their cargoes. Some had been laying there 16 months in
expectation of their slaves, and to such pitch had their patience been
wrought that the Masters had all clubbed together and agreed that in
future, every vessel should take its turn according to the seniority of
the time anchored in port. Thereby, in acting the warship, we
finessed them out of a cargo of 800 slaves.

Second, as our vessel had been built for a vessel of war, she could
not be mistaken as such, and by a little mockery, some arrogance,
and a dash of boldness, we could impose on the now and then
credulous or indolent cruisers. However, our Captain, who had
much of the chivalrous about him, ever insisted on assuring me that
we were able to fight a crusier of our same mettle. But the *Ninfa's*
engagement with the boats had taught me a different lesson.

Our Captain had returned on board with a slight attack of the
chills and fever, which confined him to his cabin most of the time.
His bilious temper suffered much from this confinement, and in a
short time he became worse and at times delirious, ever imagining
himself in fight with a man-of-war.

We had been off Cape Good Hope for several days, buffeting a
continuation of contrary gales, when after a long night of watching

and toil I was made aware that several of our slaves were discovered with the smallpox. Reader, this is one of the greatest catastrophes that can happen to a slaver. I ran to the cabin to inform the Commander of our calamity; I had not perceived that he had been laboring all night in a fit of hot fever, and still his imagination retained part of his delirious visions. His answer was, "Blow the ship up!" and as I stupidly stared at him, he again repeated the words and rising from his bed, opened his bureau. And there lay a long coil of combustible ready to ignite at will, and pointing to it, he ordered me to set fire to it.

With much trouble and gentle but forcible means, we secured him in his bed, when the coil of combustible (which connected to an iron chest in the powder magazine) was disconnected and a sentry set to watch the roving-minded Captain.

During the gale which had lasted nine days, our slaves had forcibly been neglected. Not once had they been allowed to visit the decks. The gratings had been partly covered during the gale to keep the slave deck dry from the seas and rains. The wind sails could not be kept up, and ventilation had circulated but slightly during the time.

At the first announcement that a slave had been found dead by the morning inspector, the Officer of the Watch had inspected the body, and its appearance denoted the well-known token of smallpox. It was kept silent from the slaves and the body thrown silently over the board. After breakfast I visited the slave deck with lanterns, and to my great dismay, nine of the slaves were found affected with the dreadful disease; far too many to stop the pestilence with laudanum—a fatal remedy forcibly used, but secretly and seldom resorted to.

The sick were immediately placed in the hospital (the forecastle) and every precaution taken that only those of our crew that had been vaccinated should attend them. The lower deck was fumigated, and chloride of lime sprinkled at every habitable part of the ship, and nothing was left undone that would stop the progress of the epidemic.

The abated gale lasted two days longer, and the number of the sick had accumulated to 30. The dreadful scourge was progressing with giant strides, the hospital could not contain one more, and 12 of my men had caught the distemper. Before night of this day, the number of deaths amounted to 15.

Reserve was at an end. Dead man after dead man went over the board as they expired, and the day that we conveniently opened all the gratings, our consternation rose to its climax. Nearly all our slaves had the distemper. Twelve of the stoutest were singled out to attend to the dragging out of the dead from the sick, and although they were constantly fed with rum to brutalize them in the disgusting job, still we were forced to have recourse to such of our crew as were not affected, who with tarred mittens picked up the still warm bodies to remove them to the porthole.

A further description of these horrors would disgust the reader from further perusal of my work. Suffice to say that our misfortune ended only when 497 living skeletons were left out of eight hundred prime Negroes shipped a few weeks before in good health.

CHAPTER 50th

Continuation of the Same Voyage · The Three Flags, the Three Registers · Impertinent Approach of a Small Cruiser

We had now crossed the line, and the room that the deaths had left was a great benefit to the convalescent ones, as there only remained 480 out of a cargo of 800, and our crew mustered still some few above fifty persons. The slaves had not been secured since the fatal plague. We also allowed them provisions and water in great quantity, and as I said above, with the great room and liberty they enjoyed, a few more days restored them to perfect health.

Not so with our Captain, whose debility became dangerous. The fevers had long left him, but a dysentery of former years suddenly reappeared, and his decline was visible every day. In his somewhat hypochondriac state he imagined that a dose of mercury in powder or calomel would surely relieve him. Unfortunately, our well supplied medicine chest had been left open several times during the great mortality on board, and the bottle of calomel could not be found. Once informed of the missing medicine, the invalid became more desirous for it, and nothing but these mercurial powders could save him.

In this dilemma, we kept lookout for some merchantman to obtain the drug. The next day about noon we spied a vessel two points under our lee, and as her sails were much patched and of a very dark hue, I considered her some collier bound for home and of course very harmless to us. In due time I came up with the brig *B*. of Belfast and begged him to lay to his vessel and allow my boat to board him. The ingrate did not mind my polite invitation and without answering me, continued on his course, neglecting my second and still more polite request.

Impatient at his contempt for our pendant and man-of-war appearance and not a little piqued at the disregard he paid my starboard epaulette, I ordered the vessel alongside and lashed his vessel to mine. I then boarded him with a dozen men and demanded of the Scotch Master his log book. To the Mate I commanded to write to my dictation.

I again called on the stubborn Scotchman and desired him the use of his medicine chest, offering payment for the same, which he indignantly refused. My demand and the refusal were noted by the Mate in the log book. Two of my hands with his Mate I then ordered below in search of the medicine chest, which when brought up turned out to be but a sorry rattletrap with a few old drugs. However, the desired calomel was found in abundance. I took one third and presented the Scotchman five silver dollars, which were also refused. I handed them to the Mate, who gave me a receipt and noted the same in his log. I then offered my services to the Captain and his crew, which the first treated with contempt while the others accepted with pleasure. I handed them several yams, a bag of black beans, a barrel of pork and two sacks of white Spanish biscuit. My generosity reconciled the smiles of the Scotch Skipper. We shook hands and parted friends.

Our Captain did not ameliorate with the Scotch medicine, and his end was fast approaching. Still the spirits of his hard nature did not forsake him; from his bed he daily issued his orders as usual.

Being today Sunday and according to rules established, the drum called the men to quarters, and after exercising the guns for a short while, the Captain desired to inspect the men. He was brought on the deck in a mattress, and every man filed out before him and shook hands with their sick Master. He then called them in a body and informed them that he had made his will, as he considered he should not live to see the shores.

His first article in this testamentary document was that should the vessel arrive safe, every man and officer should receive the promised gratification, and the proceeds of his vessel and cargo should be sent to Nantes to his friends.

Second, should the *St. Paul* be attacked by a cruiser and by their exertions, the crew defend our vessel and take her into port, then the half of the proceeds of the voyage should be divided amongst the officers and crew. Of the other two quarters, one should go to his friends, the other solely to myself. His consignees in Cuba and myself were his testators.

We were now to the west of the Barbados, and in every cloud we could see the constancy of the trade winds which gave us every expectation of a prosperous ending to our unfortunate voyage, and a crowd of sail was steadily pressed on the *St. Paul*. Vessels were seen daily, but none appeared suspicious. But as we rounded the Island of ———, to the westward we saw a schooner jogging under easy sails. My spyglass soon told her capacity of a cruiser. Not taking any notice of the stranger, I continued on my course, but prepared for a brush.

Not knowing what flag to hoist, I visited the dying Captain to take his last commands. Having been informed of the suspicious

craft hard in chase of us, he pointed to one of the drawers of his bureau and told me to take out the contents. I unlocked it and took out three flags well bundled up. Each contained a set of registers and documents to suit the *St. Paul.* I was desired to choose, as by his feeble words I found they were all saltwater documents.

Of the Danish, Portuguese, and Spanish flags I chose the latter and prepared to leave the cabin poop when the moribund man called me back and stretching his arms to me, begged that I would not surrender. The hard grasp of my hands satisfied him, and I left him in the arms of the Steward.

On my return on deck I perceived the schooner had neared us within three miles' distance. Her sailing was much superior to ours; she went two knots to our one. Escape was an impossibility. I determined to show the inquisitive stranger (who had fired two blank guns) my flag. I fired a lee gun and hoisted my Spanish ensign and pendant, and still kept on.

The *St. Paul* was going at the rate of six knots when another gun from the cruiser sent a shot close on our stern. All studding sails were taken in at once, and as my men had been called to quarters some time ago, I expected their appearance during this maneuver would impose on the troublesome stranger, and for a while, I expect, it did so.

Such was the velocity of the enemy that in four hours after we first saw her, she had neared us now within half gunshot, and was fast approaching with the daring of a well-fitted man-of-war. I had allowed my eleven carronades to remain unloaded and chose now this moment to intimidate the crusier by loading them under his eyes. At a word of command, all the ports went up and every cannon muzzle made its appearance. The operation of loading went through in style, and every man remained at his post.

Now all my belligerent show had not the least effect on the armed stranger. His impertinent demand showed how little he valued my war-like appearance, and when within hailing distance he called out to heave to or he would fire.

I was prepared for this arrogant demand, and for half an hour I had made my mind up how to avoid an engagement. A single discharge of my broadside would have sunk my antagonist, but the consequence would have been terrible hereafter. My object was to escape his boarding me, which I perceived was now his aim.

He still continued under full sail when he again called to heave to. We were then within pistol shot, the enemy under my lee. My answer was, "No entiendo,"[1] and I allowed the stranger to range ahead. In one moment I had him. Briefly I gave the order to square

[1] "I don't understand"

away, and putting my helm up, I struck the cruiser a little abaft his bows, carrying away his foremast and bowsprit. Not a musket was fired on our side, and such was the surprise of the stranger that we got disentangled before he took any action against us. But it was then too late. The loss of my jib boom and a few riggings did not prevent me from hoisting again all my studding sails and making off.

The following night the Captain died, and the third day after this event our cargo was safely landed nine miles east of Santiago de Cuba, and the *St. Pablo*, sent adrift, burned to the water edge.

CHAPTER 51st

My Greediness Is Recompensed with the Loss of 12 Thousand Dollars

By the Captain's will, I became possessor of 14 thousand dollars, *1829—1830 and my restless spirit did not long allow me to remain idle. The last successful voyage had created me many friends amongst the slave ship owners. Every day an offer was made me to take fresh command.

My last voyage had created a desire in me to imitate my former Commander, and as I had reserved the three different registers, I proposed to the proprietor of a large Baltimore clipper brig to fit her out on the same plan as the *St. Paul*. But wishing to surpass my old Captain and make the voyage more profitable, I suggested the idea of fighting for my cargo, or in plainer words, relieve another slaver of his cargo—a project which found immediate favor in the grasping eyes of my partner (the proprietor of the *La Estrella*).

Such was her name. As the vessel as she stood cost her owner twelve thousand dollars, I proposed to put in twelve thousand more for her outfits and become half owner.

The bargain was struck and every preparation for the projected voyage was made: armament, larger sails, additional riggings, and provisions went on board without show or ostentation. Everything was managed with secrecy and prudence. As we could not leave port without some show of cargo, several goods were taken out from the public bonds (or the customhouse) and put on board, and by night smuggled on shore again. This maneuver was a suggestion of my partner, who gained by the operation. I did not even take notice of what came on board, as it was to go ashore at night.

I shipped forty-five men and cleared the *Star* under my own name. Next morning by daybreak I was to sail with the land breeze. Everyone knows, or may guess, a sailor's last night on shore. Mine was attended with all the customary ceremonies: a parting supper, champagne here, a trip there, and an embrace everywhere, with a parting glass at each place. This was the only sober leave taking.

My time was taken up till two in the morning, when on retiring to my lodgings with a splendid headache, I found the servant at the door, who had for several hours been in search of me. The note he put in my hands informed me that my vessel had been seized by the Collector of the customhouse and that the Alcalde had issued a warrant for my person. My partner, the author of the note, advised me to secrete myself from the hands of the *alguaciles*[1] till he could arrange the affair.

Not to make this chapter longer than necessary, I will only add that my partner was himself arrested next morning and the vessel confiscated. In the brief time of 24 hours, my wings were cropped at the tune of 12 thousand dollars and my safety doubtful for several weeks. I escaped by leaving for the country and taking a new name.

[1]constables

CHAPTER 52nd

*Cha-Cha, the Celebrated Factor · Captain Lopez's Account of the Human Sacrifices of Dahomey · The Ju-Ju of Unin

The last speculation brought my funds to a very low ebb, and my   *1830
wanderings I therefore directed to Matanzas. Here, shortly after, I
took charge of a vessel for Africa. As this voyage was attended with
many incidents and misfortunes, the reader must prepare himself
for three long and tedious chapters.

My new craft was a schooner newly arrived from the United
States, and her name was the *Venus,* her burden only 120 tons. My
employers fitted her for Ayudah on the Gold Coast, and her cargo
consisted principally in rum, powder, English muskets, and rich
cottonades from Manchester; and it was calculated that I should
bring home a cargo of 450 slaves.

Having fitted her with the necessary accommodations for a live
cargo, I left Matanzas for the Cape de Verdes (the usual port of
dispatch). In due time we arrived at Praya on Cape de Verde Island,
exchanged there our flag for a Portuguese one, and proceeded on our
voyage to Africa.

Off Sierra Leone a large English cruiser gave us a long chase, and
while the breeze continued strong, she neither gained on us nor lost,
but her shots often sent spray on board, the velocity and motion
being too great to aim with accuracy. The wind luffing, we ranged
ahead of our enemy, one knot an hour. Having such a powerful
antagonist in sight, I availed myself of this consortship to find out
the best sailing trim of my vessel and kept purposely in sight for two
days to experiment with my craft.

Two days after, our mast head gave notice of a vessel ahead.
Confident of the well-experienced qualities of my vessel, I gave
chase for another trial. In a short time I could distinguish her flag
which being tricolor, I immediately took for a Colombian, and as she
hove her sails to the mast and fired a gun, it affirmed in us the idea of
her being a privateer. As I was well armed and the breeze was
strong, I took a windward position, and hoisting my Spanish flag,
sent her a shot through her jib. A second would have followed, but
for the supposed Colombian hoisting a white French flag to his peak
in lieu of his tricolors.

My spyglass soon assisted me in reading her name, *Esperance of
Bordeaux.* We both lowered our boats and met halfway. From this

1830 French Captain I first heard of the Revolution of 1830 and of the ascension to the throne of Louis-Philippe as the Citizen King. We exchanged civilities, saluting his flag by lowering mine three times, and each one went his way, him to Brazil, us to Ayudah. My cargo was landed in the factory of the famed Cha-Cha, a noted slave merchant on this part of the coast.

Cha-Cha was the native name of this celebrated Brazilian slaver, who many years ago had landed in the neighborhood of Ayudah, a deserter from some regiment in Rio de Janeiro. His first days in Africa were full of troubles and misery, but the start of the Brazilian slave trade which took place after the abdication of Don Pedro the First, Emperor of Brazil, soon placed him in a position to set up as commission agent in this traffic. His long and previous residence on the African shores, with his taste for native customs and manners, had also given him the privilege of speaking fluently the native dialect. A turn of good luck brought him into notice in the commercial slave community of Brazil and Cuba.

On my landing at Ayudah, I presented myself to this *parvenu* (I call him *parvenu* as when I handed him my invoice, he requested me to read the items). Cha-Cha, whose Portuguese name was De Susa, a Mulatto by nature, had received no education. Born of very poor parents, he had enlisted in the revolutionary troops against Don Miguel of Portugal. The cause of his desertion is not flattering, but suffice to say that his astonishing career was not due to his education, but to the influence he had gained in the country and the Interior.

I found Señor De Susa a perfect native, still retaining with the whites the manners of his forefathers. His having accepted my cargo and on conditions of giving me at the expiration of two months 480 slaves, I took my quarters with a native Manfuca,[1] visiting Cha-Cha every week but never accepting his invitations.

De Susa was noted for his generosity and hospitality to Captains and supercargo of slavers, but many of them had dearly paid for the famed prodigality, as Cha-Cha was also accused of paying them off at the long run by setting his empty warehouses on fire to avoid the payment of their cargoes.

Just before leaving Matanzas I had taken information in regard to De Susa's character, and a shipmate who had been scalded by the cunning and prodigal insinuations of this ex-soldier had put me on my guard against his machinations, and by avoiding his well-served table, his billiard rooms, and the company of his debauched sons, I

202   [1]trader, broker, or interpreter

succeeded in commanding such respect that by the end of the allotted time, I shipped my cargo.

Had I been aware that my episodes of Africa would one day appear before the public, I should have noted many occurrences that would interest the reader; I would also have visited with other Captains who by invitation from the King of Dahomey (some four days' journey from Ayudah) attended the yearly human sacrifice which takes place in May, and I can only now narrate but the description of an eyewitness who had accepted the invitation and had returned perfectly cured of his curiosity.

During my sojourn in the different parts of Africa, with the exception of the Bagar Nation at the mouth of the Rio Pongo, who adore nothing, I ever found the Ethiopian a believer in some Superior Power. The Foulhas, the Mandingos have their Koran; the Sosoo believes in good and evil spirits; one has their pray or book men, the other their Doctors or fetish men, while the first believes in a future hereafter and the latter in the transmutation of the body. The Mahometans, adoring their Maker with many genuflections and ablutions, strictly adhere to the Laws of Moses as written in some chapter of Leviticus on clean meals, leprosy, and marriages. The Sosoo respect a goat's horn or fetishes which their cunning Doctors prepare and, with many incantations, sell them at high prices to keep off the evil spirit or to render him favorable.

At Ayudah I found the natives still more Ethiopian, as they believed the good or evil spirit to exist in the living iguana. The house of my Manfuca landlord had several running about his premises, which were daily fed by his slaves and in no way allowed to be molested, even when these pet animals struck a sharp blow with their tail to a passerby. Such is the respect paid to these animals that the death of one of them in a house is regarded by the whole family as a calamity, and strangers are admonished against doing them injury. The people here had no belief but this.

The great sacrifice which was to take place at Dahomey had for its object to satisfy the virulent divinity who (they believe) once a year demands at the King's hands a torrent of blood for the benefit of his forefathers. Not having inspected this wholesale sacrifice myself, I translate the narrative of my friend, Captain Augustin Lopez.

"We started, as you well remember, for Dahomey the last day of April with the Manfucas of the King and Cha-Cha's interpreters. For three days we traveled, resting in hammocks at night and received at every village, partaking of an abundant repast prepared by De Susa's cooks.

"The day after our arrival at Dahomey, we were presented to the

King, a well-knit Negro dressed with profusions of silk shawls, petticoat, trousers, yellow Morocco boots, and a *chapeau bas*[1]. He was surrounded by a regiment of female Amazons, each holding a musket or a lance. The Manfucas and interpreters, crawling on their hands and knees, deposited at the feet of the King Cha-Cha's tribute and our presents. The first consisted of several pieces of crepes, silks, and taffetas with a large silver basin and pitcher. Our slight donation was 100 pieces of blue dungaree with 20 muskets.

"The whole was accepted with grace and the donors were made welcome by the invitation to attend his kingly sacrifice, which was delayed on account of the scarcity of victims. But we were assured that orders had been given to storm a neighboring tribe to make up the 300 slaves for the feast. In the meantime, a spacious house was given us, furnished in the European style. Liberty was also granted us to enter every hut and help ourselves with everything we chose. He gave us to understand that all his subjects, male or female, were his slaves and at our disposal.

"The 6th of May was announced as the beginning of the sacrifice, which was to last five days. Early in the morning 200 women armed with blunt cutlasses (they were naked to the waist but richly ornamented with beads and rings at every joint) made their appearance before the King's palace in a large area and marshaled before their lord, keeping pace with their rude but not unharmonious music.

"At some distance from the palace, a mud fort had been built 9 feet high, and surrounded on all sides with a pile of briars of astonishing growth. Inside this fort stood secured to different stakes 50 captives (the same that were to be immolated this day). At a gesture from the King, one hundred of these females departed at a run, brandishing their weapons and yelling their war cry, toward the fort and mindless of the thorny barricade, sprung to the top of the walls, tearing their flesh as they crossed the prickly impediment. The dispute was short, as fifty of these female warriors soon returned, each with her victim torn to pieces, and presented them to the King, who opened the sacrifice by striking with the cutlass of what he considered the bravest Amazons the head of one of the doomed captives. The same instrument was then presented to us by these females, inviting us to partake in their brutal feast. We not only refused, but left the area, never more to witness the horrors of such buchery, which lasted till noon when the Medusas returned to their kingly barracks drunk with rum and blood. And for five days we were doomed to hear the yells of the repeated storming party as they assailed the fort for fresh victims.

"Previous to our leaving Dahomey, we had a parting interview

[1]hat which he held in his hand

with the King when he received us on his royal throne, better
nominated a stool. This native chair is said to be of twenty genera-
tions or more, and each leg rests on the skull of some native king.
And such is the fanatical respect for this sedan commodity that
every three years the people of Dahomey are obliged to furnish the
fresh skull of some noted Chief or King to renew the position of the
stool."

I learnt from the interpreters that these female warriors form the
harem and bodyguard of the King of Dahomey. Their virtue and
bravery is a noted fact and is proverbial with the natives. At the
moment my friend Lopez visited Dahomey, he only saw 200, but
seldom has the King less than 300, who are generally well-built
women. Adultery and cowardice are punished by death; a jury of
themselves condemns and punishes the culprit.

I have limited the narrative of Don Augustin simply stating the
barbarous sacrifice, leaving the reader to imagine the atrocious
barbarities that were exercised after the second blow. I have noticed
that with barbarous nations, the sight of blood generally excites a
frantic desire to mutilate and fiercer blows, just as a tame tiger which
becomes furious after it has smelt blood.

My limited time at Ayudah gave me but little opportunity to
observe the customs and manners of the natives. Still I found much
similarity in habits with other tribes, the male ever lording over the
weaker sex, and polygamy here is carried to a greater perfection.
Even amongst the civilized residents, a man is valued according to
the quantity of his wives, but female chastity is not so highly insisted
upon as in the Mandingo and Sosoo country, the husband content-
ing himself with the apparent virtue of his concubines. My con-
signee Cha-Cha had eighty wives. Wonderful how a civilized man
becomes accustomed to native habits!

It is not so sixty or seventy miles south in Rio Unin or Onin. The
adulterous wife of a chief is poinarded in the presence of her relations. Here also, superstitions have instituted human sacrifice
which their "ju-ju" carries with a high hand, but not to such extent
as in Dahomey. One victim, and that a virgin, is sufficient to satiate
their revengeful deity. Having witnessed the whole jubilee, as it is
looked upon by the natives (with the exception of the victim) as a
feasting day, I can perfectly describe the horrible scene.

On the first appearance of the moon of November, the King of
Unin publishes an ordinance that his ju-ju will take his yearly tour
around the town, and it is prohibited to remain out of doors after
sundown. Such is the dread the inhabitants have toward this demon
that even the fires are extinguished in their houses.

About ten o'clock, this Satanic evil spirit issues from a sacred bush (taboo to all but their fraternity) and accompanied by ten stout men all masked like himself, enters the town, each sounding some discordant instruments whose fearful sounds strike terror to the believers. As I could not account for such dismal and terrific sound, I made inquiry from one of the initiated, and for the value of a musket, he brought at night the instrument. It was a piece of board one foot square and an inch thick with a hole in the middle, where a cord made of hide ran through, being a foot long, and when slung with velocity above the head, it creates the most abominable of sounds. And woe to the drunkard or straggler who may have the misfortune to be loitering in the streets. The heavy mace of the Devil's Committee soon dispossesses him of his life.

Every door is by order left ajar for the ju-ju's free access, and at the frightful noise, every inhabitant lies face down to avoid the basilisk[1] sight of the irritated spirits.

The choice of a premeditated victim is agreed upon before leaving the *gris-gris* or sacred bush, but to instill a Satanic fear, the ju-ju promenades the town till daylight, entering a house now and then and committing a murder or two just to create more dread. One hour before daybreak, they enter the house of the victim, which is ever the belle of the town, seize her and carry her off, the parents and friends not being allowed, under pain of death, to look up or utter a complaint. The next day the unfortunate mother must ignore the whereabouts of her child and is forced to appear perfectly contented at the choice of the ju-ju. Such is fanaticism.

On the third day the King and his fanatic subjects meet at the riverside all dressed in their best and wearing their best smiles. The band of music salutes the King, and as by magic the victim in a state of perfect nudity is brought forward by a doctor, soothsayer, or fortune teller (all these capacities are combined in one) who now acts as the executioner. The naked and living offering, no longer a maid, marches with measured steps. She is not recognizable even to her mother, as all her body and face is painted with thick white chalk. Her appearance indicates no fear, and her actions seem paralyzed. Her eyes appear fixed to a distant nothing, her arms glued at her sides, and although her head is erect, it is carried without pride.

Once before the King, she is made fast hands and feet to a bench near a trunk of a tree. The executioner then invokes a blessing on the people, and with one blow of his blade sends the head rolling into the river. The trunkless body is then placed on a mat and laid under a large tree, there to remain till the spirit carries it to the habitation of the just. At night, it is removed by the same ju-ju.

[1]fabulous creature said by the ancients to kill by its breath or look

The reader will be gratified to learn that the ju-ju, or this African divinity, is nothing more than the principal of a religious fraternity who from time immemorial (to Africans) have instituted themselves into a secret society for the purpose of domineering the more ignorant of their fellow brothers. By force of superstition, fanaticism, and bodily fear, this set of priests exact from the credulous confessions, which are in due time represented as divined by the Oracle Ju-ju. The fellows of this secret society are also masters of many medicaments which serves them to paralyze the body as well as the mind. Such resort was used no doubt with the victim I have just mentioned.

The King is the sacerdotal Priapus of ancient mythology, as the virgin's purity is first sacrificed by him, and his chiefs are generally officers in this confrerie. The costume that this ju-ju wore on the night of his promenade at Unin was well adapted to inspire fear in his fellow countrymen: he wore a long petticoat apparently made of long black hairs, a cape of the same material with a hood which covered his head, and a wooden mask. To make it more frightful to their African notions, they had given it a sharp nose, thin lips, and painted it white. The hands were covered with tiger's paws.

CHAPTER 53rd

*A Slave Revolt on Board the Venus

*1830—1831 My vessel having returned from the two months' cruise, I shipped 460 slaves and sailed homeward.

On this voyage I had no interpreters as in other voyages, and the discipline of the slaves was carried on by the force of the lash. Many complaints which could be rectified if the case had been understood were dismissed, when the complainer might have received redress. I saw a good deal of discontent among my slaves, but although I endeavored to treat them with kindness, still my goodness to them was not appreciated. A few days after, a slave in a fit of madness leaped overboard, while another choked himself during the night.

These two suicides in one day caused me much uneasiness, as in them I saw a germ of revolt. Every precaution was taken against a rising, but it finally took place when we least expected it.

We had been at sea twenty-one days, and my apprehensions against a revolt had nearly worn away. Everything appeared as peaceable as could be expected. The slaves also wore a better countenance, and when made to dance or sing, it was done with better grace than before, when the whip had had to urge them to participate in the amusements.

As I said, I was pleased at the return of their mirth, when one afternoon at the appearance of a windy squall, I called all hands to take in sails. The Boatswain's call repeated my order with his shrill silver whistle, a call well known, I suppose, to the slaves, then off deck, as a sound calling all the whites to ship duties. This moment they had chosen for a revolt.

My men had hardly got on well with their duties when a rush was made simultaneously by the slaves at all the hatches. They busted them with little difficulty, and up they came, armed with sticks of firewood and staves from broken water casks. The first guard at the main hatch was knocked down senseless, but not so with the fore hatch; the guard, finding his knife useless for the occasion, took the Cook's axe nearby him and with this weapon kept them at bay. The women in the cabin, seconding their fellow male prisoners, rose in a body on the man at the helm, who with his knife wounded several and silenced them.

The blow that knocked the first white man gave me notice of the revolution. I called on my men to desist from their duties and to arms; by this time about forty stout fellows had got on deck and with their wooden missiles disabled five of my men. However, the arms chest was at hand, and the Steward and myself kept command of the quarterdeck till some of my men could join me while the rest protected themselves and the wounded with handspikes.

The poor Cook, who had orders on such occasions to distribute boiling water on the belligerents, flew to his coppers at the first notice of the revolt and with ladle in hand, endeavored to baptize them with his slushy water. But it was some time after dinner when this happened, and the fire was then extinct; consequently, one blow of a billet of wood sent him and his ladle bleeding to the lee scuppers.

As I saw nothing short of firing into them would stop the revolt, I gave the order to shoot, but lo! Our carbine had been loaded on purpose with small buckshot. The first two discharges brought several of them on their knees. The lead had told in the parts desired, but still that did not stop the advance of their wooden projectiles. Two more discharges drove them forward amongst the greatest part of the crew who, unarmed, receded on the bowsprit. With my small party of five men I took command of the hatches and then with the arms chest in my favor, I contended a few minutes longer with about fifty men, the most part of them slightly wounded. A half dozen more firings (some blank cartridges) silenced them, and they were driven below again.

The flying sails were then attended to, and again we proceeded to the revolted slaves who now were fighting against themselves. As no one could venture below by the hatches, several men were sent well armed with pistols and cutlasses into the cabin, having previously taken the women out. Two boards of the bulkhead were taken out, and up marched my men on their hands and knees amongst the revolutionists, who boldly defended themselves with their staves.

By this time the fires had been rekindled and the water was boiling. The hatches were kept open and all the non-fighting men allowed to come on deck. But still many of the bullies, confident that we did not shoot or strike to kill, defied us with their blunt billets.

As only about sixty still remained below, I ordered my men to press them forward against the bulkhead. Then several auger's holes were bored in the deck to allow the hot water to cool them, and wonderful to relate, a few ladles soon brought them to terms. Still, two savage-looking chaps clung to their staves and dealt most dangerous blow after blow on my men. As the hot water irritated them more and more and they could not be made to give up, their sentence was uttered, and two pistol shots disarmed them forever.

Order was again restored and the wounded attended to. Two of my men were severely wounded, and 28 bullets were extracted from one wounded slave. One woman and three men died from their wounds, besides the two that would not surrender.

The cause of this revolt I never could account for, as the slaves from Ayudah and its vicinity are generally humble, docile, and gentle to manage. However, I am confident that in this revolution they were not united in one will, or we should have had harder work to subdue them. And it was flattering to me to think at the time that in their rising they had no personal ill will toward me, as not a billet was thrown at me, although I fired first amongst them.

CHAPTER 54th

We Are Forced To Administer Laudanum ·
Landing of My Cargo Under the Fire of a Man-of-war

Nothing more happened to us worthy of narrating until we made the *1830—1832 Island of Puerto Rico, when I perceived a few red pimples on the face of a youth amongst our attendant slaves. His pulse I found quick, and his eyes swollen. With a trembling hand I took him forward in the forecastle and free from the contact of anyone else, left him there incommunicado till I could take further security against the pestilence; this was a case of smallpox.

Next morning I called the Boatswain, an old tar well experienced in the trade, and requested his opinion on the present case. His answer was in a whisper. "We are lost if he is allowed to live," he said, "and you guessed correctly when you separated him from the rest."

On our return abaft, the eyes of the crew and my officers were on us. Everyone had conjectured the malady, and they all feared the result. Still such was their tremor that no one asked me a question.

The danger was great, and a speedy decision was necessary. I called my officers to a general inspection of the slaves, but not confiding to their judgment, I minutely examined every one of them. Finding that the present case was the only one existing on board amongst my slaves, I caused my men to subject themselves to the same operation. And I am sorry to say that in the second examination, no marks were found with which I could save the Black boy's life, for one more case amongst my people or the slaves would have saved me from having recourse to the same resort that Napoleon proposed to his Surgeon in Chief in Egypt, where he was forced to leave his sick and wounded to the scourge of the pest or the sure murderous rage of the Mahometans.

That evening, in the stillness of the night, a trembling hand stole a large portion of laudanum and furtively carried it forward to the afflicted boy. The poison was administered, and next morning a necessary murder had been committed. One of us, I am assured, could not eat his breakfast that morning.

A voyage attended with such misfortune could not end felicitously; ours was not prosperous, as the reader will see. From the meridian of Puerto Rico we had several gales not usual that time of the season, and it became doubtful if we could safely arrive at *211*

Matanzas, as our provision had become very scarce. On making Cape Maize, a corvette gave us chase. I was to the leeward of her, and consequently I was obliged to square away before the wind. By night I altered my course and returned on my old route. But confound the fellow, at daylight he was again windward of me and held the same maneuver the whole day.

I thought of dodging him that night by continuing on the south of Cuba, but I believe the British cruiser had smelt my track. Next day I espied him a long way astern, in full chase after me.

The wind had lulled that night and it still blew a light breeze, but the red clouds rising from the east gave notice of a strong gale from that quarter. Therefore a longer chase would have given great advantage to the enemy. My safety lay in making the small port of Uruguay, the same where I had landed two cargoes before. We were then twenty miles' distance and the cruiser ten miles astern of me. I took no delay in resolving I must lose my vessel but save my cargo. Orders were given to strike off the irons of the slaves (I had kept them all confined since the revolt). The boat was also made ready, and every man had prepared his bag for a launch.

On came John Bull, foaming at the bows, and when the full force of the breeze struck us, he was within seven miles and the friendly beach within three. The Englishman perceived our purpose and by every resort urged his vessel on. The crowd of sails he had was frightful considering the rising gale. He watered his sail with f   pumps, but he gained nothing on our light craft now that the breeze had struck us also, and sailing before the wind was our craft's bread and butter. The three miles were soon run, and with but a small movement of the helm, she was forced one third of her length on the beach, still calm from the approaching seas.

As the *Venus* struck the contrary element, her beautiful tall mast fell overboard, not injuring a single person. Our boat was in the water a moment after with a load of women and children who were given in charge of my old friend the Patroon of the buildings spoken of in a former chapter. Others of my men rigged a stage from the bows to the beach with two booms and slid the slaves and baggage into shallow water as fast as they could—but not fast enough, for the Englishman was approaching.

We had landed nearly half of our cargo when the inveterate cruiser appeared in full sail at the mouth of the haven. To back her sails and lower her boats was the affair of a few seconds; however, it gave us time to send ashore a few more, and we did not desert our

unfortunate vessel till the firing from the marines began to tell on board. The ship also began to fire on us, but it was too late. Men and slaves were a mile inland.

As a wreck, the *Venus* with about 90 slaves fell a prize to the daring cruiser, who shipped them to Jamaica and burnt the unfortunate craft.

My Sixth Trip to Africa · A Voyage of Vicissitudes, Trouble, and Imprisonment

1832—1833 My last voyage was not very profitable either to myself or my owners. Still, it gave enough to clear the first cost and fit a new vessel.

This was a regular pilot-boat-built vessel from the Chesapeake, her tonnage but 96 tons but a sweet-spirited craft. As she came into port with a large gilded eagle on her stern, we named her the *Aguila de Oro,* or *Golden Eagle.*

As usual, we sailed for Cape de Verde, but on account of some difficulties with a new Governor, we could not change our flag. Here we found the far-famed schooner *Montesquieu,* formerly a privateer out of Jamaica and on the same mission as ours—after slaves.

The pride of her Commander was such that he would not allow any vessel to compete with his in sailing. Now ours was half of the *Montesquieu*'s size, and with equal pride we contested the palm in sailing qualities. The challenge was accepted.

Each of us placed 500$ in a bag, and as I was the challenged one, the bag was tied to the end of my main boom for the challenger, the *Montesquieu,* to come up and take. Such was the agreement of the race.

We both left port in company with the understanding that once clear of the harbor, the *Golden Eagle* should have five minutes to start ahead, when we were both to crowd on all sail we could and the race should then be considered fairly begun.

As my antagonist of the *Montesquieu* had publicly boasted of this challenge, promising the bystanders to return after the victory and expend the 500$ in a *déjeuner* at the expense of the "Yankee pilot-boat," such was the name given to my small craft. Therefore on the day of sailing, the eastmost cliff of the Island of Playa was full of spectators to witness the regatta.

At the appointed time, that day, the 1000$ bag was made fast to the foot ropes of our main boom by the Boatswain of the challenger, and we both weighed anchor for sea. As we were the first out, we awaited the *Montesquieu,* and when within a musket shot ahead of her, at the mutual signal agreed upon, we kept her away sailing two points free, our best point of sailing.

214 The challenger did the same, and with the confidence of famed

superiority, did not at first spread all his canvas. But as we distanced at an enormous rate, he soon made all his sails in earnest. The breeze was then blowing steady and strong; we had cleared the island, and by keeping one point more away, we should then give our vessel her favorite position for sailing. We did so, and by sunset, adieu to the *Montesquieu*. The bag was taken in by our own Boatswain.

Four days brought us to the mouth of River Salum, an independent river between the French island of Goree and the Gambia River, in possession of the English. This river had not been visited by a Spanish slaver for many years; consequently, my arrival caused some commotion in the country.

The King's town of ――― is some forty miles in the Interior. I took the schooner up and made agreement with the King for a cargo of 275 slaves. I had just concluded my bargain with the King when I was informed that men-of-war boats were alongside of my vessel. I made all haste on board and found that one boat had boarded, but my Chief Officer had not allowed them to inspect the hold.

Five days passed without any more molestation from the French, when one morning, while arguing on the price of my goods with the King, I was seized by his own men and delivered into the hand of the Second Lieutenant of the French corvette the *Bayonnaise*. I was then sent on board of the man-of-war and my schooner taken charge of by the officers of the *Bayonnaise*. As no treaty existed between France and Spain for the suppression of the slave trade, I could not comprehend the cause of my seizure.

On our arrival in Goree, myself and crew were confined in a prison, equal for diminutive dimensions, perfect darkness, and want of air, to the notorious Black Hole of Calcutta. As we remained incommunicado for three days, I could not make any case known to several friends, inhabitants of the island, whose influence would certainly have proved beneficial.

The Chief Colonial Tribunal sits only at St. Louis in the Senegal River, also the residence of the Governor General. There we were sent on board of the *Aguila de Oro*, under an escort of a dozen marines and a competent crew and officers.

The Colony was then at war with some of the Moorish tribes 200 miles up the River Senegal. The arrival of my vessel came very apropos to the Government, who needed such a vessel to send and protect the returning flotilla of merchant crafts from Galam. Therefore my vessel was armed and sent away on her war mission the second day after our arrival, without any scruple to ascertain if she was a *bona fide* prize. Here again we were incarcerated in a military cachot to await our trial.

My arrival was made known to several merchants who had known me at Rio Pongo, and they called on me. The degrading imprisonment was immediately notified to the Governor, a brave sailor, who changed our quarters to the Military Hospital. Our quarters, although well guarded with iron bars at every opening, were made very comfortable by the Sisters of Charity who had the civil charge of this establishment. The Abbess, with that truly Christian charity which made their self-devoted institution so proverbially and universally respected, left nothing undone for our comfort.

CHAPTER 56th

The Trial and Our Attempt to Escape

Our trial was delayed a long time. Finally at the end of one month, we were notified that the Court had appointed a Sergeant in the Marine Guard for our defensor, and our trial would take place at the end of the week.

*1833—1834

As no other lawyer could be procured, we had recourse to the Sergeant, who would perhaps have made a tolerably good defense if the Prosecuting Attorney, his military superior, had not imposed silence during the defense on several occasions. My schooner had by this time made two trips in the hands of naval officers who, not understanding the quick maneuvers of an American pilot boat, had ran her on shore several times with much damage to her keel and copper. Under such circumstances, there remained two alternatives to the authorities of the Colony: either to condemn the vessel or pay for her, as it was well known to them that I would never have accepted her back. When the trial took place, therefore, even every formality of justice was waived.

In my case, it was necessary for the Government to prove that our vessel had been taken trading in slaves in the dominion of the French Colony. This being the first and only point of accusation, the Prosecuting Attorney made a long accusation worthy of all Government accusers.

Our Marine Sergeant began by proving that Salum River was independent and that French and English vessels paid tribute to its King, when the Prosecuting Attorney—a Captain in the same corps—imposed silence on our defensor with a military reprimand.

Next a Mahometan slave was allowed to swear on the Holy Evangelist against us, and to crown this misdoing, the mock Court did not allow my lawyer another word in our favor.

As the judges were about retiring, I demanded to be heard, and with some reluctance they consented. Reader, I am no orator and still less a lawyer, but in this instance I thought myself a Cicero and a Webster. I pleaded my cause to some length, till I was interrupted by the judge, when losing my temper I threw invectives right and left. Judges and captors I abused without discrimination till two soldiers forcibly made me sit down.

A few moments after, the judges returned with my condemnation, and when the President asked us if we had anything to say, I replied that we expected no justice from a French inquisition.

Finally my men were condemned to two years' imprisonment,

my officers to five years, and myself to ten years' seclusion in the central prisons of France, all without appeal. Such was then the mode of distributing justice under the reign of the good Citizen King.

The sentence passed, we were conducted to our strong lodgings to await an opportunity to transport us to France. My condemnation had aroused the indignation of several merchants in St. Louis, as they plainly spoke of the injustice used toward me. Several proposed to afford me assistance for an escape.

As visitors were still allowed to call at my imprisonment, a blacksmith's saw was introduced to me and the assurance given me that that night, the bars of my window which gave on the street should be sawed off. A boat would transport me onto the opposite side of the river, where an independent chief would be in readiness with camels to transport me to Gambia.

I know not how the Government got indication of my projected escape, but in order to frustrate it, we were sent on board the station ship, an old steamer then lying in the river. My friends did not abandon me still, but a second time proposed my escape from the station ship. It was proposed that on a foggy morning, a party of these friends should pretend to be on a shooting excursion down the river, and as they should pass the station ship, they would call on the Commanding Officer, a noted hospitable *bon vivant*, and while in the confusion of boats alongside, I should slip overboard from the foremost part of the ship and swim for the beach, only fifty yards distance, where a swift canoe would transport me to a friendly ship.

Now this thing was very feasible, as the Commanding Officer of this pontoon allowed us full liberty to ramble all over his vessel. Therefore when the letter communicating of my proposed escape was put into my hand, I called my officers apart and informed them that on the first foggy morning, I would make my escape and offered any one of them to participate in my flight. My project was much discussed amongst them, but the idea of swimming at the risk of being shot by the sentries was a chance they did not dare to attempt.

Finding them fearful of the subject, I divided amongst them some three thousand francs in Government bills and gave my gold chronometer to my Chief Mate, wishing them a speedy delivery from their condemnation.

Next day it was a foggy morning, and about nine o'clock five boats made their appearance with several sportsmen and their dogs. I was anxiously watching their approach when a friendly arm slid through mine and its proprietor invited me to a deck promenade. It was the Commanding Officer who offered this civility.

I accepted this kindness without hesitation, as he had been assiduously polite to me during the five days I had been under his guard. His first remark was, "Captain, you take great interest in those boats. I wish you could participate in their sport. Unfortunately those gentlemen will not effect their intended purpose."

I pretended I did not rightly understand his meaning and made some evasive answer, and arm in arm, I was led to the cabin poop, the private quarters of these officers. Once seated, he informed me that amongst my officers there was a Judas who had sold me, and then proceeded in telling me how they had divulged the secret of my proposed escape to his Sergeant of Marines, who had duly reported it to him.

This information struck me all aback, as I had anticipated and almost imagined my escape effected. I stood stupefied with astonishment. The ingratitude of my men had deprived me of speech for the moment, when the cabin doors flew open and the hunting party made its appearance. The Commander received them with his customary kindness and desired them to be seated.

My dress that morning was a loose one quite unusual to former days. There I stood in the cabin with nothing but a very light coat easy to tear off and loose pants without braces. My shirt was unbuttoned at the neck and vest, and no handkerchief to my neck. My feet were also stockingless and incased in a pair of loose shoes. The first remark made by the Commander to these friendly gentlemen was in allusion to my dress and begged them to forgive me, jocosely remarking that I was prepared for a cold bath, but in consequence of his advice, I had postponed it.

The hint was understood by them all, when after a moment's reflection the officer informed them of the treachery of my officers, concluding by saying that he was indeed sorry their philanthropic purpose had not been effected by the information given to his Sergeant, which he was in duty bound to frustrate. He assured me at the same time that if my escape could have been effected without his knowledge, he would have been most happy of my safety and would patiently endure a reprimand from the Governor for his neglect. He also begged my friends not to attempt any more such undertakings, as under his inferiors' present knowledge of this affair, any further attempt would subject me to a severe confinement.

My officers were then called and before the whole company made to return to me the Government bills and my watch. I was also requested by the Commander to give my word that no further attempts would be made on my part to escape while under his charge. The kind Commander, my generous friends, and the reader's humble servant then sat down to a French breakfast which lasted till dinner time, and in the fumes of the wine, we all forgot the disappointment.

CHAPTER 57th

Transportation to France

After 15 days' more detention on board this pontoon, a gunboat took *1833—1834 us to the frigate *Flora*, then lying off Senegal. On our arrival on board, the First Lieutenant, who had received letters of recommendation in my favor and had been informed of the treacherous conduct of my officers, separated me from them by placing them under a severe restriction and treating them during the whole passage as prisoners. My lot was much better. Although the principal in the condemnation, I was ever treated by the officers of this frigate with kindness and due regard for my misfortune.

Our passage to France was short, and when the moment of landing had come, I regretted leaving so many kind hearts as the officers of the *Flora*. To her Commander, Mr. Kernell, one of the best seamen of France, I am also indebted for the delicate manner I was conducted on shore at Brest, while my officers and men were paraded through the streets to the prison by a brigade of gendarmes. And I shall ever be grateful to him for the kind interest he took in representing my case to the Home Department, which immediately commuted my reclusion to simple imprisonment.

Military and Civil Prisons · Episodes of
18 Months' Incarceration

1833—1834 The following anecdote should have been inserted in the preceding chapter, as it happened in the frigate *Flora*.

There were two Sisters of Charity on board the frigate, who having completed their five years' colonial term, were returning to France to join their order. These ladies occupied a large stateroom in the lower battery built on purpose for their accommodation, and according to ministerial ordinance, they messed[1] with the Lieutenants in the ward room.

It so happened that amongst the Lieutenants there was one who at every occasion mortified the ladies by ridiculing their callings and piety. Not content with those insults which were silently but contemptuously despised, he made use of several immoral expressions at the dinner table and finished by singing a profane, vulgar song. The Sisters left the table and next morning refused to take their meals in the ward room, simply soliciting the Steward to give them the common ration of the sailors in their cabin.

The charitable nuns were soon missed at the board, and when the Steward informed the officers of their resolve to exclude themselves from the ward room, the phantasm of a court martial struck the vulgarian officer into dismay. By a mutual consent, they all agreed to send the Doctor in the name of the whole mess to the insulted ladies and implore forgiveness for their guilty companion before the Commander should be informed. It is needless to add that the apology was granted, and the ladies returned to the officers' meals.

I have narrated this anecdote to illustrate the position that the members of this charitable order stand in the eyes of the French Government. In every case, a Sister of Charity receives the same treatment, either in a military hospital or on board of a man-of-war, as a Lieutenant; and their wrongs are redressed with a most exemplary punishment.

Retournons à nos moutons,[2] as a Frenchman would say.

As my men were paraded through the streets with a brigade of gendarmes armed *cap-à-pied,* I was landed in a private boat and, simply escorted by a midshipman, led to the prison in the arsenal.

This was a strong granite-built prison solely adapted for the

[1]took their meals
[2]Let's get back to our sheep

Marine Department, and as we were condemned by a colonial court, which is subject to that department, we were incarcerated here till further orders.

My men soon joined me, and as misery creates friendship, I soon made up with my officers. This prison was then inhabited by seventy or eighty marine soldiers and sailors, and the rules and regulations were under the inspection of a Naval Commissariat.

Two spacious rooms were given us for my men and officers, and the jailor, an amphibious subject, half soldier, half sailor, very kindly informed me that the whole premises within his jurisdiction should be free to myself and crew if we conducted ourselves with propriety.

As I was promenading a spacious yard, an elderly man with a shabby uniform stopped short before me, and with a military salute requested a few moments' conversation. Not wishing to disregard a fellow prisoner, I granted the request. The intruder then begged to know if I had ever been in a French prison, as he was deputized by his fellow prisoners to inform me of the regulations of the establishment. I did not hide my ignorance on the subject and allowed my instructor to initiate me in the mysteries of their craft.

Numerous were the regulations, but too tedious to report; only two I consider worthy of the reader's curiosity.

First, I was informed that on his arrival in a French prison, every newcomer was considered bound to the "Government boarders" (such is the name the prisoners styled themselves with) to pay his footing, and as I seemed the principal of the strangers just arrived, I was expected to stand the wine for the whole company. I complied with the request, and with a 20 franc gold piece paid the footing.

The second regulation was that, as we all slept under one roof and ate soup of the same kettle, we should consider ourselves as brothers. Therefore, it was expected that all the doings of the prisoners should be kept secret from the jailor and his turnkeys. Having agreed to the condition for myself and crew, I was assured that any adventure on my part for an escape should be assisted and protected by them.

At sundown, the jailor counted his boarders, ourselves included, and we were locked up, each party in their room, for the night. Next morning I was called on by the different members of this well-secured, professional and strong-barred institute; each one offering his services according to his calling.

First appeared a well-built fellow with the undress uniform of the marine soldiers, calling himself *Caporal* Laramé, *maître d'armes* or fencing master. He offered to teach me, or mine, the broad and small

223

sword at the expense of one franc a week. Next came another cosmopolitan-looking chap, one part sailor, the other two parts landsman and bully. He called himself Grand Provost of the Single Stick (or *Maître de Baton*). He also professed to teach us the useful art of his important profession.

Several others favored me with their calls, one as a composer (or letter writer), a second as dancing master, a third as teacher of violin, a fourth and fifth as tailor and shoemaker, and many others likewise pressed services as washerwomen and barbers. I promised to accept their offers when once better acquainted with our new lodgings.

After breakfast, by invitation of the fencing master, I visited the different rooms to ascertain if in reality their offers were genuine. I was chaperoned into every cell: here were the shoemaker and tailor on their bench, mending shoes and coats out of fragments of the same. A cell contained the violinist and dancing master giving instruction to several persons in the terpsicorian art. Another cell contained the Magister silently composing a love letter for a greenhorn who, on his knees, was admiring the pointed Cupid's darts with which the writer had adorned his letter. In the middle of the same floor stood the students of *Monsieur le Caporal* Laramé practicing with two wooden swords. In the corridors I saw several shops selling cigars, snuff, writing paper, and needles and thread, and in the remotest cell I found the gambling table and the pawn shop. On retiring, I treated my Cicerone with cigars and felt convinced that nobody but a Frenchman understood the secret of killing time in prison.

On my first landing I had addressed a letter to the Spanish Consul, informing him of the present state of 22 Spanish subjects and requesting the interference of our Minister in our case. Prompt to my call, he visited on us with an eminent lawyer who undertook to stay all proceedings against our condemnation. But as our Minister in Paris never took notice of misfortune, the good will of our kind Consul and the proffered assistance of the lawyer remained without effect.

During the three months I remained in this military prison I patronized the dancing master, took two month's lessons from the Caporal and the cosmopolitan *Maître de Baton*, and necessarily lost several games at cards. I also had my shoes mended, my old clothes well scoured and patched; in fine I fully patronized the industry of my fellow sufferers, at the small expense of twenty dollars, carrying out in the meantime the saying "to do, when in Rome, as the Romans do."

CHAPTER 59th

Continuation of My Imprisonment

*1834—1835

After three long months' incarceration in this military depot, we were transferred to the civil prison of Brest, a gloomy tower in the chateau of the same city. The trajectory from one prison to the other was effected in boats. I had not the mortification of being marshaled through the streets with a file of soldiers to guard us.

On our arrival at these new quarters, the jailor gave a full receipt for our persons to the Brigadier and distributed our men amongst the malefactors of his cells. As the appearance of myself and my officers denoted better circumstances, he proposed to give us a private apartment called a *salle de distinction*, on condition that we should pay him 10 francs per month. I accepted the offer, and we were conducted to a large room with two well barred windows giving into a narrow and somber yard.

The Madame Jailoress soon informed us that she could procure us beds for 10 sous per day, and as the prison ration was only one and a half pounds of black bread and water, she would kindly introduce the *cantinière* of the regiment stationed in the chateau, who would furnish us our meals twice a day from the petty officers' mess.

The kind offers of Madame Sorret were eagerly accepted; the cantinière soon appeared with two more females from the same regiment. A bargain was struck with the cantinière for our meals, which should consist of 3 dishes per meal twice a day, at 15 sous each, payable in advance. Her two companions were Spanish women, wives of musicians of the corps who having heard that several Spaniards had been incarcerated in the tower, had availed themselves of the opportunity to visit their countrymen.

These two Catalonian women had married in this regiment when the Duc d' Angoulême marched with French troops into Barcelona and had followed their husbands ever since on their return to France. Two of my officers were Catalonians; a friendship was soon established between us, and from that moment they became our daily visitors, running our errands and procuring for us all those little comforts which women alone can devise.

I presume but few of my readers are acquainted with the treatment and fare of a French civil prison. A slight sketch will illustrate the barbarous treatment a prisoner is subject to. As I said the only fare a prisoner had during the year was bread and water and nine pounds of straw a week to lie upon. No blankets or covering were supplied, even during the winter, and as there was neither fire nor stoves, the poor sufferers were obliged to roll themselves in the broken straw or huddle together in a heap to keep themselves warm. The Government allowed them no clothes; therefore those destitute of friends or means in a few days after their arrival soon became as covered with vermin as their fellow prisoners. As this tower had a yard, we were allowed a two-hour promenade only twice a week on a piazza on the roof, well guarded with soldiers.

Such is the treatment that 18 of my men had to endure during the one year they remained in France. I believe such is not the treatment in the central prisons, where the prisoners are made to work, but in small towns when the condemnation is not reclusion but simple imprisonment, the above description is a true representation of a French prison's horrors and miseries.

My poor sailors, after having disposed of all their spare clothing to moisten their bread with a little cabbage soup, remained nearly the whole year without tasting meat. Once only, during the anniversary of St. Philippe, the Sisters of Charity gave them several bullocks' heads to feast the day of the good King of the French.

CHAPTER 60th

Episodes of a Prison

*1834—1835

As our room was the only one which the jailor had a right to dispose of in the manner I have described, several other prisoners who were able to defray the expense were often locked up with us. On several occasions we were much molested by them, but on the whole, it amused us to have their company. Many young men of good family were often put in by the police when taken on a spree.

A few weeks after our arrival in this chateau, the jailor made his appearance one day and introduced what to us appeared a gentleman. His dress was exquisite, a large gold chain adorned his neck, and his countenance was genteel and intellectual. As every new arrival in our quarters was generally greeted by me (as I was the only one that could speak the French language), I came forward and welcomed the stranger. On retiring, the jailor made a sign for me to follow. Once in his office, he informed me that the new prisoner was accused of being a counterfeiter, but on account of his gentle appearance, he had placed him in our room and begged I would not be offended.

When I returned I initiated the newcomer in the mysteries of our customs, and as it was near dinner time, I informed him of the principal and most important condition of the initiation—the wine for the company. Two bottles settled the question, and I numbered him the fifth member of our mess.

I beg to inform the reader that by this time, we had partly learned the way to kill time in prison. Our Spanish female friends had supplied us with guitar and violin, which my officers used with some musical skill, and often we gave *soirées dansantes* to Madame Sorret the jailoress and her sister (an old maid). The cantinière and her two friends were also invariably of the party, and on the arrival of the genteel counterfeiter, we could form a full cotillion.

These amusements took place Thursday and Sunday. The rest of the week was passed in reading romances, playing cards, writing petitions, and cursing our hard fate and the French Government. These fits of passion were often uttered early in the morning when the sleeper would be awoken from pleasant dreams by the tramp of soldiers and the noisy turnkey drawing his bolts and unceremoniously proceeding to count heads and sound with his iron rod the heavy grated windows.

We had now been some months in prison, and my funds had diminished to a small fraction. It was time to look abroad for supplies. I wrote to my former English partner, then in Matanzas, who never deigned an answer. Shame prevented writing to my relations, and as my trinkets and watch had gone to pay the lawyer and our board, I had recourse to an offer made by the Madame of the jail, a truly good woman, to take in scholars in the English language.

This proposal had first been suggested to her by my lawyer, who understood a little English and had formed a superior idea of my rudiments in this language. Madame Sorret offered to allow me the privilege of her bedroom to give lessons, and her two sons, boys of fifteen and nine years old, should become my scholars, for which she would give me 15 francs a month. But her kindness did not end here: she had procured me two more scholars from the chateau, sons of officers in the Army. The lawyer, the first promoter of this plan, was to send his son and a young friend; therefore, before I had consented to become a teacher of foreign languages, I had a school formed of six pupils with a revenue of nine dollars per month.

As I entered in my new vocation with the spirit of a needy professor, I soon gained by my assiduity the good will of the parents. I also added another branch to my school: the teaching of handwriting, which so pleased my protectors and scholars that they voluntarily subscribed three francs more a month each.

That my scholars made great progress I would not dare to affirm, but I can assure the reader that the parents were much satisfied even after one month's teaching, and the pupils loved me as a companion. My method of teaching was altogether my own, and as I had only six scholars, I never discharged my school till every pupil had perfectly comprehended and reasoned his lesson. After one hour's lesson, I gave them thirty minutes' dialogues, each one at my interrogation naming the most useful articles of furniture, wearing apparel, instruments, and animals of creation. As this was carried on in a jocular manner, it amused them and taught them much faster than a given lesson. My school ended daily with a story of my voyages.

As I said before, I had no pretensions to teaching, as no one is less capable of such an office as a mariner, but that I pleased both parents and scholars in a proof that on the day I was liberated, they escorted me to the ship that was to carry me a happy exile forever from France. The youngest ones parted with me in tears.

CHAPTER 61 *st*

A Short Sketch of the History of the Exquisite Counterfeiter

I have said that this fellow prisoner had a genteel and intellectual *1834—1835* appearance. His manners also were refined, but for several weeks we could not get him to participate in our confidence. His reserve toward me was more remarkable than toward my companions. However, time the great emancipator of things brought him to a sense of sociability, but not till he found our my true character. Then I was informed that he had at first signalized me as a Government spy; seeing the liberty and freedom I enjoyed by the jailor and his wife, he had kept himself on his guard.

The first advance of confidence toward me was after the following circumstance. One morning I had set myself to writing a letter to my mother and sisters when Madame Sorret informed me that the Sisters of Charity, who visited the prison to distribute work and make donations of a few comforts to the prisoners, wished to see me in the parlor.

I promptly made some toilette and repaired to the call of the philanthropic Sisters. Having heard so much in my favor from the jailoress, they had wished to offer their services, which I accepted in the shape of books.

On my return to my writings, which I had left exposed on the table, confident that no one in the room could read Italian, I again took up the pen to finish my letter. I looked over the page, and it seemed to me that I had not written so much; still, there was my handwriting. I read over the contents, and there were several lines which although in perfect keeping with the above meaning of my letter, I knew I had not written, as they contained compliments that my nature never used.

I read them over again and again; still I could not detect where was the difficulty that puzzled me. I turned and returned the sheet over, read over again the contents without better success till, out of patience, I gave it up and put my writing materials away, when my roommates burst out in a hearty laughing. I was then informed by them that M. Germain—such was the name of the counterfeiter —had added to my letter those lines which I had not detected.

After this date, Monsieur Germain became quite a companion, and as he was not yet convicted of his crime, we considered him as innocent. I repeat again that misery needs company, and his education being superior to mine, I found much pleasure in his conversation. History, religion, mythology, astronomy, algebra, Latin and Greek he was a professor of; drawing and painting he was master of, and I never saw his equal in handwriting. Therefore, a few days sufficed (after the ground was broke) for us to confide in one another the history of our former days. I recounted mine, which he very much admired and applauded, and in return he gave me his, of which the following is an abridged repetition.

Monsieur Germain was an Italian Swiss. His education, as I have described above, had been much attended to. His parents had, by some party commotion of the country, become poor, and the destined position they intended for him was lost by that changement. After traveling in search of employment without success, he fell in with a set of vagabonds who, taking advantage of his superior education, his youthful inexperience, and his master penmanship, employed him in several successful daring ventures against the law of civilization and his country. Having realized a sufficient sum, he had ventured on the present speculation which brought him in contact with the authorities of Brest, a prisoner in the tower.

The cause of his imprisonment was this: three days before the event which brought him under the strong bolts of our lodgings, M. Germain had called only a few hours before the departure of the mail for Paris on an exchange broker with 17 thousand francs in gold and requested in exchange a draft on sight on Paris. The brokers gave him the draft, deducting the regular exchange.

That same morning, M. Germain called again on the brokers, and exhibiting a letter with the post stamp of that morning's date, which letter he purported to come from his principal (oil merchants in Marseille) in which they countermanded the investments of their capital; he requested them to refund the gold, allowing them a large exchange back for their trouble, and presented them with their draft.

The principal not being in the office at the moment, the juniors declined the business till his return. M. Germain, not being familiar with mercantile and exchange affairs, offered an additional half percent to a neighboring broker, and being desirous to hasten the bargain to be in time for the diligence of 4 o'clock to evade detection, he urged the matter with an unusual dispatch, which gave suspicion.

The last broker accepted the proposed bargain and requested M. Germain to call in half an hour, when the gold would have been collected. Both brokers took counsel on the strange conduct of M. Germain, and a commissary was informed of the suspicion. Two

police officers in disguise entered his room in the hotel and seized him, but not in time to save from the flames several proofs of drafts which M. Germain, ever on the alert, threw into the fire the moment strangers knocked at his door.

The officers seized him, and the commissary, having found in his trunk several instruments adapted to engravers and a small portable press with different qualities of inks and liquids, instituted a verbal probe and committed him to the chateau.

The electric telegraph not being existent at the time, and the weather proving cloudy and rainy for three days, the semaphore to Paris could not give notice to the police there to stop the payment and arrest the partner of M. Germain. Just three days after, the post arrived in Paris from Brest, and half an hour after, a lady presented herself at the corresponding bankers and drew 17 thousand francs on a draft on sight. This lady was Madame Germain.

Therefore, the counterfeiter had taken but four hours to copy, engrave, print, and counterfeit the draft in question. And strange to say, on the return of the discharged draft from Paris, the drawers and bankers could not distinguish the right from the counterfeit one.

As no one had seen him at work or could prove any connection with the lady in Paris, whom the police never found, the case of M. Germain remained in a state of suspension till I left the chateau.

CHAPTER 62nd

Plans of Escape

*1835 As M. Germain of exquisite appearance was our roommate for nine months, I must further intrude on the patience of my reader to relate some of his plans of escape.

M. Germain had observed an intimacy between myself and Mademoiselle Sorret, the same that in some former chapter I accused of being an old maid. But now that she is to figure as a lady of my predilection, I retract my words and say that this female was only two years older than myself, who numbered then 27 winters. And as I had accepted the invitation of "Namos" in the moment a feasible chance should be offered, he proposed that on any day when the jailor and his wife would be absent, myself in my capacity as teacher should form some excuse, leave our room, seize, muffle, or gag my lady love, and taking possession of the keys from the office, open the gates and effect our escape. But as I never would have consented to prove ungrateful to the jailor and his lady, and much less would use violence with the innocent girl who I fooled with my love declarations, the plan was given up after leaving exhausted every argument that my rhetorical jail companion could produce.

Next morning M. Germain woke me long before daylight and informed me that he was glad I had not accepted the mode of escape he had proposed the day before, as we should never have accomplished it without a passport for each. He had studied a method by which we could easily be supplied with them.

My prison companion was an imaginary genius, and it amused me to hear his castles in the air which were numerous, but not of the right sort. As the present result of his night studies had relation to our escape, I begged him to go on relating his plan of procuring passports. He said that if I could induce the Spanish women to go to the prefecture and each take out a passport for Paris, he could afterwards erase by chemical process their names and signalization and put ours in their place. I consented to this, as I did intend an escape if I could effect it without bringing trouble on our kind jailor.

The Spanish women, who never refused doing us a favor, boldly demanded and obtained passports, and with them they brought the desired acids that should counterfeit the documents in our name. In two hours after, the deed was done: M. Germain was called Pietro Nazzolini, and myself Domenico Antonetti; one tailor, the other joiner.[1]

[1]carpenter

To escape without injuring our jailor could not be effected with- out breaking through the localities, and this was a difficult job, as our room was above a storeroom ever closed. Our door gave on a passage strongly guarded by several strong gates to the front en- trance; therefore the only faint hope was through the only window, which gave into a small yard and which was guarded during the night by a sentry. This yard was surrounded by a wall which if escaladed, could drop us on the parade ground of the part of the chateau occupied by the regiment.

We both set to work to mature a plan by which we could escape by this yard. Several days passed and I had done nothing worthy of Jack Sheppard,[1] but not so the intellectual Germain, now Pietro Nazzolini, who was current in all the episodes of personal escapes. Yes, his plan was formed three days ago, but it required polishing, as he said, before he could make known his design.

There was still another difficulty to surmount, which was to gain the consent of my officers, who on former occasion, the reader will remember, had proved false. This obstacle I had argued with the Italian Swiss, and we had come to the conclusion to let them participate in our escape, but that both of us should be the first. Once free of the chateau walls, we would abandon them to their resources.

We made known our intent, which was embraced with avidity, and had them prepared for a short stay. In the meantime, through the kindness of the Spanish women, we all disposed of as much linen and clothes as they could well carry out without suspicion.

Signor Pietro Nazzolini, now the commander of the exit expedi- tion, proposed that as a New Year was at hand we should choose that night for the grand evasion, and as I had retained the blacksmith's saw from Senegal, we should on that day saw one of the bars of the window, and then at eleven o'clock that night, descend by the window into the parade ground, when we could gain the walls of the chateau, which gave on the beach. To evade the sentry, the greatest difficulty still objectionable, M. Germain recommended that the women should give their friendly hand by ascertaining what detachment was to guard the prison at the appointed time on New Year's night, and as they were acquainted with the whole regiment, make some excuse that night to visit the prison guardhouse and make them all drunk with brandy. But as it was doubtful that they could accomplish so much, a reserve plan was at hand to silence the sentinel.

It was the order given to the sentinel to walk the whole hour he

[1]celebrated British highwayman

was at his post, and as the yard was very narrow, he was continually passing and repassing right under our window. Should the women fail on this night to accomplish our intent, and the sentry persist in watching our action, it was proposed, the bar once cut, to drop a lasso over his head and by the help of our band to boost him right up to the window and if necessary knock him in the head with the iron bar.

From this moment everyone went to work to make preparations, as December was in extremity. The women brought us fishing lines and carried off our valuables. Shortly and briefly, a cord was twisted strong enough to hang the whole detachment.

The New Year's day was judiciously chosen for our escape, as it is the greatest day in France, and soldiers are allowed greater liberties than any other day in the year and drunkenness is somewhat tolerated. The long-desired time arrived, and everyone trembled lest any accident should frustrate the operation of our plan. The women visited us that afternoon and promised us that they were sure of success, as the Seargeant of the detachment was the husband of one of their friends and could in her company visit the guard. A long embrace was the only remuneration the women received.

By eight o'clock that night the bar had been cut off and the lasso, well soaped, stood coiled on the window. Nine o'clock brought the sentry singing the well-known military song, "T'en souviens-tu, disait un capitaine," and half reeling, half walking, paced the yard with admirable cheerfulness.

We borrowed one hour and at ten o'clock my shipmates were placed on the floor with the end of the lasso in their hands, ready for a strong pull. The intrepid Germain stood by me, bar in hand, ready to strike.

At a given kick from me, who held the fatal lasso in my hand, my mates were to haul up, make fast, and follow us by a larger rope which lay prepared for the descent.

Silently the window was opened, and at the opportune time the lasso fell. The back kick served as a word of command. Up came the slack cord, then it made some resistance, when a musket flew up to the window with the velocity of lightning. The lasso had fallen a little sideways and scraped the sentry's nose, took his chapeau off and brought the musket as its only prize.

Prompt as the failure was, I slid the noose off and dropped the gun on the head of the now frightened soldier.

CHAPTER 63rd

I Am Liberated from Prison

The fall of the musket must have stunned the sentinel, as not a word or complaint was heard from him. Having failed in our attempt, we immediately replaced the bar, shut the window, stowed our utensils in the straw mattresses, and took to our beds in expectations of a visit from the Officer of the Guard and the jailor. But nothing of the kind took place, and we passed the night in feverish expectations.

Next morning the spirited Spanish women made their appearance, and as the turnkey shut the door on them, they burst out into a fit of laughter which to us seemed quite unnecessary. Having fully expended their risible powers at our expense, they then informed us that the poor sentinel was found at the expiration of his watch by the relieving sentries nearly frozen and in a fainting fit in the yard; and when questioned on the subject of his broken head, he had reported that an unknown hand from the store window (the one directly under ours) had struck him a blow which felled him to the ground. His report was so confused that the officer, who knew of the intoxicated state of the whole watch, gave no credence to his report, but considered it as the effect of an overheated imagination.

As we expected the daily visit from the ever-punctual turnkey with his iron rod, we secured the fissures of the window with rags and bitterly complained of the cold winds to which we were exposed by those apertures—thus preventing his opening it. The women that day carried away under their aprons the tools which now had become useless, we having given up the idea of escape.

A few days after, I received information from a relation in Paris that my petition had been presented to the King, and a prompt pardon was expected. This piece of good news reconciled us to our former good humor, even M. Germain, who saw in our liberation a faint hope for himself, as he fancied he had schooled me into a taste of his evil doings. Certainly it amused me to hear the daring of these many swindling anecdotes, and as I gave a willing ear to his future plans of robberies, he took it for granted that his tales had influenced me in his favor and that on my liberation, I would assist him to escape.

One more illustration of the fecund imagination of the swindling properties of this *ne plus ultra* of counterfeiters, and I will leave him to be disposed of by the French authorities, who on such subjects permit no bail and punish such crimes with an iron hand. We had hardly got over the alarm the failure of our escape had caused us when our mate of durance vile rose one morning and with a radiant countenance informed me that he had planned a splendid enterprise which would yield a fortune for the two who would undertake it.

This scientific cheat Monsieur Germain had made a peculiar study of that philosophy so pernicious to society and which teaches equality in its worst forms, and when he proposed telling any of his past or future exploits, he smoothed them over with a short preface of his mischievous rhetoric, ever trying to prove that by the laws of nature, one man has as much right to the gifts of this world as another. Therefore, having concluded his preamble on the question of *meum* and *teum*, he related to me only the famous projected enterprise.

In some part of Italy, I forget where, there exists a sanctuary of the Virgin Mary called the "Virgin of Loretto." This sanctum sanctorum is reputed to be one of the richest tabernacles of Catholic Europe; the jewels that adorn the altar of that Virgin are said to be valued at several millions of crowns. Those are gifts, donations, and legacies of the votaries of this image. This shrine M. Germain intended to rob on some future day, and to effect it, he proposed the following plan:

On a wintry and stormy day he would appear at the Convent of Loretto (the sanctuary of the Virgin) and as a repentant sinner from South America and a votary of the Holy Virgin, would ask the customary alms of three days' bed and board, which this convent hospitably grants to all poor travelers; during which time he would most piously attend to all of their Matins and Vespers. In the three mornings he would ask permission to serve Mass, which ceremony he knew to perfection.

On the time of departure he would feign to be very sick, when the monks of the establishment would undoubtedly place him in their hospital. Then, as his complaint increased, he would beg for a confessor, and in the ear of the credulous priest he would deposit a tale of woes and sorrow mixed up with an equal quantity of protestations of Christian repentance. In addition, he would make the convent a donation of his worldly property in South America to insure a remittance of his sins and a passport to heaven.

Once this comedy was over, he would gradually grow better, but still adhere conscientiously to his gift, and as his property was to be represented as of consequence, his treatment by the avaricious monks would be equal in value to his donations. Then as he would give into the hands of the Prior the documents of the property, a vocation would suddenly strike him, and on his knees he would beg the Superior to allow him to join their order.

Now a religionist of the convent, his devotion would be immense, and every hour of the day would find him at the foot of the altar kneeling to the Virgin, missal in hand. This continual devotion, he calculated, would enable him in two months to take the impression of all the strong locks in the sanctuarium, and as his confederate should call every market day at the convent under the disguise of a peddler, this person would take charge of having the keys made according to the impressions, at different towns.

My daring narrator thought it indispensable that his companion in this grand scheme should be a sailor, as the escape from pursuit was necessarily to be made by sea. Therefore, the keys perfected to the locks and in the hand of the false monk, the mariner companion should have a fishing felucca in the vicinity only a few mile's distance, in attendance.

At the given day, the peddler should appear with his two mules, and under the absence of the moon, in the silence of the night, perpetrate the sacrilegious deed.

Another allusion to his false philosophy concluded his dream. Well satisfied with his "masterpiece of invention," as he called it, we retired to bed, I to sleep, Germain to polish his plan. About midnight he woke me with the information that he feared his grand scheme was an abortion.

"I have considered," said he, "that the pretended jewels on the altar of the Virgin are nothing but false stones, wax pearls, and washed gold. Surely those knowing monks would not leave such an amount of property idle and to adorn a painting. No, I am positive they have sold the jewels, substituted false ones, and bought lands for their rich convents." As I felt convinced of this fact, I was glad his ingenuity had vanished in polishing the projected crime.

And now that we are to leave this swindling philosopher in prison to mature some greater act of infamy, I will add that the day before I left the prison, he had constructed another piece of rascality against the Emperor of Russia, but as my liberation took place before its finishing polish was given, I am ignorant of the particulars. However, I am positive the galleys of Brest put a stop to his notions of equality.

Our liberation came at last, in a shape of pardon; and this is the only reparation the King granted us for having unlawfully seized our vessel. As the jailor rushed into our room to announce the joyful news, his emotion was such that he could not articulate the glad tidings for a long time; his good wife and children following him in, all embraced me. This kind family felt affected into tears, and even now I imagine I feel the strong grip of the old man when he led me

*1836   forth from the iron bars and strong walls to read the act of pardon from the King. Next day, accompanied by my scholars, I went on board the vessel that was to take us to Spain and carry me forever from France. Such was the Government order.

CHAPTER 64

Cholera in Marseille

My object in gaining my liberty was to return to Africa. From Brest   *1836*
I landed at Lisbon; thence taking a Spanish name and passport, I
returned to France and landed at Marseille. Here two vessels were
fitting out for the African Colonies, but on account of the raging of
the cholera, all mercantile speculation was at a stand. I was obliged
to remain till the flow abated, when the proprietor of one of these
vessels promised me a passage.

Under my assumed name, I took board at a second, perhaps
third-rate hotel (my means being very scanty at the time) to await the
time of departure. The cholera was then in its climax, the hotels
were deserted and would have been closed but for an order of the
Préfet (Civil Governor) who issued a proclamation which deprived
of their license for two years whomsoever closed their public establishments. Therefore even when the flow raged most fearfully and
800 to 900 fell daily by the mortiferous calamity, every hotel, coffee
house, butcher and baker shop was opened.

The hotel where I took my lodgings was not much frequented
at this epoch. The cholera had driven all its inmates to the open
country, and on my arrival I only found three boarders and the
landlord sourly cursing the Préfet and his proclamation which obliged him to keep open house and face the epidemic. His reception
was not cordial, as he informed me at once that he had no cook and
that I must content myself with such fare as himself could stew up.

A seaman is seldom very *recherché* on such matters. I readily
agreed to his proposal, and as dinner was ready, I accompanied him
to his *table d'hôte*. This was a large oval table, but now nearly
deserted, as only five persons figured at this board. I took my seat
opposite a lady and near a gentleman, who soon introduced me to
the company, excusing the familiarity, alleging the necessity of such
freedom to the present case of emergency which called, during the
then existing epidemic, to stand on no ceremony. He jocosely
remarked that from one moment to another, we might be called to
forego our new acquaintances, and therefore we should make the
most of them.

I accepted the proffered introduction and having but little to lose
in this world, I feared the cholera as little as any of the present
company who except the landlord, laughed and joked at the deadly
effects of the pestilence. I called for a bottle of choice Frontignan,[1]

[1]a muscatel wine

and pledging each of my new friends in a full bumper, we soon became communicative.

I being the last arrived, I was requested to tell my history of the cause of my visit in Marseille. A few words sufficed to tell my assumed name and my Spanish origin; my complexion spoke for my profession and my half worn-out coat for my means.

My neighbor, who I shall call the master of ceremonies, patronized the conversation whenever the lady opposite was silent and informed me that his *friend* (strongly articulating the word and nodding to the lady) was like himself, from Paris, and the wife of a Captain in the Army, on her way to join her husband at Algiers. He added with some emphasis that she was also under his protection. The person on the left was Monsieur G., a lawyer also on his way to Algiers; the old gentleman with a wig at the end of the table was the speculator in horses, and himself Doctor Dujean, a medical student from the hospitals of Paris who had voluntarily visited Marseille at his own expense with philanthropic feelings to study the disease and gratuitously succor the poor.

Now it so happened that when this student of the *materia medica* named the lady and called himself her protector, her looks belied this title, and the wink she gave made me understand that the leech was hoaxing me. At seven-and-twenty I did not take jokes as peaceably as I would now, and the arrogance of his styling himself *her* friend without her permission (as I presumed) gave me great annoyance. The lady whose eyes bespoke heaven and hell, had watched the bad impression the continual conversation of M. Dujean in allusion to herself had on me, and with several negative nods, seemed to indicate a desire that I should contradict his words.

I chose the opportune time of a moment of silence, when I begged Madame Duprez to accept my arm for a walk in the balcony, remarking to Doctor Dujean that I had no respect for monopoly, and as the Madame was the only lady in the house, we were all entitled to our civilities. By this time I had the lady under my arm and on my way out of the dining room. The astonished Doctor would have considered himself insulted, but the Lawyer who had silently watched the proceedings explained to him the double dealings of the lady and quieted his offended honor.

Our Helena[1] was a complete coquette; to see us at loggerheads was her delight. We both saw it and perfectly comprehended her triflings, but still we had not the moral courage to desist from our servile assiduities, and a war of deceptions was continued by us for

[1]Helen of Troy, not the saintly archeologist

several days without any material advantage to anyone, till the affair ended in a battle.

The prefecture had announced this evening 1,200 deaths, and in defense of the scourge, our company had called for several more bottles of wine. As usual, we made merry on the frightened land-lord, who with rosary in hand, counted his Aves and Paters. The conversation fell on the art of phrenology and craniology. The mischievous lady proposed that the Doctor should feel our heads and pronounce our thoughts and passions. To set the example, she loosed her long black tresses and subjected her head to the manipula-tions of the odious Doctor.

Several bumps were explained, but others could not be pro-nounced but in her ears. I strongly objected, but the Dulcinea,[1] seeing it mortified me to have anyone else whisper God knows what in her ears, persisted in allowing the Doctor the privilege, which much amused her and the rest of the party.

The operation over, the Lawyer pleasantly allowed his cranium an investigation, which resulted highly complimentary to its owner. The man of the wig was excused out of delicacy for his feelings, and the proprietor stoutly refused any foolery with his skull. My turn had come; I made all the defense possible against a probable chance of giving the Doctor an opportunity of ridiculing me, but a kiss from the lady made me consent with the condition that the Doctor should take his turn under my manipulation, as I pretended I had studied under Doctor Gall himself.[2]

It was agreed, and the Doctor's fingers began the operation. The first bump which he said projected enormously was jealousy; the second, a complete destitution of love, friendly and moral feelings; third, immoderate drinking; fourth, avaricious to extremes; fifth, sixth, and seventh, passionate, revengeful and bloodthirsty, and so on till the lady and Lawyer cried, "Enough."

The description of the first, second, and third bumps had amused the company, but the latter had shocked them as coarse in the extreme. I rose from the mortifying operation and pointed the Doctor to a chair (rage had deprived me at that moment of articula-tion). The company stood in silence, expecting I would retaliate in the same coin of abuse, but I deceived them.

Placing myself before the Doctor, I asked him if he was ready. He having answered in the affirmative, my left hand suddenly discov-ered the bump of impudence, which my right immediately flattered with a blow in the cheek.

[1]lady love
[2]Franz Joseph Gall (1758-1828), German physician and founder of phrenology   *241*

My new method of phrenology did not please the medical student, and a few passes were exchanged, but by the interference of the company we were separated; and as the lady pronounced with the rest in my favor, my Parisian antagonist gave up the contest and never spoke to the lady forever after.

CHAPTER 65th

I Return to Africa

As the French vessel bound to Africa was now ready for sea, I took *1836* passage for Senegal, and in 27 days I had the pleasure to shake hands with those friends who two years before had labored so much in favor of my escape. But the Colonial Government stopped short the enjoyment of our meeting by ordering me off the Colony; a colonial coaster took me to Sierra Leone.

I arrived in this port in time to witness the arbitrary proceedings of the English Government toward Spanish vessels trading on the Coast. At the time of my arrival in Sierra Leone, there lay to anchor from 30 to 40 Spanish vessels seized by the British cruisers, awaiting the treaty which was about being signed by the Spanish Minister at St. James's and which gave Her Britannic Majesty's cruisers power to capture all Spanish vessels trading on the Coast of Africa. The conditions of this treaty were such that even vessels in pursuit of lawful trade were liable to be seized if sailing under Spanish flag, and many vessels were captured in the middle passage when bound from Havana to Spain or vice versa.

I have stated in some former chapter that it was currently believed at the time that the Spanish Minister received £30,000 from England for signing this degrading treaty. Two months after, the treaty arrived and the vessels were condemned. With the usual dispatch proverbial to Spanish officials, six months after the signing of the treaty, the Colonial Government of Cuba was informed by the Home Department of the existence of such contract.

My stay at this Colony was but short, as all the Spanish vessels detained here had their full complement of officers. I applied to Captain Ropes of the American brig *Reaper* for a situation. A few words induced him to hire me as Pilot and interpreter for Gallinas, a noted mart of slave and Spanish factories. As I had never visited Gallinas or the coast of Malaguetta, I begged a Spanish Captain to give me a few lessons on this Coast. The day after, the American brig left port under the charge of my new branch.

Three days coasting brought us to an anchor before the Spanish factories; and till this day I am not aware that my friend Captain Ropes knew the danger his brig had run while under my pilotage. In my second capacity of interpreter I landed with the Captain and that day sold to one factory alone (Don Pancho Ramon's) 1,000 quarter kegs of powder.

The second day we visited the celebrated Don Pedro Blanco, 243 with the object of making some trade with him. Don Pedro received us with his usual urbanity, but declined purchasing from us, inasmuch as we had not called on him on our first landing. We were aware that we had committed a fault, as we had heard much of this man's pride, but our Captain could not stand the temptation of an offer made before we landed, of a thousand kegs of powder, and at his own price.

While in Sierra Leone, I had heard much of the generosity of Don Pedro Blanco, and availed myself of the report of this good quality to induce him to purchase a large quantity of rum and tobacco that we could not expect to sell to anyone else. To effect my purpose I invented a little story which a few months after, Don Pedro readily forgave. Therefore, I am not ashamed to repeat it now.

The next day I wrote a note to Mr. Blanco and in few words explained my detention, imprisonment, and destitute position, requesting him to purchase some portion of our cargo if only to assist me in gaining the little commission the American Captain gave me on sales of my own making. Now this supposed commission was the deception I used toward Don Pedro; I hired myself with Captain Ropes in my double capacity for my passage down the Coast, till I should find employment. A prompt and laconic answer was sent back which invited me to come ashore with the invoice of the cargo. For my sake, Mr. Blanco purchased to the amount of 5,000$ in rum and tobacco, giving drafts on London for the same.

While these goods were landing, an accident took place which will illustrate the true character of this famed slave dealer. Several hogsheads of tobacco had been landed that day, and the Second Mate of the *Reaper*, who was a myope, got provoked at a Krooman (native boatman) who might have given him a short answer. The Mate sent a stave at the head of the Negro which he dextrously dodged, but not satisfied with this flying chastisement, he flew at the Krooman with another stave, threatening death to the Black fellow, who had sought refuge on the starboard side of the boat.

The now infuriated Mate still pursued him, when the hired boatman presented an oar in self-defense to the aggressor, who as I have remarked was myopic. Rage must have deducted something from his impaired sight; he saw not the blade of the oar. His upper lip came in contact with the blade with such force that it lacerated a gash into the gum, cutting the upper lip in two and knocking four teeth out of his mouth.

The Negro, on seeing the blood, ran to the bush while the wounded Mate was taken on board. That night the unfortunate man put an end to his life by taking laudanum, not wishing to survive the deformity of his harelip, as he called it.

The laws of the country condemn he who draws blood to the penalty of several slaves, in proportion to the damage done, and death in case of murder. The Krooman had been seized and now lay loaded with iron in Don Pedro's barracoons, awaiting the sentence which the whites of his establishment had already pronounced (in the shape of death), having struck a white man, which wound had been reported to have caused death.

Next morning I came ashore and was informed that the culprit was to be disposed of in the manner they had pronounced. As I had witnessed the fray, I immediately called on Mr. Blanco and explained the whole proceedings, disculpating the innocent Krooman. On my simple statement the man was liberated, much against the will of the native Chiefs, who insisted on carving out the laws of the land to their full extent. Several of the whites also pressed for punishment of the Negro, but Don Pedro, ever just to White or Black in his decisions, liberated the Krooman and sent him back on board the *Reaper*.

The perfect management of Mr. Blanco's slave establishment and his late impartial decision induced me to offer him my services, which were accepted, and shortly after I was employed as a principal in one of his branch slave factories.

CHAPTER 66th

Description of Gallinas

*1836—1837 Gallinas, in the latitude 7° 05'N and longitude 11° 35'W, the notorious slave mart of the Northwest Coast of Africa, is a river whose entrance and interior is not navigable but to boats and small crafts. Four years back, the shores of this shallow river were colonized by Spanish slave dealers who, while they remained undisturbed, accumulated several fortunes.

At the time of my arrival here in the beginning of 1836, two large factories monopolized this lucrative trade, but other minor establishments also opposed the larger ones and in time succeeded in erecting establishments as abundantly and well supplied in goods as others. However, the influence that Don Pedro Blanco had gained over the natives was never equaled by any other Spaniard.

The indigenes of this river, who are called Vye, were not numerous before the establishment of the Spanish factories, but since 1813 when several ships from Cuba landed their rich cargoes, the neighboring cities flocked to this river, and as there is much similarity in their languages, they soon became naturalized with the aborigines of its sandy and marshy soil.

Polygamy, the principal and well beloved institution of all Africans, soon leagued them into one sociable family, while their progenitors sprung up into the true owners of the land. As the new upstarts grew up educated under the influence of the rich Spanish factories, they imbibed the habits of slave hunting while they despised other occupations and in their idleness, panted but for wars and captures. Slaves in time became scarce, and the youth of the day, cradled in indolence, sought distraction in slave wars, which ever yield a rich reward.

Time brought into notice this slave mart, and merchants from Havana sent out agents to establish their deposits of goods and permanent barracoons. The double and treble call for slaves soon dispopulated the immediate Interior, when it became urgent for the natives of Gallinas to extend their wars further into the Interior. And in a few more years, this river was surrounded with wars, but as the slave factories supplied them with powder and guns, they made headway against a multitude of enemies who, not understanding the politics of alliance, fought them separately and were generally repulsed.

Still the demand increased, and auxiliary slave factories were established north and south. The Bar or Sheborough River became a tributary in slaves to the Gallinas, Mana Rock, Sugaree, Cape Mount, Small Cape Mount, even Digbay at the door of Monrovia had a deposit and barracoons belonging to whites of Gallinas.

Such a run of prosperity—as the natives now call those times —could not last long. Woman, the origin of our first sin, here caused (as it generally does in all African wars) son to rise against father, the first germ of a civil war.

This river, insignificant to commerce, is nothing more than a quantity of lagoons whose shapeless and unproductive islands give to the whole country the appearance of some importance; while in reality the principal branch of this river (which is called Soliman) extends its unimportant source to some sixty miles into the Interior, serving only as a nursery for alligators, sea cow, and the hippopotamus.

The torch of discord was first illuminated by a Black Paris who deprived his Negro uncle Agamemnon[1] of an Ethiopean Helen. Up sprung Ulysses and Achilles without number, and every small town became a Trojan City.

The configuration of the country as I have attempted to describe it isolated every family of note by its different branches of the river, and every one fortified itself in their marshy island. Two parties were formed, and the quarrel became general.

Amara and Shiakar were the two principal families originators of this civil war. Amara was a distant descendant of the Mandingo nation, and a native of Shebar. Shiakar, who was born in the river, considered himself a nobleman of the country, and although the aggressor, disputed the title of the prize. The whites, ever alert on native quarrels, wisely kept aloof from their broils and continued purchasing prisoners from each party. Many vessels carried across the ocean two inveterate enemies shackled on the same boat, while others met on the same deck a long-lost child or missing brother.

To enumerate the horrors of this war before the death of its Chief, Amara, a separate volume would be necessary. As I shall never refer to this war during my future pages, I will describe one or two barbarities of the thousand that took place between the contesting parties.

For several months, Amara (the "Paris" in the dispute) had been blockaded in his own fence stockade by Shiakar's warriors; a sortie was necessary to obtain provisions, but the enemy were too numerous for the venture. Amara called his fetish-man and demanded the propitious moment for a sally. The supposed oracle said, "When thy

---

[1]Conneau is thinking of Menelaus, Helen's husband and Agamemnon's brother. Paris stole Helen from Menelaus, precipitating the Trojan War.

hands will be stained with the blood of thine own son," meaning a youthful son of Amara who had joined his mother's family and was then far distant. The savage and superstitious Amara, seeing a child of his two years old, snatched it from his mother's arms, threw it into a rice mortar, and with the pestle smote it into a mummy.[1]

The sortie was immediately ordered, and with the pestle still warm from the child's blood, the enemy was routed. The town reprovisioned and the fortification of the antagonists demolished. The soothsayer received a slave for his barbarous but mistaken prognostication.

At another time, Amara was on the point of attacking a strong fortified town, but doubts were entertained of the success. The diviner was sent for, and his laconic answer was that Amara could not conquer till he had returned in his mother's womb. That night, Amara committed the blackest of incests, but his party was repulsed, and the false oracle received his reward by lapidation.[2]

In order not to leave the reader ignorant of the fate of Amara, I will add that after several years of bloody contest, he was conquered by Shiakar's men and taken prisoner in his own town. His captor, Prince Mana, cut his head off, and while bleeding, forced it into the fresh-torn bowels of his mother, thus verifying the double prognostication of the soothsayer.

[1]into powder. Dried human mummies used to be ground up for medicine by medieval apothecaries, and "mummy" became synonymous with pulverized humanity.

[2]death by stoning

CHAPTER 67th

Visit to Monrovia · I Land at New Sester with a Cargo for Slaves · Grand Palabra with the Prince

Not long after I had landed in Gallinas, I was sent by my employer *1836—1837* Don Pedro Blanco to Monrovia to purchase tobacco. A Portuguese schooner took me to the infant Colony. On landing, I was astonished to find brick stores, wharfs, and several small crafts on the stocks.

The Colony then dated only 14 years. Still, I found an elegant Government House, a neat public store, and long low wooden buildings which were called the Emigration House. It was adapted to those of the new-arrived emigrants whose circumstances could not afford to hire lodgings. In this capacious building I saw several families who were undergoing the acclimatizing season; I found that they were comfortably supplied with provisions whose allowance was to be continued for six months.

Two churches with competent bells embellished this village of astonishing asparagus growth. As I walked through the large and clean streets, every door was apparently open to receive me. At one place I bought eggs, at the others, chickens; beans, tomatoes, and sweet potatoes soon filled my Steward's basket. Having purchased my tobacco, I was going off when a genteel person tapped me on the shoulder and introduced himself as the Collector of the Port, presenting a printed receipt for anchor dues.

"Anchor dues!" said I. "What do you mean?"

"Twelve dollars only," was the answer. I paid the cash, considering that any printed form was worth the money. The document I took as a curiosity to Gallinas. What other town of the Coast would boast of such civilization in such a short time—a printing office managed by Blacks perhaps, but only a few years emancipated?!!

On my return to Gallinas, I was sent to New Sester[1] to establish a branch factory to supply with slaves the numerous vessels on the Coast then belonging to my employer. New Sester was then an independent principality under the power of a Bassa Chief who styled himself a Prince. My cargo was landed for the moment in a Krooman's town till a new house could be erected for me.

On my first opening trade with this Chief and his people, I found them far inferior to the Mandingos, Sosoo, and Vey People, and on

[1]or Cestros, or Sestros. The spelling finally settled down to Sester. The river Cestos in Liberia, and River Cess and Grand Cess, both on the coast east of Monrovia, also preserve the name today.

several occasions broke off communications and closed my chests. Their slaves also were inferior and the price exorbitant; however, in a few days I had collected seventy-five of them. As this was sufficient number to send off with safety to Gallinas in the vessel then at anchor, I sent for the Prince to assist me in shipping them—an operation necessarily done under his eyes, as he counted heads and received a duty. The messenger returned with the information that the Prince was annoyed at my impertinence and would not come till I made some atonement in the shape of a present.

The bearer of this dispatch was the Prince's son, a youth of 16 years who delivered his message somewhat arrogantly and for which he received a violent blow across the mouth. Bleeding at the nose, the boy returned to his princely father, and with his cries rose the whole town against the white man. The Prince immediately sent me another messenger with the order to depart from the country, adding that by the next day he would himself enforce the order if I had not gone.

Now I had been too long in Africa to be intimidated by a Negro Prince, and although I did not like the country just for the reason that he had ordered me off, I chose to remain. Therefore, that evening I made preparations to resist his orders.

At the first war intimations of the Prince, all my hired servants and barracooniers—slave watchers—had immediately deserted me. I was left alone with seventy-five slaves. In this predicament, I sent off for three white men from my schooner and secured the entrance of the barracoon.

My house was a square bamboo building to which I had added a bamboo piazza with high gratings round it. This I had done to secure the natives from pilfering me during the night. The reader must be informed that in the Bassa Country, the houses are constructed solely with bamboo; consequently the walls, which are nothing but mats of the same material, would have left my house if unprotected by this railing exposed to robbery.

In this fenced piazza was slung my hammock, and here I ate my meals, received traders, and on a deal table stood my writing materials. In this very passage I formed the plan to resist the princely order to depart.

That night I loaded twenty-five muskets and placed them in my sofa, a long trade chest. The deal table I covered with my blanket, and under its folds I hid a keg full of powder, with the head off. Nearby and under my broad-brimmed hat stood a pair of double-barreled pistols. Morning came, and one hour after sunrise the war bells announced the near approach of the Prince.

I ordered my men to open the gate of the barracoon and retire about their duty. In a few minutes the small yard was filled with armed men, and the Prince in his drummer's red coat and no breeches boldly stepped into my narrow receiving passage.

I received him with apparent cordiality and pointed out the only sitting stool in the place, which I had purposely placed at one end of this well-guarded piazza. Once seated, I had him isolated from his people; myself stood near the table and by my hat. Some of his near relations had also entered the piazza, but according to my established rules, did not advance but halfway.

As the Prince did not speak, I asked him if he had come to assist me in the shipping of my slaves, "and if so," I added, "we better begin."

His answer was, "Did you receive my message, and why are you not gone?"

I told him that as I had come at my own leisure, I would go when I pleased and that I feared him not. Then with a jerk I threw the blanket off. With pistol in hand I stood over the keg of powder and dared him to enforce his order.

In a moment the yard had been evacuated and his friends had left their now frightened Prince to discuss the preliminary of peace with a madman (I was nearly so at the time). A few moment's reflection on both sides brought the following conversation; and as the Prince could speak English tolerably well, having learnt the language on board English slavers when a boy, I will give it verbatim:

Prince: "What's matter, white man! That be fool fashion; me no come for war. Take that powder away—sit down and talk softly palavra. Me like you too much, me no like war. I hold your foot; let me go. I beg you, white man, let me go. My belly hurt me too much." Et cetera.

By this time I had taken a seat on the keg of powder and was preparing to argue the point when the Prince begged most urgently to be allowed to retire in the yard, promising to return. The fright had given him a sudden pain in the stomach; he needed air.

I plainly saw it in his countenance and took pity. The desired liberty was granted, and faithful to his word, he returned, much relieved. We both laughed at this accident and shook hands. I promised silence on the casualty, while he on his part swore eternal friendship.

His men were recalled, and as peace was proclaimed, two demijohns of rum sealed the contract. That same morning, my slaves were shipped, and the Prince remained from that day forward my good friend.

CHAPTER 68th

The "Saucy Wood" · Execution of a Slave for Setting My Barracoon on Fire

1836—1837 My bravado with the Prince had a good effect. The Krooman and fishermen inhabitants of the beach saw at once what they had to expect at my hands. The severe lesson which the Chief of the country had received served them as a moral.

Don Pedro Blanco had deputed me to New Sester for a short time only, but finding that by introducing better goods, slaves became more abundant, I was ordered to remain. And as my commission was increased to ten percent, or ten dollars on each hundred that I shipped, I went to work and built a large and commodious two-story house near the sea beach with two strong barracoons flanking the sides and a strong fence securing the whole building from intrusion. The first floor of my building I kept for store, the upper for my dwellings, and the top I adorned with a watch house which commanded a perfect view of the seas for several miles off.

Natives love to give a nickname to strangers in order to denote them from other white men, and they generally choose some peculiarity in their character or persons, often giving them the names of goods or clothes which most please them; or of any coincidence which might have struck them forcibly. Therefore my first name was "Powder" on account of the famous keg of powder, but after I had built my house and the word of "store" which they had never heard before was so often used, they baptized me "Story."

In a few months the whole country had changed its appearance. On this beach, once isolated but for a half dozen Kroo huts, now counted two moderate-size towns, and its inhabitants were amply supplied with employment from my factory. The Interior natives, confident of a ready purchase of their captives, soon found way to the beach, and in brief time the good Prince who had so strongly protested, "Me no like war," now sent expeditions against his neighbors, claiming redress for imagined grievances or payments from his great-grandfather's creditors.

This extraordinary change was not brought about without some sacrifice to humanity. Still, I have the presumption to say that during my stay here, I caused greater strides toward civilization than any other person ever did in this neighborhood in such short time.

252 On my arrival I found the natives full of their superstitious

witchcraft. Men and women were indiscriminately accused by the ju-ju man, and to prove their innocence, the "saucy wood" was invariably applied. In many cases I also found that the accusations of witchcraft were often purchased to get rid of a sick wife, an old imbecile person, or a rich relation; and as the poisonous drink is mixed by the ju-ju man, it seldom failed in proving fatal to the drinker.

Saucy wood is the bark of a tree of reddish color which when ground and mixed with boiling water, makes the poisonous draught which the natives believe has the quality to destroy witches and necromancers. Ordeals of this kind took place every day about the country, and many innocent persons were destroyed by this barbarous custom. I undertook to put a stop to this abominable practice, and on the next trial I requested that the accused should be secured in my barracoons till the deadly liquid should be prepared.

This beverage can be prepared in different degrees of strength which may or may not prove fatal. And if the accused has any friends who can purchase the concocter of the poison, then the mixture is made sufficiently weak for the culprit to reject it. But when the accused is friendless, the saucy bark is steeped with all its deadly power, and the victim dies at the second bowlful.

A Krooman was accused of having caused the death of his nephew by incantations or witchcraft; the Doctor consulted his ju-ju, who corroborated the fact; the man was seized and put in irons. Having the authority of the Prince, I demanded the accused for safe keeping till next morning when the saucy wood was to be administered.

At an early hour next day, the Doctor had ground his bark and was steeping it by a large fire. I had cause to believe that this man had an antipathy against the accused uncle; I called on him and requested him to make his mixture double strong, as I wished to ascertain if the accusation was true, adding that my own ju-ju had pronounced him innocent.

A few moments before the beverage was administered, I gave my protégé three doses in one of Tartar emetic, and I brought him forward, still loaded with irons. About a quart of the strong concocted poison was quaffed by the intrepid Krooman who, strong in his innocence and confident of the white man's superior ju-ju, swallowed the contents without a wink.

In five minutes the emetic had operated. The Krooman was liberated and the ju-ju man, astonished at the failure of his poison, retired in confusion. Once liberated, the Krooman told how I had given him beforehand the preventative, which he called "white man 253 saucy wood," and ever after, men accused of witchcraft sought refuge in the sanctuary of my barracoon. And my emetic or Epicaquana[1] never failed in saving life. In a short time, this practice was discontinued.

The English cruisers had deprived me of three vessels this season, consequently I had not shipped slaves for three months. My barracoon contained 500 slaves which required all my vigilance to retain in safe keeping. Amongst this large number of slaves I had a whole family consisting of a man, his wife, his sister, and three children. This family was sold on condition that they all should be shipped. I had passed my word in consent and awaited the first opportunity to effect it.

The father of this family had been captured by the Prince after many months of hard fighting, and his family had shared the same fate when his village was stormed. He was the discarded son of a Chief who undertook to block the public path from the Interior to the beach and collect a duty. In many instances the Prince's people had been defeated by the daring robber, who had by this time built a stockade town in the said path. Once captured, the Prince would have killed him, but in consideration of his friends, he was sold under the foregoing conditions.

This man had several times made attempts to escape, but the watchfulness of my barracooniers defeated his intents, which caused them to add at every attempt some greater restrictions to his comforts or another link to his chain. Failed in his expectations, he undertook one day to set the establishment on fire, for which attempt he was severely flogged. But on the next day, under pretense of chills and fever, he was allowed a place by the kitchen fire. When unobserved, he set the thatched roof in flames; then, seizing a lighted brand, he sprang toward the building where the powder was kept. Fortunately he was in double irons, and his motions being short jumps, he was overtaken in time and again better secured.

As the Prince visited me the day after, I insisted on his taking the savage back, but the Bassa Chief had heard of the attempt and had visited me for the purpose of putting in execution the law of his country; the incendiary was to be burnt at the stake.

No argument of mine could pacify the Prince; a savage and brutal death was the dessert for his enemy. But as I would not deliver him on such condition, it was agreed that he should be shot. And in presence of all the slaves, he was executed, his wife and sister never shedding a tear of affection on the remains of their unfortunate relation.

[1]Ipecacuanha: South American plant whose dried roots, when swallowed, induce vomiting. Still in use as Syrup of Ipecac.

CHAPTER 69th

Difficult Embarcation of 400 Slaves at New Sester

New Sester proper is no river, as some nautical charts describe it.
Two miles from the small and dangerous beach called New Sester
there exists a small river which on account of its shallowness and
narrow and rocky entrance the natives call Poor River. My factory
was at New Sester proper, and as I have said, the beach was small,
being only about 200 yards in extent and flanked with dangerous
cliffs. As it lay exposed to the open ocean and the sea breeze keeps
the beach ever dangerous to effect a landing, even in a perfect calm
day the heavy swells send mountains of water with terrific force
against it.

This beach would be impracticable but for the astonishing dex-
terity of the Kroomen, who with their canoes surmount the rolling
billows in spite of its dangers. Kroomen and Fishmen are a different nation from the Bushmen; they inhabit the beach, live separate
from other tribes, and are governed by their elders, whose rules are
somewhat democratic. These people are not allowed by the Bushmen to trade in the Interior, but in exchange for the prerogative of
the lands of the Interior, they monopolize with despotic sway the
beach trade with the shipping.

The lengthy Coast which these Kroomen inhabit is about 700
miles, and being exposed to the full blast of the waves of the ocean,
nearly the whole beach is impracticable to our European boats,
which gives them an artificial advantage over the owners of the land,
the Bushmen, who without this natural difficulty would expel them
from the land. Long practice has rendered them masters of their
calling of which they bear the name, and although one is called
Fishman and the other Krooman, still they are of the same original
family. They have the same manners, the same customs, and same
Government. The first is generally allowed to be the most expert
with the paddle, while the latter is undoubtedly the most honest.

Their canoes are made sharp-pointed at the ends, and they are
hollowed from the solid trunk of a single tree to the thickness of an
inch, which renders them exceedingly buoyant. Two men can
transport on their shoulder to any moderate distance a canoe capable
of containing four people. Men-of-war, merchantmen, and slavers
are obliged to hire this sect of men when landing on the West Coast
of Africa in general, and such is the necessity of their labors that they
cannot be dispensed with.

On my landing at New Sester, I took precaution to supply myself
with a quantity of these useful natives and to encourage the emigra-

tion from Settra Kroo. I liberated from slavery a Fishman who a "woman palavra" had brought on the verge of making a visit, passage free, to Havana. One or two more acts of kindness with my sanctuarium against the ordeal of the dreaded saucy wood caused them to seek the neighborhood of my factory, and as I gave them abundant employ and paid well for their services, in the short space of six months two flourishing towns, one of Kroomen, the other of Fishmen, sprung up by my factory. And as they acknowledged me their friend and master, one town called me Commodore while the other styled me their Consul. With such auxiliaries, I could make a shipment of slaves at most any time, even against the opposing element of the heavy seas.

Shortness of provisions sent the blockading cruiser to Sierra Leone for supplies. My well-paid spy, a Fishman employed on board the man-of-war, soon informed me of the cause of the absence of the annoying vessel. Availing myself of a clear coast, I sent a swift canoe to Gallinas requesting my employer to send me a vessel if there was one to spare.

In the brief time of five days, a brig arrived with the noted signal for embarcation. Messengers were sent to the Prince and Chiefs to assist in the shipment and collect their duties, while a general embargo was laid on all canoes, and for 24 hours not one of them was even allowed to go fishing. This precaution was necessary, as it was probable that the English cruiser kept in his pay a spy from amongst my people, as I did on board the war vessel.

The moon was on its full and the sea, as usual on such periods, was terrific. The cruiser had been gone six days, and I hourly expected his return. The shipment, although dangerous, was indispensable. Only four short hours of daylight remained to effect it. I called a council of the head Kroomen and Fishmen, and by the force of promises of double and treble pay, made them consent to venture a shipment.

Such was the surf that only the smallest canoes could be employed. The smallest men were taken to man the canoes, and a lot of youths appointed to swim off whenever a canoe should capsize. The embarcation began with the females, as the most difficult to embark; 70 were sent off without any accident. The men followed, but now a strong sea breeze had set in from the southwest which drove the rollers in with greater rapidity, and every other canoe was capsized.

Negro after Negro was rescued by the swimming party, and the sun surprised us in its descent to the horizon when only two thirds of the slaves had been shipped. I urged on the embarcation, but the canoemen, who had done wonders, now lay extended on the beach, 256 exhausted with fatigue.

Rum, which had till now encouraged their extertions, was a powerless offer to them. Night was approaching and the wind increasing, while the brig with topsail aback was making signal after signal for dispatch. Still my offers and appeals were neither accepted nor attended to. In this dire dilemma I was on the point of giving up the shipment when a thought struck me which I presumed would nerve my canoemen to new exertions.

I sent to the store for a small cask containing several pounds of Venetian beads called *corniola* or mock coral. Now this bead was the fury of fashion amongst the native women, and no greater temptation could be offered to bend them to one's will. The smiles of women in Africa have the same magical power as in any other country, and the offer of one bunch for every head embarked brought the whole female force to my aid. Mothers, sisters, sweethearts took charge of the embarcation and forced the exhausted men to fresh efforts. In fine, a hundred more were shipped while in the heat of the new offer, but darkness soon compelled me to desist. Three slaves had found a watery grave, and the charm of the beads had worn away.

I then gave up the battling of the infuriated element. The vessel was sent off 120 slaves short of her complement. Two days after, the cruiser arrived. I sent my compliments on board and begged to know if I could be of any service.

CHAPTER 70th

Assassination of an American by the Natives · I Avenge His Death

About this time a Spanish vessel had arrived from the Canary Islands loaded with fruits, having sold the greater part of her cargo at Goree, Sierra Leone, Gallinas, and Mesurado. Not finding a return freight at Liberia proper, the Captain had accepted a charter from Mr. Pedro Blanco to bring a cargo of rice from the leeward or Grain Coast, with conditions to place himself under my instruction.

On her arrival at New Sester, I had just shipped off nearly all my slaves, and my presence at my factory could be dispensed with propriety. Therefore I availed myself of this vessel to take a trip at sea and in the meantime purchase the cargo of rice for the *Brillante*; such was her name.

I called at different English factories and with cash in hand purchased several sacks of rice, and at the Kroo town deposited goods for the same produce. On my return I anchored off Senoe River for the purpose of purchasing some sea stores. Here I found Mr. Findley, Governor of this Colony, laboring under a severe illness. My medicine chest was placed at his disposal. No drug but a trip at sea could ameliorate his fast-declining health. As my vessel was in the lawful trade, he saw no cause why he should not accept my offer of a trip up the Coast. Having a strong desire to visit the Colonies Monrovia and Bassa, I assured him that my vessel was at his disposal to land him at any of the above ports. And on her return from the windward, the Captain should be instructed to call for him and take him back to Senoe, the seat of his Government.

The critical health of the Governor left him no choice but to accept my uninterested offer, and in two days we were at sea. As we were not pressed for time, we called at several native towns for livestock, giving the Governor a chance to recruit himself as much as possible by enjoying the sea air.

On our arrival at my place, I found an American vessel the *Joseph Hand* loaded with a cargo of goods consigned to me, awaiting my return to discharge them. As I could not accompany Mr. Findley any longer, I left him on board, giving orders to the Captain to proceed to Bassa, land the Governor, wait for him three days, and thence take him to Monrovia, the last place he wished to visit.

Grand Bassa or River St. John is only 14 miles northwest from New Sester. A few hours brought the vessel to that river, but as it was about sundown, the Captain proposed to land Mr. Findley next morning in his boat. But the Governor, being anxious to gain time, begged to be landed at the native towns at the cove, saying he would walk over to the American settlement which is only two miles distance, and return in two days.

At the time of landing, Mr. Findley placed in his pockets several dollars, which on going over the side made a noted jingle. The Captain remarked the effect and requested him to hide his money, but no notice was taken.

Two days elapsed, and the Governor did not return. The Captain, wishing to know how much longer he should have to wait, sent a servant of mine, who could speak English, to the settlement to the Governor. On the boy's arrival there, no one had seen Mr. Findley or had heard of him. On his return, the boy took his way by the beach, when near about midway he found a dead body floating near the rocks. A deep cut, apparently made with a cutlass, had opened a very large gash on the back of the head and which must have caused his death. The face was not recognizable, as it was defaced by the continual rubbing on the sand; still, the pants and shirt, well known to the afrighted boy, told whose body it was.

The sad information was received on board by the crew and officers with dismay. The Captain, never having landed on the Coast, was at loss what to do and dared not venture on shore to give burial to his passenger and guest. In this difficulty, a hasty return to my factory was the only determination taken. The horrible news was imparted to me by a letter from the Captain, who demanded instruction on the subject.

At this time, two Captains had landed slave cargoes at New Sester on their account, and their vessels lay to an anchor in the roads.[1] I called on these gentlemen and demanded the assistance of their vessels to put into execution a plan of revenge I had instantly formed on the receipt of the fatal letter.

My wish was granted, and that night I made preparation to take a signal satisfaction from the murderous Fishmen. Next morning I called on board each Spanish and Portuguese vessel (the two strangers being Portuguese, but owned and manned by Spaniards) and represented to them the insult the Spanish flag had received in the murder of a passenger while under its protection. I also brought forward the necessity of chastising the murderers of a white man and a native of a friendly nation; likewise informing them that their captains had lent me their vessels and I now wanted their voluntary

[1]roadsteads, sheltered bodies of water near a coast where ships can ride at anchor, as in "Hampton Roads"

services. With one voice they all offered to land with me. The American vessel *Joseph Hand*, discharging goods for me, insisted in joining my war-like expedition, and fifty muskets were distributed amongst the four crews. By eleven o'clock our squadron was underway, the Spaniard, as the best sailor, leading the way.

I had formed the plan to demand the murders of the Chief Fishmen and execute them on the grave or the same spot of the murdered Governor; their failing to acceed to my demands, I intended to land a part of the four crews and destroy their towns. In order to effect my purpose, I had suggested to the four Commanders the necessity of imposing on the natives, by a few evolutions with our vessels.

An hour before sunset we made our appearance in a perfect line, each vessel having its flags and pennants flying. We passed the native towns and when off the River St. John, tacking in good order, we returned, each one taking a position opposite the different towns as with the intent to cannonade them.

The settlers of the Colony in the meantime had searched and found the body of the unfortunate Governor, and at the moment of our arrival off the river, were discussing the best method to punish the natives for the atrocious murder. The appearance of four vessels parading about the roads and anchoring off the native towns gave them cause to believe that I had come with some war-like intent toward the Fishmen. My servant, on asking for Mr. Findley, had told them of his being a passenger on board my vessel, therefore my appearance was expected.

A few moments after my arrival, Governor Johnson of that Colony sent off a dispatch, requesting to know if the squadron was commanded by me, and requesting in such case that I would land and make arrangements to unite our forces against the natives, himself and his council having determined on punishing them.

In the meantime, the natives, who well knew we had no cannons, had flocked to the beach in droves, and as the distance from us was greater than a musket shot, they defied us by all sort of signs to a combat. On landing at the American settlement, the Governor and his military *Etat-Major*[1] agreed that early next day their forces should march by the beach, when myself and seamen would join them a short distance from the native towns. The Colonel agreed to bring a field piece with his regiment.

By nine o'clock next morning, the Colonial flag with drum and fife made its appearance on the beach, followed by about forty men dragging a short carronade mounted on a field carriage. Three of my boats immediately pushed off from the vessels to join them. By this

[1]staff of assistants

time the colonists had arrived at a rock which intercepted the beach and which the natives had possession of. By its cavities, this rock formed a secure place to the natives from the colonists' balls, and for a quarter of an hour the progress of our allies was delayed. I saw the advantage of the natives and hastened with my boats to dislodge them and open a passage to the Americans.

Not knowing what quantity of natives might be hid in the bushes only 15 yards' distance from the water, I kept my men afloat, and by several discharges of muskets, purged the rock of its warriors. One man only fell by our shots.

Our forces then joined, when Colonel Wheeler proposed that we should all march in compact body to the towns, and then, if the enemy was there, give them battle. His plan was not put in force, as the natives made their appearance long before we neared their habitations. Their plan was to keep in the bushes, and under the parapet of this native protection, shoot and run, while we kept the defensive, fired at the unseen enemy, and advanced.

Now and then the natives would appear in a large body at a safe distance from our musket shots, toss their guns or lances high in the air, brandish their cutlasses and present their backs, slap the fleshy part, and then disappear. Such game was not repeated but a second time: a colonist by the name of Bear who shouldered a heavy rifle took rest on my shoulder and with his buckshot brought one of the annoying provokers to the ground.

Our cannon and mounted blunderbusses were now called in use to scour the bushes, as the natives, confident of their hiding place, fired amongst us with more precision than was desirable. A Krooman in our party had now been shot dead, and an American officer, Mr. Washington, had received a flesh wound. Small divisions of our party advanced at a run and fired in the bushes, allowing in this manner the main body to advance, while another division did the same, and so on. We made good progress till we arrived at the first town.

Here we expected the natives would defend their roofs. A party of us took the lead and advanced, gun in hand, up the narrow path. Mr. Benson, followed by two young men, Mr. Moore and Mr. Roberts, marched in company with me to the first house, but it was evacuated. Even the doors had been carried away. The ju-ju alone was left to guard the deserted hovels, but it did not protect them against the conflagration, and five towns were burnt in a short space of one hour.

Some time before our arrival at the enemy's towns it was found that our ammunition had been nearly consumed. My canoe, which had been sent to the Colony, returned without any. This unpardonable neglect on the part of the Governor we could not remedy; a further advance was useless, and a retreat was ordered.

Till now the natives had kept on the defensive, but on seeing our retreat they became the aggressors. Our cannon with its grape kept them at bay for a short time, but our provision of shot and grape had been too profusely expended by the Colonel, and soon gave out. My men, who had no cartridge box and had received from the general chest but a short allowance of cartridges, called for more, which were not supplied.

In the urgent difficulty, availing myself of my position as second in command, I called a halt and demanded a fair distribution of the powder and balls. While in the act of inspecting a colonist's box who I found well supplied, a slug struck me in the right foot, which at the moment did not deprive me from walking, but the cold water and the sand which washed into the wound, and the loss of blood soon obliged me to seek refuge in a canoe which my Krooman kept afloat and followed our march.

On embarking I ordered my men to obey Colonel Wheeler and left them with only six loads for the cannon. The native who wounded me had watched the effect of his gunshot, and now seeing me embark, shouted to his people that "Story" (my first nickname) was wounded and on his way on board. His cry of joy was repeated by his countrymen, who now gathered in great number on the beach, tolling their war bells.

I had not reached the vessel before my Krooman informed me the Americans were in full flight, having abandoned their gun. It was reported that the Colonel, hearing the cry of the natives, had given order for this shameful hasty retreat, which caused that night the burning of Bassa Cove, a settlement on the south side of the river.

My men returned on board next morning. Eight of them bore severe marks of the previous fight, but none proved dangerous. As the Colony was in danger of being attacked, by request of the Governor I landed to his order 20 muskets and four kegs of powder, not having sufficient lead to give.

I have given a long narration of this engagement and perhaps a tedious one, but as the occurence of Mr. Findley taking passage in a Spanish vessel was at the time much vilified, representing the schooner *Brillante* as a slaver and thus maliciously "proving" the accident of his death as a calamity sent on him for having trod the deck of a slaver; and as no one ever contradicted the untruthful accusation, I have here added one or two pages more to this chapter to exculpate the reputation of a man who met a violent death while in the prosecution of his honorable calling.

CHAPTER 71ˢᵗ

Charitable Conduct of Mr. Blanco · My English Partner Taken Prisoner · I Am Windbound and in Distress · Across the Town of Monrovia with 19 Slaves

On my return to New Sester I sent the schooner to Gallinas, giving my employer a full detail of the circumstances and my accident, requesting he would send a person to take charge of the factory as I was impossibilitated by my wound. The vessel was immediately sent back with a letter authorizing me to send an enclosed draft of 500$ to the widow or orphans of the murdered Governor, but as Mr. Findley had no family, the generous gift was sent back.   *1838

The letter also gently blamed my too-prompt action in the chastisement of the guilty natives, but still lauded the motives that induced me to venture my life without the prospects of a complete satisfaction, and ended with the request that I would take things more cooly and not expose my life and his property with my hasty Italian temper. By-the-bye, the letter was addressed to "Mr. Powder," the nickname the Bassa people had given me.

The shot that wounded me had taken effect on the upper part of the foot near the ankle joint. Being an iron slug as all native balls are, it had torn the tendons and the flesh, thus making a severe wound: which accident kept me nine months on crutches.

A few weeks after, a small English coasting schooner on her passage to leeward made signal for communication with the shore. Believing she was in distress, I sent a canoe off, when her Skipper begged to see me on board, having something to communicate to me of most urgent importance. Being informed of my wounded state, the tremulous Master made bold to venture in the establishment of a slaver.

With great precaution of secrecy, he handed me a well-folded note and begged I would never tell from whence it came. The missive was from my former English partner, a prisoner in Sierra Leone. He had been captured in a Spanish slaver, taken to Havana, thence to Jamaica, now in Sierra Leone under sentence of being transported. In his letter he begged me to supply funds to purchase his escape.

The idea of my former but ungrateful partner ending his days in Botany Bay dispelled my resentment. A draft on my employer was cashed in Sierra Leone, and the day after, my partner and jailor were on their way to Rio Pongo.

263

The quick dispatch I had given to several vessels soon brought New Sester into notice. Havana, Matanzas, and Puerto Rico sent their vessels, and the third year after my first establishing there, the demand of slaves became so great that the country could not furnish us with sufficient quantity for the slavers in port.

To procure them with greater abundance, I had set up several factories at Petit Bassa and Digbay, two points a few miles off the limits of Liberia. Those factories supplied me with small slaves, which I have no doubt were half of them kidnapped a little way into the Interior. But the urgent necessity of extending my business induced me to visit my Digbay factory in person.

My boat was loaded with a choice invoice of goods, and now being able to walk without crutches, I embarked with the intent of setting a new factory, if possible, near Small Cape Mount.

On my arrival at Digbay I found my factory without a slave and the goods trusted out. This annoyed me, and without landing a piece of cloth I proceeded to the next village only a few miles distant, and there I landed my goods. The well distributed rum did its effects, and the natives promised me the exclusive patronage of their trade. In five days, nineteen slaves were exchanged for my goods and I shipped them, promising to return soon or send one of my men with greater quantity of goods and establish a branch factory.

My new boat was only 27 feet long, but sufficiently commodious to carry twenty-four persons, considering that my 19 slaves were but boys and girls. On starting, the wind was favorable, but toward sundown it had changed to the southwest, increasing to a gale with rain and heavy seas. I coasted the beach under reef sails till daylight, in the hopes of landing my live cargo at some friendly town, but at sunrise I found the beach impracticable even to Kroo canoes. The surf was tremendous.

I pushed on till I came to Monrovia, and as there was no man-of-war in port, I anchored under the cape, spreading my sails over the boat to hide my cargo. That night the wind lulled, and in the morning I made sail again. The wind and current continued to the same point, and we made no progress. At sundown I returned to my former anchorage and under the awnings made out to cook a mess of rice for my slaves. (Till then they had been fed with raw cassava.)

The next day was attended with the same adverse contrarities; at night one of the slaves died of the cramps. The third day proving still squally, rainy, and a boisterous sea, I remained at an anchor. At evening I landed at the Kroo town and hired the head man to assist me in crossing my slaves through the American settlement en route for New Sester.

This maneuver was a dangerous one, as the colonists, ever on the lookout against encroachments on the right of their Colony, would have punished me most severely if caught in the act. About eleven o'clock my slaves were landed in Kroo canoes, and escorted by six stout Kroo fellows, I took them through the town to the southeast side of the cape. The rain fell in torrents, which was in my favor; otherwise I might have met some of the colonists. However, I was prepared for the emergency, as I never traveled unarmed or unprovided with a few doubloons. Had I met a colonist and my gold could not have purchased his silence, I intended to seize him and force him with my party till my slaves were in safety.

At daylight I left my caravan, proceeding by an interior path to Petit Bassa whence my factory would supply them with the necessities to cross the other Colony of St. John's Bassa and in three days arrive at my place. On my return to the Colony, I made the people there believe that I had just arrived windbound.

No one till this day knows this circumstance, or would believe it if not told by myself. I have made this remark as the colonists of Liberia have often been accused of aiding and participating in the slave trade, and in some instances it has been publicly reported as a fact that many persons belonging to the Colony and moving in the commercial circle of Monrovia had and were participating in the profits of my traffic for the assistance they gave me. I could not then exculpate those persons, as an inference on my part would have given the vilifiers greater hold on the false accusation. But now that things are past and the slave trade is totally abolished in the neighborhood of the Liberia Colonies, I can assure the American public who have the interest of those beneficial Colonies more at heart than other nations, that in all my transactions while in the slave trade, not one colonist gave me more assistance than I could have received at any of the French or English Colonies. And every unsophisticated reader will grant that the colonist who sold me two or four pieces of cloth participated in my slave trade no more than the English, French, and American supercargo who sold me a complete and assorted cargo with which I purchased my slaves. Therefore why accuse a few poor mechanics who gave me their labor in exchange for my contaminated slaver's gold! Were not my drafts for thousands of dollars stained with the same accusation? This statement is necessary, as in some future chapter I may again refer to the Colony of Liberia.

Invitation to a British Cruiser to Visit My Factory · Detention of the First Lieutenant on Shore

On the arrival of every vessel in the roadsteads of New Sester, I invariably sent my canoe to ascertain the nature of their callings, and when a British man-of-war did me the honor to anchor off my place for the express purpose of watching and destroying my operations, a polite note would be sent on such occasions, from me to the Commander, offering to supply him with all the fresh provisions or any other commodity that the country could afford.

On one occasion the brigantine *Bonito*, one of Her Britannic Majesty's cruisers, anchored off New Sester, and a polite missive was addressed to her Captain with my customary offers. An answer was sent, politely declining my courteous offer for the present and informing me that H.B.M. brig *Bonito* had been sent by his Commodore with orders to blockade New Sester, for which purpose he had a supply of six months' provisions; and he intended not to budge from his anchorage till relieved by another cruiser. Therefore he advised me to give up the idea of attempting any further efforts toward the prosecution of my abominable traffic. He wondered how a person so well informed and apparently so well educated could not only countenance, but prosecute a traffic so contrary to humanity, and could not conceive that a Christian would consent to confine in irons and allow to perish of hunger a set of beings whom he understood then existed in my barracoons.

By the Commander's answer I saw that he had been misinformed about the real state of my well supplied establishment, and as rice was scarce that season, he labored under the idea that my slaves were suffering for want of provisions.

The accusation was indeed very mortifying to me; to be accused of countenancing the abominable traffic was an insult I could retort, and to an Englishman with double fold, who I might have accused of having taught us Spaniards the inhuman trade. But to be charged with the monstrous crime of willingly starving my slaves to death was an accusation that I hastened to disavow. Therefore I immediately sent a second note inviting the Commander or any of his officers to visit my premises and ascertain in person the fact of his error on the scarcity of provisions.

My invitation was accepted, and about noon two officers appeared off the surf in their boat with a white flag flying. A canoe

safely brought on shore the First Lieutenant and the Doctor, who
apologized for the absence of their Commander.

About this time I had in my captivity some 500 Negroes more or less, and on the arrival in my enclosure of these two officers, the customary salute when a stranger arrived was offered them; and which was for all the slaves to rise and welcome him with a long clap of the hands. This salute was intented only to Captains of slavers, who expecting to take on board as passengers the performers of this hearty welcome, invariably gave them the *douceur* of a demijohn of rum.

My Captain of the barracooniers had played this trick on the officers, expecting to receive the attending present of which he would have the lion's share. The unexpected salute somewhat surprised the officers, who seeing 500 persons rise at once and clap hands, did not know what it meant. But as every person wore a pleasant countenance, they soon understood the nature of the welcome.

My establishment was then in its climax of plenitude, seldom existing in slave factories. I had my stores full of goods, my barracoons full of slaves, and my granary full of rice, which as I said above, not often happens in establishments of this kind; an empty store denotes a full barracoon, and vice versa. The officers minutely inspected every arrangement in the premises and pronounced it perfect. My rice store astonished them for its quantity of full bags, and the well-aired barracoons, or strong sleeping houses, had their full share of praises for their cleanliness and order.

The hour for the slave repast having arrived, the customary operation of washing and singing was gone through before the British officers, who could not believe but that this was a feast day purposely got up to impress them, my guests, favorably in the treatment of my slaves. The Doctor like all of his profession, full of inquisitiveness, went about searching at every corner till he came to the slave kitchen, where the large caldron full of rice astonished his curiosity for its whiteness and quality and abundance. Calling on his brother officer, he pointed out a smaller pot full of meat and soup, from which the Doctor had picked out a piece and was eating it.

The unbelieving Lieutenant could not credit that this was the daily routine of the management of my factory, and till I brought forward the book of my daily expenditures, he could not be convinced of its reality. However, it must not be understood that I gave them meat every day, as such was not the case. For the use of my establishment I killed two bullocks a week. The blood, hide, head, feet, entrails, and the neck were appropriated to the soup for the slaves, and the arrival on shore of these officers was on the day of butchering.

As my dinner hour was at five o'clock and I wanted to honor my guests with a specimen of my cuisine, I ordered the Pilot of the Harbor to report the beach impracticable, a decree no white man should ever break on the Coast of Africa. I addressed a note to the Commander, notifying the impossibility of his officers' return on board that night; they also wrote an apology, and dinner was served.

The perambulations of my premises, its vicinity, and in the Kroo towns gave my visitors such an appetite that I saw all which "mine host" wishes to see in his guests when they are truly welcome. Fowl, flesh, and fish disappeared for the dessert and coffee. Then came the *plus café* served in thimble-sized glasses. Over this last course the conversation fell as usual on slavery, cruisers, and philanthropy.

Each one gave his opinion. The Doctor viewed the act as a philosopher and even condescended to say that he believed that slaves in the hands of white men were happier than slaves in the hands of Negroes, and would support the slavery if it could be carried on with more humanity and less bloodshed. The Lieutenant—a slave himself to Her Majesty and the service—saw nothing but obedience to the Admiralty's orders and prize money. Myself, incredulous to English philanthropy, offered to believe the boasted Christian charity of their nation for the benighted Africans, when England would cease her depredatory wars in East India, abandon the contraband and forced trade of opium in China, and stop persecuting her Irish subjects.

The evening was spent in visiting several Negro dances at the Prince's town, which amused my guests much.

About sunrise, the brig of war fired a gun calling her officers on board, and my lookout reported a vessel in the offing, and the cruiser under way. It's said that all sailors sleep with one ear cocked. The Lieutenant was up in a moment, and calling on the Doctor to follow, made for the beach, where my orders had preceded him.

The *Bonito* had not yet tripped anchor, and her signal man was flourishing his bunting in vain in order to call the officers on board. Another gun flashed as the mariner officer arrived at the beach: "A canoe! A canoe, I say! Give me a canoe!" But out of fifty spectators, no one moved.

Once more, "A canoe!" was the cry, and exhibiting several dollars, he earnestly urged the bystanders to put him on board. The only answer was, "Ask the Commodore; ask the Consul."

"Damn the Commodore and Consul too! Put me on board, and
268 here is twenty dollars for you." But no one accepted. Infuriated, he

CHAPTER 73rd

I Am Taken Prisoner by a British Cruiser

*1838 My business calling me at Mesurado, I availed myself of a Russian brig which was going north to take passage in her. On our way up the Coast and when in sight of our port of destination, a British cruiser brought us to with a couple of shots.

As our Captain had nothing to fear from a British man-of-war, his papers being in perfect order, we hove to and awaited his visit. The Commander of the *Saracen*, Lieutenant Commander Hill, on searching our vessel and finding a slave deck and a large quantity of water casks, did not consider us in such perfect order. Very unceremoniously he put an officer and prize crew on board and ordered the *Galupsic* (such was the name of our vessel) to Sierra Leone.

Being a passenger, I requested the British Commander to put me ashore. My request was refused, as my presence, he said, "was of a material consequence in the condemnation of the vessel." Some of his Kroomen had recognized me and had informed the Commander of my name; therefore Hill, having heard of my reputation as a noted slave dealer, pressed me on board.

On our arrival in Sierra Leone, the Mixed Commission Court could not try our vessel, being a Russian one. The captor decided on sending us to England. I again applied to be sent on shore at Sierra Leone, but Lieutenant Hill had imperatively decided otherwise, and as he kept the brig incommunicado, I could not write to the Governor or protest against such arbitrary proceedings.

Now to be sent to England sadly deranged my affairs. My barracoons were filled with slaves, and I had only one month's provisions in my stores. My clerk was not capable to manage my factory during the long absence which such a forced trip would detain me. All my exertions to persuade my captor to allow me to land having failed me, I took the determination to take a French leave.

Three men-of-war surrounded our vessel and kept watch against any boats or canoes accosting us. At night two marines and four sailors paraded our deck and kept a watchful lookout. Therefore, to make an escape from such vigilance was a difficult job, and nothing but a dangerous swim could effect it. The Russian Captain—a Spaniard and my intimate friend—lent me his aid, and with the assistance of his Steward and Boatswain, the escape was effected the fourth night.

270   On the day of the premeditated escape, the Steward informed the

returned to the factory and there found his companion comfortably taking his coffee.

"Doctor, I say, don't you hear the signals? We are called on board."

"Yes," was the cool answer. "But unfortunately, the vessel she's in chase of is one of Captain Conneau's vessels, and he has judiciously put an embargo on all canoes on the beach. Therefore come up and take coffee, and we will await the return of the *Bonito*."

During this dialogue I was up in my lookout house watching the progress of the chase, but as it was northward, both vessels disappeared. On my descent, I was accosted by the offended officer, who demanded of me if I intended to keep him prisoner much longer.

I told him he was perfectly free to go when he pleased, if he could find anyone to take him: he had not made his intention known to me; therefore he could not expect me to urge him off from my premises. However, he now could be furnished with a canoe, but as the vessel was no longer in the offing, he had better wait and take breakfast.

For my part, I carried the conversation in a jestive manner, in which the Doctor joined me. The affronted Lieutenant struck his countenance of displeasure, and we all sat down to breakfast.

Shortly after, their vessel returned, having given up the chase, and the officers returned on board. Next day I received a polite note from the Commander of the *Bonito* thanking me for the kind treatment I had given his officers.

crew that it was their Captain's birthday, in consequence of which a large pig was killed and double allowance of wine was allowed. The man-of-war's crew and marines participated in the fresh mess, and several bottles of brandy were distributed amongst them. The prize officer, who messed with us, was regaled during the afternoon with several invitations of cognac for which he had a peculiar liking. Still, we did not allow him to make too free till night.

With this ruse, officer, marines, and sailors were all pretty well intoxicated by sundown, but the Corporal of Marines, a sober-sided disciplinarian who never drank spirits, was the only one to be feared for his vigilance to his duties. As a compliment we had invited him to dine with us, with the intent to drug his wine, but his moderation put our attempts to complete failure.

He acknowledged that when on shore, cider only was his favorite beverage. However, accident favored us. At the dessert, a bottle of champagne was uncorked, when the officer himself called to the Corporal and in jocular manner told him to taste the *cider*. "Cider!" said the soldier. "With pleasure," and held his tumbler out. It was immediately filled.

The joke pleased the officer, and us much better. Another and another bottle made its appearance, in which the officer and Corporal participated without economy. Our dinner party broke up about dark, as it was necessary to make some preparation for my departure. The Captain in the meantime took upon himself to entertain the officer with a game of dominoes and a bottle of brandy. The Steward, a native of Mahoue who spoke English tolerably well, took charge of the Marine Corporal and led him forward, and there taking a bottle of champagne from under his coat, proffered it to him as a private present.

Smuggled goods have a peculiar taste to some people, and one bottle more of this treacherous cider conquered our sober-sided disciplinarian. A few more bottles of brandy at supper time brought Spaniards and English to seek their pillows or soft planks. The Boatswain in the meantime had prepared a sweep on the forecastle by which to assist me on reaching the beach.

At 11 o'clock I divested myself of my clothes and hat, placed them in my cabin, and also left my watch hanging at the head of the berth. In a small bundle I took a flannel shirt and light pair of pants which I tied on the back part of my neck. Then bidding adieu to my friends, I slid from the bows, placed the sweep under my arms, and under the assisting darkness of the night and a rising tornado, made for the shore.

An African tornado is a phenomenon which has been much

exaggerated by travelers, but sailors regard it as nothing more than a thunderstorm which, contrary to white squalls, gives them sufficient time to prepare for its sudden gusts. I presume "tornado" is the corrupt name for the ancient Portuguese name *trueno* (thunder) and which must have been given by them to these squalls when the Portuguese first discovered the tropical Continent of Africa. The first tornados make their appearance about the month of March at the first beginning of the rainy season, and last five weeks more or less. They take place at an interval of two or three days apart from one another. On a hot and calm day the tornado is more severe and generally rises and expands itself from meridian to sunset, but at all times the dark rising clouds give warning that this phenomenon is at hand, arriving with a heavy shower and sometimes with only a few large drops of rain, but ever attended with sudden stiff flaws[1] of winds lasting a few minutes but never over a quarter of an hour, while an abundance of thunder attends the introduction and departure of these atmospheric revolutions.

I had chosen the fourth night after the first determination of starting, as about 11 o'clock that night the tide would change and serve to drift me past one of the men-of-war that was anchored near our stern and inshore of us. I allowed myself to drift with the first of the ebb tide, and when fifty yards from the cruiser I gently struck out for the Kroo town, increasing my velocity as I distanced the man-of-war.

During the trajectory, the much desired tornado dissolved itself in thunder and rain, thus encouraging my exertions free from the apprehension of sharks. (It is supposed that sharks become fearful in thunder squalls and seek refuge at the bottom.) Only those who have visited Sierra Leone are aware of the great quantity of those dangerous animals that infest that river, and can form an idea with what pleasure I saw the black squall rising over my head and which effect was to assist me in my enterprise.

Just before 12 o'clock I landed at the Kroo town and having dressed myself, I inquired of the first person I met for a well-known head Krooman. I was conducted to his house, and this native escorted me to a free town.

Next morning, the Cabin Boy, not finding me on deck for coffee as usual, took it to my state room, when in great consternation he returned on the deck, saying I was nowhere to be found. The officer caused a search to be made, and finding the clothes of the day before with my watch undisturbed in the berth, he supposed I had fallen

[1]gusts

overboard. A signal was made to the senior officer, and in a moment *1838* the *Galupsic*'s decks were full of officers. A second search was instituted, but as it proved as unsuccessful as the first, it was resolved that the celebrated—not to say notorious—T. Conneau had fallen overboard in a fit of *mania potu*.[1]

The report of my death reached me on shore, but soon after I saw Lieutenant Commander Hill land with several marines. The old sailor was not to be caught with false colors; he allowed my death to be reported, but by his demonstrations of landing marines on shore, I saw he did not believe it himself. From behind my Venetian window I espied all movements and kept myself concealed.

[1]drunken craziness

CHAPTER 74th

A Joke on the Lieutenant of H.B.M. Brig Dolphin ·
Return to New Sester · Report of My Death ·
Anecdotes of the Prince · The Jackass

*1838 I remained absconded eight days, during which time from my hiding place I saw the *Galupsic* sail for England, escorted by the *Saracen*. In my place of concealment I received the daily visits of several friends and made purchase of a number of necessaries for my factory, and on the eighth day left on board of a Portuguese vessel which had been seized but was not condemned.

On my way to New Sester I stopped at Digbay and took on board from my factory 31 slaves, with two canoes to land them in case I should meet a man-of-war. This night proving very squally and dark, we kept under easy sail. About one o'clock the lookout espied two vessels. Supposing them to be British cruisers, we lowered the canoes and placed in each ten slaves, and ordered them to make for the shore. But before we could launch the boat and send off the remaining 11 slaves, we heard the rowing of the cruiser's boat.

Our boat was immediately capsized bottom up on the fore part of the hatch and the slaves put underneath. A sailor was also placed with them to keep them silent, and the light in the binnacle was immediately extinguished. In a moment more, the boat was along-side and with a spring, the officer was on the rail.

With another step he stood on the bottom of our boat. "What vessel is this?" said he, still remaining on the boat.

"The *Maria* from Sierra Leone," was the answer. A light was called, but as we pretended we had none, a lantern was handed from the boat. A hasty search was made of the hold by two sailors, but nothing was found to render the vessel suspicious. We were allowed to go, and early next morning arrived at my factory where the eleven slaves were immediately landed.

About noon the British cruiser *Dolphin* let go its anchor near the *Maria* and made her a prize. This was the same cruiser we had met the night before in company with a prize and who had searched our vessel. The *Dolphin* had returned in consequence of having found out from one of our slaves sent in the canoe, who in the confusion of disembarking them, had slipt overboard and swam on board the prize; and there had told how the *Maria* had hurried them off in canoes and still retained on board eleven slaves which the First

Lieutenant had not found, although under his feet. The *Maria* was
again taken to Sierra Leone and there condemned.

My landing at New Sester was hailed by the natives with great demonstration of joy. The Prince, who had heard of my death, could not believe of my return till he sent his son to ascertain the fact. Then he immediately paid me a visit.

As I extended both my hands to welcome him, he drew back, requesting I would show and count my fingers to him. I did so, and satisfying him I had the right complement, he shook me heartily by them. On inquiring the cause of his surprise, he told me that some of his men had returned from Mesurado and had there been informed by the colonists that I had been seized in the Russian brig and that the English had cut my fingers off so I should not make "more English books" (meaning writing English letters, by which the natives believed I had often deceived the English cruisers).

Many more stories had been reported on the Coast of my death at Sierra Leone, and a Captain lately liberated by the decision in his favor of the Mixed Commission Court made it his business to report to my employer my death and its disgracing cause as reported in Sierra Leone. But he was rebuked with the information that he was positive such was not the case, and that he knew me too well to be accused of drunkenness and positively believed that I had escaped and would soon make my appearance.

About this time a French vessel came to land a cargo, and as he had anchored at Cape de Verde Island, he had brought me a donkey. Such an animal had never been seen at New Sester. The arrival of the long-eared stranger made some sensation in the place, and as I had no call for such an animal, I made him a present to the Prince, who had very great desire for it. In a few days the quadruped was brought back by the Prince in person, saying he would not keep such a noisy animal whose braying, in his superstitious idea, would cause all his females to miscarry. Once this superstition spread, the poor animal was not tolerated in the neighborhood, and I was obliged to send him to Monrovia.

Confession of a Dying Sailor

*1838   For the service of my factory I employed a Clerk as bookkeeper, a Petty Officer as a storekeeper, and four white sailors to look over the slaves.

One of my sailors, who had been sick for several weeks of the dropsy and now lay at the verge of death, sent for me, wishing to communicate something of importance. I immediately attended, and at his request sent everyone nearby away.

After handing me five ounces in gold which he bequeathed to his sister, he told me he had a confession to make. I exhorted him to unburden his conscience and offered to do anything toward alleviating his remorse, if it was within my power. With feeble but distinct voice he informed me that he had been one of the crew of the Spanish vessel who a few years before had punished Captain Thompson and all on board for the murder of Don Miguel, the Spanish factor of Petit Bassa.

I had heard of this piratical revenge, but did not know the particulars. The dying man's offer to make a confession of the part he had taken in the wholesale murder of the crew of a colonial craft caused me to lend all my attention, and I am sorry I did not take it down in writing, as I could now give the correct dates when this catastrophe took place. However, I will try to repeat the words as nearly as I can translate them from memory. Translation:

"I left Havana with Captain Don Miguel on a slave voyage. On our arrival at Cape Mount, we found the place miserably destitute of slaves, therefore we continued further down the Coast. At Cape Mesurado we received information from a Krooman that at Petit Bassa, or Little Bassa, we could get a cargo of slaves in a month.

"We shipped the informer with his Kroo boys and next day arrived at Petit Bassa. The Chiefs received our Captain kindly, and having a lot of slaves on hand, we landed our goods at this place. I had made a voyage before with Don Miguel, and now I was chosen with two more men to land with him and assist him in the management of the factory.

"With the assistance of the natives we soon built up a dwelling house, a store, and barracoon, the whole well fenced with a stockade fence. Our brigantine was then sent back with a short cargo of slaves in charge of the Mate, and we continued trading till her return.

"During this time, Don Miguel supplied himself with goods from the Cape of Monrovia, paying in doubloons. The goods were sent in small crafts manned by American Negroes. Our Captain kept an

276

excellent table, and whenever those colonists landed or walked the beach from the cape to our factory, Don Miguel invited them to dinner or breakfast. An intimacy soon arose between them, and the Americans were often preferred to us, his men. Captain Thompson, a colonist, had free access to our barracoon, ever receiving some present from our Captain over the payment of his goods.

"Our vessel returned from Havana and her cargo was landed, which consisted of rum, tobacco, and powder, with a box of doubloons. The vessel was sent back to Cape de Verde to exchange her flag. In the meantime the colonists of Mesurado had picked a quarrel with the Chiefs of the trade town, and were assisted by an American vessel under the Columbian flag. With a commission of privateers, it landed the Colony's troops and there robbed the Spanish barracoons.

"The destruction of a Spanish factory was resented by Don Miguel in his kind treatment to the American colonists, and a coolness continued for some time. But the Monrovians had heard of the box of doubloons, and our Captain was again beset by their assurance of friendship, throwing the blame on the Colombian privateer for the injuries done to the Spaniards. Captain Thompson, in particular, made such sincere demonstration of repentance that our too good-hearted Captain allowed him again the same familiarities.

"Things went on pretty smoothly for some time, when the same Thompson arrived with his craft, having on board several passengers bound, they said, to Grand Bassa. They landed, and as usual the whole party dined with our hospitable Captain, which generally took place at four o'clock. At six they left for the purpose of retiring on board, receiving several pieces of salt beef and two gallons of rum for their voyage.

"About half past seven o'clock they returned, and as it was then dark, the doors were shut. They called aloud to Don Miguel to open to them and give them hospitality for the night, saying the beach was too rough to return on board. The Captain opened the door, when his guests shot him in the face. Several more shots were fired, and in a moment the premises were filled with American colonists. Don Miguel fell the moment he was shot, and a second discharge ended his agony.

"My duties were in the barracoon. On the first discharge I was at my post, but the sight of so many armed colonists soon told me what I might expect at their hands—I, who had always openly opposed Don Miguel's generosity to these men. Being hard pressed by them, I escaladed the fence and made for the bushes, where I remained till morning, when I was taken by the natives to the Prince's town.

"The Americans had a brush with the natives the next day, but as 'Tiger don't eat tiger,' I believe they divided the spoil, and the colonists returned to Monrovia. I remained with the Prince five weeks, during which time I sent a note to a friend in Gallinas who sent me a canoe in which I left Petit Bassa. At Gallinas I found the means to return to Cuba. Being the only survivor of the unfortunate four men that accompanied Don Miguel at Petit Bassa, I was also the first to relate to the owners and the brother of my Captain the piratical attack by the colonists on our factory.

"Several months after, in which time I had made a successful voyage to Africa, I met Don Miguel's brother in the streets of Havana, and I was invited to ship in his brig as Quartermaster. I accepted the offer without knowing for what part of the Coast we were bound. In a few days we left port, and one month after we made Mesurado.

"We cruised from Mesurado to Grand Bassa for five days, avoiding every common size vessel we met. On the sixth day we espied a small craft beating to leeward. We kept company for several hours and allowed her to make her long leg out to sea, when we gave chase, thus preventing her from running ashore.

"An hour before sundown, we captured her. Thompson, the cowardly Thompson, was on board. I pointed him out to our Captain as the murderer of his brother, and I seized him by the collar. He disengaged himself and jumped overboard, but our boat soon rescued him from self-destruction.

"After dark the five persons who accompanied Thompson were double-ironed in the hold of their craft, and the hatches fasten down. Thompson was then chained to some bolts driven on purpose in the deck, and his hands were nailed with spikes to the deck. Three barrels of tar were broken on the deck, and at nine o'clock precisely we set fire to the craft.

"We remained by her till she was consumed, and bilged. We then sailed for Benin, where the Captain died."

Having finished his confession, he begged to know if I would forward a letter to his sister with the gold he had given me, and request her to have a Mass said for the repose of his soul. I promised him his request, but I inquired if he had repented his murderous deed.

His answer was that he had, as far as regarded the innocent crew, but as to Thompson, he said "Never!", growing terribly passionate at the mention of the name. My endeavors to compose the last moments of the dying sinner were fruitless, as he expired a few minutes after, and his last word was "Thompson."

CHAPTER 76th

Wars at Digbay · Horrors and Barbarities of the Bushmen

*1838—1839

The reader may remember I had promised my friends at Digbay to send back a larger amount of goods and to establish a new factory. I did so and sent it in charge of a sailor.

Now these two towns had for Chiefs two cousins who for many years lived in harmony and friendship. My sending a factory to the younger cousin and placing a white man in charge there gave serious offense to the older cousin, to whom I refused goods on my last trip and who had no white man in his town to boast of. From such slight grievances and the displeasures on the subject of my goods, the two neighborly and friendly cousins became implacable enemies, and in two months from my landing, the two towns had fenced, fortified, and barricaded themselves. This done, they sent expeditions to surprise one another during the night, but as both towns kept a strict watch, nothing was effected. The kidnapping of four women and children while going wooding or watering was the extent of their depredations.

The third month, one of the cousins—he of the white man —purchased the assistance of a party of Bushmen to fight his battles. The Chief of these mercenary people was called Jenken and had acquired a certain fame in the Interior for his valor and barbarity. His wives, like himself, were cannibals, and his war men never left their home for a battle without promising to return with a large supply of flesh for their families.

Several attacks had been made on the cousin by Jenken and his warriors, but his vigilance was too great and nothing was effected. The Bushmen, tired of a contest against picket fences and stockade barricades, returned to the Interior. This demonstration of the Bushmen, with a friendly proposal from the younger cousin, soon brought them to speaking terms; and two more months passed in this apparent cool apathy.

Just about this time, business called me at Gallinas, and on my way I visited my first factory at Digbay for the purpose of giving the offended Chief a white man also as factor. As I arrived at sundown, I proposed to land some goods next morning and proceed to supply my white man at the next town with fresh goods also.

My arrival had been greeted with the customary rejoicing. My landlord, proud of his expectation now that a white man was to abide in his town, feasted his people with several gallons of rum and fired many discharges of powder to celebrate the event. The dancing, drinking, and firing lasted till midnight, when everybody retired to rest.

About three in the morning the sudden cry of women and children woke me up, when several discharges of muskets announced to me and my Kroomen boatmen that the town was beseiged or attacked by the enemy. Presently we heard a loud knocking at our door requesting me to open and fly. It was the Chief, who was on the point of abandoning his town, as he could not make resistance. His men, only few in number, were too intoxicated to oppose the dreadful enemy.

I was on the point of complying with the request, but my Kroomen dissuaded me from venturing in the melee of a flight, assuring me that the enemy was the treacherous cousin who had only temporarily discharged the Bushmen to deceive our landlord, and that such being the case, I and them had nothing to fear but a temporary captivity and a redemption for all, which would be gladly accepted by the captors.

In a few minutes a rush was made through the town, attended with the well-known war cry and yells of the conquerors. Yell after yell succeeded, till our door was burst open and Jenken, torch in hand, made his appearance and declared us his prisoners.

In the meantime his men captured, seized, and murdered every living thing that came within their reach.

The storming of the town had taken place about four o'clock, and till daylight we had been kept prisoners under the guard of Jenken himself, who from our house issued his commands of destruction. When day appeared, nothing more was heard but the groaning of the wounded and the moaning of the women and children now prisoners.

At the return of the warriors from the pursuit of the fugitives, several wounded old men were dragged in by the feet and piled up, ready for execution. Our habitation was fronting the only palabra house, and as we remained still prisoners, we were forced to witness the brutal massacre of the wounded victims.

On invading the town, some of the warriors had found in the Chief's house several jars of rum, and now the bottle went round with astonishing rapidity. The ferocious and savage dance was then suggested. The war bells and horns had sounded the arrival of the female warriors, who on the storming of a town generally make their entry in time to participate in the division of the human flesh; and as the dead and wounded were ready for the knife, in they came like furies and in the obscene perfect state of nakedness, performed the victorious dance which for its cruelties and barbarities has no parallel.

Some twenty-five in number made their appearance with their faces and naked bodies besmeared with chalk and red paint. Each one bore a trophy of their cannibal nature. The matron or leader, Jenken's head wife, a woman of forty, bore an infant babe newly torn from its mother's womb and which she tossed high in the air, receiving it on the point of her knife. Other Medeas followed, all bearing some mutilated member of the human frame.

Rum, powder, and blood, a mixture drunk with avidity by these Bacchantes, had rendered them drunk, and the brutal dance had intoxicated them to madness. Each was armed also with some tormenting instrument, and not content with the butchering outside of the town of the fugitive women, they now surrounded the pile of the wounded prisoners, long kept in suspense for the *coup de grâce*. A ring was formed by the two-legged tigresses, and accompanied by hideous yells and encouraging cry of the men, the round dance began. The velocity of the whirling soon broke the hideous circle, when each one fell on his victims and the massacre began. Men and women fell to dispatching the groaning wounded with the most disgusting cruelties.

I have seen the tiger pounce on the inoffensive gazelle and in its natural propensity of love of blood, strangle its victim, satiate its thirst, and often abandon the dead animal. But not so with these female cannibals. The living and dying had to endure a tormenting and barbarous mutilation, the women showing more cannibal nature in the dissection of the dead than the stronger sex. The *coup de grâce* was given by the men, but in one instance the victim survived a few minutes when one of those female furies tormented the agony of the dying man by prostrating herself on his body and there acting the beast of double backs.

The matron, commander of these anthrophagies, with her fifty years and corpulous body, led the cruelties on by her example. The unborn babe had been put aside for a *bonne bouche*, and now adorned with a string of men's genital parts, she was collecting into a gourd the brains of the decapitated bodies. While the disgusting operation went on, the men carved the solid flesh from the limbs of the dead, throwing the entrails aside.

About noon the butchering was at an end, and a general barbecuing took place. The smell of human flesh, so disgusting to civilized man, was to them the pleasing odor so peculiarly agreeable to a gastronomer. A fresh cry of joy was heard at a distance, when there appeared impaled on a strong pole the well-known person of my landlord's first wife, who had been found hid in a neighboring bush. Life was not yet extinct, and the bearers, three in number, carried her in an erect position through the town, singing their abominable war songs. A hole was dug and the pole planted in it, then a large fire was made around, but before it was lit, life had departed. This woman would have been saved, as she was still young and handsome, but in her hatred of the enemies of her husband, she had spat on her captors, daring them to take her life. This was her terrible punishment.

The barbecuing over, an anthrophagous repast took place, when the superabundant preserved flesh was packed up in plantain leaves to be sent into the Interior for the warriors' friends. I am silent on the further cruelties that were practiced this day on the unfortunate infirm and wounded that the different scouting parties brought in during the day, supposing the reader to be sick enough at heart at the above representation.

Towards evening myself and the Kroomen were taken to the conquering town, where I paid the value of two slaves for myself and a slave for each of my Kroomen as a ransom for my party. In this chapter, the public will see that I freely accuse myself of being the cause of these wars, and I would not pardon myself if I had caused them with the knowledge of their consequences. I do not disculpate myself, nor would I be thought a willing promoter of these barbarities.

CHAPTER 77ᵗʰ

I Return to Gallinas · The Tornado and the Shark Pendant

Once free from the hands of these savages, I swore that never more would I send goods to Digbay. Early next morning I left for Gallinas, where I was anxious to meet my employer before he left Africa forever.

*1838—1839

The moon was on its full, and the surf was roaring. My boat could not be launched, but two things hastened my departure from this place. First, the horrors I had witnessed; second, the hasty departure of Don Pedro Blanco. In perfect disgust of the traffic, country, and myself and without consideration, I divested myself of my outward garments and against the will of my men I stepped into a fishing canoe and with only one man to manage my bark, dashed through the infuriated swell.

My provisions consisted of three bottles of gin, a small jug of water, and a basket of raw cassava. My luggage I carried with my account books in a small tight keg.

Free from the breakers, we proceeded tolerably well on our way, my man paddling and I bailing, gin and cassava refreshing our exertions now and then. At ten o'clock that night we made Cape Mount, but it would have been madness to have ventured a landing, such was the state of the surf on the beach. On we pulled for our destination, the moon assisting us with her bright rays.

By daylight, the paragua (umbrella), a noted tree at Soliman Point, gave us our true position. My Spanish friends on shore soon espied with their excellent telescopes my well-known dress—the Panama hat and red shirt. But instead of running to the beach to welcome me or drag me from the water in case the canoe should capsize, they hoisted on the signal staff the black flag, signal of danger, the same as used to warn slavers off the Coast. My faithful Krooman had prognosticated a difficult landing, and now the signal from the shore assured me of the impossibility of affecting it in a canoe.

Then for the first time it came to my mind that the sun was near the Equinox, when the bars are ever unpredictable. I then also understood the unwelcome signal, which would never have been made by my friends but when forced by strong necessity. The breakers for half a mile rose mountain high and in regular rotation, leaving that distance white with foam. As our little canoe was lifted by the heavy swell, I could see the Spaniards waving their hats in sign for me to depart southward toward Cape Mount.

I had often swum longer distances, and this fact was well known to my friends. Therefore I could not comprehend why they now insisted on my returning. My pride began to feel that sting which pushes men often into acts of madness, and if success attends him, makes him a hero for a day; but if the attempt fails him, makes him a fool forever.

I arose on my knees to have a better inspection of the danger, still intent on venturing through, when the black flag was lowered down three times in token of adieu. Soon after it was hoisted again over an enormous shark. The friendly Spaniards had recourse to this signal to manifest to me the true cause of danger.

To return to Cape Mount was a great distance for the wearied limbs of my Krooman, who had now been paddling twenty-four hours. Only two choices remained to us: to await the arrival of a friendly vessel, or the subsiding of the surf. Therefore we took our last meal of cassava, and my Krooman stretched himself in the canoe and comfortably went to sleep, half of his body soaking in the water while the upper part scorched in the sun. With my paddle I watched and steered till sundown, when the well-known black clouds from the southeast obliged me to arouse my African and bid him prepare for a tornado.

My sleepy Black partner woke and looking round at the second danger, began to invoke his fetish slung round his neck to spare me from a wet jacket and him from an equal misfortune to his skin. These black squalls are a most disagreeable event to Fishmen and Kroomen when caught at sea in a tornado, as the heavy rains that fall from them chill their body, whose only covering is a single handkerchief which in their aquatic excursions is kept rolled round the head to keep dry.

The appearance of the black clouds brought shivering sensations to my Krooman, and the last bottle was broached to battle the expected cold element. Had we been in company with other canoes, we would all have collected together and by holding to one another, secured ourselves against the gusts of wind, and the short sea. (This is the manner in which the Fishmen of Cape Palmas and thereabouts valiantly ride out a tornado.) But we were alone. The great vigilance and expert arm of my ignorant African was the only defense we had to oppose to the thunderstorm.

On it came with its accustomed fury, but my able Krooman, keeping bow-on, nobly resisted the shocks and gradually we fell

back by the impulse of the irritated waves. Thus we stood it till the heavy clouds discharged their impregnated loads of cold rain on our shoulders. The shower in part relieved the Krooman of his labor, as it put the sea down, but it gave me an additional work, as to keep the canoe free, my Panama hat took the place of the native bailer, an instrument comparable to a wooden spoon.

The squall and wind over, the sea resumed its placidness, and we were left to shake off the chills of the cold rain. My flannel was wrung, but my sable friend having none, an extra kiss at the bottle was the only covering I could give him.

This last dram was the forlorn hope, as like the former, it only burnt with artificial heat to the stomach, leaving the body ten minutes later still more chill and neglected. The last drop was swallowed with regret, and the next half hour passed away under the stupor of the effects of the alcohol. My head swam with a feverish independence, feeling and seeing nothing, but it soon died away, leaving me a helpless mortal half senseless and wholly benumbed.

But here again Providence rescued me from this dangerous position, which one moment's reflection would never have placed me in a canoe when the Equinoxials were at hand. The tornado had brought a light land breeze, and with it came down toward us a vessel. The sharp eyes of the Krooman soon espied her, but prognosticated her a man-of-war—an enemy, of course, which I could not board with my slave accounts.

What to do I knew not, but a sacrifice was necessary as my Krooman still pulled for the vessel. I threw the keg overboard and in a faint voice hailed the schooner. She hove to, and by Providence! it was a Spanish vessel bound to Gallinas. I was recognized and hoisted on board to astonish the officers with my imprudence.

Two days after I landed, and my Soliman friends then told me that had I ventured through the breakers on the day of my arrival, I should certainly have perished by the sharks. Such was the avidity of these animals, since 127 slaves had been lost by a shipment made a few nights previous, that they even sprang from the water to attack their prey. The one that served as a signal two days before had been lassoed while devouring the body of Negro near the shores of the river.

My trip proved a labor in vain, as Mr. Blanco had left a week before my arrival.

CHAPTER 78th

Departure for England

1839 I had now been in the slave trade several years. The furor for changes and emotions had cooled off, and the desire for a roving life had subsided to a degree of negligence for new sceneries. The losses, troubles, and imprisonment never had deterred me before, but to witness the late barbarities inflicted on the wounded in a war of which I was the involuntary cause had sickened my heart with the slave trade, and humanity spoke louder every day in favor of a lawful traffic.

A visit to Cape Mount where I had gone to restore a child to his father, the King of the country, had inspired me with an idea to abandon the slave trade and settle there a lawful factory. Receiving his son from slavery, the King in his gratitude for my liberality offered me the best spot in his dominion to establish myself whenever I wished.

The situation of Cape Mount was, and is, one of the most pleasant places from Sierra Leone to Cape Palmas. This point I chose for my future residence; from this moment my sole study was how to give up a traffic for which I had contracted a great dislike, but in which I was so far involved that my whole fortune was at stake.

My employer had just retired a millionaire from Africa, and the circumstance of my short detention in Sierra Leone had prevented me from seeing him before he left the country. Therefore I made this an excuse for abandoning my factory and paying him a visit to Havana, but my object was to visit England and make arrangements to set up a commercial factory in Cape Mount. Having arranged my business for a long absence and provisioned my barracoons, I left Africa in the English schooner *Gil Blas* with Captain Herbert for London. Our passage was dull and long till we arrived at the capes of the English Channel, when a strong wind rose from the south-southwest and drove us up to Dover before the wind.

It was about nine o'clock when I was called from my bed to see the red brilliant face of the Dover clock signalizing the hour. A few moments after, I heard the voice of our Captain calling for the lantern. The Black boy handed it, and informed me that a steamer was coming down on us.

Presently I heard the Captain again, giving order to hard up the helm, and shortly after calling out with his speaking trumpet to some vessel, "Port! Port your helm or you will sink us!"

286 I had no time to hear more, as a tremendous crash which sent me

reeling to the lee side of the cabin informed me that we had come in contact with the steamer. I was then *en déshabillé*, or vulgarly said, in my small clothes. In this state I made for the deck, when I saw a huge black wall bearing on the side of our little craft, whose main mast lay over her stern, carried away by the steamer's bowsprit, which still stood domineering with contempt over our quarterdeck.

In the shock, the steamer had carried away part of her cutwater. The remaining upper part, pressing hard on our gunwale, bore us down two or more feet. This gave our schooner a sinking appearance which at once caused everyone to scrabble on board the steamer. In the meantime the order was given on board the steamer to back-water, giving us just time enough to save ourselves.

On our arrival on board the steamer, with the assistance of the Mate, I collected all our crew. A Black boy was missing. Presently we heard him cry from on board the schooner for assistance. Our Captain had been struck by the main boom and now lay quite helpless on one side of the steamer's deck. But not so his Mate, a noble English tar who hearing the voice of our Black boy, called to the Commander of the steamer to send a boat, offering his services to save the boy.

No article was taken of his demand, and the schooner was allowed to drift clear of the steamer. The steamer, whose name was *Royal Adelaide*, had now repaired her few damages and stood on her former course down channel, being bound to Dublin. No notice was taken of us, but a kind soldier invited us in the fore cabin. As we descended, the Mate protested against his Captain's inhabiting such a place, and with an intrepid step he placed himself on the poop and addressed the Commander in no very measured terms, demanding that his Captain and passengers should be furnished with room in the after cabin.

Shortly after, the Captain and I were conducted in the gentlemen's cabin, and as I still wore my cotton undress, I was given a shirt and pants fresh from the slop-shop. My Black boy followed me in the cabin, when a volley of coppers were given him from several passengers.

Early next morning we were informed that a boat was in waiting to land us at Cowes. As I was about stepping over the side, the Steward demanded a pair of slippers I had picked up about the cabin. Therefore, having no hat on, I landed without shoes or hat. Our sailors had fared much better; their brother tars had profusely covered the nakedness of those that needed, and the soldiers and few women of easy virtue that were passengers in the fore cabin had supplied them with coin enough to help them up to London.

On landing at Cowes we formed a procession of 14 persons, I alone doing penance in my bare head and feet. It was still too early for our Captain to visit Lloyd's agents.[1] We stopped at a small tavern where our sailors treated their superiors to a cup of coffee. A crowd had collected around us to inquire the nature of our appearance at such an hour, when a servant man dressed in silk stockings, red vest, and livery coat made way through the crowd and demanded to speak to our Captain—and with all the foppyish importance that only a liveried valet can assume, presented him with one sovereign on the part of his master, my lord the Marquis of W.

Our Hibernian Captain, disdaining to accept the scanty alms, told the man of plush and silks to tell his Irish master that 14 men had no need of *one* sovereign, exhorting the bearer to make tracks or he would show him the road.

The agent of Lloyd's supplied our Captain with £20, which took us to London. Two days after, the papers announced the taking into the port of Ostend the schooner *Gil Blas* by the pilots of that place. She was discovered early the morning after the collision, drifting by the pier of Ostend and now in charge of the pilot, who claimed a salvage of one thousands pounds.

Our Black boy was never heard of, although when she was taken into port, one hundred or more parrots were found on board still alive. On the arrival of the schooner in London, the vessel's table cloth was found in her pump-well, full of blood, which induced us to believe the boy had been made away of in order to secure a larger salvage.

[1]to report his loss to representatives of the famed London insurance firm

CHAPTER 79th

A Slave in London

As I never had visited England, I proposed to see London above and September, below stairs. My three years' economies in Africa placed me in a 1839 state to enjoy this wish in moderate extent.

My Black boy, which I called Lunes (Monday), I habited in a suit of marine blue with a profusion of anchor buttons. His vest was of red velvet slightly edged with a gold cord. This was intended, with his cap of blue cloth and a red band, to denote his valet occupation. With this subject of aristocracy after me, I visited, directory in hand, the principal places of the celebrated Capital of Capitals. I shall not intrude on the reader's patience by reenumerating the sights of London; these are daily described and are now as familiar as an everyday walk down Broadway in New York. My object is to describe Africa and Africans; therefore I shall only detail low anecdotes of my African slave servant.

"Monday," who was a well-built boy of 15 years with a pleasant countenance, often attracted much notice by his naive remarks when I visited any of the institutions. I remember one day I took him with me to Greenwich Hospital, and while on board the steamer I called his attention to the cupola of St. Paul's and remarked to him that the day before, we had both been in the golden ball.

My explanation was carried on in an African English, which caused the bystanders to collect in numbers around us. My argument could not convince the boy, when he answered, "No, no, my father. You lie. True, I be Black, but I no be damn fool! Which way two men can live in t'at small t'ing?" His incredibility caused great merriment to the company, and for the rest of the short trip he was the lion of the moment.

At another time I took him to Ashley's Amphitheatre, representing *Mazepa*. The boy, who sat before me (in England and Europe, Blacks are allowed to mingle with the whites) admired much the play, but not with that impression I had expected.

The piece over, the arena opened to a new performance, when an elephant was introduced. The animal had arrived nearly in the center of the circus before the boy saw it; his attention had been diverted to the upper tiers. And on looking down, seeing the huge monster so near him, he gave a spring back and cleared the three hind benches, then calling on me, begged I would run or "T'at big-bush-meat" would kill me.

As I stood laughing, the boy again cried out at the top of his voice, 289

"My father, come, come. T'at t'ing he be bad t'ing, he can kill people. Come, come my father, I love him too much. I look him first time in my country; he can kill man, I tell you! Come! Come!"

This African dialogue, carried on with an affrighted demonstration and in imploring loud voice, suspended for a few minutes the evolutions of the circus; and those that were at a distance and could not see or hear the amusing discourse roared, "Turn the nigger out."

I arose to protect my servant from the ready grip of a policeman when several gentlemen politely invited me to remain, taking charge of the Black boy on their bench and amusing themselves with his remarks on "white men foolishly troubling themselves with wild beasts."

On several occasions Lunes had inqured of me what Jim Crow meant, having often heard that name applied to him in his solitary walks up the Strand. Not knowing myself the meaning, I told him it was a name of a "big" Black man. ("Big," in the English patois of Africa, means rich or powerful man.) But on passing the next day the Adelphi Theatre, I saw advertised the representation of *Jim Crow* by Rice. Wishing to give the boy an ocular illustration of the technical name, I gave him a half crown and left him at the door of the theatre. As he knew the way back to my lodgings, I told him to return as soon as the play was over.

At breakfast next morning I was informed that my servant had not as yet returned. This information gave me great concern, as I was afraid he would give me some trouble if he acknowledged himself a slave to a magistrate. I employed an officer to make a search, and about noon he was brought in, his clothes all in rags, and without his cap.

By his account it appeared that the play of Mr. Rice did not please him, and in his uncivilized ignorance he pronounced his opinion a little too loud. The gentry of the third tier, not comprehending his murderous English, ridiculed him and called him Jim Crow, whose personification now understanding, he disliked. He therefore resented the proffered insult with such forecastle language as his stock of English could well supply him and which brought him a severe chastisement from the crowd. A short fight issued, and the darky was taken in charge.

The loss of his cap and red vest with the sound thrashing he had received, and one night in the watch house completely ruined his good opinion of the English, and from that moment forward he refused to visit any public amusement and never heard of Jim Crow without trembling with passion.

As I was making preparations to embark him for the Coast, I gave

him two sovereigns to purchase presents for his fellow servants at
New Sester. His purchases were soon made in the shape of long
German pipes, brass ear and finger rings, and snuffboxes for which
he paid an exorbitant price. A few days before his departure, the
ladies of the house, with whom he had become a great favorite, made
him several presents, and the white servants in the employ also
supplied him with many trifles. His joy at the idea of returning to his
native country was so expressive that everyone who knew his condition of slave could not comprehend how a free boy as he apparently
was then could return to slavery with such demonstrations of pleasure.

One evening at tea, the conversation fell on the boy, who had
accidently let fall a dish full of cakes. The lady immediately excused
him by remarking that since he had packed his trunk, the boy's mind
was distracted with the idea of his return home. Several questions
were put to me in regard to him by several ladies present, when I
referred them to the boy himself.

As he was present, a gentleman asked him why he did not like
London. His answer was that it was too cold, and he did not like to
wear "stockings on his hands,"[1] or shoes, which he could never
abide. A lady then asked him why he preferred returning to his
country and be a slave to remaining in England and be free. As his
answer was extempore and caused some merriment and a little
confusion to the lady, I will repeat it in his own English.

As he then stood facing the lady, he drew himself up. "True," he
told her, "I be slave, but me be slave for white man, a proper
Spaniah." (Spaniards in the slave regions of Africa are believed the
richest men in the world.) "I no be nigger for Black man! I like my
country best; me no like this thing." (showing his shirt collar) "He
trouble me too much. Me no like shirt, me no like this" (showing his
pants) "Me like my country fash'." And taking his handkerchief out
of his pocket, he rapidly gave the inquiring lady a demonstration of
African economy in the covering of their nakedness, by placing it
where it is most necessary. Resuming then his conversation, he
informed the blushing party that he liked his Master because "When
me be proper man, my master he give me plenty wives."

The last sentence was received with a roar of merriment, and he
was allowed to retire. His master, laughing in his sleeves, peaceably
finished his tea.

[1]gloves

CHAPTER 80th

A Few More Days in London · Three Days in Havana · My Return to Africa

November, 1839

November is not a favorable month for strangers to visit London. Its damp and foggy days soon sicken a foreigner from the dullness of the gloomy city. I had now been in England two months, during which time I had visited the most noted places of the island; therefore my desire was accomplished, and as I wished to hasten my voyage to Havana, I set about in search of a respectable merchant who might assist me in putting in operation the principal object that had brought me to England—the establishing of a lawful factory at Cape Mount.

The unfortunate *rencontre* of the *Gil Blas* with the steamer had given me the opportunity of becoming acquainted with her owner, a highly respectable merchant of Lime Street, London: George Clevering Redman, Esquire. Mr. Redman at the time owned three vessels in the African trade, and I chose this gentleman to whom I might make my proposals.

As I had been introduced to Captain Herbert as a lawful trader, I did not wish him to continue in ignorance of the true character of my traffic. Therefore on my first visit on the object of my proposition, I unmasked myself and signified my intent of giving up the slave trade with the desire I had to form a connection with some merchant to enable me to establish a factory in Africa. I also described Cape Mount as the most proper place for such an enterprise and mentioned the existing friendship between the King of that river and myself. I even proposed to purchase the country from the natives if necessary.

Mr. Redman, being an enterprising person, heard my proposal with interest, and after few days' consideration, proposed to enter himself in negotiation with me as soon as I would give proofs of having abandoned forever the slave traffic. No contract was written or document signed, as I still should have to continue in the trade till I could withdraw from my employer and settle my accounts with all other persons engaged with me in the slave trade. Then, if necessary, I was to return to England and enter in the anticipated engagement.

Having so far compromised myself, I hastened to leave London, taking with me the good wishes of Mr. Redman for the realization of my future plans. A French vessel took me from France to Havana.

On landing in the capital of the Queen of the Antilles, I found my

292

employer in no humor to accede to my philanthropic views, and as an American vessel had been chartered to carry a cargo of goods for the Coast, I was ordered to take my passage on board as supercargo for part of the goods consigned to me. And on the third day of my arrival in Havana, I was obliged to march off to the Coast without having effected my purpose.

Perhaps it will well be asked why I did not give up my situation and thus free myself from any further engagements in the slave trade. My answer is that I had still too great an amount of property under my charge at New Sester which could not be given up till invested in slaves. Thus my engagement stood, and only when fully complied with could I be entitled to demand a settlement of my employer.

The *Crawford* of New York was the ship that now was to conduct me to Africa again on my old mission, which was no longer a voluntary act but a necessity. The goods under my charge had been shipped under the name of José Arreste, therefore I was introduced to Captain Joseph Brown under that name.

On leaving the harbor, two Black women were sent on board by my employer, with a request that I would take care of them and land them with their relations. These females, having paid their cabin passage, lodged in one of the forward cabins, but were allowed to visit the after cabin. And as they were under my and Captain Brown's care, we allowed them all those privileges indispensable to females but which are seldom granted on board of American ships when the female is colored.

The oldest of these women was about forty years and of very corpulous nature, the other much younger and apparently a companion to the first. This respectable Black woman was returning to Gallinas on a visit to her father, King Shiakar, after an absence of twenty-four years. It appeared that when about the age of fourteen she was taken prisoner and sent to Havana. She was then purchased by a citizen who employed her for years in selling cakes and pies. In time she partly paid for herself, when she gained the privilege allowed by law of renting herself out, paying to her master a stipulated daily sum which the Cuban law judiciously taxes. A few years after having accumulated a sufficient sum to liberate herself altogether, she paid for her freedom, and her proprietor was obliged to receive her value and give up his title.

A few more years of frugality, industry, and exemplary conduct made her proprietress of a house and egg stall in the market, when chance brought her in contact with a cousin who had lately arrived from Africa and who informed her of the existence of her father and brothers. The desire to see her parents had induced her to take passage to Africa to visit them. Her pure filial motives and an unreproachable conduct merited her the strong recommendations she bore to Captain Brown and myself.

Forty-two days' passage took us to New Sester, where I landed my goods and sent the *Crawford* with her female passengers to Gallinas.

On her arrival on shore, her friends were informed of her landing and sent a deputation to receive her with all the pomp that natives love to use on such occasions. Several canoes made their appearance with flags flying, firing muskets, and running short zig-zag races. As they landed they formed a procession, bearing with them a large bullock as a present to Captain Brown.

The older brother headed the procession in the middle of several other inferior relations, and on being introduced to his civilized sister, he extended his arms to embrace her. But to the astonishment of the public, she drew back and only extended her hand, refusing any further demonstration of her affection till he should appear modestly dressed.

The rebuke kept the numerous relations at bay as the brother could not boast of pants, the indispensable that caused the unsisterly reception. After ten days, sojourn amongst her native friends, this Princess left them without regret to return to Havana, disgusted with the manners, the customs, and uncivilized habits of her fathers.

CHAPTER 81st

Difficult Correspondence with the U.S. Brig Dolphin

During my absence in England, Governor Buchanan had applied to the Prince of New Sester to drive the slave traders away from his territory and enter into a treaty of commerce and friendship with the Colony. The Prince accepted the friendly treaty but refused to molest the slave factories. *March, 1840*

Governor Buchanan, availing himself of the presence on the Coast of the United States brig *Dolphin*, induced the American Commander, Lieutenant Bell, to visit New Sester, himself accompanying him. On their arrival there, a letter was sent to the Prince signed with Lieutenant Charles R. Bell's name, in which the American Commander informed the Prince that he wished him to send off all the Spaniards in his territory then holding slave factories.

The Prince, I was informed, answered a short but strong rebuke to the assumed rights of the Commander to dictate to him in his own territory, when the following letter was sent on shore to the Spaniard residents there:

> U.S. Brig *Dolphin*
> New Sestros
> March 6th, 1840

Mr. A. Demer & others,
New Sestros
Coast of Africa

Sir:

I address you in consequence of having received a note from you a few evenings since, but I wish it to be understood that this communication is intended for all or any persons who are now in New Sestros engaged in the slave trade.

I have received information that you now have in your establishments on shore several hundred Negroes confined in barracoons, waiting for an opportunity to ship them off. Whether you are Americans, English, French, Spaniards, or Portuguese, you are acting in violation of the established laws of your respective countries, and therefore not entitled to any protection from your Government. You have placed yourselves beyond the protection of any civilized nation, as you are engaged in a traffic which has been made piracy by most of the Christian nations of the world.

As I have been sent by my Government to root out if possible this traffic on and near our settlements on the Coast, I now give you notice that you must break up your establishments at this point, in two weeks from this date; failing to do so, I shall take such measures as I consider necessary to attain this object. I will thank you to send a reply to this communication immediately, stating your intentions and also sending an account of the number of slaves you have on hand. I am, etc., etc.,

(signed)
Charles R. Bell
Lieutenant Commander
U.S. Naval Forces, Coast of Africa

I know not what answer was made to the above letter, as no copy was kept, but on my arrival a few days later, my Clerk put into my hand the American Commander's letter. Being the principal and oldest factor on shore, I made the following hasty answer, which I sent by dispatch to Colonel Hicks at Monrovia to be forwarded to Commander Bell:

New Sester
2 April, 1840

Charles R. Bell, Esq.
Lieutenant Commander of the U.S. Forces
Coast of Africa
Monrovia

Sir:

Your letter of 6th March directed to the white residents of New Sester was handed me on my return to this country, and I am sorry I cannot make but the following short answer.

First, sir, you seem to take the supremacy over the most civilized nations of the world, and under the doubtful pretext of the authority of your nation, you threaten to land and destroy our property on these neutral shores. Next you are pleased to inform us that *all* Christian nations have declared the slave trade piracy; and that we are not entitled to any protection from our Governments.

Why then do the Southern states of your great republic allow slavery, public auctions, transportations from one state to another not only of civilized American-born Black subjects but of nearly white Christian citizens? Such is the case, sir, in your independent and free country, and the slave trade is carried on in the U.S. of America with more brutality than in any other Colony of the West Indies; and still I hope you are Christian!

To your third article where you mention "having been sent by your Government to root out this traffic near your own settlements on this Coast," allow me to have my doubts on such orders. Your

Government could not have issued them without making them previously known publicly; and permit me to say that those Christian nations you are pleased to mention are not aware that your nation had set up Colonies on the Coast of Africa. They were always led to believe that these settlements of Liberia were nothing more but Christian beneficial societies, humanely formed by private and philanthropic individuals to find a refuge for the poor Black American-born that the free and independent laws and institutions of the United States cannot protect in their native country.

If this my argument cannot convince you that you are not justified in molesting a harmless people on these desolate shores, allow me to inform you that should you put your threats into execution and should you have the advantage over us, many factories here would suffer by your unjust attack, which would give them an indisputed right to claim high damages from your Government.

Most of the whites now residents here are and have been friendly disposed toward Americans at large, and some have been educated in your country. It would be the saddest day of their life if obliged to oppose by force of arms people of a nation that they love as much as their own countrymen! The undersigned in particular would wish to observe that the same spirit that led him to avenge Governor Findley's murder will support him in the defense of his property, although much against his inclination.

I remain very respectfully, your servant

Theo. Conneau

A few weeks after, not satisfied with the fruitless attempt to drive us out from New Sester, Governor Buchanan, ever hasty in his military parades, called out volunteers to march against New Sester. I know not why the expedition failed, but this is the only time that I came in contact with the authorities of the Colonies during the ten years I sojourned in their neighborhood.

Great Distress of Rice in the Country · Expected Famine in My Barracoons · I Am Relieved by Doctor James Hall, Proprietor of the Trafalgar

1840   During my absence, the chargé of my establishment had sent off a cargo of 300 Negroes which arrived safe, bringing me about 9,000$ net profits. And there still existed in my barracoons one hundred and fifty slaves ready to ship off.

The new cargo of goods landed from the *Crawford*, which was the last cargo I intended to invest in slaves, was soon exchanged with the natives, and in two months I found myself again surcharged with 600 slaves. Two other factories in my vicinity also were crammed with slaves and like myself were daily expecting vessels to take them off, but unfortunately a fresh set of men-of-war had just arrived from England and had swept all slavers from the Coast.

Provisions became every day more scarce, and the horrors of a famine was the daily topic of our conversation. Every exertion to gain provisions or economize them were resorted to; boats and canoes scoured the Coast for rice and cassava, but I had the mortification to see them return without any. I doubled and trebled the prices of provisions, with as little success. The natives themselves were nearly in a state of starvation and would often apply to me for food.

The great scarcity of provisions and the little prospects of a prompt relief had forced me to discard the oldest and most infirm of our slaves from my barracoon. Still, I could not afford to give those in irons but one meal a day, and even this short allowance could not be continued but twelve days, when all my resources would be at an end. Anticipating the expected difficulty, I had called the native Chiefs and demanded their opinion when the dreaded day should appear. I had made my mind up to keep my slaves till the last meal had been expended, when I would liberate them; and such, I had told the Chiefs, was my intent.

The idea of liberating so many enemies took them by surprise. They could not allow to put the country into war, as the liberating of my 600 slaves would surely cause a revolution amongst their own people. I was implored not to take such a step, and they would assist me and relieve me of part of my burden. It was then agreed that each one would take a share of my female slaves and all the youths from my hands. This proposition of the Chiefs relieved me of 255 mouths.

Ten days more elapsed under this dreaded expectation, and I was on the last few rations when the American brig *Trafalgar* of Baltimore made its appearance in the roads. On my arrival on board I purchased several goods, and all the biscuit, rice, and provisions that could be spared. Then I made my case known to her owner, Dr. James Hall, former Governor of Cape Palmas, and informed him of the destitute state of provisions the whole country was in, and begged him to relieve my very difficult position, offering to sell him a large cutter-built boat which I knew was much needed by Governor Russwurm of Cape Palmas in exchange for rice.

The kind Doctor, seeing my great distress, assisted me in this great trouble, and in a few days returned with 700 measures of rice in payment for the cutter *Ruth*, and for which disinterested kindness a noble-born British officer nearly broke up his voyage.

Five days after the departure of the *Trafalgar*, the *Volador*, a slave vessel of 165 tons and of great fame, made her appearance; and that night I succeeded in shipping 749 slaves. This vessel not only took all my slaves but the best part of the two other factories', their proprietors abandoning in disgust the invalids and those of the slaves that could not be shipped. The factors took passage themselves in the *Volador*, and this is the last cargo I shipped. Having still a few goods left, I invested them in slaves, fully determined that it should be my last of the slave traffic.

CHAPTER 83rd

My First Proposition to Abandon the Slave Trade

With the determination of abandoning the slave trade, I had established a separate store in the vicinity with the exclusive purpose of trading only in produce, and this establishment was given in charge of a young colonist.

Her B.M.'s brig *Termagant* was then permanently blockading New Sester and did not allow even a boat to communicate with my factory. Early one morning the *Termagant*'s boats gave chase to a strange sail who being hard chased, made for the beach. The natives, believing her to be my boat, ran to the beach to protect her, and finding support from shore, the stranger landed his boat and hauled her up on the beach. The cruiser's boats followed, and a small brush took place with the natives. But finding it was not my property and the English pressing too hard on them, they abandoned the contest after robbing and breaking the boat up in pieces.

This affray took place only two miles from my lawful factory. Not knowing the cause of such firing, I ran to the place of the contest, believing my employees in difficulty with the natives. On my arrival I found a Spaniard, the proprietor of the boat and the cause of the foregoing disturbance.

He was the bearer of a letter from Gallinas informing me of the safe arrival of the *Volador* in Havana with 611 slaves. This letter also apprised me that my employer Pedro Blanco still persisted in sending me out goods and by no means accepting my resignation. It also acknowledged a fresh credit in his hands of $13,100, being the amount of my commission on the 611 slaves of the *Volador*.

The bearer, not being known to the natives, had been robbed by them, and I was on the point of enforcing a restitution of his clothes when the report of a cannon caused me to believe that some aggression was being made against my establishment. Two more shots, and the proximity of the man-of-war to New Sester proper convinced me that the *Termagant* was conversing with my factory through the interpolation of her artillery.

I hastened back to my principal establishment, when I found my premises full of natives. The three shots from the Englishman had brought them down from the Interior. The following letter was then handed me by my people, which had been received some hours before the *Termagant* had begun firing on the place. It was addressed to me and had been sent on shore by a fishing canoe. These are the contents:

Her Britannic Majesty's ship *Termagant*   *5 November,*
off New Cestros   *1840*
November 5th, 1840

Mr. Conneau
New Cestros

Sir:

   The natives or Kroomen of your settlement having this day fired on
the boats of Her Britannic Majesty's ship under my command while
in chase of a Spanish boat with seven men going to New Cestros, I
therefore demand the persons who fired on the boats to answer for the
same; and should this demand not be complied with, I shall take such
steps as I deem proper to procure satisfaction.
   I have addressed you on this occasion, judging by the interference
of those Blacks in your behalf, that they are instigated by you.
   I have the honor to be, Sir, your obedient servant,

Lieutenant Commander H. F. Seagram

It was now only one hour before sunset, and the *Termagant* was
still under easy sail, perhaps discussing if another demonstration
with her 36-pounder was necessary to enforce an answer from me. A
short note was immediately written proposing to call on board next
morning and give entire satisfaction, but when about sending it off,
no Kroomen would undertake the job; such was their fear that the
firing had impressed them with. The surf also was impractical to
boats; therefore I determined to visit the British Commander myself, and as a Krooman in my company could have nothing to fear,
two of them consented to take me on board.

   On my arrival there, the roughness of the beach had not allowed
me to put on but shirt and drawers. I introduced myself and informed Lieutenant Seagram that I had come in person to give the
desired satisfaction.

   Having supplied me with a dry suit, he received a full and true
explanation of the contention of the natives with his boats, I assured
him that the interference of the natives in protecting the Spanish
boat was not instigated by me, in proof of which I demonstrated the
haste I had made in going myself to the place of contest. My
argument was supported with the assurance that I had given up the
idea of carrying on the slave traffic any more.

   Lieutenant Commander Seagram gave full credence to my argument, and as it was then too late to land, I was requested to remain
till next morning when himself would visit my establishment with
the intent of conversing with the Prince, having a communication to
make from his Commodore.

Next morning our landing created the greatest confusion amongst the natives when they saw me in company with an officer who the day before had fired into my premises. In the first place, they could not understand how the night before I had trusted myself on board after such a hostile demonstration toward me, and now they could less comprehend how an enemy, such as an Englishman was believed to be to me, was politely invited to my factory. The Prince, on seeing an officer sitting in my house, observed that I must possess some powerful ju-jus to attract the confidence of my enemies. But his astonishment had no bounds when Commander Seagram in a long discourse proposed that the Prince should abandon the slave trade, which argument was supported by me—I who for four years had carried on that traffic with such energy and perseverance.

The Prince, believing I was only deceiving the Englishman for some cunning purpose, readily agreed to every proposal toward the extinction of the slave traffic, and a promise was made on his part to sign a document to that effect. Now the reader must be informed that I allowed the Prince to deceive himself on this occasion, as it afforded me an opportunity of bringing him in contact again with Commander Seagram, which intercourse once established, I knew, would have the good effect to induce him to adopt the proposed measures much better than if carried by me and unsupported by the British officers.

Lieutenant Seagram also availed himself of the apparent good intentions of the Prince, and a treaty was signed in which the slave traffic was abolished by the Prince and myself at New Sester forever. As I was the principal mover in this treaty, on the day the document was signed I voluntarily gave up one hundred slaves to the British Commander, for which I was to receive the protection of the British forces in removing from New Sester.

A few days after these occurrences, the Honorable Captain Joseph Denman, Senior Officer of the British forces, landed at Gallinas with 200 men, burnt and destroyed all the Spanish factories there, by which opportunity the natives gorged themselves in abundance with all the Spanish property to the amount of £200,000. Such lucky event could not pass unnoticed by the natives, and in a few days the arbitrary proceedings of Captain Denman were known to all down the Coast.

The Prince of New Sester, seeing that I was not molested by the English cruisers as were other Spanish factors, began to repent his contract with the British Commander, as it not only deprived him of robbing me but bound him to protect me in my new vocation. Vexed at the disappointment, he clandestinely called a meeting of his Chiefs and appointed a day when the *Termagant* should be from the roads to rob my establishment and punish me for having abandoned the slave trade and for having induced him to accede to a treaty so detrimental to the welfare of his country.

This hostile meeting took place without my knowledge, although it was well known to all my slave domestics whose silence had been purchased by the Prince, and the surprise would have taken place on me if a Krooman—the same whose life I had saved from the saucy wood—had not given me timely notice.

It had been agreed between Lieutenant Seagram and myself that in case I wanted any assistance from him, I should hoist the British flag. Availing myself of the gratitude of this Krooman, I wrote a note to Lieutenant Seagram, who was then at Trade Town some ten miles distant, informing him of my present danger, and in the meantime I fortified myself.

I had still in my employ five white men and four extra sailors awaiting a passage home. With this party and my household servants I proposed making a defense against the Prince's forces, and on receiving the information of the premeditated and treacherous attack, I immediately armed my men and placed the four cannons at every angle of the barracoons. My slave domestics I also armed, each with a musket, but the first night following these preparations, they all deserted me. My own servant Lunes, the one I had taken to England, left me with the rest, carrying my double-barreled gun.

Next noon my faithful Krooman brought me the following answer from the British Commander:

> Her Britannic Majesty's
> brig *Termagant* off Trade Town
> 23 January, 1841

Mr. T. Conneau
New Cestros

Sir:

In your letter of yesterday date, you request the protection for your property and inform me that you are in danger from the Prince. I regret indeed that such should be the case, more especially as they have pledged me their words and signed a "book" to the effect that they never would again engage in the slave traffic. But as I have found that you have acted in good faith since I commenced to treat with you on the subject, I shall afford you every assistance in my power and will land an armed party of twenty men before daylight on Monday.

I am, Sir, your obedient servant

> *H. F. Seagram,*
> Lieutenant Commander

The return to anchorage of the *Termagant* next morning caused the Prince and his armed party to postpone their evil intent, although about two thousand men had now collected around the premises. About noon his men began to be impatient for booty, but still fearing my guns, dared not attack and resorted to set the stockade on fire. A conflagration would have given them a superb opportunity to rob me, therefore I made the convened-upon signal of distress —the English flag "Jack down," with a blank gun.

Three boats immediately landed an officer and twenty-five men who marched up to my factory to the great consternation of the natives, who had been kept in ignorance of the expected assistance and who now only awaited the night to set the factory on fire.

At sundown the Commander sent the following written orders to the officers commanding the protecting force:

> Her Britannic Majesty's brig
> *Termagant* off New Cestros
> January 25th, 1841

Mr. Henry Hannant
Mate of H.B.M. brig *Termagant*

Sir:

You are hereby required and directed with the officers, seamen, and marines under your command to take charge of the factory of Mr. Theodore Conneau and protect it during the embarcation of his goods and property. No man is allowed outside of the factory, and you are to take especial care by frequent musters that none of them straggle.

The natives are in no wise to be molested or interfered with unless they should openly attack you, when of course your endeavors must be used to repel them. At sunset a watch is to be set for the night, and the men mustered in their blankets or warm clothing. The Kroomen of the ship under your orders you will employ to assist in sending off the goods, and I have confidence in you to leave all unwritten orders to your judgment.

> *H. F. Seagram,*
> Commander

This night was passed in expectation that some of my treacherous servants would return and fire the premises, but the Redcoats had paralyzed their courage. No one even appeared in sight. Next day the embarcation took place, and 600 kegs of powder were first embarked.

Governor Buchanan, having been officially informed of my

danger, now abandoned all resentments against me and generously *1841* came down with his barge and ten men to protect, in company with the British forces, the embarcation of my goods. It took us four days to ship them, and three English merchant vessels very kindly and generously transported my property free of cost to Monrovia.

A Naval Engagement of Peculiar Nature to Me

1841   Having now voluntarily given up the traffic, I immediately visited Cape Mount with the object of forming the establishment proposed with Mr. Redman of London. Lieutenant Seagram, now more friendly than ever, offered to conduct me to Cape Mount and preside at the intended purchase, thus making the title more valuable to me, as the treaty would be signed and witnessed by a British Commander, while on the part of the natives, the epaulettes and sword of a Naval officer would give the affair more importance.

Availing myself of the friendly invitation of the British Commander, I took passage in the *Termagant* and at sundown of the same day, we anchored off Cape Mount. As the breeze had disappeared with the sun, leaving a beautiful clear horizon at the west, the mast heads called out, "Sail ho!"

This is a magic word on board a cruiser. Every man dropped his tin-can pot of tea to stretch his neck toward the desired object. Briefly a Petty Officer who had gone in the fore top with a telescope reported her to be a brig with raking masts and white sails, therefore she was pronounced a slaver.

The anchor came up without drum or fife, and the *Termagant*'s head was put to the west. I said the breeze had disappeared, but with a light fanning breeze from the land and the ebbing current from the river, we gained three miles on the supposed slaver. A perfect calm obliged us to anchor again in 30 fathoms of water. At daylight we were in sight of one another and within seven miles distance; still it continued a dead calm.

The appearance of such a large slaver, probably armed, had aroused the well-known courage of the British tars, and from one end to the other, nothing was heard but their whispers, some praying for wind, others wishing for breeze, while the Commander, Doctor, and Purser were mentally cursing the calm and their hard fate which deprived them of promotion and a large share of prize money.

I have only mentioned the Commander, Doctor, and Purser as at this moment the Master's Mate and Past Midshipman were off on duties in the ship's boats, the first cruising off Gallinas, the second on the same errand off New Sestros.

The first of the morning was passed in expectation of a breeze, but after breakfast the Commander could no longer stand the temptation of such a rich prize. The hands were mustered, and the yawl and the Captain's gig were lowered and manned to board the slaver. The yawl was only a 14 foot boat, and she was manned with six seamen and two marines. The Commandant of this craft was a Master's Mate on his way to join a cruiser who had volunteered his services. The Commander's gig was 25 feet long and narrow as all fancy boats are. Here Lieutenant Commander Seagram crammed four marines and five sailors, himself taking command.

As this diminutive flotilla was about starting, the Boatswain begged to be allowed to fit out my canoe, a tender and delicate shell which only Kroomen know how to manage. The consent was given, and our bold marine satyr and lord of the forecastle manned this native bark with the only two remaining Kroomen, himself sitting in the middle with a musket and cutlass.

On leaving the ship, the Commander recommended the Doctor and Purser to follow the boats in case the breeze should spring up, but recollecting that neither were sailors, he begged me to point out the necessary maneuvers in case of need.

The moment the slaver espied this hostile armament, she ran her sweeps in, and hoisting the Spanish flag, fired a blank gun, thus giving warning that she was armed and ready to meet the engagement. A faint hurrah was heard from the boats, who now pulled with a steady long stroke to the enemy. Another gun was fired from the slaver, but this time it was a shot, which striking the water near the first boat, rose *en decouche* several times till it spent itself within 20 yards of the canoe. This time we could not hear the hurrah from the boats, but from our tops we distinguished the hasty strokes of their oars pulling in two divisions towards the Spanish craft.

A third report told us that the engagement had begun, but the rolling of our vessel deprived us of using the telescopes on the tops. Still, a glimpse now and then assured us that our expedition had been beaten off. As the dense smoke cleared away, we espied one of our boats and the canoe only, returning loaded with men.

A light air had just given headway to the *Termagant*, and I shaped my course toward the retreating boats. In the meantime, the slaver picked up her boat, which she had nobly thrown overboard and offered to the British Commander, ran her sweeps out, and with the faint sea breeze, shot out to sea as fast as possible.

As the Commander stepped on board, he was bleeding at the head. He had been knocked overboard from the rail of the slaver with a handspike. Two men were missing, and three had been seriously wounded by a grapeshot from the stern chaser of the slaver as the dinghy crossed her stern to board the enemy on the port side, and which fire had immediately sunk the boat. The Boatswain returned intact, and if I must believe subsequent reports from one of the Spanish belligerents of the *Serea* (Portuguese for mermaid), his fire did more execution than the whole musketry of the six English marines. The Boatswain's nutshell had been observed by the Boatswain of the slaver, and in a contemptuous manner he proposed to sink her with a large top block lying nearby. The canoe came alongside with the velocity peculiar to Kroo canoes, and as the Spanish Petty Officer rose to throw his missile, John Bull's musket ball penetrated his head. Both had their wish, as both had fired with unerring aim, and the canoe returned with the heavy top block in her bottom.

The Commander of the *Serea* was named Miguel Olivares. By the report of Commander Seagram, the Spaniard acted most generously with him and his men. Seeing the boat sunk and the men floating near his vessel, he lowered his boat and bade him take it and return on board of his own vessel.

I have described this engagement as an illustration of the different vicissitudes a man often encounters in a short time. Here I was, placed on the deck on a British armed brig with the trust of her maneuvers while in chase of a vessel who for what I knew then might have been consigned to me. Had she arrived twenty days sooner, I would probably have given her a full cargo of slaves. This day, circumstances had placed me in a position to assist in sinking her if necessary; such was then my determination. I had given my hasty word to the Commander on his leaving his ship to sail her, and certainly I should not have abandoned her decks if an engagement had taken place. But I was indeed happy to see the Spaniard make off from us, as my heart rebuked me at the idea of taking arms against men who had perhaps broken bread at my table.

CHAPTER 85th

Purchase of Cape Mount

February, 1841

Next day I landed at Cape Mount and visited the King, Fana Toro, at the town of Toso. My object was soon explained, and with the assistance of his son Prince Graye, the agreement was made, when it was stipulated that the purchase money should be paid in presence of his full council and the title given in presence of the officers of the *Termagant*.

The appointed day arrived, and according to agreement, the following title was signed by King Fana Toro and Prince Graye and witnessed by Lieutanant Commander Seagram and his officers:

Title Deed of Cape Mount

Know all men by these presents that I, Fana Toro, King of Cape Mount and its river, in the presence of and with the full consent and approbation of my Chiefs, in council assembled in consideration of a mutual friendship existing between George Clevering Redman, Theodore Conneau & Co., British subjects, and myself, the particulars whereof are under written, do for myself, my heirs, and successors give and grant unto the said George Clevering Redman, Theodore Conneau & Co., their heirs and assigns in perpetuity all the lands under the name of Cape Mount, extending on the southeast side to Little Cape Mount and on the northwest side to Sugaree River, comprised with all the islands, lakes, brooks, forests, trees, waters, mines, minerals, rights, members, and appurtenances thereto belonging or appertaining, and all wild and tame beasts and other animals thereon; to have and to hold the said cape, river, islands with sides of the river and other premises hereby granted unto the said George Clevering Redman, Theodore Conneau & Co., their heirs and assigns forever, subject to the authority and dominion of Her Majesty the Queen of Great Britain, her heirs, and successors. And I also give and grant unto the said George Clevering Redman, Theodore Conneau & Co. the sole and exclusive right of traffic with my nation and people and with all those tributary to me, and I hereby engage to afford my assistance and protection to the said party and to all persons who may settle in the said cape, river, islands, lake, and both sides of the river by their consent, wishing peace and friendship between my nation and all persons belonging to said firm.

Given under my hand and seal at the town of Fanama this twenty-third day of February One Thousand Eight Hundred and Forty-one.

Witnesses:

Harvey Frowd Seagram		his			his	
Lieutenant Commander	King	X	Fana Toro	Prince	X	Graye
George D. Nobbs		mark			mark	
Clerk in Charge						
Thomas Crawford						
Assistant Surgeon						

of Her Majesty's Ship *Termagant*

Proprietor now of this African dominion, I visited in company with the officers of the *Termagant* the upper part of the river. From Toso, the King's residence, we entered the lake of Cape Mount, so far famed for its excellent barracuda and mullet fish. The sea breeze being fresh, we took a reef in our sailboat and steered for two hours east-northeast in search of a spot which the King had recommended as a suitable place for my settlement. Prince Graye, being our pilot, took us a short distance up a creek well wooded with mangrove trees and there pointed us a landing still bearing marks of civilization, as we trod on decayed steps made of English bricks.

As we proceeded on through the bushes and young trees, our princely conductor pointed out several larger trees forming a large circle which had formerly been an enclosure to an English slave factory. As the British officers doubted the words of our African Cicerone, he took us to a large orange tree and told us to read some marks on the bark, which without any trouble we read:

T. WILLIAMS: 1804.

I complimented my guests on the subject, which joke was digested with merriment by the officers, and after inspecting still further in the Interior without meeting any place suitable to my taste, we returned to Toso to sleep.

Next day we ascended to the top of the cape, which is 1200 feet high, expecting to have a fine view of the like and the sea. But the great and rich vegetation disappointed us, as from the moment we began to ascend till we returned on the opposite side, we met continually with large trees whose tops monopolized the heavens, depriving us at the same time of the perspectives we were in search of.

As we descended toward the seaboard, we encountered at the foot of this mountain a flat spot of rich ground with a brook of delightful water nearby. As the spot was near the entrance of the river and but a short distance from the beach, I chose this for my future habitation. My pioneers having divested a large palm tree of its green bushy head, the English jack was hoisted on it and the place was named New Florence.

A hasty hut was soon constructed, and two days after I paid the King and his Chiefs in Council the following goods as payment for their territory: six casks of rum, 20 muskets, 20 quarter kegs of powder, 20 gallons tobacco, 20 pieces white cloth, 20 pieces blue cloth, 20 iron bars, 20 cutlasses and wash basins, with 20 of many other trifling articles.

Now in full possession of my territory, I endeavored to procure laborers from the King and the neighboring Chiefs. For two days, forty men and boys hired at the rate of 20 cents per day and their food, worked with admirable cheerfulness and activity. But a continual work of felling trees, digging out roots, and clearing ground was an unusual thing to them. They all declared that they could not stand it, and all but a dozen slaves remained with me, while the free took their payment in rum and tobacco and retired from what they supposed was a Herculean labor to the *dolce far niente* of the Africans, which is to bask in the sun from morning till night.

Two days more of labor drove away the remaining slave laborers, and on the fifth day I was left alone with my servant in my solitary hut. On remonstrating with the King on the indolence of his bondsmen, his answer was that white men were fools to pretend that a man should work from sunrise to sunset, and that every day. He said that was not Black men's fashion and I could not expect it, adding that on his part he could not conceive how a man like myself with such great quantity of goods as I had could take such trouble and work as I did.

His argument was not encouraging, but I could not expect a more favorable one. All native Africans have an antipathy to hard labor, and this was an illustration. Even higher wages could not induce them to work but one or two days at a time, and the amount of four men's labor was not equivalent to one day's work of a European. With such poor prospect before me, I left a man in charge of my hut to continue the labors, and I returned to Monrovia.

Liberia

1841 It would be ungrateful for me to pass unnoticed the Colony of Liberia where the hospitality of the City of Monrovia was kindly tendered to me by Governor Buchanan when the barbarity of the Chiefs of New Sester drove me from their shore, arms in hand.

It is not my object to tire the reader with the history of Liberia, as I presume everyone has heard or read the condition of those thriving philanthropic settlements which now extend over 300 miles of Coast. In my former visits to Monrovia I had been looked upon as an intruder, and the Government officials ever kept a watchful eye over all my proceedings. And when my character as an established slaver was ascertained, the port was interdicted to my vessels and my stay in that town prohibited. But now that I came as a fugitive, as I may say, every door was opened to me, and every hand extended in friendship.

The Governor and his Council allowed the landing of my slave goods on deposit, and the two servants who had remained faithful to me were secured by the Court as my apprentices. This is another instance of those great changes I have mentioned in the former chapter: a month ago the inhabitants of this quiet town were disturbed from their midnight sleep by the roll of the drum calling volunteers to march against the slaver Conneau; today I dine with the principal officer of this Colony. Such is life, and this was one of those hasty and changeable vicissitudes which characterize this work, and which critics perhaps will not fail to point out as too often repeated.

At Monrovia one finds all sorts of mechanics. The inhabitants have imported with them that Yankee mechanical genius which characterizes Americans in general—their former Masters. With the assistance of a few carpenters, sawyers, and blacksmiths, in four months I built a small craft of 25 tons and which I called *Termagant* in honor of the English war vessel that had supported me in my troubles. I have mentioned the construction of this vessel only to prove what can be done in that Colony, as when the barque was launched, the only article of foreign manufacture were chains, her copper, and sails. The riggings were made there, the pindles and gudgeons were cast there, the leather for her use was tanned there, and her pumps and masts were also the product of the country and of their mechanical genius as well as her anchors. Having described the

312 upper order of mechanics, the reader will easily conceive that in-

ferior ones are found in abundance, and had nature endowed the River of Mesurado with better harbor or an entrance fordable to large vessels, Monrovia would have been now only second to Sierra Leone.

Of their Government I am silent, inasmuch as they now enjoy a constitution copied from that which sustains the great Union of the United States, and their President Roberts can be well titled their Washington, having merited the honorable epithet in the field, in council, and in the unreproachable conduct of his life.

A look in the map will inform the reader that the Mesurado River is a small branch of the St. Paul, a much larger river, but still impracticable to large vessels, its entrance being obstructed by dangerous rocks. Following up the border of this larger river only five miles from the town of Monrovia, the eye extends on plains full of vegetation, and at the sight of the wild stout grass and tall trees, a botanist would pronounce its soil the most fertile. Full and palpable proofs have been given of the fertility of the soil in the product of the sugar cane, coffee, and cotton, having myself seen cane 14 feet long and as large as any I have ever seen in India or Havana. The coffee trees there grow much larger than those of the West Indies, and I have known one single tree to yield 16 pounds of coffee, being seven pounds more than the average of the coffee plants in the West Indies.

Throughout the whole continent of Liberia, from Cape Mount to Cape Palmas and St. Andrew River, the soil is equally productive. Native fruits such as cocoa nuts, orange, mango plum, sapodillo, granadilla, sour and sweet soap, plantain, banana, guava, tamarind, ginger, sweet potatoes, yams, cassava, corn, and pineapples are found in abundance in their proper season. And of late years, the industry of American settlers have added the breadfruit, the avocado pear, the rose apple, and patanga, water and musk melons, mulberry and sorrel; while in many gardens can be found turnip, beets, cabbage, French and lima beans, tomatoes, squash, etc.

Rice, being the staff of life on this part of the coast, grows in abundance and is cultivated with profit by the natives who reap by its sale to the Colonists many European luxuries which formerly were only supplied to them by slave ships.

Much has been said of the pestilent climate of Liberia, but if any disinterested person will read over the true reports of the colonization journals, they will find that mortality amongst the newly landed emigrants has diminished of late years to one half of what it used to be ten years ago, and this is accounted for by the great care the agents of the Colonization Board have instituted toward the first acclimation of newly landed emigrants. Now the Colony is perfectly supplied with every accommodation to receive them, and colored Doctors have had sufficient time and practice to understand the nature of these African fevers which have deterred many families from emigrating to Monrovia.

Ten or fifteen years ago, the Government of Liberia could not supply even with great expense the necessary fresh beef so needful to the sick or convalescent; a bullock was then a rarity, and such was the demand for fresh meat that poor mutton or beef was sold at private sales at 25 cents per pound. Today, now that all the slave factories have been broken up, good beef can be purchased at the public market at 8 and 10 cents per pound. Fowls and fish are no longer a dainty morsel for the rich. The poor mechanic can at moderate price supply his family, and I have no hesitation in asserting that within the three past years, native provisions have diminished in price one half of their value.

Having so far deviated from my object in the description of Liberia, let me finish this chapter with a line or two on the opinion I have formed of the inhabitants of that Colony.

Some men are of the opinion that colored men in general are not fit to rule themselves. It is also believed that few are capable of attaining superior intellect. I differ much from those skeptics, as not only can the men of color, if educated, represent a distinguished position, but even native Africans as I have seen in their difficult palavras, are capable of delivering such correct judgments that our best jurists would pronounce them perfect Solomons. My argument will be sustained in regard to the capabilities of the colored race when we find the present Colonies of Liberia governed by men of their own color, and those men but a few years back were either slaves or despised citizens of the United States. Liberia at present can boast of several distinguished men who but for the prejudice of their color could adorn any society, and those who have been personally acquainted with President Roberts, General Lewis, Judge Benedict, Mr. Teague, Beverly Yates, Mr. James B. McGill, Mr. Benson of Grand Bassa, and Governor McGill of Cape Palmas can bear testimony that nature made no distinction with them but in color, and endowed them with the best qualities that superior white men are made of.

The prosperity and the ultimate result of this Colony may be still considered a problem. If the generous, philanthropic, and benevolent feelings which have created it with such laborious and Herculean consistency should at the most critical moment—the present—relax or abate, the consequences would retrograde the surprising advancement of these establishments, and the benefac-

tors of the Colonization Society would not see their excellent *oeuvre*
completed. Let every helping hand pull at the ropes—a sea
phrase—for 20 years longer; let every effort be made to multiply the
Colony with fresh emigrants, a grateful Liberia will become in a few
years the model school of African Christianization.

England and France have not only acknowledged their republic
but given them material aid, and Queen Victoria has given her a war
vessel, and Napoleon[1] a valuable present of arms. If the Constitution of the United States deprives the head of the Government of the
prerogative of any acts of generosity to her outcast colored children,
let not the charitable and the Christian abandon the prosperity of
their colored countrymen and namesake.

Amen!

[1]Napoleon III, who became Emperor in 1852, shortly before Conneau was
writing

CHAPTER 87th

*A Lesson to H.B.M.

1842—1843 Intent on my grand object, in a few days I returned to Cape Mount with several American mechanics and a lot of goods to assort my stores, and by force of double pay, several natives sent on their domestics and inferior relations to give the finishing stroke to New Florence.

My factotum had with much labor cleared the virgin ground of its forest, and now with my civilized colored Americans, the principal building and the stores were erected, while the native laborers were employed in the formation of a garden whose celebrity has been duly appreciated by the officers of the different Naval Stations then in Africa.

I had now removed my furniture and property to New Florence. I still continued embellishing the place and drumming through the country for business. My Pilot was also ever on the alert to board vessels in the offing and praise the prosperity of his Master and Cape Mount, while my native brokers scoured the neighboring tribes, chanting the praises of the white merchant.

My long and leisure hours I employed in framing my vessel and the cultivation of my garden, but a sudden dispute had arisen between two large towns, where Fana Toro was called in as an umpire. The palabra lasted several days, when the old King returned not having succeeded, and of course taking part against the dissenter of his judgment. The unhappy event brought a perfect stagnation in the country trade, and now more than ever I desired the expected assistance from the British Government. On the arrival of every war vessel, my boat boarded her offering my services and inviting the officers on shore. My offers were generally kindly received, and while I enjoyed the luxuries of their company, I reaped a liberal profit in furnishing the Pursers with fresh provisions and the ward room with small stores.

An occurrence took place about this time which might illustrate how a branch of the slave traffic is brought about. Her Britannic Majesty's sloop ——— was in the harbor, and three of her officers had landed with their fowling pieces to shoot a boar, but as it rained the whole day, it was postponed to another day.

Their having receipted my invitation to dine, we sat down in my long piazza as the coolest part of the building. Shortly after the soup, a great rush was made into my yard, causing a good deal of rumor and annoyance. On inquiry, my servant told me that one of the head

316

Bushmen had brought Soma, a young native man and a noted gambler, fast by the neck and wished my storekeeper to purchase him, or he would kill him.

This being a good opportunity for the British to inspect an instance of African barbarity, I caused the Bushman and the gambler to appear in the piazza. Soma had previously been in my service as an interpreter and was nearly related to the King. I had discharged him as a vagabond and for having gambled and sold his younger sisters away, and which I had reclaimed from Gallinas.

On questioning the Bushman, he said that the scoundrel Soma had played with him at the well-noted native game with cowries (*pair et impair*[1]) and had first lost his gun, then his cap and clothes. Insisting on playing still more, he had pledged himself limb by limb, losing his head the last, and as none of his friends would redeem him, he had brought him to me to sell him. But if I refused to purchase him, he would take him to the waterside and cut his throat, Soma having lost with him several times but never paying his gambling debts.

There stood with an imploring countenance the unfortunate gambler, divested of all garments, with a cord round his neck and his hands pinioned behind his back. I flatly refused to redeem the scoundrel and told him in English (Soma spoke English) that I had no pity for him, and he must stand the blunt of abominable propensity, thus giving a chance to my guests to exhibit their philanthropy. I even told his new Master to take him away and use him as he chose.

Twenty dollars would have saved his life. That amount was not offered, and the gambler and Bushman were allowed to depart. A wink to my interpreter sufficed; the Bushman returned to town with a demijohn of rum and twenty pounds tobacco, and Soma was conducted with the same rope around his neck to Gallinas, and I presume he is now playing *al monte* in some plantation in Cuba.

[1]roulette term: odds or evens

*The Building of New Florence

*1843 My labors continued for several months, but at the recapitulation of my expenses, I found that to continue at such high rate of wages would soon prostrate my finances. And with the advice of Lieutenant Seagram and Captain Tucker, Commanding Officer of the African Naval Station, I petitioned Lord Stanley to grant me one hundred liberated Africans to till my ground. After several months delay, the following answer was sent me by the Governor of Sierra Leone:

> Government House
> Sierra Leone
> 28th October, 1843
>
> Sir:
>
> I beg to acknowledge the receipt of your letter dated in August last, enclosing the copy of a petition, the original of which you transmitted to the Acting Lieutenant Governor Fergusson for the purpose of having it forwarded to Her Majesty's Government.
>
> And in reply, I have to acquaint you that by the receipt of a dispatch from the Right Honorable Lord Stanley, Secretary of State for the Colonies, bearing date the 8th April, 1842, His Lordship states that he cannot sanction a compliance with your request to have a number of liberated Africans as apprentices in tilling your grounds, and further that he could not recognize the purchase of Cape Mount as placing that district under the protection and sovereignty of the British Crown.
>
> I beg to add that I am glad to have been informed by Captain Oake that regarding the vessel alluded to in your letter which you had been unable to dispatch for want of a license, that you had obtained one for that purpose from the Governor of Monrovia. I am, Sir, your obedient servant.
>
> *G. Macdonald, Governor*

The reception of this official letter put a damper to my prospects, and my castles in the air tumbled down with all the philanthropic schemes. The curtain that my imagination had figured with so many pleasant days in the prosecution of a lawful commerce fell, leaving in the distance a dull and cloudy hereafter.

This fatal letter not only put an end to my future expectations, but broke at once the correspondence with my generous friend

George Clevering Redman of London. I dropped the unwelcome
missive, and my next step was to strike the English jack, never to be
saluted by me again, and in my fit of vexation, even the palm tree
was chastised to the roots. The day after, a new pole commanding
the full view of the harbor was erected, and there I hoisted a large
tricolored banner with a white star in the center, which I caused to
be saluted in presence of the King with a salvo of 20 guns from my
eight cannon.

I am not naturally of a vindictive character, but am peculiarly
sensitive to an insult, and that Lord Stanley refused to extend his
Government's protection to my purchase after my having been
flattered into that belief by the Commandant of the British Naval
Station certainly annoyed me. And for the first time I repented the
confidence I had placed in the expectations and assistances promised
by the officers of the squadron.

For several days I was at a loss what to determine, either to
abandon Cape Mount and return to my former traffic, or continue
on my own resources to cultivate the lands and follow the more
honorable but less productive lawful trade. Two insurmountable
difficulties presented themselves before me. One was the want of
hands to work the ground, the second the practical knowledge of
cultivating the soil.

Another visit to the fertile shores of the lake convinced me that
with good will and much industry, even a sailor could become a
planter. Therefore, without more useless reflections, I took the
plow for my device[1] and by the first of the month, I had ordered
from England a large number of farmer's tools. Next thing I did was
to purchase 40 youths which I would employ in a coffee plantation,
while others would be yoked to my plows till I had raised animals to
replace them.

A new spot of ground was cleared. Several huts were also immediately erected with a comfortable house for the overseer. This
office I entrusted to my former Boatswain, who had lived with me at
New Sester as manager of the barracoons.

Unfortunately, this Petty Officer, although an excellent disciplinarian and master of his trade when on sea, on a slave deck, or in
a barracoon, was but a sorry manager on land cultivation. His men
were ever conducted by the sharp call of his silver whistle, and the
simplest work could not be done but with the systematic marine
procedure, chastising with his cat for every trifling offense. In
a month, four of his crew were placed on the sick list and five had
deserted (as he called it).

[1]emblem, coat of arms

I replaced him with an American colored man who on his turn made free with my slaves, and the plantation was neglected. In a year, I found that my farming speculation was a failure and that it was easier to plow the ocean than the land.

As I had divided my new-purchased slaves into two sections, reserving for my own service the most intelligent, the others were placed, as I said, in the plantation. With my crew of 20 large boys I laid out a shipyard, a blacksmith shop, and a sawpit, placing at the head of these different establishments a colonist from Monrovia to instruct for each a given number of my slaves. In the meantime, the natives in the neighborhood had received my runners informing them of the new factory established at Cape Mount.

By the return of the next dry season, New Florence had within its fences a population of 100 souls, 25 buildings, and nothing was wanting but a stock of cattle which my craft soon brought me from Kroo country. English, French, and American vessels began to visit Cape Mount, while the men-of-war of the stations were supplied by me with wood and fresh stock.

Thus things went on for three years, peaceably and prospering, till a native war broke the amicable intercourse with the neighboring tribes, and which caused many difficulties to my enterprise and brought me in direct contact with the enemies of King Fana Toro.

I cut short this chapter to give a description of this Chief and the natives of Cape Mount.

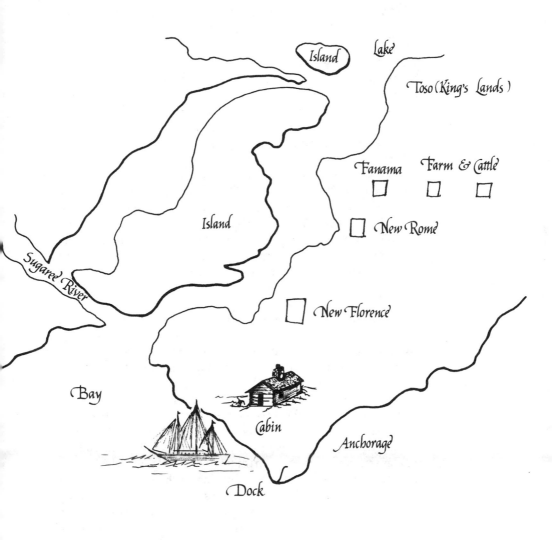

Island

Lake

Toso (King's Lands)

Fanama   Farm & Cattle

New Rome

Island

Sugaree River

New Florence

Bay

Cabin

Anchorage

Dock

CAPE MOUNT COAST, Etc.
(After a sketch in the manuscript)

CHAPTER 89th

*A Description of the Vey People, the Ceremony of the Gree-gree Bush and Their King, Fana-Toro

*1843 The promontory of Cape Mount stands in the latitude of 6° 44' North and in the longitude 11° 35' west and is seen forty miles at sea. This headland, slightly noticed in maps, is well set down in nautical charts and serves as a point of fresh departure for navigators.

The bar of this river is very changeable, having at some seasons eight feet, while at others only 4 and 5 feet of water, although inside of it and up the lake, there is depth enough to float a common-size brig or a schooner. This lake forms the horizon in some parts, and its extent may be 30 miles round. Three flat islands of two and three miles in extent rest in the center, with a rich vegetation of wild grass and African peach trees. During the former wars, it is said these islands were the neutral ground for the Mandingo for their palabras, and both hostile parties respected religiously the neutrality of the ground. I would have chosen this spot for my future domicile, but to carry on commercial intercourse with the shipping, it was too distant from the seaboard.

The productions and the soil of the neighborhood of this river are not inferior to those of other parts of Liberia. Cotton, coffee, and sugar cane grow with equal success as in other tropical climates, and the Vey Nation cultivates with abundance all domestic productions for the daily animal food.

The inhabitants of Cape Mount are called Vey and are not inferior in aspect to the Day or the Gorah people. Their dialect differs slightly but is understood by all, and their habits are the same. The men as well as the women are generally well built, of a regular size, and of erect deportment. Their religion differs but little from the Sosoo of Rio Pongo, believing in the spirit whose power when invoked through their greegrees or fetishes can be rendered favorable, but generally inclined to mischief and obstinacy. They also believe in the transmutation of body; the just and good to be rewarded hereafter by transmutation into a favorite animal, while some believe they will regenerate into a white man, and the white into black. But their true creed is impossible to define, as they have no standing dogma. Not being either Caffree or Mahometans, they still observe the absurdities of both: Mahometanism having intro-

duced amongst them through their traveling and cunning doctors a faint *croyance*[1] of a Superior Deity, which can only be invoked by the *1843 medium of their fetishes.

The Vey proper of the Interior, far from the contact of the Europeans, are like other Ethiopians, and from their most tender age are brought up with the savage neglect of the African parent, crawling perfectly naked about their miserable villages. The male at that age only covers his nakedness when his cunningness has taught him to steal something with which to do so; and when he envelops his loins, it is not from a sense of pudor, but to imitate his betters. The female, less bold, remains in her natural state of nakedness till she becomes a woman, or her future husband presents her with a short fathom of cotton. And neither one uses the scanty rags as a covering, but as ornaments, having no regard to shame. Their genitors give the example by lying promiscuously on the same floor and in the same hut, in perfect state of nudity, sometimes ten or fifteen males and females under a roof whose walls are only fifteen feet square.

A bushman Vey, lulled in indolence true to African custom, rises in the morning to eat his meal of rice or cassava and returns to his couch which in daytime he poses in the sun, and there remains till midday when another wife serves him a second meal. The rest of the day is spent in gossiping and a second siesta. At sundown, someone of his wives or female relations helps him to wash his body. He takes a third meal and retires to a blazing fire to stretch his worried limbs, to renew the same operation next day. The wife or wives, with the slaves, form the working class of a Vey family. As in all savage nations, the woman when married has to support and labor for her husband.

The Vey woman from her most tender age helps the mother in her domestic works, while the privileged brothers follow the indolent example of the father. The female task is a laborious one, as she not only furnishes the wood, water, and provision for the lazy males, but sows, plants, and reaps with her rude instruments the farms which the husband has condescended to clear and burn the bushes off. A young Vey female when at the age of nine or ten years old is taken from the paternal roof to be lodged for a space of time in the greegree bush, which is nothing more than a school for prostitution. On the reception of the Vey maid, her whole body is immediately painted white, and an operation is performed on the girl which is equivalent to a Jewish baptism or the Mahometan purifica-

[1]belief

tion of their males. Then, as a clean member, she is admitted in the female confrérie of the greegree bush where she is taught that which only a wife or a mother learns with blushes and experiences with natural female shame.

The greegree bush[1] is a sacred and a secret spot, chosen in the heart of a thick bush—sacred because the operation performed on the virgin is a sacrifice necessary to their fickle and contrary spirit, to render him favorable to the fecundity of the victim; secret because those mysteries taught in this reclusion are repugnant even to an African man. The female adult remains within the green walls of this brothel till her husband claims her at the hands of the father, when a handsome present is made to the matron, and the husband receives her in his arms—a maid perhaps, but certainly not a novice, whom he treats more as a mistress than a blushing virgin.

These institutions exist in many parts of Africa, and such is the desire to join them that three or four young females of poor parents who cannot pay the fee of admission club together, kidnap a young slave, and with it, gain admission, no native power having a claim on them or the stolen slaves when once within the sacred bush.

No man is allowed in this secret spot, nor even women that are not initiated or have undergone the ordeal. An infraction in the premises would be punished by death to the male and a rough treatment if a female; such is the power given by the customs of the country to the women managers of this female society. I have said no man is allowed to enter this bush, but the Grand Devil or ju-ju has free admission, and is the medium by which husbands exact obedience, respect, and the confessions of their frail peccadillos. This fearful ju-ju is personated by a man; therefore I correct my statement and say *man is* allowed. Even a white man, if introduced under the bushy garb of the forest Devil, can enter after the payment of a substantial present, and behold, unknown to the parents and town people, such mysteries that cannot be divulged without a blush.

The ju-ju here at Cape Mount, as in Unin (Rio Lagos) is personated by one of their initiated. Men also have their greegree bush which is conducted nearby in the same secret manner. Having visited the above-mentioned female establishment, I had no curiosity to see the abominations of men, but my informer, who was himself a grand officer in both establishments, gave me to understand that the one as well as the other of this greegree bush were indisputably necessary to the country: the male institution admitting all to the purifying operation, initiating but few in the mystery

[1]Conneau notes, "Since I wrote this, I have found a description of the greegree bush on page 212 of Vol. I of the *Maryland Colonization Journal,* . . ."

and just enough to keep up the institution in perfect secrecy to make the females profitable wives and bring them up in fear of the Bush Devil, which they are led to believe inspects all their infidelities. Father Loyola the Jesuit could not have invented a better check on the amorous temper of the African female, who is doomed to share with many others the stale embraces of an old man.

By the greegree bush is also understood a reserve dense bush near every town which is prohibited to all men and solely reserved to females. This secret bush serves the female community as hospital of midwifery. Women when near their labor are taken by the matron of the village to this spot, when in a few minutes the mother issues forth with her babe and makes for the nearest brook, returning to the management of the household affairs often in shorter time than one hour. When Doctors do not interfere in cases of *accouchement*, difficult cases are surmounted by female experience, and when the case is desperate, the intruder is forced into the world by tormenting the mother with burning coals. Still, but very rarely the Ethiopian mother falls a victim in the contest of the fulfillment of the orders of nature.

Forty or fifty families form a town, and sometimes less. The Government of these communities is ever in the hands of the oldest men, who administer justice or redress grievances by a palabra held in public where the oldest only have the saying. These villages subject themselves willingly under the protectorate of larger towns, whose Chief arbitrates as supreme and without appreciation in all disputes between the towns under his protection. But as his judgments are not always satisfactory, the disgusted party desert their huts and join another Chief's town, building their village in the vicinity.

In the time of King Fana Toro, the town of Toso was the royal residence, protecting six towns and 15 villages, Fana Toro ruling over the inhabitants more like a father than a King. At the time I contracted for Cape Mount, his age was 77 rains, equivalent to so many years. He was small, meagre, and erect, proud of his age and of the respect his people treated him with. His younger days had been noticed for his firmness and intrepidity, retaining for his enemies that resentment which often led him to the most atrocious barbarities.

Shortly after my installment in Cape Mount, I had cause to see the savage temper of this old man fully illustrated. Some trifling country affair had caused me to pay the King a visit. On landing from my boat at Toso, I was informed he was not in town. But as a white man I had admission in his house, and not believing the report, I entered his premises. Not finding him there, I went to the palabra house, and there I found him surrounded by a large mob holding perfect silence around the infuriated King, who with a bleeding knife in his hand and his foot on the body of a man, was still addressing the carcass of his enemy.

Nearby stood a pot of boiling oil, in which had been fried the heart of the conquered antagonist. My unexpected presence raised his choler to a greater anger, and kneeling on the dead man, he called me forth and, stabbing it several times, told me with trembling rage that this was his bitterest enemy of 20 years' standing. And dealing a fresh blow, he accused him of having violated his daughters, butchered his sons, sold his people, and burnt his towns, dealing a blow at every accusation.

The unfortunate prisoner had been kidnapped by treachery, as he was too brave to be taken alive. As he could not be made to walk, the King's men had made him fast and cooped him in a basket wrought to fit the live body. In this lattice coffin they had brought him down on their shoulders. When in the presence of Fana Toro, his first word after three days' silence was of abuse, and dared the King to do his worst.

He was then placed in the palabra house, his heart torn from him, fried, and eaten by the King and his warriors. The body was afterwards burnt in order that, according to their belief, it should not take the form of some wild beast and still disturb the King's old days.

And this was the only act of barbarity I can accuse this old man of: on other occasions I have ever found him just and even kind, and I think I have no cause to blame him for what he could not remedy. He followed the example of his forefathers and obeyed the ferocious dictates of an African nature.

Of his boldness, courage, and self-endurance I will cite the following anecdote of him: some twenty years ago, several mercenary tribes had joined his enemy, and in a few days they devastated his territory. Nothing but the strong and treble stockade of Toso had stood the shock of his allied enemies. A vigilant blockade had been formed round his town, and his people were locked in without water or food. Thirst and hunger compelled the inhabitants to demand a surrender of Toso, when the King proposed a sortie.

All his warriors cried against such a mad proposal, as they had expended all their ammunition. A contest arose in which it was determined to depose him and choose the bravest amongst his warriors to replace him. A candidate was found for the kingship, 326 when Fana Toro, deserted by all, demanded of the new-elected

King if he was as brave and self-enduring as himself. And calling for   *1843
a pot of boiling palm oil which stood by, he held his forefinger in it
till the flesh was consumed to the bone, never moving a muscle of his
countenance.

I have no need to say that he was saluted again as their King and
friend. Availing himself of their enthusiasm, this African Scaevola[1]
issued from the wooden ramparts of Toso, drove off the blockading
enemy, conquered several battles, obliging the assailing allies to sue
for peace; and to the day I left him, the mutilated hand of the King
was the boast of his people.

---

[1]Muncius Scaevola, a legendary Roman. Captured in his attempt to assassinate
Porsinna, an Etruscan King beseiging the city, Scaevola proved his indifference to
pain by letting his right hand burn off in a brazier and was set free

The Funeral of Prince Graye

1843 The Vey people observe with some ceremony the two principal epochs of human life: its birth, and its death. Both these events are saluted with much firing of muskets, eating, drinking, and dancing, when the friends are rich, but the burial ceremony is of much greater consequence, children sometimes ruining themselves to inter an aged parent with pomp.

At the death of Prince Graye at Cape Mount, his sons having but little to bury their father and no slaves on hand, they pledged their town of Fanama (near my place, New Florence) to me to assist them in defraying the expenses of the funeral. In the meantime, the defunct body was wrapped up in twenty full large country sheets, then was wrapped round the body twenty full pieces of Manchester cottonade of all colors. He was then placed on a catafalque in a dark hut where three of his wives continually watched and added new fuel to smoke the body of their lord.

After two months of moaning and the needful supplies ready for the interment, a notice was sent within 40 miles inviting everybody to the funeral. On the appointed day, the body was brought from the hut, a perfect bacon.[1] His twenty wives had their heads shaven and were wearing but just enough cloth round their loins to replace the fig leaf; the more affectionate ones showing the less regard to hide their charms, estimating them valueless since the death of their husband. The oldest wife appeared covered with bruises, gashes, and burns, self-inflicted to denote her sorrow, and chanting in chorus with the others the praises of the defunct.

The body was then laid out in the palavra house on a new mat, his fur or silk hat adorning the lump which denoted the head. The war shirt (the Prince was a warrior) was thrown over near the hat, and his greegrees and fetishes were placed by his side. His sons stood in the next veranda receiving the consolations of the invited guests, who according to custom deposited presents of rice, palm wine, and other luxuries to help out the merrymaking.

At the death of Prince Graye, I was at Mesurado, but a dispatch from my Clerk informed me of the unfortunate event. Graye was not only my neighbor, but my friend. His death was a calamity to me in my grand speculation of Cape Mount. The respect shown to my deceased friend, I knew, would assure me the affection of his

[1] i.e., a smoked ham

sons, young men of some note in the country. Therefore by the time this semi-mournful, semi-joyful ceremony was to take place, I arrived with an enormous coffin covered with blue dungaree, studded with a profusion of brass nails and all the gilden brass ornaments that I could purchase at Monrovia. My craft also brought four bullocks (a rarity then) and several barrels of rum.

I had chosen my time to make a display, and the tide helping me in, I arrived at the landing of Fanama at 10 in the morning, the two brass pieces of my boat speaking my arrival. Coffin, bullocks, rum, all marched before me in silent procession to the gates of the town. The appearance of the white friend of their father, lord, and husband was greeted by a loud and long cry. I was carried high from the ground in the arms of the women in tears, and deposited near the body. My gifts and the rich coffin had brought forth all the tokens of gratitude these semi-savages were capable of. Each relative, male or female, had a tear of gratefulness.

At noon the bullocks were killed and the blood offered in a white basin to the dead. A salvo of musketry was then fired, and the body was stowed in the coffin without regard to position, such was the shapeless bundle of cloth that it could have been a difficult job to tell the true position. Six men took the body to the beach, and it was buried under a cluster of cotton trees regarded as the royal cemetery.

On our return to the town, the oldest son was saluted as Prince by the people, and father by all his relations, his brothers and sisters regarding him as such. A large repast was then served, every stranger claiming a platter of rice and palabra sauce to himself. At sundown the twenty wives appeared in full dress, all adorned with beads and their shaven heads anointed with oil. The oldest son took to himself six of his father's women, then dividing the rest amongst his brothers and the other relations. His mother he gave to his father-in-law. The division over, he very courteously offered me the choice of one of the six in return for the honor I had paid his father, but as I never cared to be related to natives, I declined the offer.

CHAPTER 91st

*Fana-Toro and the "White Man Grass" · I Am Coolly Received by Commodore Jones

1843—1846 I had now installed myself permanently in Cape Mount, and my youthful and native mechanics had acquired a tolerable use of the axe, the adze, the sledge on the forge, and the whipsaw. With only their help and one or two American colonists to guide them, I undertook to build a brig of one hundred tons. The keel was laid in due time, and in six months the world of Cape Mount was astonished at the erection of the mighty fabric.

My plantation went on slowly, but my garden became the curiosity and wonder of the Europeans while the natives, not comprehending the nature of so many different sorts of "gass,"[1] as they called it, stood confounded, not understanding the use. Still, they admired the symmetry of the beds and the harbors. To water my garden I had turned a brook which canal surrounded the perfect square of the garden, and as this canal was completely lined with wickerwork of interwoven willow branches, the Samsonian labor had spread wonder through the country.

The aged King was also aroused from the couch of his abigails[2] to view the seven wonders of Africa. Fana Toro, on viewing the current of water turned from its former course, struck his breast in amazement and demanded what it was a white man could not do. As he was inquisitive, every different vegetable was to be explained, and its use made comprehensive, and which brought forth many exclamations of surprise at the trouble the white men took to satiate their gourmandizing appetite.

The use of flowers he could not understand. At 10 o'clock the bell called all hands to breakfast. We returned to the house, and in company with my Clerk and an English Captain, we sat down to our *déjeuner*. The first course over, salad and roast was served. As the old gentleman had a capital tooth and an excellent appetite, a plate of the salad was presented him, which he promptly refused, telling the servant in his native language that he was not bullock; he would not eat grass. But as I insisted, threatening to inform the English Captain how he had eaten the heart of his enemy (an action he repented, I had ever known), he took the plate and demolished the contents,

[1]"grass"
[2]lady's maids

330

calling for more, and insisting on adding some of those green and yellow grasses (meaning the flowers).

In a few days I had cause to regret my having insisted on his devouring the salad. His messenger was daily sent for a mess of the "white man grass" with the "sharp water on" (meaning vinegar). Such requisitions became too often repeated, to the annoyance of my steward, who after a few days sent him horse radish leaves, thinking the peppery taste would cure him of salad. But false esperance! He sent a larger recipient for a double dose of "t'other white man grass who bite me mout'."

Everything prospered at New Florence but the farming and trade and my cattle. On my first arrival I had formed an idea that I could in one or two years open trade with the Interior, but by this time I saw that such could not be the case. The slave traffic only was thought of by the natives, and the little produce that is food in the vicinity was only brought down when slaves were sent to the beach. I also came to the conclusion that the Interior tribes in the neighborhood of Cape Mount had no commerce with the other tribes further east, but for slaves; in consequence of which that river will never become a commercial port as Sierra Leone, Rio Pongo, Rio Noonez, and Bassa, those places having direct communication with the great tribes of the Interior and commanding gold, ivory, wax, hides, and tea. Therefore I hastened the building of my vessel to dedicate her to the exterior or the coasting trade.

About this time there arrived on the Coast an American vessel called the *Atalanta*. She was loaded with tobacco, powder, American rum, and cotton goods. The Captain, not understanding the mode of trade or the Spanish language, engaged me to transact his business in Gallinas. I accepted the proposal and in a few days I disposed of all her cargo. The taut appearance of the brigantine had struck a Spanish trader on shore, and an offer was made through me for the vessel as she stood. The tempting offer was accepted, and an agreement centered on, that she should be sold and delivered to me on such a day, which was the day before Christmas, and the birgantine left to finish her trip at the Gaboon.

In undertaking to furnish this Spanish slaver with a vessel and the necessary apparatus for a slave cargo, I considered I was directly aiding the traffic, and in controvention with my promise with Lieutenant Seagram of H.B.M. brig *Termagant*. On a mature reflection, I came to the conclusion that in taking the agency of this vessel and covering her with my name till delivered to the Spaniard, I was no more amenable to a rebuke than many respectable merchants in

Sierra Leone, Acora, or Anamaboo who daily sold all sorts of English manufactured goods to noted slavers.

The appointed day arrived, and the vessel made her appearance, exact to the hour. My smoking semaphores announced the brigantine's arrival at Sugaree, 3 miles from Cape Mount. That same day the American Captain surrendered his vessel to me, taking his paper, his flag, and crew on shore. In taking charge, I made all the hasty preparations necessary to receive her cargo, and next morning by sunrise, I delivered her to her Spanish owner, who embarked seven hundred slaves and succeeded in evading the well-guarded Coast, landing in Cuba after a remarkable short passage of 27 days.

This shipment made so near my place gave umbrage to the British cruisers, who sent messages to question me on the subject. As I refused to give satisfaction or any information on the subject, a coolness was the result, and the British armed vessels deserted my establishment. A few months before this, the old ship *Crawford*, but then a Spanish ship, shipped at Gallinas one thousand slaves in defiance of two armed British boats, and even succeeded in getting off clear of the Coast after a close chase from H.B.M. brig *Ferret*, receiving several shots through her sails and hut. This miraculous escape was partly laid to me, although I knew nothing of the event when it took place. But as I would not demean myself to give the desired information against my former companions, I was considered an enemy to the squadron.

Till now the British cruisers had made Cape Mount their rendezvous, and my establishment supplied them with fresh provisions twice a week. At the reception of Lord Stanley's reply to my petition, which as I have said deprived me of the British protection and caused me to haul down the British ensign, the officers who I am flattered to say had given me many tokens of their esteem regretted the occurrence, and our intercourse was from that moment allowed to diminish into a perfect *éloignement*.[1]

By advice of two friendly Commanders, I wrote a letter to Commodore Jones, commanding the Naval Station of Africa, representing my position and requesting him to petition the Government a second time to place Cape Mount under British protection and grant me liberated Africans to till my lands. The Commodore was then in the offing, and next day I received a verbal message to call on board his ship, the *Penelope*, a stream frigate.

Commodore Jones received me on his decks, but without that gentility that characterizes the English officer. I saw at once that his

[1]antipathy

temper had been soured by some injurious report against me. Having introduced myself, I begged to be informed if he had considered my petition, but he cut my discourse short by telling me that before he would answer my question, he had several to put to me, and according to my answers, he would regulate his. Commodore Jones then requested me to inform him who was the Commander of the *Crawford*, what number of slaves she took, and who was her agent on shore.

My reply was that I was totally ignorant of the whole affair, not being at New Florence when the shipment took place. The incredulous smile played on the lip of the Commodore, and turning to one of his officers, he presented me as the Machiavelli of Africa. I accepted the compliment by uncovering myself and remarking that the subtle plenipotentiary was born in Florence; consequently a countryman.

The next question was more pointed, as he taxed my veracity by telling me that I could not make the same excuse in the case of the *Atalanta*, which had shipped within the limits of Cape Mount, and requested me to inform him how it took place.

The first abrupt question had prepared me for the second, and without hesitation I told the British Commodore that had I known that such questions were to be put to me, I should certainly have declined his invitation, and he could not think me a gentleman if he considered me capable of divulging the secrets of men who were on friendly terms with me and who every day broke bread under my roof. British pride was mortified, but containing his passion, the Commodore again addressed his officer, saying, "Two such men would give work enough to the whole British Navy."

I again made a grand salaam and left the ship, convinced that all intercourse was at an end with the English cruisers.

CHAPTER 92nd

* The Orang Otango, the Leopard, and the Elephant

The portion of Cape Mount where I had built New Florence had not been peopled since the wars I have mentioned, and the leopard, the catamount, the orango-tango, and the cavalli or wild boar had since that epoch taken full possession of its dense forest. A few days after my landing, a small native boy in my employ had been chastised by the overseer, and fearing a repetition of the punishment, he stole some cassava and made for the Mount. His absence was noticed shortly after, but expecting his return, he was allowed to rove.

Not returning on the third day, a search was instituted, and after some trouble the body of the dead child was brought down to the factory, every limb dislocated and covered with bites apparently made by a human mouth. The natives reported that the boy had been the victim of a troop of orang otangs. This supposition was correct, as when I visited the spot, several footprints of this semi-animal were found near the bruised basket, and the skin of the cassava was also found in all directions, as peeled off with the teeth.

The leopards were my greatest annoyance, as their darings were ever attended with great losses. Not a live animal could be allowed to rove without the fences, even in daytime, and my laborers could not venture out at night or unarmed in daytime. I resorted to fall and spring traps, but such was their cunning and strength that they all escaped. I also tried to poison them by arsenic, leaving stale meats sprinkled with the poisonous salt, but here again I failed. Two of my best bloodhounds had been maltreated by one of them in daytime when one of these leopards was making off over the fence with a sheep on its back. The only mode in which I succeeded in destroying them was to place a piece of meat on the mouth of a musket which I secured on two forked sticks eighteen inches from the ground, and having it fenced in such a manner that the animal could not bite it off but end on, when a string attached to the meat would pull the trigger and the load discharge itself into the beast's mouth.

In this manner I purged the vicinity of these unwelcome intruders. The orang otang naturally retired to the Interior. The cavalli was spared but when short of meat, when my hunter would in a few hours pick one with his musket to replenish the butcher shop, and such was the certainty of his success in the hunt of them that I never allowed my hunter to kill but one at a time. The catamount was driven away from the premises by my intrepid dogs, and in two years my cattle roved in perfect safety at all parts.

The elephant had for a long time deserted the promentory, but still lived on the shores of the upper part of the lake, and whenever killed by the natives, the King and I had our share of the spoil; if a male elephant, we received the snout or feet; if a female, the udder, these being considered kingly morsels and a *bonne bouche* for the white stranger. The elephant is considered a public property, the huntsman alone claiming the tusk, and the short tail is the prerogative of the King. But the flesh belongs to everybody, and such is the avidity for the flesh of the monster animal that severe quarrels take place at the cutting up of the body.

The hunting of this giant of the forest is performed by one single person, and much importance is placed on the bold huntsman, as it often happens that several persons take shares in the speculation. Per example, a noted huntsman wishes to undertake a venture in the bush for an elephant. He associates himself as a whaler would to fit out his ship for the South Pole. He finds a partner to furnish him with three regulation soldiers' muskets or long buccaneer guns; another to supply him with powder and iron bolts instead of balls, and a third to put up his provisions, and a boy to carry his armament. Once this fit-out is ready, the hunter's ju-ju is invoked by some fair promise which, like the Neapolitan *lazarone* to his titular Santo Gennaro,[1] is never kept. He leaves the town accompanied by his wives, who at parting wish him good luck.

The African elephant is smaller than the Asiatic and, I believe, more astute, cunning, and wild. The hunter has to dodge his game for severals days, as this animal is ever on the alert when near the populations and scents the huntsman with a peculiar instinct, allowing unarmed men to pass him without taking flight or showing battle. To entice the monster near a safe retreat, the huntsman strews for a long distance pieces of pineapples, which grateful smell the elephant will follow, when the African, behind some tree, discharges his bolts always near the center of the head, drops his gun and discharges another; drops that again and then runs to his hiding place, which is generally a tall tree, where his boy and provisions await him.

[1][Conneau's note] Santo Gennaro is the patron saint of the Neapolitan *lazarones* and fishermen. A good anecdote is told of a Neapolitan fisherman: while at sea fishing with his son, a severe gale overtook him before he could make a safe harbor, the boat laboring heavily against the sea, shipping a quantity of water and nearly swamping several times. The father, having exhausted all his prayer to the favorite saint, as a last resource promised Santo Gennaro a silver lamp if he would deliver them from the present danger. The boy, who knew his father's circumstances, asked how he would pay for a silver lamp. "Hold your tongue," said the old fisherman. "The danger over, the Saint may go to the Devil for a lamp." The Italian is "*Passato il peliero, gabbaro il santo.*"

*1845—1846   It seldom happens that the animal falls at the first or second shooting, the powder used being so inferior that the shot strikes with little force. The wounded quadruped searches for his enemy in vain, and in his agony wanders far away to die several miles from the place of contest. The afrighted huntsman then sends his arms bearer to the town to inform his friend that the monster has been shot, when the whole town issues forth in search of the beast, which will cause the pot to boil for several days.

Sometimes they are disappointed, as the animal, receiving but a slight wound, changes his quarters and is never seen. At other times it lingers for many days, when the chase is given up in despair, and the beast is only discovered long after by the collection of vultures and buzzards who hover over the animal's dead carcass.

Again the townspeople issue forth, guided by these birds of prey, and fall on the half putrid flesh with more avidity than the feathered tribe. Many severe battles have been fought and many slaves have marched to the beach, captured on the dead body of an elephant.

CHAPTER 93rd

*I Take Fana-Toro's Part

In a few months the wars had spread through the country, which caused the natives to give all their attention to them, and the consequence was that the slave traffic was again revived with greater energy.

The reader may imagine my difficult position: just established in a country and surrounded by war. I could not remain neutral, inasmuch as New Florence was situated on the same side of the river with Toso, the King's town, while the enemy held the other border. The failure of my petition to the British Government and the coolness of the men-of-war toward me was well known to both parties; therefore to protect myself and not give umbrage to Fana Toro, I took his part.

In a few days I erected a new fence, and my cannons were made ready for an attack, or to support the King in my boats. This preparation I made more to inspire fear than to make a real use, as in my whole establishment we only mustered three white men and two colonists from Monrovia. The forty or fifty native servants I perfectly knew what dependence to put upon; I had learnt at New Sester the fidelity of a slave for his Master.

Several engagements took place, and many prisoners were made by both parties. The King insisted on my purchasing his share, a thing I had determined not to do, except as I would employ as my servants. But such were the solicitations of Fana Toro that I agreed that a factor from Gallinas should send one of his Clerks within my limits with slave goods to purchase the King's prisoners. I would not have consented even to this arrangement, but was forced by strong necessity. The King's enemy on the right side of the river sold his prisoners to Gallinas, and furnished himself with powder and ammunition, while our old Fana Toro had no *débouché*[1] for his captives and without my assistance would have been conquered.

With these auxiliaries on both sides, the belligerents kept up an open war which lasted two years, ending by the surrender of the King's prerogative. In the meantime, Commodore Jones had so well blockaded Sherborough River, Gallinas, and Cape Mount with his steamers and sailing vessels that no shipping could run in and take cargoes, and the slave factors had recourse to building their own crafts. The brig *Atalanta* when sold to me had a longboat which was

[1]landing place

left in my charge. The scarcity now of vessels brought this boat in requisition. Her owner from Gallinas sent his carpenter, and in few days she was decked, rigged, and equipped for sea.

Her measurement was 23 feet long, with five feet of beam, and 3 feet deep, and her tonnage could not have been over 4 tons when decked. In a dark night she left the river with 33 Negro boys, a Navigator, and two men. On my arrival in Bahia some time after, I saw the same boat there; she had arrived safe and landed her whole live cargo after a trip across the ocean of 38 days. Her Captain told me that they would have perished of thirst but for the fortunate rencontre of a vessel who supplied them with water. This astounding daring in the slave trade was initiated by three other boats next season, which likewise arrived safe.

CHAPTER 94th

I Sail for Little Sester · The Difficulties of Converting the Heathen

During this time, my intercourse with the Colony of Liberia was *1845—1846 most friendly, and my cutter *Termagant* continued to navigate under the colonial flag, commanded by a young colonist named Horace Smith, who I had trained into a sailor from his boyhood. The *Termagant* had only left the river five days for a long trip to the Leeward Coast in search of cattle when my lookout announced her return, and soon after, my youthful Skipper made his appearance on shore, informing me that the Fishmen of Little Sester near Saucy Town had made an attack on his vessel. But being on his guard, he had shot two of the aggressors and now returned to make his protest and take fresh orders, deeming it prudent not to proceed till better armed.

This, then, was the season for difficulties; war on shore near my factory and war at sea with my cutter. The wars on shore did not annoy me further than they stopped the lawful trade, but the attack on my craft by the Fishmen who ever owned me as their friend I considered a most ungrateful act, and without a moment's delay, I fitted the *Termagant* for a fight, taking the command myself. But as she sailed under the colonial flag, I made a declaration to the Governor of Monrovia, Mr. Roberts, of the assault and the result of the defense, informing him of my intention to proceed to Little Sester to settle the affair amicably or give the natives a second chastisement if necessary.

With the permission of the Governor, I left Monrovia in my double mission of war or peace.

On my arrival at Little Sester, I sent a message on shore inviting the Chief of the town on board to talk the palavra. The reader has been informed in a former chapter that for many acts of kindness, the Kroomen and Fishmen had styled me Commodore. Even the Spaniards at Gallinas, knowing the influence I had with them, called me the Kroomen's Consul. My message was kindly received, but as they had been the aggressors and they feared my hasty temper, they cunningly evaded the acceptance of the invitation on board and referred the settling of the palavras to the Governor of Cape Palmas and King Freeman of the same place.

I accepted the invitation, as Governor Russwurm was noted to the whites, the colonists, and natives for his integrity and his just *339* dealings. I was also happy they had referred the adjucation of the case to the American Governor of the Colony of Maryland, in the case where a white man was in contest with a native, giving Mr. Russwurm the supreme respectability of a judge and an umpire.

The whole country had heard of these difficulties, and the natives having heard only the sound of their own bell, had heard but one tune—that is to say, believed the report of their countrymen. Governor Russwurm appointed a day for the palavra, but King Freeman, having heard a correct statement of the case, signified to the Governor that he was satisfied his countrymen were in the wrong and begged him to dismiss the case, as he was ashamed the Governor and the white man should investigate a cause of so much ingratitude.

After such full acknowledgement, I presented the parties with a bullock in token of reconciliation. This is another instance of the rectitude and just dealing of some native Chiefs, although very few are found like King Freeman of Cape Palmas.

A few days after, a vessel landed the Roman Catholic mission headed by the Right Reverend Dr. Baron and the Reverend Father Kelly. Being Catholic myself, I welcomed their landing at the Governor's House and was delighted to find that the President of the Maryland Colonization Society, Mr. Latrobe, had permitted them to set a mission in the Colony, and which was not allowed by the American Colonization Board of Monrovia. Mr. Russwurm had received them with his accustomed benevolence and granted them all the privileges that other missions enjoy there.

A few days after, a French man-of-war arrived in port. The Commander, by order of his Government, immediately offered his services to the reverend gentlemen. Dr. Baron, availing himself of the opportunity, chose the following Sunday to offer his thanks to Heaven in the presence of the natives. In the meantime, the carpenters had erected an altar in a schoolhouse which the Governor had generously tendered them.

Sunday morning arrived, and the Governor with the French officers in full uniform and attended by their boat's crew attended the Mass. The native Chiefs, by invitation of the Governor, attended also. The schoolhouse had been decorated with a rich altar and profusion of candles. On the walls hung 12 handsome engravings representing the birth of Our Savior, his passion, and his death. Precisely at 10 o'clock Dr. Baron appeared in his rich sacerdotal robe, followed by a layman bearing the missal. The ceremony of the Mass was performed in perfect decorum of the congregation and

with amazing wonder of the natives, who at the first appearance of the revered and decorated priest had struck their breasts in pleasing astonishment and at every new genuflection or action demonstrated a respectful approval.

The Mass over, Dr. Baron, with the assistance of the Governor's interpreter Yellow Will (a true African Cicerone), explained to the native Chiefs the meaning of the 12 engravings—no easy job, as few natives understand pictures or engravings at first sight. But Yellow Will was there, and with the help of a cane, every object was pointed out and perfectly transmitted by him into the dull comprehension of his countrymen, who at the third engraving began to recognize the well-known features of Our Savior, often referring to the second picture for the countenance of the Infant Jesus.

The description went on till the representation of the flagellation, when one of the natives demanded why the white man flogged his god. But Yellow Will did not interpret this and imposed silence on the intruder, called him a fool, and told him to go on board of a man-of-war as he had done for six years; then he would know all about it.

At parting, each Chief received a present, but during the ceremony of the Mass, King Freeman had espied the wine and begged a description more illustrative of the holy ceremony; which was immediately attended to, each receiving a bottle of white wine. On retiring, Yellow Will reported that it was the general opinion of all the natives that Dr. Baron was the best man, as he "savvy god palavra too much." The book they had seen—the engravings—was a "proper book," that the "New Pray Man savvy book pass all t'other book men."

In a few months, the reverend gentlemen erected a large mission house and a church, but the climate proving fatal to the new missionaries who took charge after the above-named gentlemen retired, this Catholic mission was abandoned.

CHAPTER 95th

*A Brief Description of Cape Palmas

*1845—1846 During the few pages that will end this book, I shall not refer again to the Colonies, but as Cape Palmas is the property of the Maryland Colonization Society, and as I am now in Baltimore, the friends of this noble institution will perhaps digest a very short chapter on the description of this Colony.

Cape Palmas stands in 4° 20' North and 7° 48' West, and the principal colonial town, called Harper, is pleasantly situated on the promontory, commanding an imposing view of the sea while its elevations dominate over the native towns in its neighborhood. The climate of this Colony is the best of all the Coast, being free from the miasmas attending large forests, stagnated savannahs, and deep rivers. Here the country is slightly undulated with hills in the midst of large, fertile valleys, and its rocky and sandy shore leaves at low water a clean, wholesome beach. The emigrant on his first landing may pay a slight tribute to the change of climate, but the African Fever here seldom proves fatal.

The soil is even more fertile than that of Monrovia. The rains, not being so abundant and of less duration, allow vegetation to take its natural strength, ripening by degrees into its perfect growth. The dry season, which parches everything in Mesurado, here is relieved by frequent showers of rain, while the continual sea breezes in daytime maintain the thermometer at 76° to 83° Farenheit.

The soil is remarkably productive, and the Colonization Society of Maryland could not have chosen a better spot than this headland of the Grain Coast to situate the subjects of their bounty, inasmuch as they placed them with the intent that they should dedicate themselves to farming, and ocular demonstration now shows the benefit of these measures, since the colonists of Harper and Latrobe have never known as yet a year of scarcity, while the Windward Colonies have often suffered from the failure of crops. With equal success the planter can here grow the sugar cane, coffee, indigo, et cetera. Corn grows to greater perfection than at Mesurado, having less rain to contend with. All kitchen vegetables here obtain their full maturity, and like other Liberian Colonies, the inhabitants supply the shipping in the season with an abundant profit to themselves.

This Colony has also a great advantage over the other Colonies, as the country round is well stocked with cattle and the sea with fish.

The natives also are more industrious, while are less prone to quarrel, and look upon the colonists with far different feelings than the Vey, the Day, the Bassa, and the Kroomen look upon the Monrovians. The legislative laws of the Colony have wisely prohibited the introduction of spiritous liquor in the Colony, which with other just as correct laws will prove the true-founded mental principle of its welfare. The mode of Government as first dictated by the Colonization Board and now so fully carried out by their Governor, Doctor McGill, has proved to this day the true source of its present prosperity.

*Disappointments and Reversals

1846   I continued my voyage to Saucy, Druin, and St. Andrew, purchasing cattle and rice which I effected in short time, returning to Cape Mount with my stock of animals. On landing, I found my establishment in a perfect state of revolution.

A colonist whom I had taken from misery and want and whom I had employed as blacksmith deserted my establishment, carrying with him several of my servants, and had joined the enemies of the King. My craft, which I intended to call the *Poor Devil*, had remained in status quo during my absence; the King also had made several attacks which through treachery had all failed. A number of vicissitudes had now accumulated about me which in part disgusted me of an African life.

Since the first establishing of New Florence, everything had proved a failure, and to put the climax to my growing disgust, my cutter *Termagant* went on shore on the bar, losing vessel and cargo. As misfortune never comes alone, the sudden death of an English Captain from Sierra Leone caused me a loss of 3,000 dollars. In despair at so much bad luck, I went personally to work on the *Poor Devil*. The bends were put on with great difficulty, as the African timber was hard to bend. Still, her frame was completed. Nothing remained but the decks and planking, which I expected from the United States with her spars, sails, rigging, and chains and anchors. I looked forward with some pride to the day when this bark would carry me away from Cape Mount, such was the disgust I had formed of my new abode.

About this time a colonial craft landed a very respectable and reverend gentleman, Mr. A. D. Williams, a former Governor of Monrovia, who was deputied to Cape Mount by the Principal of the Methodist Episcopal Mission of Monrovia. Mr. Williams handed me the following letter:

> T. Conneau, Esq.
>
> Dear Sir,
>
> This will be handed you by Rev. A. D. Williams, a minister of the M.E. Church with which you are so well acquainted that I need not introduce him to you. It is a matter of regret to me that I am so situated that I cannot accompany Mr. Williams to Cape Mount. It would have afforded me pleasure to have visited your establishment,

as well as it might have facilitated our mission operations, could I have done so. Permit me, however, to bespeak for Mr. Williams your attention and patronage, both of which you have so kindly in our conversation on the subject promised.

Our object is to elevate the natives of Cape Mount, to establish a school for the children, to have Divine Service regularly performed every Sabbath, and thus to endeavor to introduce among the people the knowledge of the only and true and wise God and the blessing of our common Christianity. Such is the immense influence which you have over the Cape Mount people from the fact of your owning so large a territory that a great deal of the success of our effort I will depend on you, Sir.

To your efforts for our prosperity and final success we look, then, very anxiously. In the course of a few months, should circumstances warrant the expense, I intend to erect suitable buildings for the missionary and his family and Divine Service. In this case we shall have to intrude on your land on which to build. I shall endeavor to visit the Cape Mount as soon as possible. I remain, my dear Sir, yours truly,

John Seys

The principal of the M.E. Mission could not have chosen a better person for the sacred duty and one whom I would prefer in obliging. Mr. Williams was worthy of his mission, but he had chosen a bad time to establish his school: the wars still continued, and the native towns were depopulated. But as I had promised my assistance to the Reverend Mr. Seys, I introduced him to the King, who in very courteous terms represented to Mr. Williams the difficulties of the country and the danger existing, but promised should the war speedily end, to send him a notice, when a missionary or a "book man" would be received with pleasure.

To give a better proof of the scarcity of people then in the country towns, I sent messages to Toso, Fanama, and Sugaree for the inhabitants to meet at New Florence next Sunday to hear the "God palabra." Sunday came, and the Reverend Mr. Williams only preached to my Clerks, mechanics, and servants. I wrote to Reverend Mr. Seys of the mortifying failure, and Mr. Williams returned to Monrovia.

The long-expected planking, spars, and sail finally arrived in the schooner *Patuxent* chartered from New York for that purpose. Her cargo of deck planks could not be discharged. The September month had set in with its usual strong gales from the southwest. The porthole on her bows could not be opened on account of the heavy seas. I sent her to Cape Palmas to take in a few tons of rice; my winter provisions had been lost with the cutter on the bar. On her return, she was seized by an American cruiser and sent to the United States as a prize; her crime was having a quantity of rice and a slave deck. The United States Court of New York could not condemn her, inasmuch as these decks which gave such umbrage to the Commander of the cruiser proved to be a load of 4-inch lumber from 40 to 60 feet long and such as used for ship decks, and not a slave deck of common one-inch pine board.

I Visit New York to Reclaim My Wood Cargo and Return to Find My Luck Worsening

It was ordained that the *Poor Devil* should be in reality the poorest of devils, doomed from its infancy. Had she been allowed to float, I believe she would have turned out a second Flying Dutchman. The tricks of misfortune seldom deterred me from further operation. I was bound to finish my hobby craft with its fancy name and sail her, and the loss of the lumber to finish her would only retard her launching by six months. With this determination, I embarked for New York in search of another load of lumber to coat the ribs of my African craft.

*1846—1847

In New York I found the *Patuxent* had not been condemned, but a "probable cause for seizure" had been given by the Judge, which *jeu-de-mot* deprives the aggrieved party of redress and protects the captors from a just prosecution from damages hastily and inconsiderately inflicted, while the U.S. Court is left to pay the expense of the prosecution. A wonderful phrase, this "probable cause for seizure."

I had not visited the United States since 1836. The imposing sight when one enters the harbor of New York in the month of July may be termed a phenomenon; the eye sees so much that the memory cannot retain it.

In a few weeks, my object had been accomplished. The bark *Chancellor* was chartered for one year. In her I shipped another portion of lumber, rigging, sails, et cetera and an assorted cargo for the Coast. Our passage was short and agreeable, and everything announced a change of fortune. But the Blind Goddess had reserved me a grand surprise. On landing, I found the King had been obliged during my absence to make a treaty of peace with his enemy "the upstart."

This would be the Chief who had assumed the name of George Cain. He was a native of the vicinity of Cape Mount and somewhat related to the old King. Having served some time with the colonists, he spoke the English language well. The aged King had been compelled by treachery of his own subjects to effect an apparent friendly arrangement with Cain, who now called himself Prince George. My treacherous blacksmith, who having taken as his third wife Cain's sister, acted in this affair as his adviser, and on my return from New

York, I found them both domiciled on the beach and of course near my premises.

Both these men were my sworn enemies. Cain—or Prince George—could not forgive the assistance I had given to the King in the war against him, and the colonist blacksmith, whose name was Curtis and who had long ago brutalized himself in amalgamizing with natives and had renounced his creed and civilization, added ingratitude and followed the enmity of his native brother-in-law to work the destruction of Cape Mount.

Having established themselves on the beach by degrees, they communicated with the British squadron, and as the Commanders still held a strong prejudice against me, the astute and defaming communications of my two enemies were not only believed but sought for. In a short time I was made as black as themselves. No crime but I was guilty of: the Spanish factory in favor of King Fana Toro was denounced as mine; the shipment of the *Atalanta* and the fitting out of her boat was a private speculation of mine; the schooner *Patuxent* was also reported as a slaver. These and a thousand more absurdities were poured with the gall, bitter, and malignant animosity of a native character when spurred by the aid of an obliged and civilized villain into the willing but not ignorant ears of the British officers, and New Florence was reported to the few English friends that still remained to me a slave mart. But now, even at this moment, it is a gratification to me to be able to challenge my worst enemy to accuse me with having directly participated while at Cape Mount in the purchase of slaves for shipment since the end of 1839.

From the moment that the first post was erected for the fomentation of New Florence, the most rigid rules were observed in regard to morality. My premises were kept pure from that libertinism which is familiar to other factories on the Coast of Africa. Even at New Sester with five or six hundred slaves in my barracoons and from 5 to 10 white men to watch them, the discipline of my police was the object of my ambition. I have been visited at Cape Mount by French Commodores, by British and American Commanders, by white and colored missionaries and merchants of all nations, and no one can today bring a blush to my forehead.

It was not so on the beach after Cain and Curtis became the friendly informers of the cruisers. The beach of Cape Mount became the rendezvous of amusements where sailors and marines without regard to grade found a recreation for their passions.

Such was the state of things I found on my return to Cape Mount. My arrival in an American bark soon created new suspicions. Her

cargo was reported to the men-of-war as a slave cargo, and her lumber as a second slave deck by the host of these brothels, and the *Chancellor* was watched from anchorage to anchorage by an English cruiser. *Fama volat et fama noxit,* as the Latin said: fame flies, but fame injures. Such was the case in this instance. My return was heralded for miles along the Coast, my former friends the British cruisers taking the trouble to report the *Chancellor* as a suspicious vessel of the United States to the brig *Dolphin,* then at Mesurado.

In a shorter time than twice twenty-four hours, the American bark *Chancellor* was boarded by an American officer who reported her to Captain Pope of the *Dolphin* as a regular merchantman, but such had been the malicious representation of this vessel that the *Dolphin* remained a month in the same anchorage.

The *Chancellor*'s repairs over, we proceeded to Gallinas to sell our cargo, the American man-of-war following us there. Our next trip was to the leeward of Palmas in quest of palm oil and ivory, a course quite contrary of the *Dolphin,* which was bound to windward (I believe Cape de Verde). As we parted company with the American cruiser, a British war brig took charge of our escort, anchoring when we anchored and getting underway when we did, finally following us into every nook and harbor, much to the annoyance of both parties. At Grand Buttoa I took the *Chancellor* within a reef of rocks, and here we were left to proceed on our course, the cruiser returning to Cape Mount.

1847 It was on the memorable day of March the 15th, 1847 that the Commander of the same cruiser who had taken the trouble to escort us to Buttoa landed at New Florence with a Lieutenant and six sailors and *sans ceremonie* proceeded to search my premises for slaves. Not finding any, he took two bars *de justice*, the same as used on board all men-of-war to secure disobedient sailors, and carried them on board. Next day about eleven o'clock, several boats' crews and marines landed headed by Captain ———— of H.B.M. sloop *Fevo*————[1] and Lieutenant Commander Mr. Murdoc of the cruiser *Contest*, and without provocation or giving notice, these Commanders ordered the premises on fire, my man in charge not being allowed even to save his wearing apparel.

As I was not there at the time, I cannot vouch for the correctness of this statement, but my Clerk Horace Smith made oath in protest extended soon after on Monrovia to that effect, adding that the marines and Kroomen of both vessels helped themselves without scruple of whatever was not destroyed.

The ill-fated *Poor Devil* was destroyed by the flames. The conflagration was extended to all the buildings, leaving New Florence a mass of ashes. Prince Cain and his civilized brother Curtis attended this work of philanthropic destruction, and in invitation to their white English friends, spread their devastation even to my garden and plants, cutting all my valuable fruit and coffee trees imported at great expense from Rio and Bahia. The poor cattle also were captured by them, to be sold next day on board the *Squadron*.

It is painful for me to chronicle the conflagration of Cape Mount and the destruction of my property. I would have willingly ended my work without a murmur on this subject, if this hostile act had not been performed during my absence. Even this day I am ignorant what authorized such unheard-of-despotism. Not a word was left me wherewith I could trace a justification to exculpate the authors of my ruin.

Three days after this unhappy event, the old King died. His last breath was extinguished with my name, and a few weeks after, the natives, awaking from their stupor and missing their white man and his house, the pride of their land, rose in a mass and called for retribution. Cain, the vilifier and false traducer, was butchered with his son, and his associate Curtis was poisoned. Both perished victims for their false accusations which to this day the natives suppose induced the British Commanders to destroy New Florence.

[1]The manuscript page is torn, obliterating these names.

Captain Conneau's Letters to Brantz Mayer   *1854*

> Saturday evening
> Baltimore

Dear Sir,

I have been in bed since Monday, bound down by the two knees—Rheumatism. Can you let the bearer have *all* the corrected work you have on hand?

Buena pasqua, su servidor,[1] etc.

> *Theo Conneau*

> 9th January 1854 Monday
> Baltimore

My Dear Sir,

If my animal powers were in as good order as my physical ones, I should be the bearer of my own message and would avoid giving you the trouble of writing the answers to the many questions you will find in the next lines. The only apology I can make to you is that an invalid is as full of curiosity as a Yankee traveler.

First, how are you? 2nd, Have you seen our London friend from Washington? 3rd, How is Doctor Hall? 4th, What progress in Capt. Canot's memoirs etc? Is your opinion on the work the same? 5th, When do you intend applying to Mr. Harper? Or have you made your mind to go to New York on the same affair?

The bearer will deliver you the last portion you gave for the copyist. Please give him all you have ready. The description of Ama-De-Bella's sister Beelgu and her escape from a watery grave is beautiful. By-the-by, I am better and receive my friends in the parlor. Hurrah for Homeopathy!!

> Believe me Sir,
> Your obt. sert.,
> *Theo Conneau*

> Susquehanna House
> 24 January 1854

Muy Sr. y Estimado Amigo,[2]

I am somewhat better, and now I can walk about in my room and go downstairs to the sofa. What news have you for me? I am most

---

[1] Merry Christmas holidays, your servant . . .

[2] "Most distinguished and esteemed friend . . ." The body of this letter is wholly in Spanish, possibly because of the content of the second paragraph. This text is a translation.

curious to know anything about our undertaking—Did your friend from Washington arrive?

If I become better pronto, I will first have to attend to a project whose idea has come to me—Cuba and her Emancipation.

Send me any book you may have on hand to pass the time.

Su servidor y amigo,
Theo Conneau of
Rheumatic misery

Liverpool 3rd April 1854

Dear Sir:

In fulfilling my promise, I know not how to extend a whole page, as I have but little to say in regard to my voyage or my arrival here to you, who have traveled so much and are perfectly *au fait* of all the events of a sea voyage and the locality of this Smoky City. Still allow me to inform you of an occurrence which I never met before in thirty years of a sea-faring life.

Four days out from New York, we fell in with a field of ice and imprudently continued on course till we met long after dark with an ice-berg (I should say an ice island), and such was the proximity that it became perfectly calm after passing it. The danger soon brought our Racing Captain to his senses, and our course was changed for a retrograding one, but we still continued the whole night in plowing the icy fields to the great damage of our stem and paddle wheels. The first we carried away down to the water's edge, the other were found next morning minus several buckets. I am not a great coward, but in my dreams that night, with every thump we gave against the ice, I imagined John Bull again after me. Fortunately we did not give in with one of those floating mountains, else the writer would address you from H. or H.

Of Liverpool I have but little to say. Take away her docks and American shipping, and the City would remain an insignificant, gloomy, and chilly place. Of its inhabitants I dare not say a word; I should be too severe a judge. But let me assure you that they are generally what I told Lord Byron, and I like them not. I would not give an inch of Baltimore or an acre of the most desolate or deserted spot of the United States for the whole of the Perfide Albion.

Tomorrow I sail or steam again for the belle France. I go direct to Havre from here. My brother's sickness lashes me on in preference to my business in London, but I intend in two weeks to visit the Smoky Metropolis when you will again be molested with my second letter, which I hope will be more interesting.

I make no apology to you for the hasty manner I scribble these lines. As you have perused six hundred pages of my bad English, I presume you take bombshell proof against bad composition and murderous language. Therefore, my dear Sir, take the good intention for the deed—a tribute of my regard.

You will please direct still your letters to Paris, Hotel des Etrangers, Rue Joquelet, as I intend returning there from London and I pray forget not to forward me all the blessings and the curses on the work as soon as possible.

Pongame, amigo mio, a los pies du su amable y estimadisima Señora y creame su muy atento amigo y seguro,

Servidor,[1]
Theo Conneau

By-the-bye, I met on the *Arctic un original* (as we français would say), a self-styled Doctor Collyer who pretended to know you: the fool made himself so perversely disagreeable on board that long before our arrival here, everyone had given him the cold shoulder. I pray, who is this babbling and charlatan Dr. Collyer; is he the one that first introduced in the United States the model-artists?

2nd P.S. I leave this letter to be forwarded after my departure. Should it arrive safe, oblige me to call on the good Dr. H. and tell him I am off for Paris.

T.C.

Paris 21st April 1854

My dear Sir:

Since my arrival in Paris, I have been detained by my brother's illness, but now will proceed on my way to London. I called on Mr. Alexandre Vattermare, and his reception was most cordial, it is with delight that he spoke of you, and he retains a most lively remembrance of you and yours. M. Vattermare said he has much to say to you, but will not write till he can give you a full detail of what concerns the library—that is to say, when the donation is publicly accepted by the Chief Magistrate. He expects it will take place the 4th of July, when all the Americans here will be invited and the Emperor if possible. It appears that the present Préfet has fitted out at the expense of the City a large hall in the Hotel de Ville in preference to the one in the Place de la Bourse, and which he did not think sufficiently grand for the honor of such gift.

M. Vattermare wishes also for the reports of the last four years on Liberia; pray ask them of Mr. Latrobe. M. V. has expressed a wish to see the only 250 pages of the book *Capt. Canot;* I shall satisfy his curiosity as soon as my brother has gone through it. An Englishman,

[1]Place me at the feet of your amiable and esteemed Missus and believe me to be your most attentive friend and secure servant

a Scotch nobleman Captain Trotter, has read the work and likes it very much. Had I the rest, I should certainly have made the greatest haste to London to see Mr. Bently. However in a few days I will be there, when I hope he will make me a good proposal. But it is the opinion of my brother and M. Vattermare that no agreement will be entered upon with only the perusal of 250 pages.

M. Alex Vattermare has inquired most minutely into the health of all members of your kind family, of Mr. Charles Mayer and your nephew the artiste. I shall probably condescend to accept some Government situation, my brother having taken the necessary steps. You will kindly oblige me by sending me as soon as possible the proof sheets corrected or uncorrected, so that I may at once strike a bargain with Mr. Bently, who I am afraid will do nothing till he sees more of the work. Please send it by Adams Express to my brother at the following address: Monsieur le Docteur Conneau, Médecin en Chef de l'Empereur. Palais Royal, Rue St. Honore No. 216 Paris. Have you forgotten you promised to write me very soon, and send me the puffs or critics on the book. *No se olvide.* Be pleased to present my respects to your Lady, and croyez votre serviteur tres humble.

Theo Conneau

You will receive this through the Doctor's kindness.

Paris 26th May 1854

My Dear Sir:

Yours very obliging of 28th April with the 120 pages proof sheets has just arrived in my possession as I returned from my trip to London, but before I proceed any further, let me inform you what I have done since my arrival in France. First and foremost (as we sailors say) I met my brother, quite recovered and married to a much younger woman than my wife. (Mind the Doctor is my senior.) Well, this much esteemed brother was really glad to see me. He was always so, but his many occupations and his indolent ways kept him from answering my letters. Truly, I only wrote him the first and the second; then I damned his silence and sent him to David Jones without regard to his title, his decorations, his crosses, and his money. However, I was wrong and have since found out my mistake. Indeed, his position near the Emperor, the many occupations and his matrimonial duties (him a sober-sided most virtuous old bachelor) have and still keep him not only mentally but bodily occupied, to the great annoyance, I suppose, of my young sister-in-law.

Let us drop that subject and *retournons à nos moutons.* I soon informed my brother of the shattered circumstances of my affairs, my dubious prospects, and the cause of my journey to Europe, keeping a stiff upper lip on the exact water mark of my *bolsillos*[1] and proudly

[1]pocketbook

avoiding any illusions of expecting any assistance from him; I still felt the mortification of his long silence.

By-the-bye, I forgot to mention that our first interview took place at my own room at the hotel. Distaining to call on him first, I had sent him a note informing him of my arrival. In two hours after, we had embraced. That evening I was presented to his wife and her relations, with a numerous pass of friends purposely invited to see the sailor Captain. Knowing my own value, I do not blush to say that my Aesculapian brother was proud of me. As I had previously told him that the object of my voyage was the publishing of my memoirs on Africa, and as during my trip to Europe I had translated 150 pages of the work into French, I was requested by the company who knew the fact to narrate part of it. The *brouillon*[1] was sent for and briefly, the tales of my first sailor days, my curious family rencontre in Spain, my piratical uncle in Cuba, my trip in the *Areostatico*, and the description of Esther's Mulatto love made me the Lion of the Evening, to the delight of my Imperial brother.

As I came to the blank pages and to a full stop, the disappointment of the company was magnificent great in the inquiring countenances of my hearers. I was immediately beset by the ladies and a shower of questions was indiscriminately put to me. One wanted to see my eye, the other wanted to know if in reality the Dutch Female Commander had fallen and I remained a Joseph; a third was most enthusiastic about Esther and wanted to know why I did not free her from her impotent lord and bring her to France. The men disputed my French accent: one found it English, the other Spanish, while the whole felt jealous of the favorable impression the recital of those pages had made on their wives. At parting I was made to promise to send immediately to America for the rest of the work, and a *beautiful* Creole lady from Bourbon (who passes for 26 while she is a good 32) kissed me in full company for speaking well of her country, bananas, and pineapples. Mind I say beautiful because it is the first female kiss I have received since I left my wife, and I would not have sacrificed myself but to a beauty.

I drop the subject, as I imagine you are laughing at my last phrase—the first kiss—and *sacrifice!!*—and continue in a more sober and interesting narration.

My arrival in Paris was not noticed in Galignani's Columns,[2] but my astute brother, with the Italian tact worthy of Cardinal Mazzarini, informed the Emperor while at breakfast with his Empress that his brother had just arrived from America. He begged permission to retire that morning half an hour sooner. The Emperor has a perfect good memory and immediately asked about me, whence I came from, and what had brought the *contrabandier* to France. The Doctor, availing himself of the opportunity, answered that I had come to see France as I had seen it at my birth, *un Empire*. I will tell

[1]synopsis
[2]*Galignani's Mesenger*, founded 1814

you verbally what the Emperor said to his beautiful and accomplished Eugénie about me; it is too flattering to write it down.

Next day I was permitted to see Napoleon the III, his Majesty having previously informed the Doctor that as I had a spirit for *les grands voyages*, I might be appointed as colonial agent to New Caledonia. I saw the Emperor *dans la Salle des Maréchaux*[1] at the Tuileries in Paris. His salutation (extending his hand) was, "Well, *Africain, tête étourdie*,[2] are you still intent on your perilous voyages? And are you not tired of the sea?" A long conversation took place about my electric telegraph and what would I next undertake. I told him I was ready to obey his commands and was willing to go to Caledonia. In shaking hands again, he assured me that my appointment should be made out.

I shall see him once more before I depart for New Caledonia, the place of my destination.

Next Sunday after Mass, I was by desire of the Empress presented to her. At the appointed hour, my brother and myself were chamberlained into her august presence. We found her sitting on a center divan with two *dames d'honneur* who immediately retired. Her Majesty rose to meet us, and the Doctor kissed her extended hand, then presented me. My grand salaam was answered by a most pleasant inclination of the Imperial head. "Well," said her Majesty, "you must be very happy at meeting the good Doctor, ho! He tells me you speak Spanish: *"Estuvo Ud. en España, y en que parte?"*[3] Then followed a long conversation in both languages. Her Majesty, in twenty minutes, went over the whole American Continent, spoke of all the Republics, their products and revenues, the United States and Cuba. Lopez and the filibusteros were duly noted; Spain and the American Minister Soulé[4] (to whom she gave fits, as we Yankees say) were not forgotten. My expected voyage to New Caledonia was next brought in the tapis, and her Majesty wished to know if I was *soltero*.[5] I had to describe my wife most minutely: her age, complexion, place of nativity, date of marriage, and oh God! how many children? (I wished I could have borrowed a couple of yours to make myself more interesting!) I took advantage of her curiosity to inform Her Majesty that I should be most unhappy if the *Ministre de Marine* did not permit me to take my wife to New Caledonia and begged her to intercede for me. My petition was granted on the spot. My Eliza will have to don the Bloomer Costume at the crossing of the Isthmus of Panama, as I am to join the corvette *Avanture* at Valparaiso.

To describe to you the beautiful Eugénie, no pen (even mine, a

[1] in the Hall of the Marshals of France
[2] you thick headed African
[3] Have you been in Spain, and in what part?
[4] Pierre Soulé (1801-1870) fled France under Charles X and became a U.S. Senator. In 1854, he was Minister to Spain and intriguing to get Cuba away from Spanish Control.
[5] unmarried

diamond-pointed gold one) can do it. I leave to your rich imagination
the Herculean task. Only fancy to yourself the most regular features,
centered by a straight, Grecian, and aristocratic nose, a divine mouth
with a set of teeth of inimitable whiteness which lets the words out
with a most angelic music, a *chevelure* of light auburn abundantly
spread and leaving a clear, honest forehead to gladden the inspector.
Her stature is something more than five feet, not stout but round and
bien potélée[1] and elegantly formed, with an enchanting mole cunningly
placed on the left side of her cheek. Add to this a very superior
intelligence, a noble mind, an exceedingly pleasant address of speech
with an indescribable, amiable, affable deportment. All these
qualities are guided by the best, the kindest and charitablest heart in
Europe (and those are in my idea only one half of her perfections).
You who write so well and are such a connoisseur of the noblest and
best part of creation could, if once in the presence of our noble
Empress, describe the Pride of France in her true light.

As I have accepted this Government situation which will
immigrate me from Europe for two years at least, I determined to pay
a filial tribute to my aged mother who I had not seen for 30 years.
Nice is the place of her present residence, and which I attained by the
way of Marseille. At Nice I met a sister from Florence who had come
to see me. I had left her a child of six years old; she is now the mother
of five brats. On my presentation under the maternal roof, Mother,
Sister, no one would know me although aware of my arrival: my aged
Mother refused to find in her boy of 13 years old, auburn hair, and
clear skin the aged son of a thousand vicissitudes. Not a single
linament could be recognized; the poor soul wanted to see an Adonis
in my hard, sea-beaten features.

I treated myself to three days of motherly and sisterly affections,
when I returned to Paris. Here again I was not idle: theatres,
promenades, balls, races, dinners, etc., with a few sober and most
virtuous night ramblings completed the week I had allotted myself to
visit Paris *comme il faut*. Then I attended to business, which will be
narrated in the following lines.

As you requested me to call on M. Alexandre Vattermare, I did so
the second day of my arrival here. I found him in Rue Clichy No. 39.
His reception was most cordial; in fact it will prove to us most
beneficial (as without his assistance our book might have slept in
eternal death). I wrote you of our meeting and his answers to your
query. I begged M. V. to see the work which he pronounced very
interesting, and thinks if transplated in French would sell well
(by-the-bye, I wish the French were as enterprising as us Yankees). I
see many stumbling blocks before me. My brother has also read the
book, or the 230 pages, and likes it much.

I am, or M. Vattermare's father is, about hunting up a publisher to
contract with him for a publication in France. M. Vattermare (son)

[1]pleasingly plump

proposes to translate it, but wants cash in hand, and I have none. He is perfectly capable, and it will be a pity that for want of capital we should not be able to publish it here. More anon.

The 14th of the present I arrived in London with a bundle of letters of recommendations. Mr. John Mitchell, publisher to the Queen and the *Empéreur des Français*, introduced me to Mr. Richard Bently (by-the-bye, those two gentlemen publishers are good friends). My letter or yours from Mr. Hoffman was duly noted and the M.S. accepted for perusal. But as Mr. Bently the father was not then in London, I was politely requested to call in a week. As my new appointment only permitted a few days' absence, I returned to France to await Mssrs. B.'s answer. Yesterday it arrived, to my brother's address, and here I transcribe a true copy:

"London, New Burlington St. May 27th 1854. Sir: We shall be happy to undertake the publication of *Capt. Canot or, Twenty Years of a Slaver* on the principle of a division of profits, guaranteeing me from risk of any loss that may arise. I shall be glad to hear from you that the above terms are agreeable. I am, Sir, yours respectfully, George Bently. To Capt. Conneau."

I have written to Mr. Mitchell, who most kindly proposed to be my friend and assist me in this affair, that the only terms I wished to accept were to make a sale right out of the book, or at least and last resource to accept so much in hand, say 500 pounds, and divide the profits. I now await an answer.

The 30th inst. I shall return to London en route for the United States, then I will close this business with some publisher if Mssrs. Bently do not accept my terms. My next from London will inform you of my final arrangements in Paris and in England on the subject of the book, but I again repeat to you that had you allowed me to take more of the work, I could have probably met with more success and better advances. This is the opinion of M. Vattermare, Mr. Mitchell, and my brother.

I will also answer in my next your very kind letter of 28th April which I cannot do today as I am well tired of committing mistakes, but you are used to my bad English. Let me congratulate you on the eighth happy progeniture and present my respectful regards to your good Lady, to whom I wish perfect happiness as for all your family.

I have no time to write to my good, and good indeed, friend Doctor Hall. Therefore I pray you read him this *short* amazing letter and say I propose to be at his table by the 20th of next month. Request him if he should meet my old friend Thurston to tell him of my whereabouts and all he knows of me, as I do not write but to you this post, not even to my better half.

Let me end these lines by again praying you to remember me most kindly to your brother Charles Mayer Esquire, and the nephew artiste Mr. Frank Mayer[1] and tell him that I am taking 1/2 dozen

[1]who illustrated Mayer's Captain Canot

lessons in *photographie* to take sketches at New Caledonia, as I wish to 1854 give some pictorial statements of those savages to my friends on my return amongst them.

My brother promises you the autograph of the Emperor. He is not in town now, or I would send it. Te acabo! Amen! Believe me, my dear Sir, yours very truly and in haste,

Theo. Conneau

One turn only of the rheumatic vice since my departure, and that very gentle! Adios—Correct yourself my errors and forgive them.

Paris 12th June 1854

My Dear Sir:

Your obliging letter of 13 May with the second envoy of the proof sheets has arrived safe, and my brother has it in hand to peruse it. Tomorrow I will send it to Mr. Bently in London when I hope he will warm up to some bargain, as he has not yet struck the right chord. Mr. Amyot the French publisher, to whom M. Vatterman has introduced me, will (when I shall send him) have the whole proof sheets say, and if he likes the work, make the following agreement, *viz.* to translate and print it on his own account and divide the profits. This, you see, is the same bargain that Mr. Bently offered if I delivered him the whole proof sheets of the work immediately (which I could not do). Since this offer I have not heard a word from him, but now in sending him the whole 258 pages, I hope he may come to some terms.

Next day after tomorrow I return to London when I will again write you more on the subject.

There is here under the press and will appear very soon a work nearly of the same nature, called *La Vie d'un corsaire et épisodes d'un Negrier* (Romance).[1] I hope this may not interfere with our work.

In my last letter I did not fully answer your seven octavo pages of 28th April. I will now do so in rotation to the said obliging letter.

First, No result from the "*Arctic* Adventures." Second, My brother is perfectly restored and full of business in the Palais in the morning, and at the Chambre des Députés in the afternoon. 3rd, You say I will be naturally curious to know the progress of the memoirs: yes, certainly, but you do not satisfy my curiosity, as you do not say when the work will appear. 4th, "How much better it would be to send directly to England the proof sheets." Certainly, if the bargain was made and signed; I hope my next letter will make that request to you. 5th, About the drawing, I have partly engaged with Messrs. Bently and Amyot that in case we came to an agreement, you would send copies of the plates to each of them. 6th, My brother laughs not at Homeopathy, but smiles in his sleeves at the flattering results I give on my complaint; he believes they (Drs. in Homeopathy) do no harm and sometime some good. But he does not practice it himself. 7th, I am glad Dr. Hall has sent his son to sea. It appears sea air is more congenial to his delicate health. 8th, I knew not you intended to dedicate the work to anyone. I wish you had sent me the copy of the dedication. What have you done in regard to my preface? 9th, Why *can't* you have a stout boy, while you are about it? Mrs. Mayer, I know, would prefer *un hériteur*.[1] 10th, In regards to "my trip to France may prove auspicious," I have informed you what I have done since my arrival: I have accepted a situation, as I told you in my last, of colonial agent for New Caledonia; not a lucrative place for the present, but a stepping stone for advancement, which my brother promises to look to. You know I have had many things to contend with, and the publishing of the memoirs was the greatest. I will tell you all about it in Baltimore: the Emperor himself has created this employ in the Marine (no colonial agent ever existed in that department). 11th, You say Baltimore is as dull as usual. I differ from you: I never found it so. I love Baltimore and its generous inhabitants; I have there two good friends indeed!! 12th, Your demand of the Imperial autograph will be delivered personally, but not that of Eugéne Sue or Louis-Philippe. My brother is not obliging enough to collect the autograph of persons he does not like.

13th, I am sorry the spirit of filibusterism exists against Cuba and hope the Americans will never countenance it, as a day of retribution may come at last. The European Powers will never permit a friendly power to be trampled upon by a mighty nation: we have an example now of Russia's arrogance. 14th, About your President Pierce, I never thought him a statesman but an upstart and low democrat, a slave to his party. I am in opinion a Whig and a wholesale Federalist; "The Union" is my motto. 15th, Monsieur Vattermare is well, and has assisted me much in the operation of our book, but my dear Sir M. Vattermare is somewhat like my brother, full of calls boarded on each quarter: port, starboard, forward, and stern; never answers no one without calling personally. 16th, I have told you already about "Sending something of real interest." Last of all, you may expect me by the 30th of June, when we will have a long chat (feet under your mahogany) about Paris and my adventures in Europe. Again, "the wars"—nothing of interest. The papers are dumb, but something is expected very soon. Sweden will be gained over, then adieu to Kronstaad. Oh Nicholas[2], how blind his politics; England and France must rule the European world.

Will you favor me by forwarding the enclosed to their directions, and when you call on Dr. Hall remember me to him; he has ever been my sheet anchor in distress.

[1] an heir
[2] tsar of Russia

I begin on your kind letter of the 15 May. 1st, Mr. Vattermare will himself answer your demand about M. Fernaux-Campans. 2nd, My brother the Doctor will do for me as much as his timidity will permit him, but all that glitters is not gold. My reputation as a slaver and my actions against the French Government are still fresh; I have been noted in the Black Book. 3rd, Nicholas must either abdicate, be murdered, or disgraced in his bellicose wars; all Europe is against him. 4th, the European powers will let all questions remain dormant till the Russian campaigns are over. 5th, No more turns at the vice. Rheumatics are nearly vamoosed (as the late conquerors of Mexico expressed). Surely 284 pages cannot be the ¾ of 470 pages; have you curtailed the work still more? The Empress is much better, but the Emperor is too much preoccupied to amuse himself at the bellows (to create heirs). Still, it is the sincere wish of all France. Napoleon is indeed very popular. I have seen him on foot several times at the public works, without guards or soldiers. The cheers were enthusiastic to extreme. I do not understand your word "divorce." Surely [   ]¹ of the *New York Herald* has not fabricated a Ba [   ] bug. I am indeed happy Madame Mayer is up, although very feeble. My best wishes for her prompt convalescence and the new Mayer, likewise for all your admirable family.

Adios, hasta nuestra tra pronta entrevista, su amigo y su servidor.²

Theo Conneau
in haste 3 P.M.

London 24th June 1854
Picadilly, Hatchett's Hotel

My Dear Sir,

Having just concluded the contract with Mr. R. Bently for the publication of the book, I hasten to approve it and hope you will think as I do that I have made the most out of a bad job. It is through the great influence of Mr. John Mitchell, Publisher to the Queen, that Mr. Bently has undertaken to publish the work at all, and at his own terms ("Dividing the profits, expenses paid") with the condition that Mr. Richard Bently shall receive the last proof sheets 15 days before the work shall be published in America. I have consented and tonight we are to sign the contract. You will therefore stay the publication in New York till my arrival, which will take place on the 22 of July, as I start from Havre in the *Franklin* on the 5th of said month.

Of course you will not write me any more, and await my arrival to forward the other or the rest of the proof sheets. With this same date I write and send Mr. Alexandre Vattermare the manuscript sheets to

---

¹The original stamps have been torn from the one-sheet folded letter, removing these words.
²Good-bye until our next visit, your friend and servant,

be delivered to M. Amyot the French publisher who has partly agreed to publish the work if we furnish him the proof sheets in time for him to translate and print the work at the same time as Mr. Bently of London. I have also agreed and shall request my brother and M. A. Vattermare to sign that agreement on my part. Therefore for a double cause you will necessarily stay the publication, as I said. I will bring the copies of both agreements for your inspection. The originals will be left with my brother, as M. Vattermare refuses to have anything to do with the money matter.

I have Napoleon's autograph for you in a shape of a letter to my brother about the affairs of Boulogne with a certificate of my brother's accompanying it. Nothing more but adios, su amigo in double great haste,

Theo Conneau

Please to franchise and forward this letter. Let the Doctor know of my success in the publication of the book in France and England: I know he had very little hopes when I left Baltimore! I shall not write him, you, or anyone else till my return.

Merchant's Hotel 20 July
Courtland St.

My dear Sir,

I have just arrived in New York safe and sound, and whole luggage also safe on shore. The cause of my not writing to you before is that I stuck to the rake till all hopes were lost of getting her off. I could not desert a poor fellow in distress.

I am detained here on account of a bale of instruments belonging to the French Government, which are to go with me to New Caledonia. Till I have possession of it again, I may not visit Baltimore. I wrote to the French Ambassadeur on the subject. Write me soon and let me know something of the book. You will perhaps send me a letter of introduction to Messrs. Appleton & Co.[1]

By the 25th instant I will dine with you or vice-versa *lo mismo*.[2] God preserve you from cholera.

Yours ever truly,
Theo. Conneau

Philadelphia 26th July 1854

My Dear Sir,

I have surrendered myself for 24 hours to Petticoat Government, an agreeable durance after an absence of four months, but I will

[1] the New York publishers of Mayer's book
[2] the same thing

forego the matrimonial couch to fly to Baltimore tomorrow evening,
and you may expect me at your office by 11 o'clock the day after.

I say, the Messieurs Appleton, they treated me very civilly and
gave me flattering words about the book, which they say will come
out the middle of September (just what we want). I am invited to call
again when the older brother will be in town.

Yours very respectfully,
Theo. Conneau

Philadelphia 7th August 1854

My Dear Sir,

By Adam's Express you will receive 4 books: 3 *oeuvres de Napoléon*
and one history of Napoleon III. The engravings of the Emperor and
his Empress with the charts of the seat of war, I sent them enclosed
with a set of engravings, etc., etc. to Doctor Hall. Please call for
them, as I informed him they are for you.

Forget not my tobacco question.

Yours in haste,
Theo. Conneau

Be kind enough to send me the letter for Mssrs. Appleton.

Philadelphia 18th August 1854

My Dear Sir:

Your most kind of 12th inst. arrived just in time to find my right
hand scalded to the flesh, and this is the cause why I have not
answered it. I thank you for the *American Farmer*. I have bought the
book on the South Seas.

Mr. Appleton has very kindly given me *two* full copies of the book
with the engravings which are now navigating for London and Paris.
When you start for the Modern El Dorado, leave a letter for me with
the Doctor and write me from there to Paris. I will be happy to hear of
your success. Please present my best regard to your Lady and of your
handsome girls and excuse my haste, while I pray you to believe me

Yours very respecting
and truly,
Theo. Conneau

I will not relieve you of your promise to send a copy of the work to
the following persons:

one to my brother
one to Mr. Theo. W. Man, Exchange Building, Baltimore

one to Mr. P. Thurston, Fountain Hotel
one to Mr. James Henry, Reading Depot, Philadelphia
one to the Doctor as soon as it comes out. You will charge for the
same on my share.

Theo. Conneau

At sea, coast of Peru, Frigate
Avanture, 17th Oct. 1854

My dear Sir,

I intended writing you from Panama, then from Lima, and again
from Valparaiso, but time and my natural negligence have deterred
me from keeping my promise with you. My trip from New York to
Valparaiso was performed in 37 days, remaining one day at
Aspenvale, four at Panama, one at Guayaquil, and two at Lima.

The passage all along was excellent, but the treatment on board the
Empire City abominable, and as you have to travel the same road on
your way to California, I will describe some of my troubles. First of
all, the *E.C.* is a very slow boat and very neglectfully kept. Her dining
saloon being in the lower deck, passengers are deprived of light, air,
and ventilation during meal times. The berths are well enough, but
full of insects and vermin.

The table is certainly the worst served I have ever seen on board of
any packets. The servants (Black Devils) are the greatest sauciest
rascals in creation, and as their Chief is also a damned mustachio'd
Negro, things are conducted with filthiness, impertinence, and
neglect. Such is the imprudence of those demons that if a passenger
calls for a drop of water during the day and does not place a shilling in
their greasy hands, he is sure not to get it. I have known a second class
passenger to ask for a glass of water, when a Mulatto rascal told her to
go and get it.

At meals, passengers were so crowded that only one hand could be
used, and if you are not placed at the extremities of the table presided
by the Captain and Mate, you partake of all the spoiled dishes without
the consolation of knowing or seeing what you eat. It is an
impossibility to procure a seat near the ends; those places are reserved
for the Captain's friends and the men of importance (the Express
men). There the best dishes are served and seen at discretion, while
the poor stranger, although [as much] a gentleman as the Express
men, is left without recourse to grab in the dark what he can lay hold
of, sometimes eating fish for flesh and turnips for potatoes.

I would advise a passenger going in the *E.C.* with ladies to procure
himself an introduction with the Captain before starting. Then he
may enjoy some of those privileges that men of importance
monopolize—have at any time a glass of water ad libertum to drink,
eat breakfast and dinner by candlelight, with the distinguished
privilege of partaking of a free lunch in the Commander's Sanctum
Sanctorum, while the other passengers, less lucky, are obliged to

swallow burnt and spoiled meat in total darkness, drink muddy warm water, and heavily pay the Steward for a morsel of bisquit and cheese at lunch.

I have mentioned "a clean glass of water," as during half of our trip we had dirty water, not only red with iron rust, but muddy—an unpardonable neglect on the part of the officers. I had forgot to mention that the Black gentlemen servants reserved for themselves the privilege of monopolizing the ice, serving and selling at pleasure, thus depriving others of the scanty portion the vessel allows for the Cabin cooler.

I would also put passengers on their guard against employing the Ship's Doctor in case of sickness, who if he does not kill you, at the end of the voyage you are presented with a bill, sufficiently exorbitant to purchase a medicine chest. Should you undertake your trip to California, pack your luggage in your worse trunks (valuable ones would be ruined). Cover them with gutta percha and mark them at both ends and top with your full name, an indispensable precaution through the Isthmus and on board the steamers. You must not place confidence in the promises of the Steam Company Clerks, as the number of your berth cannot be secured on the Pacific side, inasmuch as there is no certainty what steamer will take you. Never engage your passage across the Isthmus from the Express; you are liable to be left behind as I was, and when once on the end of the railroad, the Express man leaves you in the mud with a valueless ticket in your hand that no muleteer will take, preferring cash to a draft seldom paid. Once in Panama, your Spanish language will carry you through and if your pockets are well filled, you may procure a good sherry toddler and a bad beefsteak at a restaurant.

Having trespassed on your patience and time with my troubles and advice, permit me to close these most insignificant lines with a kind adieu and my best wishes. By-the-bye, we are on our way to Callao for our last dispatches, thence to Tahitee, Marquesas on our way to New Caledonia, and if I am not roasted like St. Laurence, will write you again from there. The last news we have from my Gambia Island are that they (the inhabitants) would have kidnapped the Admiral if timely notice had not been given him; they coveted his corpulency and would have made such a meal as they made two years ago on the bodies of 12 men belonging to the boat's crew of a French man-of-war. The New Caledonians are fond of French flesh; fortunately I am an Italian and may not meet with their gastronomic taste.

What of the book? Write me soon, addressed to the French Consul at Valparaiso, M. Casote, and pay post. I have written this in great haste and in the lower deck, lighted by a single bull's eye.[1] If you can make it out, it is more than I can do, so goodbye and adieu again.

Yours very truly,
Theo. Conneau

[1]window of blown glass often with the blowpipe scar remaining

Index

DISCARD